AMBROSE OF MILAN:
DEEDS AND THOUGHT OF A BISHOP

Visit our web site at
www.stpauls.us

or call 1-800-343-2522
and request current catalog

Ambrose of Milan
Deeds and Thought of a Bishop

Cesare Pasini

Translated by Robert L. Grant, PhD

ST PAULS

Library of Congress Cataloging-in-Publication Data

Pasini, Cesare.
 [Ambrogio di Milano. English]
 Ambrose of Milan : deeds and thoughts of a bishop / Cesare Pasini ; translated by Robert L. Grant.
  p. cm.
 Includes bibliographical references and index.
 ISBN 978-0-8189-1341-9
 1. Ambrose, Saint, Bishop of Milan, d. 397. 2. Christian saints—Italy—Milan—Biography. I. Grant, Robert L. II. Title.
 BR1720.A5P29413 2013
 270.2092—dc23
 [B]
                                   2012039231

Produced and designed in the United States of America by the
Fathers and Brothers of the Society of St. Paul,
2187 Victory Boulevard, Staten Island, New York 10314-6603
as part of their communications apostolate.

ISBN 10: 0-8189-1341-X
ISBN 13: 978-0-8189-1341-9

© Copyright 2013 by the Society of St. Paul

Printing Information:

Current Printing - first digit   1   2   3   4   5   6   7   8   9   10

Year of Current Printing - first year shown

2013   2014   2015   2016   2017   2018   2019   2020   2021   2022

Table of Contents

List of the Writings of St. Ambrose vii
Introduction to the English Edition, 2013 ix
Introduction to the First Edition, 1996 xi
Bibliographical Note xiii
Chronological Dates xv
Translator's Notes xix
Abbreviations (From the Italian version) xxi
Biblical Abbreviations xxii

CHAPTER I:	Episcopal Election of Governor Ambrose	1
CHAPTER II:	Family Roots and His Youth	15
CHAPTER III:	His Early Formation and "Father" Simplician	25
CHAPTER IV:	"Take Heart, Heal the Ills of the People"	39
CHAPTER V:	Guide to Monks and Consecrated Virgins	55
CHAPTER VI:	Marcellina and Satyrus	69
CHAPTER VII:	Aquileia: September 3, 381	81
CHAPTER VIII:	Roman Tradition and Christian Innovation	99
CHAPTER IX:	A Contested Basilica and a People Bound to Their Bishop	115
CHAPTER X:	"Because I Don't Deserve to be a Martyr, I Have Acquired These Martyrs for You"	133
CHAPTER XI:	Augustine, Son of the Church of Milan	149
CHAPTER XII:	Anti-Semitism?	165
CHAPTER XIII:	An Effective Aid to Social Life	181
CHAPTER XIV:	"I Have Loved This Man"	195

CHAPTER XV:	In the Service of the Word	209
CHAPTER XVI:	Concern for the Churches	223
CHAPTER XVII:	Effusive Fragrance and Sober Inebriation	239
CHAPTER XVIII:	The "Encounter"	255
CHAPTER XIX:	Saint Ambrose	269

Endnotes 285
Endnote Index of Works Cited 313
Index of Names 317
Modern Era Bibliographical Index 321
Index of Selected Topics 323

List of the Writings of St. Ambrose

I offer a list of the writings of Ambrose, following the subdivisions proposed by SAEMO (*Sancti Ambrosii Episcopi Mediolanensis Opera*, a bilingual (Italian/Latin) edition of Ambrose's complete works). For certain works, described in great detail in this volume, I indicate the page (or pages) in which they are presented.

Because there are no standard English titles, and some works have yet to be translated into English, the Latin titles of Ambrose's works are included.

Exegetical Works
The Six Days of Creation/Hexameron: SAEMO 1.
On Paradise/De Paradiso: SAEMO 2/I.
On Cain and Abel/De Cain et Abel: SAEMO 2/I.
On Noah/De Noe: SAEMO 2/I.
On Abraham/De Abraham: SAEMO 2/II.
On Isaac or the Soul/De Isaac vel Anima: SAEMO.
On a Good Death/De Bono Mortis: SAEMO 3.
On Jacob and the Good Life/De Iacob et Vita Beata: SAEMO 3.
On Joseph/De Ioseph: SAEMO 3.
On the Patriarchs/De Patriarchis: SAEMO 4.
On Avoiding the Temptations of the Times/De Fuga Saeculi: SAEMO 4.
On the Trials of Job and David/De Interpellatione Iob et David: SAEMO 4.
Apology on David to the Emperor Theodosius/De Apologia Prophetae David ad Theodosium Augustum: SAEMO 5.
Second Apology on David/Apologia David Altera: SAEMO 5.
On Elijah and the Poor Man/De Helia et Jejunio: SAEMO 6.
On Naboth/De Nabuthae: SAEMO 6.
On Tobias/De Tobia: SAEMO 6.
Explanation of 12 Psalms/Explanatio Psalmorum XII: SAEMO 7-8.
Commentary on Psalm 118/119/Expositio Psalmi CXVIII: SAEMO 9-10.
Commentary on the Gospel of Luke/Expositionis Evangelii Secundum Lucam: SAEMO 11-12.

Moral Works

On the Duties of the Clergy/*De Officiis Ministrorum:* SAEMO 13.
On Virgins/*De Virginibus:* SAEMO 14/I.
On Widows/*De Viduis:* SAEMO 14/I.
On Virginity/*De Virginitate:* SAEMO 14/II.
The Education of a Virgin/*De Institutione Virginis:* SAEMO 14/II.
Commendation to Virginity/*Exhortatio Virginitatis:* SAEMO 14/II.

Dogmatic Works

On Faith/*De Fide:* SAEMO 15.
On the Holy Spirit/*De Spiritu Sancto:* SAEMO 16.
On the Sacrament of the Incarnation of the Lord/*De Incarnationis Dominicae Sacramento:* SAEMO 16.
Explanation of the Creed/*Explanatio Symboli:* SAEMO 17.
On the Sacraments/*De Sacramentis:* SAEMO 17.
On the Mysteries/*De Mysteriis:* SAEMO 17.
On Penance/*De Paenitentia:* SAEMO 17.

Discourses and Letters

On the Death of his Brother/*De Excessu Fratris:* SAEMO 18.
On the Death of Valentinian II/*De Obitu Valentiniani:* SAEMO 18.
On the Death of Theodosius I/*De Obitu Theodosii:* SAEMO 18.
Letters/*Epistulae:* SAEMO 19-21.
Letters Outside the Collection/*Epistulae Extra Collectionem Traditae:* SAEMO 21.
Acts of the Council of Aquileia/*Gesta Concilii Aquileiensis:* SAEMO 21.

Poetic Works and Fragments

Hymns/*Hymni:* SAEMO 22.
Inscriptions/*Inscriptiones:* SAEMO 22.
Titles/*Tituli:* SAEMO 22.
Commentary on the Prophet Isaiah/*Expositio Esaiae Prophetae (fragments):* SAEMO 22.
On the Sacrament of Rebirth or on Philosophy/*De Sacramento Regenerationis Sive de Philosophia (fragments):* SAEMO 22.

Introduction to the English Edition, 2013

Many persons have expressed to me an interest and admiration for Ambrose of Milan. Presenting and communicating something of his writings and describing some aspects of his life, or even offering to the reader this volume in its initial Italian draft has sufficed to make them acquainted with him. Perhaps Bishop Ambrose strikes one as an integrated personality, multi-dimensional, lively, frank, always ready to probe more deeply than that which is obvious, but never distracted from daily life by ancillary problems. Or perhaps we find ourselves unable to remain indifferent to certain of his concise expressions, incisive in the clarity of their prose and often enveloped in poetic finesse, almost like slogans, that nonetheless express the authentic substance of truth. A model citizen when it came to public duties, but furthermore — and above all — a Bishop totally dedicated to the mission entrusted to him, this is how Ambrose appears in the eyes of those who know how passionate about life he is, passionate in his roots, passionate in his love for that "Christ the Lord" who in his discourses he likes to evoke *ex abrupto*. But isn't this simply a spontaneous interruption, or more, the flowering, in simplicity and splendor, of an interior presence continuously alive in him?

In the Introduction to the first edition of this volume I laid out the criteria to be followed in the structure of this biography. I won't repeat it, but simply confirm it. This translation substantially retains the Italian text from that time, with the only exception to add certain additions or corrections suggested by recent research on the subject.

The places of origin, however, have changed. The text was born in Milan, in the Biblioteca Ambrosiana, where I was working in those days. This translation joins together two locations: Rome and Davenport, Iowa. The Biblioteca Apostolica Vaticana, where I now labor, has made me aware of Ambrose in his Roman background: it is the environment in which, many centuries ago, the young Ambrose was formed and it is the environment where — I can attest with happy surprise — there continues to be a lively interest in his personality and his spirituality. Davenport and the university dedicated to St. Ambrose, is the place in which this translation was born in the care of Fr. Robert Grant. To Fr. Robert we owe not only the achievement of rendering the text, previously published in Italian, into a new language, but also an intensive study and indefatigable energy in advancing an environment of research toward a suitable awareness of Ambrose. So his work and the willingness of ST PAULS/Alba House are making this biography available to the entire English speaking world: I am deeply appreciative!

To be thorough I must touch on one last location: The *Sacro Monte di Varese*, not far from Milan, home of the *Romite Ambrosiane*. This contemplative monastery which for more than five centuries has been nourished by the spirituality of St. Ambrose was already mentioned in the preceding Introduction. Here I wish to confirm the importance of the witness of these cloistered sisters who, together with that of the entire diocese of Milan, speak as if St. Ambrose remains alive and real. I hope that the readers of this volume will also be able to realize this happy experience for themselves.

Rome, July 12, 2012

Introduction to the First Edition, 1996

How is a book born?

I remember... as a baby, then as a boy, with Mom and Dad and the whole family... December 7th was the day of the "oh bèj, oh bèj" festival set up in the streets around the Basilica of San Ambrogio. We made the rounds among the booths (more to look than to buy), then made the inevitable visit to the "scurolo" or crypt of the Saint, in his church, where he rests between the martyrs Protasius and Gervasius, a "Milanese" encounter, that drew people to this slightly mysterious personage who was, for us at least, very important.

Another recollection from not so long ago: in those years the Romite Sisters of the Order of San Ambrogio ad Nemis del Sacro Monte di Varese invited me to make a presentation on the figure of the Bishop of Milan, to whom they loved to link their monastic tradition and from whose instruction their spirituality drew. Thus were born the initial steps in my study of Ambrose, preparing the first notes. The reading of the writings of the Bishop led me to the discovery of profound and fascinating passages, and the energetic attention of the sisters augmented my taste for research.

Today those notes have become a book. From the Biblioteca Ambrosiana, in which I now find myself working and which through the will of the founder, Cardinal Federico Borromeo, was named for the great Bishop of Milan, I am pleased to offer to readers the final development of that which — unbeknownst to me — had begun to be born in those far off days. I would like to communicate a bit of that congeniality which Bishop Ambrose himself was known to possess because an encounter with a real person never ceases to fascinate and the nearness of an authentic believer continues to offer itself as a guide and provocation.

What criteria do I have for this biography?

Substantially my intent was to put into relief the episcopal ministry of Ambrose, letting this emerge as the fundamental and unifying aspect of his life. Consequently, I have given less weight to his ties to the political goings on of his day emphasized rather amply, perhaps excessively, in the "classic" biographies by Jean-Remy Palanque, F. Homes Dudden and of Angelo Paredi. Indeed, Ambrose was above all a Bishop, and his whole life revolved around this episcopal ministry, assumed on the 7th of December 374 and placed in the hands of the Father and of history on April 4th, 397, the day of his leave-taking from this world. As I write, we are approaching the vigil of the seven hundredth anniversary of his death. This book, then, hopes to recount his episcopacy, pivoting on the years in which he was Bishop of Milan and retelling his life from the perspective of his ministry.

Moreover, I have chosen to let the texts speak for themselves: those of the ancient witnesses that history has left us and especially those writings and items handed down to us by Ambrose himself. Obviously, I have not overlooked, out of awareness of their status, the biographies already mentioned and much studied, both recent and of earlier vintage, dedicated to him: to these I am deeply indebted. In any case, it seemed to me that approaching the texts and directly reading their testimonies better reaches into the soul of the protagonist of these pages. Occasionally this method, which is used both by re-expressing the contents and by frequent use of citations, requires great patience in research and reading. The fruit, then, that is drawn seems to me more lively, less of an artifact, and also more immediately verifiable. I hope that the reader is able to enjoy savoring the words of Ambrose and the other texts reported here, and if they come to the impression that the author of this biography is, in the end, too withdrawn from the work, willingly leaving the protagonist to fill in for him... that would be a most appreciated consequence!

Finally: I have also tried to invoke Ambrose, so that he might aid me in the enterprise of which he was in part the cause. I am sure that my request has not been ignored. But I do not want to implicate him in that which I have written here.

Milan, April 4, 1996

Bibliographical Note

For the citations of the works of Saint Ambrose I make use of the Italian translation (tacitly corrected where I have thought it necessary) proposed in the recent bilingual edition published by the Biblioteca Ambrosiana of Milan, by the publisher Citta Nuova di Roma (cf. SAEMO, in *Abbreviations*). [The same edition was used in the English translation, while retaining the 'tactful corrections' of the author.]

I avoided overloading the notes with excessively numerous references. Thus, besides the indications of the cited texts and respective editions consulted, I reduced to a minimum references to biographies of Ambrose and other studies.

Here are listed the biographical references most commonly used. First of all, the classic biographies of Palanque and Homes Dudden: J.-R. Palanque, *Saint Ambroise et l'Empire romain. Contribution à l'histore des rapports de l'Église et de l'Etat à fin du quatrieme siècle*, Paris, 1933; F. Homes Dudden, *The Life and Times of St. Ambrose*, Oxford, 1935. Further, the famous biography of Paredi remains an obligatory point of reference: A. Paredi, *S. Ambrogio e la sua età*, Milan (Hoepli) 2nd ed. 1960 (3rd 1994); a partial redaction has gone out with the title *Sant'Ambrogio*, Milan (Rizzoli), 1985. English translation: *Saint Ambrose: His Life and Times* (M. Joseph Costello, S.J., tr.), Notre Dame, IN (University of Notre Dame Press), 1964. And finally, certain more recent biographies: N.B. McLynn, *Ambrose of Milan. Church and Court in a Christian Capital*, Berkeley (University of California Press), 1994 (who presents, however, an elusive and a bit of a Machiavellian Ambrose); H. Savon, *Ambroise de Milan (340-397)*, Paris (Desclée), 1997; E. Dassmann, *Ambrosius von Mailand. Leben und Werk,* Stuttgart (Kohlhammer), 2004.

The work *Cronologia ambrosiana: Bibliografia ambrosiana*

(1900-2000) is a most useful tool for the chronology of the life and works of Ambrose and for the entire reference bibliography — which refer to him, almost always tacitly, along the entire corpus. Edited by G. Visonà, Milan (Biblioteca Ambrosiana) — Rome (Città Nuova), 2004 (for all the works of St. Ambrose see pp. 25-26). Bibliographical additions for the years following 2000 are published in the review *Annali di scienze religiose,* beginning with number 1 (2008) of a new series. Finally, I note the new review *Studia Ambrosiana,* issuing with number 1 in 2007 as a product of the *Accademia di sant'Ambrogio* (today the *Accademia Ambrosiana: Classe di Studi Ambrosiani*).

Chronological Dates

303	Martyrdom of Soteris, ancestor of Ambrose, in the persecution of Diocletian.
325	Council of Nicea: condemnation of Arius and proclamation of the Word of God is *of the same substance* with the Father.
340 (circa)	Birth of Ambrose at Trier, third born of the imperial government official of the same name; Ambrose was preceded by his sister, Marcellina, and a brother, Satyrus.
340	At Aquileia, Constantine II is murdered by his brother Constans; the family of Ambrose leaves Trier for Rome; perhaps in those situations the father of Ambrose died.
352 (Dec. 25) or 353 (Jan. 6)	Marcellina takes the veil as a vowed Virgin by the hand of Pope Liberius.
355	Council of Milan: through the intervention of the Emperor Constantius II, the Bishops refute the faith of Nicea; Dionysius of Milan is sent into exile. To his post the philo-Arian Auxentius is insinuated.
365 (circa)	Ambrose and his brother Satyrus go to Sirmium to practice law.
370 (circa)	Ambrose is transferred to Milan to assume the governorship of the province of Liguria and Aemelia under the authority of Valentinian I.
374 (Autumn)	Death of Auxentius and the election of Ambrose.
374 (Nov. 30)	Baptism of Ambrose.
374 (Dec. 7)	Episcopal ordination of Ambrose.
375 (Nov. 17)	Death of Valentinian I; the western part of the Empire was divided between his sons Gratian and Valentinian II, while the East remained in the hands of the Emperor Valens.
376 (circa)	Intervention of Ambrose at Sirmium for the nomination of Bishop Anemius.
377	Publication of the treatises *On Virginity* and *On Widows*.
378 (early months)	Death of Satyrus. Ambrose delivers his two funeral discourses: *On the Death of his Brother*.
378 (to Aug. 9)	Valens dies defeated in the battle of Hadrianopolis against the Goths. To ransom the prisoners Ambrose breaks the sacred vessels. Valentinian II and his mother Justina move from Sirmium to Milan, obtaining from Gratian a basilica for their philo-Arian cult.
378	Publication of the first two books *On Faith*.
379 (Jan. 19)	Gratian chooses Theodosius as Augustus for the Orient.
380 (Year's end)	Publication of books III-IV of *On Faith*.

381 (Spring)	Gratian restores to Ambrose the sequestered basilica. Ambrose publishes his treatise *On the Holy Spirit*.
381 (May-July)	Council of Constantinople: reconfirms the faith established at Nicea and proclamation of the divinity of the Holy Spirit.
381 (Sept. 3)	Council of Aquileia under the guidance of Ambrose. The philo-Arian (*homoean*) Bishops Palladius of Rateria and Secundus of Singidunum are condemned.
382	Council of Rome under the presidency of Pope Damasus, with the participation of Ambrose. Ambrose publishes his treatise *On the Mysteries*.
383 (Aug. 25)	The Emperor Gratian is assassinated. In the West, the Empire is left to Valentinian II.
383 (Autumn)	Valentinian sends Ambrose to Trier to meet with the usurper Maximus.
384 (Summer)	Opposition of Ambrose to the request of Symmachus for the replacement of the Altar of Victory in the Roman Senate.
384 (Autumn)	Second mission of Ambrose to Trier. Augustine arrives at Milan as a teacher of rhetoric. He makes contact with Ambrose.
385	Valentinian requests a church for a group of philo-Arians (*homoeans*) led by Mercurinus Auxentius and supported by the Empress Justina; first resistance of Ambrose.
386 (Spring)	Renewed request for a church by a group of philo-Arians (*homoeans*). Serious contest toward Holy Thursday, April 2. In Holy Week of 386 or one of the subsequent years Ambrose preaches the homilies *On the Six Days of Creation*.
386 (June 17-20)	Recovery and translation of the remains of the martyrs Protasius and Gervasius.
386	After having resigned from his position, Augustine retreats to Cassiciacum to prepare for baptism.
386/387	Publication of the treatise *On Virginity*.
387 (April 24-25)	During the Easter Vigil Augustine, prepared by the rich Lenten catechesis of Ambrose, receives the baptism by the hand of the Bishop.
388 (Aug. 28)	Defeat and death of Maximus by Theodosius who, the following October, enters victoriously to Milan as the effective head of the whole Empire.
388 (Year's end)	A synagogue at Callinicum is burned by a group of Christians. Ambrose blocks Theodosius from punishing those responsible and to reconstruct the synagogue at State's expense.
389/390	Publication of the *Commentary on the Gospel of Luke*.
390	To punish an uprising, Theodosius subjects those responsible to a terrible massacre at Thessalonica. The Emperor agrees to undergo the penance proposed by Ambrose and the Bishop readmits him to the Church on Christmas that year.
392 (Beginning)	Council of Capua, presided over by Ambrose. On the question of Antioch and on the anti-Marian doctrine held by Bishop Bonosius.

Chronological Dates

392 (Easter)	At Bologna Ambrose delivers a homily for the veil-taking of Ambrosia, published the next year under the title *The Education of a Virgin*.
392 (May 15)	Death of Valentinian II; in the following August Ambrose celebrates the funeral at Milan.
392 (Aug. 22)	General Arbogastes proclaims Eugenius as Emperor. Ambrose avoids having contact with him.
393 (Early Months)	Council of Milan against Jovinian and the defense of the value of monastic and Virgin's consecration.
393 (Spring/ Summer)	In order to not encounter Eugenius who is approaching Milan, Ambrose begins a voluntary exile in Bologna, Faenza, and Florence, towards the end of August and the following year. At Bologna Ambrose assists at the recovery of the remains of the martyrs Vitalis and Agricola.
394 (March-July)	At Florence Ambrose dedicates a church built by the widow Juliana. The homily pronounced on that occasion was published later the same year under the title of *Commendation to Virginity*.
394 (Sept. 5-6)	Victory of Theodosius over Eugenius in the battle of Lake Frigidus. Ambrose intercedes for those who were complicit with Eugenius.
395 (Jan. 17)	Death of Theodosius. Leadership of the Empire is left to his two sons, Arcadius and Honorarius. In the funeral discourse delivered on the following Feb. 25th, Ambrose recommends the young Augustii to General Stilicho.
395	Recovery of the remains of martyrs Nazarius and Celsus.
395-396	Probable preaching and publication of the *Commentary on Psalm 118* and of the treatise *On Isaac or the Soul*.
396	Letter to the Church of Vercelli for the election of the new Bishop. Ambrose went to Vercelli.
397	Composition of *Commentary on Psalm 43*, interrupted by the initial aggravation of an illness that will lead to the death of Ambrose.
397 (April 4)	In the first hours of the day, Ambrose died, assisted by Bassianus of Lodi and Honoratus of Vercelli.
397/400 (circa)	Death of Marcellina.

Translator's Notes

The goal of this translation is to get this very important text, revised by the author from the original Italian edition, into the English speaking world, which is otherwise lacking a book of this scope and value on the life of St. Ambrose of Milan. The challenge has been to retain the personality of this most congenial author while rendering the text as if it had been written in English. This is impossible, but worth the effort. If forced to choose, the translation favors the English reader over the literal Italian. Several decisions had to be made, including these:

- Altering Italian syntax to conform to normal English language expectations.
- Retaining the bibliographical references in their original languages since that is the only way for an interested reader to track them down.
- Using standard English-language choices in rendering proper and place names; thus "Rome," not "Roma," Ambrose, rather than "Ambrosius," but "Paulinus."
- I have translated Biblical citations directly from Ambrose's Latin, since these can be idiosyncratic. For example Ambrose says: delexi ("I have loved") where the LXX simply uses the Aorist "I loved." (Both Italian and English Bibles, interestingly, use the present: "I love.") Abbreviations and citations of the Bible are as found in the New American Bible.
- Translating quoted sources directly from their original languages.
- Substituting Pasini's Latin/Italian sources for Latin, Latin/English, or in rare cases, English only. Thus, besides the sources Pasini used, I have used the following:
- CCEL: www.ccel.org (Christian Classics Ethereal Library)

- DCO: www.documentacatholicaomnia (Documenta Catholica Omnia)
- NA: www.newadvent.org (New Advent)
- FC: *The Fathers of the Church*, ed. Roy J. Deferrari, et al. The Fathers of the Church Inc., New York, 1953.
- PLD: www.pld.chadwyck.com (Patrologia Latina Database)
- TLC: www.thelatinlibrary.com (The Latin Library)

Abbreviations
(From the Italian version)

BHG = F. Halkin, *Biblioteca hagiographica graeca*, I-III, Bruxelles, 3rd Ed. 1957 (Subsidia hagiographica, 8a); and ibid., *Novum auctarium Bibliothecae hagiographicae gracae*, Bruxelles, 1984 (Subsidia hagiographica, 65).

BHL = Socii Bollandiani, *Biblioteca hagiographica latina antiquae et mediae aetatis*, Bruxelles, 1898-1899 (Subsidia hagiographica, 6); and H. Fros, *Biblioteca hagiographica latina antiquae et mediae aetatis. Novum supplementum*, Bruxelles, 1986 (Subsidia hagiographica, 70).

CCL = *Corpus Christianorum. Series Latina*, Turnhout-Leuven, 1953 ss.

CIL = *Corpus inscriptionum latinarum*, Berlin, 1869 ss.

CSCO = *Corpus Scriptorum Christianorum Orientalium*, Paris-Louvain, 1903 ss.

CSEL = *Corpus Scriptorum Ecclesiasticorum Latinorum*. Editum consilio et impensis Academiae Scientiarum Austriacae, Wien, 1866 ss.

MGH = *Monumenta Germaniae historica*. Edidit Societas aperiendis frontibus rerum Germanicarum Medii Aevi, Hannover-Leipzig-Berlin, 1826 ss.

NBA = *Nuova Biblioteca Agostiniana. Opere di sant'Agostino*. Latin/Italian ed. Cattedra Agostiniana of the "Augustinianum" of Rome, Rome, 1965 ss.

PL = *Patrologiae cursus completus. Series latina*. Ed. J.-P. Migne, Paris, 1841-1864.

RIS = *Rerum Italicarum Scriptores. Raccolta degli storici italiani dal Cinquecento al Millecinquecento*. New revised, amended, and corrected edition, Citta di Castello, 1900 ss.

SAEMO = *Sancti Ambrosii Episcopi Mediolanensis Opera. Tutte le opere di sant'Ambrogio*. Bilingual edition edited by Biblioteca Ambrosiana, Milan-Rome, 1977 ss.

SC = *Sources Chretiénnes*, Paris, 1941 ss.

SCA = *Scriptores circa Ambrosium. Complementi all'edizione di tutte le opere di sant'Ambrogio*. Bilingual edition edited by Biblioteca Ambrosiana, Milan-Rome, 1987 ss.

For the books of the Bible I have adopted the abbreviations used in *La Sacra Bibbia*, Italian version for liturgical use, edited by CEI, Rome, 1971.

Biblical Abbreviations

OLD TESTAMENT

Genesis	Gn	Nehemiah	Ne	Baruch	Ba
Exodus	Ex	Tobit	Tb	Ezekiel	Ezk
Leviticus	Lv	Judith	Jdt	Daniel	Dn
Numbers	Nb	Esther	Est	Hosea	Ho
Deuteronomy	Dt	1 Maccabees	1 M	Joel	Jl
Joshua	Jos	2 Maccabees	2 M	Amos	Am
Judges	Jg	Job	Jb	Obadiah	Ob
Ruth	Rt	Psalms	Ps	Jonah	Jon
1 Samuel	1 S	Proverbs	Pr	Micah	Mi
2 Samuel	2 S	Ecclesiastes	Ec	Nahum	Na
1 Kings	1 K	Song of Songs	Sg	Habakkuk	Hab
2 Kings	2 K	Wisdom	Ws	Zephaniah	Zp
1 Chronicles	1 Ch	Sirach	Si	Haggai	Hg
2 Chronicles	2 Ch	Isaiah	Is	Malachi	Ml
Ezra	Ezr	Jeremiah	Jr	Zechariah	Zc
		Lamentations	Lm		

NEW TESTAMENT

Matthew	Mt	Ephesians	Eph	Hebrews	Heb
Mark	Mk	Philippians	Ph	James	Jm
Luke	Lk	Colossians	Col	1 Peter	1 P
John	Jn	1 Thessalonians	1 Th	2 Peter	2 P
Acts	Ac	2 Thessalonians	2 Th	1 John	1 Jn
Romans	Rm	1 Timothy	1 Tm	2 John	2 Jn
1 Corinthians	1 Cor	2 Timothy	2 Tm	3 John	3 Jn
2 Corinthians	2 Cor	Titus	Tt	Jude	Jude
Galatians	Gal	Philemon	Phm	Revelation	Rv

AMBROSE OF MILAN:
DEEDS AND THOUGHT OF A BISHOP

CHAPTER 1

Episcopal Election of Governor Ambrose

"I have been called to the episcopacy from the discordant quarrels of the courts and from the dreaded power of public administration.... I knew that I was not worthy to be called Bishop, because I was given to this world. But through your grace I am what I am, and I am, without doubt, weak (cf. 1 Cor 15:9), among all the Bishops the least worthy; anyway, since I too have faced certain difficulties for your holy Church, protect the result. Don't allow me to lose, now that I am a priest, that One who, when I was lost, called me to the episcopacy."[1] So it was, at the beginning of 390 or a bit earlier, that Ambrose recalled with some emotion the seminal event of his life when he was called from the governance of Milan to the episcopal seat of this same city. The tone of the cited passage, with the humble prayer addressed directly to the Lord Jesus, seems to indulge excessively in self accusation both in reference to the transgressions of his earlier life and regarding the assertion of his inadequacies in his current service to the Church. Indeed, just a few months before his death, he vividly recalled to the people of Vercelli all the foot dragging that he attempted in order to escape, or at least forestall, his ordination: "What resistance I put up not to be ordained! In the end, because I was forced, I begged, at least, that the ordination might be postponed. But it did no good to propose exceptions; the violence done to me prevailed."[2] But the story of the choice of Ambrose hinged, as we well know, on the fact of the high esteem that the citizenry harbored for their governor.

It is worth pausing briefly over such moments in order to grasp the richness of the various elements in play. The events may be located in the autumn of 374, on the death of Bishop Auxentius. For nearly twenty years he had occupied the episcopal seat of Milan after having been forcibly imposed on it by the Emperor Constantius II in 355 following a Council held in the city which concluded with the banishment into exile of the legitimate Bishop Dionysius.³ Auxentius, who had opposed the doctrine of the consubstantiality of the Word and the Father as was proclaimed at the Council of Nicea in 325, had instituted in Milan a moderate form of Arianism (*homioism*) which, in a few years, and thanks in part to imperial support, can be shown to have prevailed over the orthodox doctrine. The phrase *homeo* prevailed in the Milanese Council of 355, notwithstanding the opposition of Bishop Dionysius and a few others. Thus, with the advent of Auxentius, the Milanese Church, which until that moment had been solid in adherence to the Nicene Creed, became deeply divided. The gradual return to orthodoxy of the neighboring sees had progressively left Auxentius in clear isolation, rendering his position increasingly more anachronistic. It was natural that at his death the tensions exploded between those who wished to restore to orthodoxy the venerable Milanese see and those who, having risen under the guidance of the Arian Bishop, intended not to lose such a prestigious bulwark of anti-Nicenism.

Among the narrations which describe such tense moments, I think the one that interprets better than any other the play of sentiments, reflections, and reactions of people is that which, decades after the events, was preserved in the *History of the Church*, by Sozomen, a Byzantine historian of the 5th century who wrote in the '40s of that century. His account, furthermore, is presented as agreeably sober and concise, and is, therefore, useful as an initial arrangement of the facts. Here is the passage in question: "With Auxentius dead, the crowd found itself in serious conflict because they were not able to agree on a compromise person who could exercise the episcopal ministry in the Church of Milan. The city itself ran a grave risk! One group, in fact, threatened to throw everything into chaos if they could not succeed in their desired goal. Ambrose, who was then governor of the province, fearing the agitation of the people, entered the church and exhorted the congregation to desist in their conflict, reminding them of the laws, the wellbeing, and the benefits that derive from concord.

He had not finished speaking to the people regarding these themes, when everyone, who had abandoned themselves to a fit of mutual rage, suddenly came together in their choice of a new Bishop, namely, the one who had advised them to seek peace."[4] Let's be clear: they may have felt it opportune to entrust to the governor, who had come to speak to them of peace, the responsibility for a new period of reconciliation and reconstruction which the Milanese Church community was yearning for after the long episcopacy of Auxentius. In the reaction of the congregation one may intuit the communal appraisal of this political man who, governing the city, had given remarkable proof of impartiality, balance, and honesty. They thus intended, by choosing him to guide the Church of Milan, to recreate harmony in the ecclesial community so worn out by the doctrinal divisions of the preceding decades and to lead it back to unity of intent and faith.

If, from Sozomen, we go back to the sources closer to the events, not only might we find new details concerning the exceptional event of this layman spontaneously called to such a demanding an episcopal seat, but we might discover other aspects of the unfolding of the events that are pleasingly embellished without, however, tainting the veracity of the story. Our informers are Rufinus of Aquileia and Paulinus of Milan, to whom it is right to be introduced before being ready to listen to their interesting stories.

To Paulinus we owe a biography of Ambrose written in 412/413 or, more likely, in 422.[5] He had been a copyist and secretary to the Bishop during the last years of his life and thus was able not only to enter into personal contact with him, but also to collect useful information concerning his deeds and his writings. Furthermore, having been a deacon in the Milanese Church, he had gone to Africa with authorization to administer the resources which it possessed in that region; it was thanks to this mission and to his prolonged stay in Africa that Paulinus, coming into contact with Saint Augustine, was ultimately prevailed upon by him, still full of memories of the "father" of his conversion, to draw together into a biography something of the volumes that he knew of the Bishop of Milan. Thus was born the *Life of Ambrose*, a precious source of knowledge about the protagonist of these pages. It is valuable because it was based on oral and written documentation of the first order, including the reflections of those who had seen the Bishop, most especially those of his sister Marcellina, also certain letters and other works by Ambrose. These sources are added to what was known directly by the author.[6] To be sure, in reading it, we must at times prudently sift through Paulinus' enthusiasm for the marvelous deeds and wonders which he derived, if only in limited and controlled measure, from the great models of this literary genre (initiated with the *Life* of the hermit Anthony written by Saint Athanasius of Alexandria in Egypt).

Rufinus of Aquileia, in contrast, is the first of those who refer to Ambrose in the context of a work on history. Better known as a translator into Latin of the masterpieces of Greek spirituality (especially Origen), Rufinus was also familiar with a version of the *History of the Church* by Eusebius of Caesarea and added two chapters to it in his own style, carrying the story up to the death of the Emperor Theodosius. It was in this section, redrafted in 402/403 that Rufinus refers to the incidents involving the Bishop Ambrose, beginning with his election. His testimony is even more reliable since he had direct contact with the Milanese environment, and was in Milan, among other times, in 400, a scant three years after the death of the great Bishop.

Let's listen to Rufinus first. When he presents the scene of Ambrose entering the church to placate the souls there, we discern in his words an alluring vivacity: the spontaneous consensus of the people, following the soothing discourse of the governor, is described as an uproar: "At a stroke the unanimous voice of the people, previously discordant and divided, erupted in a shout, asking for Ambrose to be Bishop. They shouted that he should be baptized immediately… and they nominated him their Bishop. There would have been no other way for them to become a single people with a single faith had Ambrose not been chosen Bishop."[7] A few lines earlier Rufinus had emphasized the mood in referring to the serious gravity of the contrast between the two factions, having spoken of a "catastrophe" that irrevocably threatened the city; in these expressions he emphasizes the contrast with the new situation and, with enthusiastic participation, he describes their rediscovered unity, attributing the cause of this unity to the prospective episcopal consecration of Ambrose. The overall effect expressed in that "roar" seems to be at one and the same time the affectionate exaggeration of a devout memory and a most understandable manifestation of a healthy liberating outburst.

In his version Paulinus, presenting the same episode with a prudent "It is said," recounts that it was a child who, by suddenly calling out "Ambrose Bishop!" had roused the attention of all the people and the choral repetition of this same exclamation.[8] The outcry of the child-prophet has been commented on in various ways. It is first of all connected with numerous celestial oracles manifested precisely in reference to the voice of children. One thinks of the episode of Augustine when, in the garden attached to the house, tortured by his own thoughts, he heard "a voice, like that of a little boy or girl, I don't know which, who spoke singing and repeating many times: 'Take and read, take and read.'" He interpreted "that this should be treated as a divine command to open the book and read the first verse" that would be found.[9] But the episode described by Paulinus, without necessarily losing this symbolic value, is also interpreted as a joke made by a random urchin, sprung out of nowhere from among the adults in that serious and conflicted "assembly." This proposal triggers the memory of another incident, although occurring a dozen years later, during the extremely tense struggle between Ambrose and the Emperor for the possession of a basilica, when children, who were meant to be playing, tore down the "curtains" with which the Emperor had claimed the Portiana Basilica for himself.[10] Perhaps it is not worth the trouble to complicate the study after the fact: we sense all the inventiveness of the brief scene of Paulinus, we note that it may not be unlikely, and above all we remember that the prank of a child doesn't really prove to be too much of a problem, any more than the swift agreement of the people to such an unexpected idea.

And it remained to the people not to cede the victory when the "candidate" himself opposed their request in every possible way. We have already heard from Ambrose himself that he tried to resist, or at least to delay his ordination, surrendering only, in the end, to the "violence" done to him. In such moments there must certainly have prevailed in him a strong sense of indignation, such as we have seen emerge with great intensity again many years after his ordination. If we add to this his lack of theological preparation and his pastoral inexperience, of which he was well aware, we can well imagine a natural displeasure with such an unanticipated life change, or further, we might even call it a truncated career. More than that, his was an instinctive and understandable defensiveness in the face of an offer that promised nothing easy and was extremely exacting: he was asked to dedicate his life and his energies, his heart and his intellect, to this chaotic Milanese Church: Why accept? Why pay the price? Was it an opportunity or perhaps a duty? Did this call come from on high?

Beyond the sober expressions of which we are already aware, Ambrose never expressly confided what passed in his thoughts and feelings in those days. Certainly he also needed to reflect on other contingent, but not trivial, aspects. How firm was the impulsive popular conviction? Should he lean toward weakening the initial enthusiasm or toward a maturing confirmation of the decision already made? What did the Emperor think, to whose service Ambrose was bound by having assumed the office of governor? And what about the priests of the city and the Bishops who normally gather for the election of a new Bishop: would they confirm the popular will? To these questions Ambrose was able to respond only gradually. And we also ought to confront each of these aspects in order, picking up immediately from the pivotal role of the people, which was, without question, central and determinative. Ambrose himself, celebrating the eleventh anniversary of his episcopal ordination on Sunday, December 7th, 385, would turn to the faithful gathered to listen, remembering the role which they had played in all the events: "You are for me like parents, because you gave me the episcopacy: you, I repeat are like children or parents, each of you a child, all together parents."[11] Certainly, if we believe Paulinus, they were "parents" not only in the initial acclamation but also in having known how to refute, blow for blow, the various excuses that Ambrose employed in order to escape. In this matter

Chapter I: Episcopal Election of Governor Ambrose

too, the account in the biography[12] is shown to be most likely true and worthy of being valued and followed. This is without, of course, forgetting that in telling it Paulinus touches on traditional hagiographic themes, namely those of Cyprian of Carthage, Pope Cornelius, and Martin of Tours, to cite only a few examples, who became models of refusal on account of a sense of personal unworthiness and of flight as an extreme attempt in opposition. The first stratagem was the use of torture in the proceedings: that is, Ambrose wanted to demonstrate a cruelty that wasn't his habit in order to try to dampen the enthusiasm of the people; all the more so since ecclesial legislation tended to block access to sacred orders to those who had exercised a political function, precisely because they had the power to shed blood and render unjust judgments. A second attempt was that of "giving himself to philosophy" specifically — as this not particularly lucid passage is interpreted — to that of Neo-Platonism, or in some school that was opposed to Christianity, thus rendering him inadmissible as a Bishop. Even more likely, he intended this gesture in the sense of a positive and profitable mediation between classical thought and Christianity, but taken up full time and thus considered as an alternative to episcopal ministry.[13] The next attempt also failed. We don't know how, but Ambrose supposedly schemed to allow "women of ill repute to enter his house, in full view of everyone, only so that, seeing this, the will of the people might be dissuaded." Beyond the reaction that Paulinus attributes to the people in the first instance regarding torture (they were supposed to have exclaimed, "May your sin fall on us"), it is interesting to note that in this latter case there existed an ecclesial legislation that refused sacred orders to those who had succumbed to sinful desires in their sexual conduct.

Then he tried the most desperate strategy of fleeing, indeed a double flight. The first time, in the middle of the night, he headed for Pavia but, with bitter surprise he found himself the next morning not far from Milan near the Porta Romana. A second time he hid in the house of Leonitus, a person of Senatorial rank. The dismay Ambrose felt about the first flight can be imagined without too much difficulty, if we assume the uncertainties of disorganized exit in the dark of night and then with a snowfall, frequent in the final months of the year in that region, which offers the advantage of passing unobserved but does not exactly facilitate one's orientation. Walking in a southerly direction, he was in fact headed southeast, along the road that leads to Rome. It is more interesting still to note the recurrence in Ambrose of a consistency of comportment in other similar situations: in the year 390, wanting to avoid meeting Theodosius, guilty of the massacre of Thessalonica, he chose simply to absent himself from Milan at the arrival of the Emperor to the city; and in 393-4, in order not to have to take sides officially in the contest with the usurper Eugenius, at his approach he undertook a long trip to parishes in the country far from Milan: to Bologna, Faenza, and Florence.

After the first flight, Paulinus again recalls, once Ambrose was "discovered, he was put under surveillance by the people, a letter was sent to the most lenient Emperor at the time, Valentinian, who appreciated with great joy that his delegated magistrates were sought after for the priesthood."[14] This note merits comment. Valentinian I, successor of that Constantius who had imposed Auxentius on the Milanese seat, was not an "interventionist" in the field of religion as was his predecessor. While personally professing the Nicean faith, he was in fact disposed to remain neutral in religious questions, remembering that it was not licit for a layman to make decisions in matters of faith.[15] On the other hand, Ambrose had undertaken a civil career that he could not interrupt without at least rendering an account of the fact; and the election of the successor to Auxentius, whom Valentinian had left in the seat and respected as Bishop until his death, could not be considered to be of no interest to the Emperor. If it is not easy to interpret the degree to which this correspondence was official, the decision to inform him of the goings on was certainly very advisable and, as we have seen, desired even by Ambrose himself. Besides, Rufinus expressly connects the two features, adding more emphasis to the response of the Emperor: "Given that (Ambrose) was reluctant and put up a stout resistance, the desire of the people was referred to the Emperor, so that order may be satisfied with every consideration. It was the work of God that a spontaneous transformation should

Chapter I: Episcopal Election of Governor Ambrose

return the discordant faith of the people and the divided souls to a unanimous consensus and a single purpose."[16] Valentinian, at that time, resided at Trier, and sent his response from that city. We may note that he maintained neutrality, as was his style. He resolved the situation, ratifying that need for concord that we have seen as being central since the beginning of this narration. The will of Ambrose was, in any case, left in straits, because the people had further confirmed their conviction to have the governor as Bishop, and the Emperor, neutral in respect to questions in the ecclesial area, had never expressed a liking for interfering. At the arrival of the response of Valentinian, the Vicar (the imperial functionary at the civil diocese of Italy and with residence at Milan) arranged to retrieve Ambrose, still hiding with Leonitus. "With the publication of an edict," Paulinus indicates, "everyone was invited to consent, if they wished to protect life and property."[17] He was immediately resigned, not so much because of the proffered threat, but rather because it signified that Valentinian would be forced to discover the secret refuge of Ambrose with Leonitus: if he was to respect the imperial opinion, he knew there was no point in remaining hidden any longer.

At this point in the narration Paulinus introduces an expression, very beautiful in its simplicity, profundity, and substance: "Because (Ambrose) understood the will of God in respect to himself and that he was not allowed to resist any longer,"[18] he chose to be baptized. Thus ends all the reluctance of a candidate before a decision that cannot be revoked and thus is the interior disposition of one who, at the end of much drama and wandering, personally embraced the "violence": throughout this whole week he did not remain indifferent, obstinate or passive, and the parable begun with the outcry of the congregation (or of the child) is concluded now with the resolute decision to receive baptism and then in turn, episcopal consecration.

Throughout this entire episode, right up to this minute, the Bishops and clergy remain excluded. Let's take a look at this oddity that we can't quite thoroughly explain. Perhaps, we can speculate, the popular action was so forceful as to leave in the shadows the role of the clergy in the choice of the right Bishop, and we may simply need to imagine both the deacons and the priests to be divided at first and then marvelously in agreement on the name of Ambrose, with a disposition similar to that of the large crowds. Certainly a part of the clergy had received their sacred orders from Auxentius and so shared his convictions. Others, on the other hand, had distanced themselves from his doctrine and his actions: we can speak of the priest Philastrius, head of the Milanese pro-Nicean cell, and of the Milanese deacon Sabinus, who had represented the orthodox community of Milan at the Roman Council which, sometime around 370, had condemned Auxentius. But what was the percentage of those from the opposing forces? And what was the reciprocal state of mind? And why didn't Rufinus and Paulinus make their position known? We don't know for sure.

As to the Bishops, the 4th canon of the Council of Nicea requires all who belong to a given ecclesiastical province, or at least three of them, to convene to nominate a new Bishop: they are empowered to render definitive the popular designation, confirming the election and proceeding to the ordination of the candidate. No indication has come to us specifically which and how many Bishops may have been present in Milan. In any case, they would have wanted not only to express a favorable point of view, but beyond that, to overcome any impediment that might have been created because of the anomalous situation of having a neophyte as a candidate. Indeed we ought to remember that, like many of his era, and though raised in a family of strong Christian tradition, Ambrose had not yet received baptism. To consent to the episcopal ordination to someone such as he meant therefore to admit to orders one who, in effect, had only recently embraced the way of faith. Previously the Apostle Paul had taught that the Bishop should not be "a neophyte, lest he become conceited and thus incur the devil's punishment" (1 Tm 3:6); and the consular canons, the 2nd of Nicea and the 10th of Serdica (343), had transformed this suggestion into a disciplinary norm. Anyway, cases of exceptions in similar dispositions were not rare, especially in the East, and Ambrose was aware that among his peers even the Westerners functioned in the same way. This is expressed in the letter to the people of Vercel-

Chapter I: Episcopal Election of Governor Ambrose

li, already cited: "The Bishops of the West with their judgment, and those of the East with their example, approved of my ordination" and after having recalled the opposing expression of Paul, adds, delicately interpreting the motive for the exception: "If the ordination was not delayed, that was due to an act of force by whoever constrained me; if the humility required for the episcopacy isn't lacking, where one is not the cause, guilt cannot be imputed."[19] By now persuaded of his candidacy, Ambrose might have still willingly delayed the reception of sacred orders, but he must have had to give in and move this moment forward.

"Once baptized, he exercised, as much as possible, all the functions of ecclesiastical ministry. And on the eighth day he was ordained Bishop, with the highest approval and joy on the part of everyone."[20] Thus Paulinus describes the week of grace that saw Ambrose made a Christian on Sunday, November 30, 374, and consecrated Bishop of the Church of Milan on the following Sunday, December 7.[21] As for the "functions of ecclesiastical ministry" that he was to have exercised in that brief span of a few days, even if the expression is broadly interpreted as indicating the passage of Ambrose through certain levels of orders before succeeding to the episcopacy, perhaps it is intended more simply in the sense of an initial and symbolic exploration of his new duties and pastoral responsibilities: the granting of all the sacred orders in such an abbreviated sequence might reveal, in fact, a preoccupation with formulaic completion, anachronistic by that time.[22]

By the explicit request of Ambrose the rites were celebrated by a Catholic Bishop: "He chose not to be baptized if not by a Catholic Bishop" attests his faithful biographer.[23] He did not wish to camouflage the peace which the community so desperately needed with a doctrinal compromise and he signaled which direction he wanted to move to reconstruct the desired unity. But who was this Bishop? Neither Ambrose nor other historical sources, and nothing of the Milanese tradition, have left us his name. Not a few have thought it Simplician, whom Augustine called "the father of Ambrose by the grace received through him"[24] but he, however, was a priest and so would have served in some subordinate ministry in the celebration of the baptism.²⁵ Another suggestion comes instead from the tradition of the Church of Vercelli, which has preserved the name of its own Bishop Limenius as the one who administered the baptism and the episcopal ordination of Ambrose. The theory is provocative and deserves to be examined in some detail,²⁶ even if it cannot be considered a confidently positive proof. An ancient Vercellese calendar, which was adapted to the Roman Rite in 1576 by the Bishop of Vercelli, Giovanni Francesco Bonhomini (Bonomi), in any case conserved the commemorations in a manner typical of the local tradition, registering on the date of 30 November and 7 December respectively the record of the baptism and episcopal ordination of St. Ambrose, adding in both cases the expression "by the hand of Saint Limenius, Bishop of the Church of Vercelli." Limenius was the successor of St. Eusebius to the Vercellese cathedra and was the predecessor of St. Honoratus, the one and the other strictly certified in the Milanese succession: the first for having collaborated with Dionysius of Milan in the Council of 355, the battle in favor of the Nicene doctrine, and for also being as quickly exiled; the second for having been elected thanks to the conciliatory intervention of Ambrose, again on the vigil of his death, as we will have occasion to describe later.

In any case, the silence of Ambrose in regards to this is striking, considering that he sent an extremely long letter to the Church of Vercelli on the occasion of the election of Honoratus, in which he recalls the succession of Dionysius and of Eusebius and, as we have seen, his own election. The rest of this whole letter describes a situation of serious disagreement and confusion at Vercelli, leaving us to presume that such failures were produced in the final years of the episcopacy of Limenius; as a matter of fact, by not expressing himself openly, Ambrose seems not to deny whatever responsibility there was on part of that same Limenius, whom he never named, as if drawing attention to a deliberate omission. The question arises as to whether, in the eyes of the Bishop of Milan, the image of Limenius might have been tainted or even deserved criticism. If so and thus motivated, the name of the one who in theory had conferred baptism and episcopal

Chapter I: Episcopal Election of Governor Ambrose

ordination was systematically erased in this letter and in his other letters and even from the biography of Paulinus.

Ordained by a Catholic Bishop, Ambrose began his prolific and laborious ministry in the Church of Milan.

But who was this governor so unexpectedly plucked from the political scene to pastoral service? What were his origins? What family shaped his human character and formed his religious faith? What can we learn of his growing up and of the roots out of which he developed? Before taking up the story, let us pause to look back, to recall the interesting details of his past.

CHAPTER II

Family Roots and His Youth

When he became Bishop, Ambrose would have been less than 35 years old, having been born around the year 340. The scholars, to tell the truth, have for a long time oscillated between this date and another, which puts his birth forward to around the year 334, in this case, envisioning the episcopal election when he was of a more mature age, around 40 years old.[1] Recently, however, Hervé Savon[2] has drawn attention to an expression found in the *Apology* addressed from Palladius of Ratiaria to Ambrose following the Council of Aquileia in 381 (a text to which we will have reason to return in later chapters). Contentiously turning on Ambrose, Palladius rebukes him saying: "You, without even stopping to think, have claimed to be able to make judgment in the space of an hour on persons whose episcopacy, of a long duration and, so far as consented to by human conscience, irreproachable, surpasses the years of your sordid lasciviousness. In fact, one of them, after 11 years as a priest, was noted for being Bishop for 35 years."[3] By this, he means that the number of years during which Ambrose was not yet baptized (identified as the years of "sordid lasciviousness"!) were fewer than the 35 years in which Palladius was Bishop (who speaks here in the third person).

It is a matter, substantially, of interpreting two sources: a letter that Ambrose wrote to Bishop Severinus of Naples and a tiny bit of news furnished by his biographer Paulinus. The chronological interest in the letter to Severinus consists in the dual reference first to a certain "barbaric incursion" and to "the tumult of War" to which Milan found itself exposed in that moment, and hence to his correct age of fifty-three. It remains uncertain to which tragic events Ambrose was alluding, to the invasion of the usurper Maximus which took place in 387 or to another by Eugenius in 392. We are still left therefore with the two dates for the birth of Ambrose.

We are thus drawn back to consider the year 340 as the year of the birth of Ambrose. The biographer Paulinus tells us, that "Ambrose was born while his father Ambrose (after whom he was named) executed his official functions at the prefecture in Gaul." We do not know whether the expression used in the biography[4] means that the father was effectively prefect of the Praetorian Guard or that he simply executed some other responsibility in the prefecture. In any case from this phrase we are able to derive precious information: because the prefect of the Praetorian Guards of Gaul resided at Treveri, this ancient Roman city (today Trier, in Germany, in the Rhineland-Palatinate) must be considered the birthplace of Ambrose and the place of his infancy.

This last hypothesis permits greater latitude in the extension of the phases in the life of Ambrose and above all allows us to imagine his nomination as Bishop to have taken place when he was of a more mature age.

When he was born, the family of Officer Ambrose had already enjoyed the arrival of two other children: Marcellina, the older sister who would be consecrated to God and who would become the confidant of her brother in the most anxious moments of his episcopal ministry, and who would survive him for a brief period of time; and Satyrus, to whom Ambrose was bound by a very lively affection, whom we will see leave this life a few years after the episcopal ordination of his brother. But the serenity of this cheerful nuclear family was immediately broken by the premature death of the father. Paulinus hints at this when, skipping intermediate events, he passes from the infancy of Ambrose directly to record the moment in which, "already an adolescent," he resided "in the city of Rome with his widowed mother and sister,"[5] which may be said to be the *domus Ambrosii*, still preserved in the Rione or District known as Sant'Angelo in Rome, on the Via di Sant'Ambrogio.[6] In all likelihood the return of the family to Rome, their city of origin, would come to be linked with the tragic imperial events of 340. In that year, in fact, the Emperor Constantine II, who, at the death of his father Constantine the Great (337) had received the governorship of Britannia, Gaul, and Spain,

Chapter II: Family Roots and His Youth

establishing his residence precisely at Trier, invaded northern Italy in a vain attempt to overthrow his brother Constans, but he died defeated at Aquileia. The family of Ambrose the officer may not have been able to remain without being implicated in that fall, and it is highly probable that precisely in that situation, with Ambrose merely an infant, they would have left Trier. As a matter of fact, it may even have happened that the father went missing after having returned to Rome. It is equally possible to theorize that he may have already died during the campaign of Constantine II or perhaps at Trier due to the violence that would have followed the death of the Emperor.

But the moment has come to become more familiar with the ancient roots and fundamental characteristics of this family which left such a strong impression on the interior disposition, the deeds, and the thought of Bishop Ambrose.

His was certainly a family of ancient Christian tradition. From among the ancestors on his father's side was numbered a martyr, Saint Soteris, probably condemned during the persecution of Diocletian (303), buried along the Via Appia and commemorated in the liturgy on February 11.[7] Ambrose speaks about her in the conclusion of the three books *On Virgins*, the first work he composed, published in 377. Soteris, we read, "at the time of the persecutions, scaled the height of suffering, even suffering outrages reserved for slaves, going so far as to offer her face to the executioner, which, while her body had been subjected to torment, alone had been preserved from injury; and rather than simply bearing it, she wanted to suffer; so strong and patient was she that she offered her soft cheeks to the punishment. The executioner exhausted himself striking her before the martyr yielded to the blows. She did not bow her head or turn away, nor did she let a single tear fall or allow herself to be conquered by her suffering. Finally after having resisted every kind of punishment, she discovered the sword she sought." In his description, Ambrose has probably mingled common narrative elements that apply also to other Christian martyrs with the memories of the family. In any case, it is certain that Soteris was not a stranger to Ambrose, nor to his sister Marcellina: in this passage, interpreting the decision of his sister to consecrate herself to

God and turning herself to Him, the Bishop had rightly remembered her as being "educated by an inspired tradition of hereditary chastity, infused in you by a martyr relative."[8]

In the recollection of Ambrose, alongside her supplication to die by the sword, the face of Soteris captures his admiring attention: for the firmness that she maintained, for the calmness which remained undiminished by her trials and, one might add, for that noble beauty which dared to immolate and sacrifice itself to a supreme ideal. Emphasizing this last aspect in a homily delivered at Florence many years later, in March of 394, Ambrose would return to describe Saint Soteris: "So beautiful in countenance and virgin of a great noble family, she considered the consulates and prefectures of her ancestors in the holy faith and would not consent to the order to sacrifice. The cruel prosecutor ordered her to be slapped in such a way that the young virgin would yield either to pain or to shame. But she, as soon as she heard this order, exposed her face, unveiled and uncovered for martyrdom only, and willingly ran to meet the offence offering her face."[9] We have already met Marcellina following in the footsteps of Soteris. The virginal choice of the sister of Ambrose, matured in the profoundly religious climate that the family breathed, culminated with the imposition of the veil by Pope Liberius, it is believed either on the day of Epiphany in 353 or on Christmas day in 352.[10] Perhaps the great Bishop of Alexandria, Athanasius, an exile from Rome in those years, strenuous defender of Nicene orthodoxy and resolute advocate of the monastic vocation, had blessed that decision and rekindled that spiritual climate. The description that Ambrose makes of the vows of Marcellina in the 3rd book of *On Virgins* reveals certain similarities with an analogous work of Athanasius, the *Letter to the Virgins*;[11] but in any case, the entire treatise of *On Virgins*, expressly dedicated to Marcellina, and the other works on virginity that the Bishop would compose show without any shadow of a doubt what a deep influence the words and the example of his sister had on Ambrose and on his teaching.

Marcellina continued to live out her consecration within the family, as was usual at that time, together with a friend who shared

Chapter II: Family Roots and His Youth

her choice. The house would have been frequently visited by religious personalities, even by Bishops (certainly by Liberius, possibly by Athanasius, and by still others). We get an anecdote from these visits, retold by Paulinus: Ambrose, seeing the diffident kissing of the hand that his mother and sister and her companion offered in meeting the visiting Bishops, "in jest, offered his right hand saying that he, too, was worthy of such a homage, thus relating that he would become a Bishop one day." The biographer continues, explaining that in Ambrose "the Spirit of the Lord had spoken, saying that he would be raised to the episcopacy." We may find the reaction of his sister's companion to be more natural, as Paulinus observes, "She did not listen, thinking that he was just a boy and that therefore he didn't know what he was saying."[12] Nevertheless, it remains to add that Ambrose never forgot the reaction of the virgin: going back to Rome a few years after his ordination to visit, Paulinus — as usual — records, "while she was kissing his right hand he said, smiling, 'Look, as I told you, you kiss the hand of a Bishop.'"[13] If we return to the playful boy of this anecdote, we notice that he grew up in a healthy environment and that he would have had as a result an adolescence and a serene childhood, fruitful in its results.[14] There is no indication, either in Paulinus nor even in Ambrose himself, whom we have seen in other places to have been such a severe judge of himself, to lead us to imagine in his background upsetting or anguish producing experiences such as those of his illustrious disciple Augustine.

It is not possible to fully understand the figure of Ambrose unless, along with the Christian roots of his family, his Roman origins are also highlighted, more precisely his membership in the senatorial nobility of the city. It is not impossible that his remote ancestors may have come from Greece or more simply had had contacts with the Hellenistic world, as are hinted at in the names Soteris, Satyrus, and Ambrose which remained in use among the members of the family; but the insertion of the family into the Roman environment would have occurred in very ancient times, because even in recalling the martyrdom of Soteris, ancestor from his father's side, we have seen the Bishop make mention of consuls and prefectures, among whom would have been listed certain members of his family.

His belonging to the Roman senatorial nobility explains the high office exercised by his father at Trier. Furthermore the full name of the saint — Aurelius Ambrosius — suggests the hypothesis, generally considered plausible, that from his mother's side of the family he may have been bound to the *gens Aurelia*. And an even tighter link with the noble family of Symmachus is attested to by the exchange of letters in the episodes in which Ambrose intervened with Quintus Aurelius Symmachus and which are signs of a persistent friendship between the two beyond their differences over the attempts on the part of Symmachus to restore paganism.[15] Finally, as with every senatorial family, that of Ambrose also had to possess enormous wealth: a series of dates and clues permit one to affirm that he would have had properties both in Sicily and Africa. Satyrus, the brother of Ambrose, will appear in these regions to take care of such possessions; and these are the same goods which, donated by Ambrose to the Church of Milan on the occasion of his episcopal ordination, constituted a secure patrimony for it in the following centuries.[16] We shouldn't marvel, then, that a member of one of the most prestigious Roman families would have had a public career and would have, further, landed at Milan as a *consularis*, that is, governor of a province. For this information too we are in debt to Paulinus: Ambrose, he attests briefly, "left the city to practice [the profession of lawyer] in the audience hall of the prefecture of the praetorian," and "argued cases so splendidly that he was selected by the illustrious Probus, then prefect of the praetorian, to sit in Council. After this he assumed the badge of *consularis*, to administer the province of Liguria and Aemelia, and went to Milan."[17] While Sextus Claudius Petronius Probus was prefect of the praetorian at Sirmium, Ambrose would have exercised the profession of lawyer in this city on the banks of the Sava, capital of Pannonia Secunda (today Srijemska Mitrovica). His presence at Sirmium can be fixed to the years 365-370; the promotion as a member of the prefect's Council would have occurred specifically in 368, when Probus took the seat, or a little after. Paulinus says that the prefect, in saluting Ambrose upon his leaving

Chapter II: Family Roots and His Youth

for Milan, would have given him instructions, according to custom, recommending that he: "Go and act, not like a magistrate, but like a Bishop."[18] This peculiar prognostication, and in general the favorable attitude of Probus in his dealings with Ambrose, allows us to allude to the prefect's Christian roots (who, unfortunately, was otherwise less noted for amassing evangelical goods than for grabbing power and wealth), or even better to the influence on him by his wife Anicia Faltonia Probus, whose sincere religious sensibility is beyond doubt.

Having described the family of Ambrose with its unique characteristics we want to move on to also sketch out the steps that led its illustrious son from Trier to Rome, to Sirmium, and finally to Milan: at the point, that is, at which they can be connected to those of the preceding chapter. It remains to note that, alongside the substantiated elements that stand at the basis of the formation of Ambrose, only rarely have we found interesting news and direct information concerning his family. To tell the truth Paulinus records an episode which would allow us to see the whole family reunited (excluding, however, Satyrus, because the biographer never mentions him). At Trier, he recounts, while Ambrose, "still a baby, lay in the crib in the praetorian's courtyard sleeping with his mouth open when suddenly a swarm of bees came up and covered his face and mouth, such that there was a continual coming and going on the part of the ones who went in and out." Ambrose's father was present, "walking nearby with mother and daughter." He didn't want the nursemaid to chase the bees away, although he "pondered with paternal worry how this prodigious event might end." When the bees finally "rose together high in the air so that they could no longer be seen by the human eye," then, "impressed by this event, he exclaimed: 'If this baby lives, he will be someone great.'" Paulinus concludes by interpreting the presence of the bees as a portent of the writings of Ambrose which, like sweet honey, "would have announced the gifts of heaven and raised human minds from earthly things to heaven."[19] What is there to say? It provokes diverse judgments from the commentators:[20] some say that it was a naturally explainable fact; others that it was an episode of symbolic value or perhaps a singular anecdote or a dubious tradition. Certainly the story, rich in symbolic significance, had already been retold of famous personages of classical antiquity (beginning with Plato and Pindar) and successively it would have been used also for Christian writers (for example, Isidore of Seville, in the 6th/7th century). In its principal lines it may have some basis in reality or it may have been totally reconstructed as a symbol. In the case of Ambrose, noting that the episode had provided a series of two non-convergent interpretations, the one attributed to the father and the other provided by the biographer himself, causes one to think that on the one side it may have been derived from something that made the father formulate an explanation quite generic on the "great" future of his son, and on the other side that Paulinus, in line with the tradition and with his own taste for the marvelous, had further enriched the episode underlining the symbolism of eloquence, sweet and nutritious like honey, that fascinated and gave strength to the hearers.

But even in this narration the parents of Ambrose, the mother above all, make a very brief appearance. Of Marcellina and Satyrus the brother speaks more fully in his writings, and we turn to discuss them in the next chapter. But Ambrose never mentions his parents: perhaps because they were prematurely departed, perhaps out of a sense of modesty and a delicate reserve in their regard. Nevertheless, from them he had received his great Christian values and Roman tradition, and in their household he would have had taken and tasted the sense of family and admired the generous dedication of his parents. If we take up the homily which he delivered on December 7, 385 on the eleventh anniversary of his episcopal ordination, we saw how he turned to the faithful calling them his parents, we read there an attitude of appreciation toward parents and a portrait of mothers marvelously and delicately alive, which perhaps suggests to us something of his own mother.

Let us listen to what he said: "'Honor your father and your mother'...honor them with demonstrations of respect in such a way as to abstain from every offense, so that not even with a facial expression should you lack in reverence for your parents.... Honor nevertheless does not consist only in the manifestations of respect, but also

Chapter II: Family Roots and His Youth

in generosity... honor signifies giving aid according to the merits. Take care of your father; take care of your mother. And even when you have taken care of your mother, you will never be able to make up for the sorrow, you will never be able to make up for the pain she has suffered for you; you will never be able to compensate for the love with which she carried you in her womb, nor the nourishment she gave you, pressing her breasts delicately to your lips with tenderness and affection; you will not be able to make up for the hunger that she bore for you when she refused to eat anything that might do you harm, nor touch anything that might adversely affect her milk. For you she denied herself the food that she deserved, for you she ate food that she did not like, for you she has kept watch, over you she cried: and could you then allow her to live in need? Oh my son, what terrible justice you call upon yourself if you do not support her who gave you birth! You owe what you have to that one whom you owe what you are."[21] The person whom the people of Milan had chosen as their new pastor was truly equipped for the work to which he had been called: from the family he had acquired a solid foundation of Christian values, and also thanks to the family he had received his noble Roman heritage and thus was able to rise to fulfill his responsibilities in civil society, acquiring an experience of considerable value. He had, further, a delicate sensibility, of which we have only recounted a few enlightening examples: the same sensibility that he will affirm, continuing the phrases which we read in the preceding chapter: "Since I too have taken on certain work for your holy Church, protect the results. Do not allow to be lost, now that he is a Bishop, one who, when he was lost, you called to the episcopacy, and give me, first of all to be able to share in intimate participation in the pain of sinners. This, indeed, is the highest virtue... as a matter of fact, every time I care for one who has fallen, permit me to provide compassion and to not absolutely chastise them, but groan and weep, so that, while weeping for another, I weep for myself."[22] Ambrose, through his family, presents himself in this way. And now we have reached the moment to see him at work, beginning with that intense preparation which he had to and wanted to undertake in the first months of his episcopacy. Before concluding, however, it is only right to add a word about his physical appearance. I base my comments on the mosaic of the 5th century which portrays him between the martyrs Protasius and Gervasius in the chapel of S. Vittore in Ciel d'oro (today annexed to the Basilica of S. Ambrogio): in the features of the mosaic, in fact, scholars have recognized a record of a real resemblance to Ambrose.[23] Angelo Paredi in his commentary notes, in the portrayal of the face, "the slight asymmetry of the eyes, the short cut of the hair, the mustache and dark colored beard tending toward chestnut." Elsewhere, completing a sketch of the physical appearance of Ambrose, also revealed in that portrait, he describes him in this fashion: "He was short in stature, with an elongated and thin face, his black beard and mustache making the delicate white of his features stand out; large suggestive eyes were rendered more attractive by a slight asymmetry, such that the right was a little lower than the left; his pose, finally, was calm and relaxed, revealing the Roman aristocrat, declaring that he possessed in his blood the art and the ability to command."[24] The slender and strong figure of Governor Ambrose is now coming to lead the people of Milan who had stubbornly wanted him as their pastor.

CHAPTER III

His Early Formation and "Father" Simplician

Governor Ambrose had his own good reasons for at least wanting the episcopal ordination to be delayed. We know that he was not listened to, so, confessing to his readers in a passage which has become famous: "I was torn from the court and the trappings of the magistrate to the priesthood to teach you what I myself had not learned. And thus it was that I had to teach before I began to learn. I must, therefore, simultaneously learn and teach, since before now I had no leisure to learn." This passage can be found at the beginning of his treatise *On the Duties of the Clergy*[1] which was published in 389/390. By the time the Bishop published this text nearly 15 years had passed since those difficult moments.

Closer to that time we find his impressions expressed in the first book of his treatise *On Virgins*, which we know was already circulating in 377. Ambrose introduces the topic in his discourse recalling the Gospel parable of the talents. If the servants are required to increase the capital they have received, the Bishop recognizes, then "I too, though given scant intelligence, have the greatest duty of making the word of God increase in the minds of the people who have been entrusted to me." Further, "The Lord asked us to be zealous, not successful." Furthermore, he foresaw that he would need to be better prepared for a time when he might have to offer an oral argument. Ambrose confided in having chosen the written form of communication because at least "the book does not blush." With humility and wit the Bishop compared himself with the ass of Balaam, which, upon the sight of the Angel of the Lord, had miraculously begun to speak (cf. Nb 22:22-35). Thus, with his writing, he finally managed to loosen "the tongue which had long been mute" (and this was, in fact, the first work he published). Further he remembers the staff of Aaron, which had miraculously produced buds and caused flowers to bloom in the tent of the commandments (cf. Nb 17:16-26), and explains the fidelity with which in the same way God can "easily cause a flower to blossom in the holy Church, even from our nodes." Finally, he proposes the similarity with the bush from which God had spoken to Moses on Mount Horeb (cf. Ex 3:1-6), and imagined "those who, even in my brambles, will be seen to shine with a certain radiance," as well as "those by whom my voice is heard from the bush who loosen the sandals from their feet," and are freed to walk. At this point of the oration the Bishop notices himself using an illustration that does not reflect that sense of incapacity and of unworthiness with which he had intended to present himself. He seems even to have attributed arbitrarily to himself "the prerogative of holy men." But he corrects himself immediately. Alluding to two Gospel images, one about Nathaniel who rests under the fig tree (Jn 1:48) and above all that of the sterile fig which, after three years, the master wanted to cut down but which the farmer chose to leave one more year (cf. Lk 13:6-9), he thus invokes a prayer: "Oh that Jesus for his part might wish to look down upon me, who is still lounging under a barren fig. Perhaps, after three years my fig tree too will bear fruit." Obviously the three years are those suggested by the parable, but even these allude to the brief episcopacy that Ambrose had up to that point. The illustration continues with one last application, in which the Bishop reveals once again his own modesty as well as an agreeable earthiness: "Oh that the cultivator of the vineyard of the Lord, of whom the Gospel speaks, who may have already received the order to cut my fig tree down, might be merciful yet this year, first digging around it and laying down a load of manure, who knows but that this tree might lift the needy up from the dust with strength and raise up the poor from the ash heap (Ps 112/113:7)"![2]

What do these doubtlessly sincere outpourings of Ambrose mean? What Christian formation had he had, other than that basic training received at home? He was certainly "instructed in the liberal arts," as Paulinus attests.[3] But this brief reference from his bi-

Chapter III: His Early Formation and "Father" Simplician

ography attests only that Ambrose had followed the regular course of studies in the ancient world. After his elementary studies he had then attended the school of *grammatica* and then higher education taught by a *rector* learning specifically the "liberal arts" by which is understood, as is noted, the three literary arts of grammar, rhetoric, and dialectic (the *trivium* of the Middle Ages) and the four scientific disciplines of arithmetic, geometry, music, and astronomy (that is the *quadrivium*).

In the pastoral activity of the Bishop, Ambrose will be able to make use of the fruit of these studies. In his hymns, which made him famous in future generations, we perceive that his musical preparation was at a high level. In his treatise *On the Six Days of Creation* we see the ripening fruit of his awareness of natural phenomena and of the animal and vegetable worlds. In general in his writings we recognize echoes of his literary studies and of his taste for the classics, which he loved to cite, sometimes explicitly, but even more so to imitate and recall them by means of veiled allusions. The list of authors directly noted by Ambrose, or known by him through collections of literary pieces, such as poems, short stories or plays, would be quite long: we can at least list the names of Virgil, Cicero, Sallust and Seneca of the Latinists, and Homer, Plato, and Xenophon of the Greeks. Regarding the Greek language, it is worth noting that Ambrose had a good command of it, because not only does he demonstrate his knowledge of classical and Christian authors whom he quotes in this idiom, but not infrequently he cites their Greek words or expressions, stopping then to explain shades of meaning.

But let us return to the lack of pastoral and theological preparation to which the Bishop had admitted with such disarming humor. Certainly, his specific preparation was clearly limited, as recently demonstrated by Chiara Somenzi.[4] In his youthful years at Rome Ambrose participated in a lively debate between the local Christian community and that of the local Jews, provoking the latter with a Latin translation which was an engaging rewriting of the treatise *On the Jewish Wars* by Flavius Josephus. Thus, early on he developed an important awareness of the Hebrew world which he would then have brought to bear on his exegesis of Scripture. In any case his theological and pastoral preparation lacked that experience and those investigations that other clerics would have possessed. He does not give up in the face of those difficulties, but wanted to and knew how to prepare himself. In particular he dedicated himself with care to biblical and theological study, plunging into the Scriptures and reading the works of the great Fathers, his contemporaries and his antecedents.

Jerome of Stridon, the famous monk exegete and translator of the Bible, seems rather to have taken Ambrose's expressions of modesty literally, and with the fiery character which set him apart, he was prone to form cutting judgments on the literary production of the Bishop. Perhaps the supposed involvement of the Bishop of Milan in the serious humiliation which the Roman clergy inflicted on the Dalmatian monk in 384 exacerbated his reaction in his dealings with Ambrose. Jerome had been the collaborator of Pope Damasus and his de facto successor designate, but now instead he found himself put aside and practically forced to leave Rome for the East.[5]

Here it is necessary to report Jerome's most serious judgment, which he expressed just two or three years after that incident. In his *Preface to the Books of Didymus on the Holy Spirit*, a work he translated, alluding to Ambrose without naming him, he claimed: "I prefer to appear to be a translator of the work of another rather than of that disgraceful prattle, to try to make myself attractive with the colors of others as certain people do! I recently read the books of one such individual on the Holy Spirit and, as the comic poet (Terence) said, I saw works drawn from good Greek into bad Latin. I found neither nuance nor virility nor distinction… but it was all flaccid, soft, showy and ornate." His reference is to the treatise on *On the Holy Spirit,* published by Ambrose in 381. Jerome concluded by inviting the reader to consult his translation of Didymus and not that unworthy work of plagiarism, and thus to "recognize what the Latins stole" and to scorn "the rivulets of the gutters, having begun to draw from the fonts themselves."[6] Such acerbity leaves one at a loss. Rufinus of Aquileia, whom we know to have translated and extended the *History of the Church* of Eusebius and who had personally suffered the

Chapter III: His Early Formation and "Father" Simplician

attacks of Jerome, felt the duty to defend Ambrose and, in his *Apology Against Jerome*, referring to the preface already cited, observed: "You have heard how… he shamefully tormented him and claimed that he who had been chosen by God for the glory of the Church of Christ, who in order to give testimony to the Lord had spoken in front of persecuting kings and was not refuted, had nothing of manly virility. Saint Ambrose wrote of the Holy Spirit not only with words, but also with his blood." Rufinus is even convinced that Jerome had translated the work of Didymus precisely in order to pick a fight with the Bishop of Milan.[7]

Rufinus wanted to respond. Ambrose, however, kept silent, perhaps so as not to elevate the dispute, perhaps out of an instinctive sense of pride which kept him from getting swept up in the brawl. Or perhaps acting out in person the patience in humiliations that we find spoken of in one of his mature homilies of 395-6: "Whoever is humiliated must not be dejected or discouraged but above all derive from the humiliation the motivation for spiritual progress, in a way as to appease the proud man with one's own humility… and to wipe out the offenses with one's own patience." He should, in fact, imitate Christ the Lord, who did not avert "his face from the humiliation of the spitting, and because of this he taught everyone with his forebearance."[8] But, in the bitterness of these disputes, certain serious questions remain open: could there not be, perhaps, something true in Jerome's criticism? Was Ambrose an unprepared writer, a vulgarizer of the thoughts of others (if not exactly a plagiarizer)? And, to expand the context of these questions: was he merely an organizer and an effective and generous functionary, or was he more to be known for his advanced speculative abilities? Beginning with more circumstantial observations, we at least have to admit that certain improvisations, even unusual or forced exegesis[9] are to be found in the work of Ambrose. But individual and partial errors certainly do not condemn the entirety of his work. Furthermore, beyond improvising, he admits the lack of time for finalizing and organizing his thought. Ambrose was a pastor and was never able to systematically collect his theological reflections. Still he was an intelligent assimilator who, without embarrassment, made use of what he had learned from his reading: he does not habitually cite his sources, a practice readily accepted in the ancient world. In any case even restating that which he found in others, he never missed a chance to add a personal touch, either in order to adapt it to the pastoral situation which he was addressing or, perhaps because of his sharp mental instincts, to keep him from being an annoying repeater, which led him to appropriate unusual brief phrases from others.

In one well documented and compelling study, Raniero Cantalamessa, while making specific reference to Ambrose's reflections on the subject of the Trinity, expresses a judgment which we can hold to be of value in general: "Ambrose is recognized, to a very notable degree, for his capacity to seize on problems, to assimilate some solutions and to find for them (in this excelling his teachers) clear formulations, in which the ecclesiastical orthodoxy is laid out in perfect form.... But above all Ambrose is recognized for his basic coherence and his authentic theological personality which was able to take in and organize the conclusions of the theological work developing around him."[10] In this last sense it is possible to affirm that the Bishop, on certain themes, knew how to develop treatises with a genuinely personal interpretation which constitute an effective progress in the field of theological reflection.

Prescinding from these general considerations, let us turn to describe something of Ambrose's initial preparation remembering that it would have entailed, beyond the field of theological studies, his spiritual and pastoral formation as well.

In this regard a brief expression of Saint Augustine in his *Confessions* comes to our aid. Speaking about the priest Simplician, to whom he went in order to receive enlightenment on his journey toward conversion, he presents him as "father through the grace of Bishop Ambrose, which I received from him," adding that Simplician was "'loved like a father' by the Bishop."[11] We know that that expression specifically indicates Simplician's participation in the celebration of baptism in some subordinate ministry. But we understand that the relationship between the two cannot be reduced to that moment.

Chapter III: His Early Formation and "Father" Simplician

Indeed, it was up to Simplician to guide the inexpert governor in the mission with which he was entrusted. First, however, he needed to prepare him spiritually to receive the sacraments of Christian initiation and of Sacred Orders. Further, he helped him to take steps in pastoral action and in biblical and theological formation.

It is worth the effort to get to know this noble personage better[12] who, on the death of Ambrose, was for a brief time his successor to the Milanese see. Born around 325, possibly in Milan, and having become a member of the Milanese clergy, he spent some time in residence at Rome. In this city he was put in contact with Marius Victorinus, the originator of Latin Neo-Platonism. Simplician played a preeminent role in his conversion to Christianity.

It is surely most likely that, while at Rome, Simplician met the young Ambrose and frequented his house, as other ecclesiastics were seen to do as well. This would help better explain why the governor, put in a bind by his surprising nomination to the episcopacy, would have turned to him for insight and assistance during this crisis, going to Rome specifically for this purpose. "Expert" in conversions, since he had led Marius Victorinus and later also guided Augustine, he was well positioned to support Ambrose in this delicate transition. Furthermore, his association with Marius Victorinus guaranteed Ambrose a rigorous philosophical preparation. In Milan Simplician would later give life to a Neo-Platonic circle, of marked spiritual bent, whose most eminent representatives would be Augustine, Flavius Manlius Theodorus and other esteemed men of culture. That same group would have been able to take upon itself Ambrose's theological preparation, in particular regarding the Arian question. Indeed, in Rome Simplician would have been in contact with Athanasius of Alexandria who, as we have seen, was living in exile in that city. He was, moreover, surely in contact with Marius Victorinus following his conversion and would have consulted the writings which he composed against the Arians.

Simplician, therefore, was well prepared to be a potent teacher for Ambrose. But what pedagogy did he adopt in the instruction of the new Bishop? Our point of departure is with the four letters sent by the Bishop to his master,[13] all of them observations on biblical passages. In these, it is notable that while Ambrose appears to be the one who is carrying out the role of teacher in these dealings with Simplician, in reality the opposite is true. It is with this method, above all, that with such fine tact Simplician guided his disciple, inciting him to undertake personal research.

This art of teaching was a characteristic aspect of the personality of Simplician: Gennadius Massiliensis informs us that in the only writing of which we are aware, entitled *Letter with Texts to Develop,* "he teaches by asking questions as if wishing to learn."[14] Simplician, that is, to use a well chosen definition of Aimé Solignac, "belonged to a category of those who do not write, or who write little, not because they lack ideas, but because they have too many, or rather their fine intelligence carries them to consider any formulations whatsoever as inadequate in respect to the truth."[15] But despite this they never cease from being formidable guides and careful exhorters of their disciples: in the writings of the latter, in fact, his thoughts are found and, in a way, that is their publication. In this sense, it is to Simplician that we owe the work of Ambrose.

We could add here something about the teaching techniques of Simplician with Augustine, but we press on to learn something more about Ambrose, his intellectual preparation, and his mode of study.

Indeed, Ambrose loved silence. He cultivated it as a fertile ground for his reflection and study. It is curious to note in his treatise *On the Duties of the Clergy,* immediately after expressions concerning his personal lack of preparation (about which we read at the beginning of this chapter), he develops the argument for silence.[16] Almost as if to indicate the desire for silence which pervaded him, he expresses his conviction that only by means of concentration is it possible to penetrate into the depths of one's conscience. The famous passage of Augustine is most eloquent where he describes how Ambrose, in moments when he was free from the needy crowd, "restored his soul by reading." And he adds, "In reading, the eyes scan the page and the heart penetrates the meaning; but voice and tongue remain at rest."

In reference to this, Augustine, when he had entered the room

32

Chapter III: His Early Formation and "Father" Simplician

to pay a visit to Ambrose and found him thus absorbed, as if interpreting a tacit desire of the Bishop, did not dare to interrupt: "Who, in fact, would have dared to disturb him in his concentration?" Regarding this practice, it was not usual among the ancients to read without pronouncing the words. Augustine interpreted the motive to be either that the Bishop wished to avoid an unnecessary loss of what little time he could dedicate to reading due to interruptions by listeners interested in the argument, or that he intended "to save his voice, which was easily weakened." The general impression that one gets from this narration is, in any case, that of a great concentration: as a result of this Ambrose bore abundant fruit in the reading he did; and he managed to assimilate a great deal, even while finding himself immersed in such an active and intense life. Augustine concludes the passage that we have been reading with a gentle and respectful concession: "In either case, whatever may have been the intention for which (Ambrose) behaved like that, certainly in a man such as he it could not have been anything but good."[17] I might ask whether the central motive might not have been precisely the desire to be able to finish a text undistracted, fully immersed in the text and persistently engaged.

Ambrose's study was pursued, thus, in a climate of silence. The Bishop was not able, in any case, to content himself to cultivate just this one aspect, no matter how profitable and necessary it was. Simplician had certainly suggested to him a deeper concentration: that is, to look for and to desire with his whole being, in his studies, that wisdom which comes from on high and which God alone can offer. To use the expressions more consonant with the language of Ambrose and which we find adopted in his teaching to the faithful, we can refer to the image of the "desire to meet" with God, with his Mystery, with the Son and with his living Word. We can sense something of this interior preparation of Ambrose, which animated his study of the Scriptures and his reading of the great ecclesiastical masters and writers. In an interesting passage from the *Commentary on Psalm 118,* in which the Bishop describes the desire for the Word to be experienced by certain people, he points out such models to his listeners.

The Bishop interprets verse 82 of the Psalm to them, where a longing expectation is spoken of, for which "the eyes" of the one praying "are worn out." Ambrose comments: "Is it not perhaps true that, when we desire and expect the arrival of someone, we keep our eyes fixed on the point where we expect him to come? And thus we tire them in the long tension of daily waiting." As Anna for example, the mother of Tobias, who "scanning the road anxiously, keeping watch, expected the arrival of her son" (cf. Tb 10:7); or also as David who, fearing for his son Absalom, "as a concerned father, stationed a lookout in the tower in his impatience to hear that message which would come from the course of battle, notifying him regarding the safety of his son (cf. 2 S 18:24)."

But the most beautiful example is that of the young wife who "from the shore waits with untiring watchfulness the arrival of her husband and, with every ship she sees, she imagines that her husband will be found on board and fears that someone other than she will be the first to enjoy the sight of her beloved and it won't be she the first to say 'I see you, my husband!' Therefore, as that woman who wants to be found waiting the arrival of her husband and thus sets aside all her domestic preoccupations to keep a watchful eye on the path beaten down by travelers and their footprints, so the prophet (David) left all his preoccupations at that time and, as a constantly vigilant guardian, kept the gaze of his internal eyes fixed on the word of God until its fulfillment." The passage ends with a formal declaration: "We too, then, fix our hearts on the objective of understanding the unfolding of the Scriptures and we invoke God that the Word might come to us and give us understanding. If someone has seen the Word of God from afar with the eyes of the intellect, in a way not yet clear and distinct, he discerns with his interior eyes the ship of the Word approaching his own soul. When he begins to see more distinctly, how much more will he hurry to approach that landing place of truth, to be as close as possible to make out its cargo?"[18] In this spirit Ambrose approaches and examines the Scriptures. It is more than appropriate for us to pause specifically in order to learn his method of commenting and presenting the Word. With the very same passion he ap-

Chapter III: His Early Formation and "Father Simplician" *[immersed himself in the Greeks]*

proached and read the commentaries and other writings of Christian authors. As with the classics, the list would be quite long; he studied the Greeks almost exclusively, save for Hilary of Poitiers, whom Ambrose used with a certain frequency. The Greeks begin with Origen, who will become his principal guide in the second phase of his literary output; then Athanasius of Alexandria, Basil of Caesarea, and his friend Gregory of Nazianzus, Eusebius of Caesarea and Didymus the Blind in following whom Ambrose earned from Jerome the label of plagiarizer. Another Greek, finally, is the important non-Christian author, the Jewish Philo of Alexandria, upon whose writings the Bishop drew frequently for his biblical exegesis. *[Philo]*

Studious Ambrose. And the fruit of these labors was Ambrose preacher and writer. If, at the beginning of his episcopacy, he had confided in having attended more reassuringly to written communications, because "the book does not blush," it remains true that his life as pastor called him to preach and that later his homilies and catechesis frequently gave birth to commentaries and treatises of various types. The relationship between the oral preaching and the written draft of his works deserves a bit more attention at this point.

In reading the writings of Ambrose it is not rare to come across indications of the oral phase from which they are born, such as cross references to biblical texts only just proclaimed in the liturgy, references to situations of the moment, or the immediate reaction of the listeners. Still prior to the written circulation of his works, one may catch a revision, more or less substantial, and occasionally also the introduction to references and events and to situations subsequent to the moment of the oral proclamation. Because of this the exact dating of the works of Ambrose is extremely complex. One must identify, in sequence, from the origins, both the moment of the preaching of certain homilies which make up the writing (verifying whether they were delivered in sequence or in different periods) and the time of the definitive publication of the text. In certain cases scholars assure us that the presence among the works of the Bishop of copies of writings of similar content is due to their exceptional conservation and dissemination, alongside the work regularly published by the Bishop after sufficient revision, even the stenographic text of the oral preaching. This is verified in particular in the treatises *On the Sacraments* and *On the Mysteries*. The first comes to us in a spoken style rich in questions and repetitions, with aspects of disorder and improvisation. The second is in the usual careful and re-elaborated form.[19] I have clarified these aspects so as not to lead the reader into a maze of arid inquiry, but to encourage the careful comprehension of certain assertions. Thus, for example, one may speak of "a homily preached to the faithful on that day or year" and further of "a work published in a given period," or also because the Bishop's style may at times be very carefully prepared and at other times more uneven, in certain cases quite lively and in others more pedantic: these certainly influence the extent of the revision to which the original oral word was subjected.

I would like to present at least one example of the echoes of the oral rendition that remain in the written works of Ambrose, choosing it from among the many good-humored expressions of the self-deprecating style that the Bishop not infrequently engaged in. In his homilies *On the Six Days of Creation*, delivered in the course of Holy Week in 386 (or a little bit later),[20] commenting on the fifth day of creation, Ambrose, already well along in his talk, suddenly notices that he had spoken only of aquatic beings, neglecting to speak of the birds as well. So, taking up the discourse after a brief interruption, which the stenographers have indicated in their notes and which, extraordinarily, is left inserted into the text, he jokes with his listeners: "We had forgotten, my beloved brethren, how indispensable it is to treat of the nature of birds and our talk on that subject had flown away together with them.... For this reason, while I took care not to neglect that which is submerged in the sea and did not forget that which is covered by water, I missed all the birds because while bending over to examine the depths of the marine whirlpools, I did not raise my eyes to the flights taking place in the sky above, and I was not even averted from my observation by the flashing of wings which was surely able to be reflected on the water." Thus, notwithstanding the lengthy homily already given, he felt it necessary to go back to that which he had inadvertently omitted.

Chapter III: His Early Formation and "Father" Simplician

Ambrose for his part was confident that the faithful were listening to him without being distracted: "I do not fear that in following the flight of the birds there will creep upon us the boredom that had not crept up on us while scrutinizing the abysses or that someone among us might fall asleep in the course of the exposition, because he would then be awakened by the song of the birds. But without doubt it seems impossible to me that anyone who would manage to remain awake among mute fish, is allowed to sleep among birds, being stimulated to remain awake by such an attraction."[21]

And now to two examples provided by Ambrose himself regarding the diligent revision of his writings, which were not only made the object of personal review but were also sent among friends with the prayer for them to express all the observations which they deemed advisable. We find the first example in the letter to Sabinus, Bishop of Piacenza. "You have returned to me the pamphlets which I value mostly on account of your judgment. So I have sent you others, not because I am pleased with your favorable judgment, but because I have been won over by the frankness that you promised me and that I requested of you." It is necessary, insists Ambrose, that "those things which by chance leave you perplexed be evaluated by your judgment before being published since they cannot afterwards be withdrawn from circulation…. I do not want you to read the works that I have already been able to publish, but that they first be subjected to your opinion prior to their publication."

The Bishop recognizes in fact that, even "prescinding from the fog of incompetence which envelops me, everyone overlooks the defects of their own writings and they pass unperceived by the ear, much as ugly children are still dear to its parents, so too do the least worthy works please their author." Thus the preemptory invitation to Sabinus: "Consider each detail; examine my talks word by word, to see that in them there be no seductive eloquence and persuasive words, but sincerity of faith and sobriety in its presentation. Make a note beside each word of uncertain meaning and dubious value."[22] The second testimony he reports to "Father" Simplician. Ambrose, in one of the letters he sent to him, makes reference to his own treatise

On Jacob and the Good Life (published in 386) and he wants to know whether, as with other works of his, it had been subjected to the vigilant and loving judgment of the master: "Regarding that which I have proposed sketching in one of my discourses an image and ideal of the blessed life, I think I have offered a comprehensive picture that will not displease many, certainly not by you who loves me, even given how much more difficult it is to satisfy your judgment than that of many. You nevertheless make light the weight of your judgment out of fondness and for this it is rendered more pleasant to me."

At the beginning of the letter the Bishop had mentioned his own preaching on themes treated in the Letters of St. Paul and the encouragement he had received from Simplician on this subject. This passage is worth referring to because it also bears the genuine expressions of affection and recognition that Ambrose nurtured toward his wise master: "It isn't much, while we are talking between us intimately with the familiarity of a long standing affection, you mentioned to me the pleasure which you felt when I sent you certain passages on the writings of St. Paul for my instructions to the people.… In your own words I recognize the affection of an old friendship and that which is even more valuable, the love of a kind father — in fact a long-standing friendship establishes a relationship which may be shared with many, but not paternal love — no — rather, since in the past I have never done what you asked of me without results, I will obey your will" to continue my preaching with dedication.[23] Disciple and master had intensified their mutual confidences and friendship: thus the disciple grew and formed himself in the pastoral service to which he had been called.

CHAPTER IV

"Take Heart, Heal the Ills of the People"

"Take heart, man of God, because you have neither received nor learned the Gospel of Christ from humans. Rather, the Lord himself has taken you from among the judges of the earth to seat you on the chair of the Apostles: 'Fight the good fight' (1 Tm 6:12), to heal the ills of the people. If there is someone affected by the curse of the Arian insanity, restore him to the ancient path of the Fathers."[1] With this warm exhortation the great Cappadocian Father Basil of Caesarea addressed the new Bishop Ambrose shortly after his election. In his letter, Basil indicates that he had received from Ambrose news of his nomination as the leader of the Milanese Church: in this regard it may have been premature to respond so cheerfully to him. He assured him, moreover, of having "glorified our God, who in each generation chooses those who are worthy," as he had done in antiquity with King David and the prophet Amos. In this age, Basil predicts, God has chosen Ambrose, obtaining "for the care of the flock of Christ a man of the imperial city who was assigned governor of the whole people, a person of high spirit, admired by everyone for his nobility of birth, splendor of virtue, and vigor of eloquence. He has refused all the advantages of earthly life and considered these a loss for the sake of gaining Christ (cf. Ph 3:7-8)."[2] To our modern sensibilities this praise appears frankly excessive, but ancient rhetoric loved such exaggerations. In any case, this isn't our interest in the letter. Nor does news that Basil seems to know about the nomination of the Bishop of Milan assume any particular significance, which corresponds to that which we already know. Besides, he may have taken these details, beyond those he got from the letters of Ambrose, from the couriers themselves who delivered the letter. Beyond all that, the central message must be discovered in the exhortative part that I cited at the beginning of this chapter, in which we find the emphatic call to heal the malady of the people who may have joined "the curse of the Arian insanity." While the expression used by Basil seems to betray an uncertainty concerning how prevalent was the Arian presence in the Milanese territory, the resolute tone of the phrase, the encouragement to "take heart," and the call to restore the ancient norms of the Fathers, suggests that the Cappadocian Bishop was well aware of the situation at Milan. Besides, he had maintained contact with notables connected with a group of Nicean Milanese, viz., the Deacon Sabinus and the layman Evagrius, of whom more will be said later.

The importance of Basil's intervention may be further appreciated if we consider the ecclesial works developed by him during the years of his episcopate. Indeed, Basil himself had assumed the exhausting undertaking of leading back to full orthodoxy those in the East who had not adhered to the faith proclaimed at Nicea in 325, and he had, in broad strokes, tried to draw the churches of the East and those of the West closer together, their having been divided from one another in their judgments on certain particular situations. More specifically, and it is worthwhile recalling it now as we must return often to the argument, he had sought to establish a common understanding in regards to the Church of Antioch, which was simultaneously claimed by two Bishops. One was Paulinus, who from the beginning had professed a rigorous fidelity to the Nicean orthodoxy but could count on the backing of only a small group of the faithful. The other was Meletius who, after being elected thanks to Arian influence, had gradually drawn closer to the Nicene positions and was engaged in gathering to himself the great mass of the community. In any case the question seemed to remain unresolved because the Westerners (among whom was Ambrose) had continued to support Paulinus, while among the Easterners it seemed illogical to remove their support from Meletius. Significantly, in closing the letter, Basil asks Ambrose to continue the epistular relationship just begun: this is not merely an expression of courtesy; it is seen above all as an invitation to this important Bishop "of the imperial city" not only to make it his duty to return the Milanese Church to Nicene orthodoxy, but to promote the very strained relationship between the East and the West besides.

Unfortunately, as far as we know, the exchange of letters between the two had no follow up, and the request of Basil was only partially acknowledged by Ambrose because of the premature death of the Cappadocian Bishop in 379. Indeed, it is true that, after Basil's death, the Bishop of Milan became interested in questions concerning the Eastern Churches much more frequently but, we must note, he did not correctly perceive the elements in play and lacked the necessary tact to confront such intricate matters which, furthermore, were not dependent on his authority. Nonetheless, Ambrose accepted, with all his might, Basil's invitation to lead the Church entrusted to him back to the orthodox Nicean faith, liberating it from the "curse of Arian insanity."

But to better understand his action in this regard, it is necessary to know certain fundamental facts regarding the doctrinal question in play, on the specific *homoean* position of his predecessor, Auxentius, and on the Milanese situation at the time of his episcopacy. This is what I now propose to make clear.[3] We have seen that the Council of Milan in 355 ended with the banishment into exile of the Bishop Dionysius. But the sacrifice of that pastor, venerated as a saint for his conduct, was more than justified because the object of contention was extremely serious. In the first twenty years of the century, in fact, the Alexandrian priest Arius had preached a doctrine that, in its most radical formulation, debased the Word of God to the level of a creature contrary to the Council of Nicea in 325 which defined the *consubstantiality* of the Son with the Father. Moreover, while the Western Churches followed the Nicene faith nearly *en masse*, the East produced a quite diverse front of 'Arian' opposition, and consequently there was created a grave division among the Churches. The Emperor Constantius II, in his attempt to get on top of this sad situation and to reestablish unity, sent Athanasius of Alexandria into exile for his uncompromising defense of Nicene orthodoxy and chose to maintain an apparently intermediate doctrinal position, around which to recreate a broad consensus. This new interpretive line asserted, very imprecisely, a *likeness* between the Son and the Father, and for this reason became currently called *homeoism* (from the Greek term *homoios = similar*):⁴ the Bishops gathering in Milan in 355 were forced to bend to this doctrine and it was accepted with conviction by the successor of Dionysius, Auxentius, who had been ordained a priest in Alexandria by Gregory, rival and substitute for the exiled Athanasius. In *homeoism* then, the opposition to the definition of Nicea, though less obdurate and contrary, was in any case equally fractured and gravely erroneous: by *likeness*, in fact, it held that one can intend something different from *consubstantial*. In either case the Divine Word who had come into the world was not in any way understood as true God as is the Father. As a consequence, in line with then current Greek philosophy, it came to affirm a God neither fully nor really involved in the economy of salvation, but rather a kind of inferior god (a Demiurge) through whom a relationship with humanity was initiated. Confronted with such a doctrine, it is no wonder that the more conscientious part of the laity and clergy along with those who, for whatever reason, did not wish to abandon the Nicean faith constantly professed by the Milanese Church, opposed the new Bishop imposed by the Emperor, judging that he followed the "Arian" heresy.

In truth, Auxentius did not have an easy episcopacy. From the start, Constantius II had to provide him with an armed escort: moreover, since he was of Cappadocian origin and ignorant of the Latin language, he was considered by the Milanese to be a foreigner and an intruder. When the Emperor passed away, on the 2nd of November in 361, the whole apparatus that he had constructed was found to have been improvised without support. Indeed, it is true that in 359 the *homoean* doctrine was approved with strategies similar to those imposed on Milan four years earlier by a Council of four hundred Western Bishops gathered at Rimini and in a parallel meeting of Eastern Bishops gathered at Seleucia. Further, we even know that the following year a Council called at Constantinople had conferred an apparently definitive seal on those pronouncements. But when, on the death of Constantius, many Bishops, having been forced to adhere to *homoeanism*, were able to return to profess Nicene orthodoxy,

Chapter IV: "Take Heart, Heal the Ills of the People"

Auxentius, who had enjoyed an important role at Rimini, began to find himself progressively more isolated.

The laity and the members of the clergy who had been opposed to his appointment thus had a better chance of demonstrating their dissent. They found their leader in the priest Philastrius, who later would become the Bishop of Brescia. His successor Gaudentius records that at Milan Philastrius had been the "effective custodian of the flock of the Lord, battling against the Arian Auxentius" and seems to attribute to the period of his action against the Milanese Bishop as his "being subjected to beatings and having carried in his body the stigmata of our Lord Jesus Christ (cf. Gal 6:17)."[5] Another opponent of Auxentius, and a member of the Milanese clergy, is the deacon Sabinus whom we know to have been in contact with Basil of Caesarea[6] and who may quite probably be identified with the future Bishop of Piacenza.[7] Representing the Nicean community of Milan, he, in fact had participated in the Council called in Rome around 370, in which an explicit condemnation of Auxentius was formulated; Sabinus, moreover, was charged by the Council to carry the synodal letter to Alexandria.

Interventions from outside were also carried out to expel Auxentius from his seat. As early as 364 or 365 a group of about 10 Bishops, among whom were Eusebius of Vercelli and Hilary of Poitiers, standard-bearers for Niceanism, formed a Council in Milan. These Bishops had presented a charge against the Bishop to the Emperor Valentinian I, but they achieved nothing because of the able way in which Auxentius was defended and because of the prestige that he was known to have won. On another occasion Evagrius also intervened. He was a nobleman of Antioch whom we have seen to be in contact with Basil and who, at Antioch, may have become Bishop of the splinter group of faithful of which Paulinus had been head. In one unclear testimony of Jerome we conclude that the vigilant action of Evagrius "enabled him to bury, if I may say so, before his death, Auxentius…"[8] that is (it may be interpreted) while still quite alive, Auxentius was drastically limited in the range of his influence.

The situation that Ambrose found in the city on the death of

Auxentius was therefore extremely complex: there remained a devoted group of Niceans who had never been suppressed by the strict *homoean* position of the Bishop, but certainly there had risen a substantial group of anti-Niceans, instructed and formed by Auxentius according to the his own doctrinal line. It is not for nothing that Ambrose, toward the end of his life, while recalling to the people of Vercelli the figure of the Bishop Dionysius who died in exile, remembered that he had requested "in his prayers to die in exile rather than find, on his return, the sentiments of the clergy and people distorted by the norms and habits of those miscreants." His prayer was heard, because, "thanks to grace, he carried the peace of the Lord with him in serenity of soul."[9] In the early days of his episcopacy Ambrose, who, even though he had demonstrated his choice of camps with no uncertainty by requesting to be ordained by a Bishop of the Nicean faith, still acted with much prudence in his dealings with the Arian problem in general and more specifically toward his clergy and toward the faithful. These persuaded him to have an attitude similar to that which he had in reference to his initial lack of competence in the field of theology, which would be enhanced only gradually through the instruction of Simplician and through his personal study. Besides, he may have wanted to avoid unhelpful irritations.

Regarding the clergy, in particular, a notation of a most unusual origin assures us that "Ambrose, of happy memory, accepted those who had received ordination from Auxentius, his predecessor at Milan." We owe this assertion, formulated around the year 400, a scant three years after the death of Ambrose, to the pen of Theophilus of Alexandria.[10] Writing to ninety year old Bishop Flavian, successor to Meletius as leader of the greater part of the Church of Antioch, Theophilus suggests that they put an end to the schism that had divided the city for many decades, avoiding any inappropriate disciplinary harshness and so welcoming among the ranks of his priests even a dissident group that had made its chief, first the Bishop Paulinus, and later his successor Evagrius. "To an old man like you," he added, "you certainly know that our fathers resolved situations far more difficult than these and thanks to wise reflection they were able, with those

Chapter IV: "Take Heart, Heal the Ills of the People"

who had no laws, to become as those who are outside the law (cf. 1 Cor 9:21): thus, they provided a solution to a situation which was hard to resolve and did not upset the whole body of the Church."[11]

It is surprising to find a suggestion so balanced and comprehensive from Theophilus, the fiery Bishop of Alexandria who, called to Constantinople in 403 to answer for certain excesses, instead, supposedly by means of intrigues, had John Chrysostom, pastor of that city, deposed. As far as Ambrose was concerned, however, he was nevertheless a trustworthy witness because we know of direct contacts exchanged between the two, in particular in the aftermath of the Council of Capua in 392, as we will have occasion to describe in its own place. And we remain pleasantly ignorant of the happenchance that resulted in the note just cited finding its way to us. Concerning the letter of Theophilus to Flavian, lost in its complete form, there remain preserved only two fragments, citations made a little more than a century later, probably in the year 513, in a letter of the Monophysite Bishop Severus of Antioch. This was written to encourage him to assume a more conciliatory attitude in his dealings with those returning to the bosom of Monophysitism. But even the letter of Severus is not intact in its original redaction in the Greek. To understand it we must refer to a Syriac translation, completed a century and a half later, in 669, by the priest Athanasius of Nisibus. It is here that, fortunately, we find preserved the precious reference to Bishop Ambrose.

Thanks to that reference, we can confirm what we already know of him: with this choice he demonstrated such balance and such capacity for reconciliation that had already fascinated the Milanese and that had induced them to claim him as their pastor. One thing, in fact, was extremely necessary: not to too broadly or sternly challenge those clergy and faithful who were in some way compromised by Arianism, but rather to instruct them and aid them to form a correct sense regarding the themes concerning which Arianism, in all of its expressions, had proposed and spread erroneous solutions.[12] Ambrose, then, needed to concentrate in his study of these subjects in order to then propose them to the people in the preaching and writing he would be promulgating. In these the Bishop first of all described the doctrinal position of his *homoean* adversaries, making little effort to determine their thought with exactitude, instead finding it simpler to trace them to their Arian roots. Further, he will respond with detailed arguments against their accusations and he will refute the interpretations of scriptural texts that they had adopted. Above all, he will propose to his listeners and readers the grand Trinitarian themes, putting them together in a truly original theological synthesis.[13] In any case, it is not possible to lay out all of these arguments here. Therefore, after having completed the description of the initial contacts that Bishop Ambrose may have had with Arianism (including anti-Arian interventions carried out by him in nearby regions and aspects of the Arian presence in Milan in those years) I will limit myself to making known how his publications on this subject came to be, then to move on finally to present certain of their more salient passages.

First let us deal with the intervention at Sirmium over the nomination of a new Bishop, the anti-Nicean Germinius having died around 376. We know that Ambrose had practiced as a lawyer there before coming to Milan and it is not difficult to imagine that he had known of the religious situation of that Church, and of Illyria in general, strongly influenced by the Arian doctrine. He came to Sirmium and managed to impose as Bishop one Anemius, a Catholic of clear Nicean convictions. Paulinus, to whom we owe this notation, adds that Ambrose had to endure the charges of the Arians and recounts the anecdote of "one of the Arian virgins" who, "more impudent than the others, ascending into the sanctuary, seized the vestments of the Bishop as she wanted to drag him into the part reserved for women and, after having been knocked about herself, was driven from the church." We can pick up the account following this scene: the Bishop reproved the assailant while expressing the fear that she might fall victim to some curse. The Arian virgin died the next day. Ambrose then "accompanied her to the tomb, repaying her offense with kindness."[14] It is also conjectured[15] that Ambrose was present at Sirmium to take part in a Council of clear Nicean cast, at which the Arian Bishops of that region were deposed. The meeting would have taken place in 378 and, it follows, it could be made to coincide, tweaking one or the

Chapter IV: "Take Heart, Heal the Ills of the People"

other of the two dates, with the arrival of Ambrose for the election of Anemius. But all of this remains uncertain, and among these hypotheses one should not overlook one which places the synod much earlier, in 374-5, excluding every connection between it and Bishop Ambrose.[16] Likewise, the conjecture that the Bishop of Milan may have been present at a Council celebrated in Rome toward the end of that same year, 378 lacks elements of probability.[17] Among similar uncertainties, there remains only the assurance of his intervention on behalf of the nomination of Anemius, according to Paulinus.

Turning to this episode, we recall from the biography a final assertion. The Arian reaction against Ambrose, Paulinus asserts, was orchestrated by the Empress Justina, the second wife of Valentinian I. We find here the name of this sovereign for the first time, which frequently appears linked to her Arian sympathies. In fact, when, on the 17th of November 375, her husband died, whom we know to have been a Nicean though a non-interventionalist, she was freer to manifest her genuine ideas in religious matters and to intervene in defense of her position, thanks to the power that came to her as the mother of the new Emperor Valentinian II, still a child. Perhaps Paulinus exaggerates by connecting the first chapters of the *Life of Ambrose* so strongly with the conflict between the Bishop and the Empress. But it is none the less certain that she, by transferring her residence from Sirmium to Milan in the autumn of 378, would resume the conflict with Ambrose. In the end this led to the culmination of their battle during Holy Week of 386.

An earlier episode in the conflict between these two is found in the period that we are dealing with, a little after the arrival of Justina and Valentinian II at Milan. They had left Sirmium because of a serious threat from the Goths at the border of the empire. Opposing the Goths were the forces of Valens, Augustus of the Eastern part of the empire. In order to assist him, Gratian, the Augustus of the West, older son of Valentinian I and his first wife Marina Severus, mobilized his forces moving from Gaul to Illyria. But Valens, in his impetuosity, did not want to wait for his colleague and on August 9, 378 he confronted the Goths in an open field near Hadrianopolis. He was resoundingly defeated and killed. Gratian, therefore, settled at Sirmium in order to take the situation in hand. On the following January 19 he chose as Augustus for the East that Theodosius whom we will see entering into a long and friendly relationship with Ambrose.

Because of these events, Justina and Valentinian II would have arrived at Milan, accompanied by the court and not a few refugees from Illyria who professed the same Arian faith as Justina. For the sake of all of these as well as for the Arian sympathizers already in the city, the Empress claimed a church which was promptly seized by Gratian. In the spring of 381 Ambrose, recalling this episode in a treatise *On the Holy Spirit* dedicated to the Emperor Gratian, affirmed that the Emperor "had seized (the church) that he might test" the faith of the Bishop and that consequently "having obtained the proof, restored" the basilica; adding further that the restitution was spontaneously decided by the Emperor, without the intervention or suggestion of anyone. He concludes, turning directly to Gratian: "You made it clear to everyone... that whereas the seizure was not yours, the restoration was."[18] The awkwardness of the Bishop regarding the attitude of the Emperor in authorizing the seizure is evident: in that period, historians assure us with conviction, Gratian had adopted a policy of religious tolerance, similar to that followed by his father Valentinian I.

Moreover, Milan must have had to support another pro-Arian presence in those years: Julian Valens, Bishop of Pettau (or Ptuj) in Pannonia, accused of having delivered the city of Mursa to the Goths, then, having had to leave his land, sought refuge in Milan, joining the *homoean* group in the city. In the letter sent to the Emperors by the fathers of the Council of Aquileia in 381, we have indication that they requested that Julian should at least be expelled from Milan.[19] Further, if we read a parallel letter, he "upset the Milanese church with detestable plots." Furthermore, Ursinus, a contender against Pope Damasus for the seat of Rome,[20] was also united to the Arians.

In a situation thus divided, in the midst of which Ambrose demonstrated much patience and added an indubitable clarity of position, the Emperor Gratian sent to the Bishop requesting a clarification regarding his faith. In the response that Ambrose provided,

Chapter IV: "Take Heart, Heal the Ills of the People"

consisting of the first two books of the treatise *On Faith*, he in fact began by declaring: "You, holy Emperor Gratian... wanted to hear of my faith."[21] Recent scholars do not agree on the explanation for why the Emperor had questioned Ambrose, but they are united in refuting the traditional explanation that made Gratian to be an Emperor exceedingly attracted to religious themes and Ambrose an excessively submissive disciple of the master. Without wishing to enter into the details of this question, it may be enough to recall how the articulate and powerful *homoean* presence in the city constituted a ready coterie to persecute the Nicean faith professed by the Bishop. In a similar situation he was not permitted to exempt himself from defending and justifying with adequate motives the faith to which he adhered: "You advised me to express my faith in a book, not that you might learn but that you might approve" he said, completing the phrase cited above.[22] It was most likely for this reason that Gratian made this request to Ambrose.

In the two books of *On Faith*, addressed to the Emperor perhaps in 378,[23] Ambrose espouses the Nicean faith in one God, who has one name and in whom "one is the power of the Trinity," he taught "the perfect Father has begotten the perfect Son" in such a way that "the Father and the Son are one being not thanks to any confusion, but by the unity of nature"; and further, defending himself from the accusation of affirming three gods, he specifies that "we confess the Father and the Son and the Holy Spirit in such a way that in the Trinity are perfected the fullness of divinity and the unity of power."[24] He went on, further refuting certain Arian theses: The *homoeans*, as I have pointed out above, had come to be assimilated to their Arian roots and therefore their doctrine of the *likeness* of the Son to the Father came to be compared without half measures with that more radical term *unlikeness*.

Entering into this theological struggle, Ambrose, in the months following, apparently continued to write regarding these themes, judging from the reaction of renewed attacks by his adversaries in response to a further invitation of the Emperor. The reaction of the *homoeans* was given voice by Palladius, Bishop of Ratiaria in Illyria:

in 379 he had circulated his own contemptuous polemical writing against the two books *On Faith* in which he contested the interpretation of Ambrose that *homoeanism* was strongly tinged with Arianism, and in any case he was opposed to the Nicean faith in the *consubstantiality* of the Son with the Father. Ambrose began to respond immediately in preaching to the people; and already by the end of 380 he had finished an actual revision, having been able to collect these homilies into three books that were joined to the two already composed in his treatise *On Faith*.

His reference to Palladius is perceptible even in the introduction to this new section: in it the Bishop, addressing the Emperor, remembers the actual composition of the two preceding books and so explains the motive for continuing them: "Since, O most clement Emperor, you have charged me to write something on the faith that might be able to instruct you and despite my reticence, you yourself encouraged me, for this reason, as if in preparation for battle, I wrote only two books.... The perverse minds of certain individuals, determined to concoct a discussion, stimulated me to carry to conclusion the work with a more thorough treatise. The religious concerns of your clemency also encouraged me to complete the task.... I have decided, therefore, to treat a little more fully those questions that were touched upon in few words."[25] As was natural, the contents of this new section confirm and carry on the themes treated in those preceding. In this case Ambrose sought this time to give greater attention to the thought of his adversaries and above all he wanted to analyze with care the biblical texts that they thought supported their theses. The Bishop, furthermore, was less preoccupied by the judgment that may have been given to the Emperor, being more calmly secure in the acceptance which would be forthcoming.

Indeed, Gratian, in the first months of 379, sent a letter to Ambrose in which, besides explaining his own enthusiastic satisfaction with the first two books already completed, charged the Bishop to write another treatise: specifically "a dissertation on the Holy Spirit in conformity with the faith," in which the Bishop "with arguments from Scripture and reason" would convince him, as he had adequately demonstrated for the Son, that the Spirit is God.[26] This request, as

Chapter IV: "Take Heart, Heal the Ills of the People"

we recall it in passing, does not simply show a desire for competence; it is to be placed above all in the area of reflections on the third person of the Trinity that were developed in those months in a particularly focused way in the East in reaction to a group that had denied the full divinity of the Holy Spirit. In 381 the definitive response would be made at the Council of Constantinople, with the affirmation that the Holy Spirit "is Lord of life and is adored and glorified with the Father and the Son." During the summer of 379 Gratian was in Milan for a few weeks, where Ambrose probably met him in person. For his part, Ambrose responded to the Emperor with a quite affectionate letter, full of his recollection of and appreciation for the faith professed by him. In his own words: "You have restored to me the peace of the Church, you have closed the mouth and, would heaven have willed it, even the heart of the impious; and this you have done with a faith no less authoritative than your power."[27] It seems to mean that for Ambrose peace may have returned because those attacks that had made his position as the leader of the Church in Milan less secure had already lost their force and fearsomeness: Gratian himself no longer felt the uncertainty that had provoked his earlier request for clarification, and Ambrose was thus able to dispose himself to listen to the Emperor's request with a more reassured spirit, even though he was in no hurry to do so. Only in the spring of 381 was his treatise *On the Holy Spirit* delivered to the Emperor who had returned to the city in March of that month.

We are already aware of the deep dependence of this writing on a similar treatise of Didymus the Blind, given that the ruthless critique of Jerome had not omitted mentioning it. Here I would like to add that, according to interpretations more accepted at this time, this indicates to us, in the account of the recent takeover of the basilica requested by the Arians, that a decisive change had taken place in the political religion of Gratian. If in fact already in 379 the Emperor had manifested his firm adhesion to the explanation of the faith provided him by the Bishop of Milan, he now also chose to intervene directly in the defense of that faith. For this reason, as we read, of his own free will he had chosen to restore the church. Again for this reason, the Bishop and the Emperor agreed upon the imminent Council that was to be held at Aquileia on the following September that would decree the condemnation of Palladius of Ratiaria and of his companion, Secundus of Singidunum. But with these matters we are entering into a new phase to which we will return shortly.

Now, though, as promised, we want to read some passages from these writings of Bishop Ambrose, retrieving from them, according to the beautiful definition of Raniero Cantalamessa, those "precise formulations which Church orthodoxy holds as its perfect expression."[28] Here is an initial formula regarding the distinction between the unity and the singularity of God which permits Ambrose to hold to the oneness of the divine substance without having to renounce the trinity of persons or to fall into the affirmation of more than one God. He cites above all the expression of Jesus: "I am not alone; but it is I and the Father who sent me" (Jn 8:16). Hence he comments: "He indicates the Father and the Son but does not attribute to them a plurality, nor does he divide the unity of the divine substance. It is evident that that which is of but one substance cannot be separated even though we are not dealing with individuality but of a unity.... Individuality has to do with the person, unity with nature."[29]

It is worthwhile mentioning this other passage also, somewhat longer and more detailed, in which we find along with the usual definitions an appeal to safeguard the mystery, because Ambrose, and the Fathers with him, when they put their capacity for penetration at the service of a more precise knowledge of the truth, nonetheless never forget to mention the transcending merit of the divine reality. Here is the text: "The divine substance of the Trinity is, so to speak, indistinct but the Trinity is distinct, incomprehensible and inexpressible. We have in fact determined that there is a distinction between 'the Father and the Son and the Holy Spirit' (Mt 28:19), without confusion: a distinction, not a separation; a distinction, not a plurality. We have thus determined that in this divine and wonderful mystery the Father always subsists, the Son always subsists, and the Holy Spirit always subsists: there are not two Fathers, nor two Sons, nor two Holy Spirits.... Thus have we understood it, thus do we read it, thus do we keep it in mind. We recognize the distinction, but we are ignorant of its secrets; we are unable to search into its cause, but we hold fast to

Chapter IV: "Take Heart, Heal the Ills of the People"

its mysteries."³⁰ Ambrose was proclaiming these and other affirmations vigorously before these "Arians" who, though in a veiled way, preached the inferiority of the Son with respect to the Father. In any case the Bishop did not wish to alienate anyone. In these same books *On Faith* he expresses the desire to be able to gather everyone around the same doctrine, and exhorts the faithful to show understanding toward the anti-Nicean group. In the passage I am going to cite, Ambrose had just described the kind of submission and obedience that the Lord Jesus expressed to the Father by means of the human nature assumed by the Word in the Incarnation; he furthermore expressed the example of Jesus' humble submission to Mary and Joseph; and he drew this application: "Let us also conduct ourselves benevolently, let us convince our adversaries of that which would be useful to them, let us beg and 'weep before the Lord who had created us' (Ps 94/95:6). We do not wish to conquer, but to heal; we do not behave insolently, but admonish mercifully. Those who will not bow before the truth or to reason will bow to sentiments of benevolence." Recalling then the parable of the Good Samaritan, he concluded in this way: "All those therefore, who wanted to be healed, came to him and received the medicine that he brought from the Father and that he had prepared in heaven."³¹ It is precisely in this context that Ambrose lays the foundation for developing a theme which is quite dear to him and to which he returns, with touching emphasis, at various times in his works. We have seen that in Jesus the Word made flesh, the weakness of human nature also emerges. Against the Arians, the Bishop emphasizes that we should not be scandalized by this fact, which shows the Son to be inferior to the Father: they are, rather, evident signs of the reality of his incarnation and not reasons that support heresy. In these signs — and here we find the point lovingly contemplated by Ambrose — we rather admire the marvelous condescension of God for man; his humiliation is bound up with his sharing. We again take up the letter in which the Bishop invited all to come to be healed. "This medicine," he explains, "does not sprout from soil, because in all of nature we do not find this prepared." It is, in fact, quite otherwise: "Thanks to a divine plan the Word takes on this flesh of ours, to conquer as a man teaching men." Because, Ambrose adds, I would not have considered it as taking advantage "had he manifested his power as God since he would only have shown his inviolable divine nature" or had he failed "to attempt the condition of my nature and of my weakness." But "he had to be tempted; he had to suffer together with me, so that I might know how to conquer when I am tempted, how to escape when I am suffering with him. He conquered by means of his dominion of self, having contempt for riches; he conquered through faith; he trampled ambition, put intemperance to flight, and sent into exile all lack of moral restraint." This is the medicine that cures man and that makes Ambrose exclaim: "O faith, more precious than all treasures, O truly efficacious medicine healing us of our wounds and our sins!"

The Bishop is not embarrassed, at this point, to observe that "it is as advantageous for us to believe as it is worthwhile," and he confirms this by taking up (in a form slightly adapted) three biblical expressions that illustrate the divine condescension in favor of man: "He took upon himself my weaknesses" (cf. Mt 8:17), "He became sin for me" (cf. 2 Cor 5:21), and "For me he became a curse" (cf. Gal 3:13). Based on these certainties, while also suggesting that man imitate the example of Christ the Lord, Ambrose is thus able to conclude: "He wept so that you, O man, would weep no longer; he submitted himself to offense so that you might not suffer from your offenses. It is a great remedy to have in Christ one's own consolation. He bore these things for us with great patience, and should we not thus be able to suffer these things patiently for his name? Who, beaten, would not learn to pardon from the moment that Christ, even when he was bound to the cross, prayed for his persecutors? Don't you see that what you suppose to be Christ's infirmities are his power: his tears wash us, his weeping cleanses us, his doubt confirms us so that you, if you begin to doubt, might not despair. The greater the offense that he suffered, so much more moving is the gratitude that is owed him."[32] In listening to these words of Bishop Ambrose his response to the invitation of Basil is symbolically completed: he "had healed the sickness of the people" not only by banning the Arian error but by rightly following and pointing toward the Doctor who had humbled himself "for us."

CHAPTER V

Guide to Monks and Consecrated Virgins

In his *De Vita Solitaria (On the Solitary Life)* Francesco Petrarch recounts that "by the will, even the command, of God, Ambrose was entrusted with the care of the large population of Milan. While not daring to continue a solitary life, aware of an office so important and of such great responsibility, he still revealed his aspirations all the time and in every manner that was afforded him." To do this he chose as his residence a place "apart and completely alone," which the poet imagines was situated near today's Basilica of S. Ambrogio. "Furthermore, every time he saw himself free from his episcopal cares and liberated from the heavy and continuous labors that he had to confront in order to expel the Arians from the church, for all the time that he was able to remove himself and almost steal himself away from his occupations, that holy man went to a very secret retreat. There was a woods near the city, but nonetheless suitable for contemplation; in the middle was a small house adapted for a big yet humble man, that had been converted into a temple, though quite small.... Now the woods have been developed and the place changed in appearance, preserving only the name "Ambrose's Woods" (*Ambrosii nemus*) as it is commonly called.... There, as I have heard it said and as I imagine, he scattered the sweet flowers of his books, of which today, in all the gardens of the Church, is to be found the pleasant taste and fragrant scent."[1] Petrarch had composed *On the Solitary Life* in 1346, but we must attribute the cited passage to a later period, during or after the residence of the poet with the Visconti in Milan between 1353 and 1361. In this way he is a witness to us of the pious traditions that circulated in regard to Bishop Ambrose in Milan in the 14th century. From these we put together the image of a pastor in love with the solitary life who, part monk or hermit, went to recollect himself in an oasis of silence at the margins of the city in order to dedicate himself to contemplation and to the laborious composition of his writings.

By the time of Petrarch this vaunted tradition had already been around for several centuries: in the *Passion of the Holy Milanese Martyr Arialdo* (d. 1066), composed in 1075 by the blessed Andrea da Strumi, a precise reference is made to the "place called *Nemus*, one mile distant from the city" where the deacon Arialdo had gone to celebrate the Easter vigil together with his confreres. The biographer takes care to inform us that in this place "there was yet a church constructed by Saint Ambrose and dedicated to him where, according to the tradition, Ambrose himself used to go alone to escape the chaos of the crowds and dictate his books."[2] The chapel, it is nice to remember, though reconstructed at various times, is preserved even till now, at the *Porta Comasina*, and still retains the title of S. Ambrogio ad Nemus.[3] In the 14th century, moreover, in places next to the church, there lived religious who were tied to this pious tradition. We know that in 1375 a regular community known as the Order of S. Ambrogio ad Nemus was established there that came to be approved by the See of Rome. With the growth of the members of the community, both men and women, who were called to this Order and who characterized themselves by taking up the Ambrosian rite in the liturgy was born the exigency of regrouping themselves into a single congregation, officially constituted in 1441 under the guidance of the convent of S. Ambrogio ad Nemus.[4] When in the 17th century the congregation became extinct, there remained alive only the women's community of Sacro Monte di Varese, officially constituted in 1474, which has kept the tendrils of the Order of S. Ambrogio ad Nemus alive even to our own day.[5] The religious experience described ideally fits that of Bishop Ambrose; and therefore, one may imagine an uninterrupted arc of monastic presence at the chapel of S. Ambrogio ad Nemus throughout the entire Middle Ages[6] — a pious conjecture without objective confirmation, we must admit. But also a starting point for more research: Did Petrarch have a point in presenting us an Ambrose thus inserted into the monastic context? And did the Church of Milan enjoy any earlier experience in this regard?

Chapter V: Guide to Monks and Consecrated Virgins

We can begin with the last question. We know in fact that, under the episcopacy of Auxentius, Martin came to Milan. He would become the Bishop of Tours and is held to be the founder of Western monasticism. His biographer, Sulpicius Severus, recalls that Martin, disciple of Hilary of Poitiers in the defense of the Nicene doctrine, on his return from an anti-Arian mission to Illiricum stopped at Milan, it is thought around the year 358, to initiate a monastic-ascetic experiment there. But Auxentius "bitterly persecuted him and, after he had assailed him with many insults, violently expelled him from the city."[7] In reference to the Arian question, this episode confirms to us the force which the Bishop organized against any Nicene challenge in the first years of his rule; regarding, then, the argument that I am treating here, this simply indicates that Martin "established his residence in a hermitage"[8] and that, because of the intervention of Auxentius, he quickly had to end this attempt, leaving the city. We can deduce from this that nothing must have remained of this first monastic presence in Milan.

Regarding the time of Ambrose we have, however, two testimonies preserved by St. Augustine, the one in the *Confessions* and the other in two books on *Customs of the Catholic Church and Customs of the Manicheans*: two extremely brief, but truly interesting publications. The first took place in the months just prior to the conversion of Augustine when he received a visit from Pontician, one of his compatriots, a fervent Christian "who held a high post at the palace." Their talks centered on religious themes, and Pontician took the opportunity to recount the life of the famous Egyptian hermit Anthony, whom Augustine had not yet come to know. The subject thus became narrowed down and Pontician was able to continue by broadening the argument to include "flocks of monks, their lives… and the productive solitude of the hermit." He also wanted to describe the edifying episode of two of his friends who, at Trier, having read the life of Anthony, had immediately embraced the monastic vocation with firmness. But before beginning this new account, Pontician also made reference, as if in passing, to monastic experiences in the region around Milan. We find precisely here the dispassionate news that we were looking for and which Augustine reported in this way: "At Milan, outside the walls of the city, a monastery existed, supported by Ambrose and populated by good brothers, without our knowing it."⁹ The phrase speaks of a community of monks which Ambrose cared for, assuring them of his support, which had to include the material as well as the spiritual aspects.

The other news is inserted in a treatise on *Customs of the Catholic Church and Customs of the Manicheans,* composed by Augustine a few months after having received baptism, while at Rome awaiting to embark for Africa: with the enthusiasm of a neophyte, he described the numerous positive manifestations of the Catholic Church, contrasting them to the negative behaviors observed among the Manicheans, with whom he had been involved until just a few years earlier. Augustine records in particular an experience of "those who live in the city, but apart from the life of the world" and inserts the specific testimony that interests us: "I myself saw a number of holy Milanese, more than a few, who were led by a great and highly learned priest."¹⁰ The community, we can confirm in all likelihood, is the same which had been alluded to by Pontician: Augustine, therefore, after having heard him speak, went to visit them himself before leaving Milan.

Nonetheless there remains something of a mystery concerning this institution, and the brief notes that we have do not resolve all our doubts in this regard: they refer, in fact, to monks to whom Ambrose gave watchful attention but whom in any case he never names. While on the one hand we see them preach at most a few retreats for consecrated virgins, they seem to be calling themselves back to a deeply rooted and not passing experience, structured within the heart, but on the other hand they have left no trace behind and seem not to have had a significant following.

Constrained to address the argument from a more general point of view, we are able at least to remember that Bishop Ambrose valued the monastic life and more exactly that form of communal life among members of the clergy which will be established for the first time by Bishop Eusebius in the Church of Vercelli a few years later. Indeed, in a letter written to this church, which I have already recalled on

Chapter V: Guide to Monks and Consecrated Virgins

various occasions, Ambrose, taking a position on the choice of the new Bishop of the city, records that the candidate to that ministry must possess "two quite different qualities... continence proper to a monastery and discipline proper to the Church." He also explains that it is precisely "here, then, for the first time in the West, that Eusebius of blessed memory brought together qualities so different from one another such that while living in the city, he maintained the customs of the monks and governed the Church with the sobriety of one fasting."[11] Priestly ministry and monastic life: Ambrose very often returned to this combination in the course of that long letter and one can understand that he approved of the choice made by Eusebius at his time and that he would have wanted it to continue on in the Church of Vercelli. The question is therefore raised as to whether the Milanese monastery which Augustine tells about might not have been thought of in terms of these criteria as well. The concern of Ambrose would thus result as having been yet more clearly motivated. And one could hold that occasionally the Bishop would share with those monks some moments of recollection, just as Petrarch had imagined drawing upon the tradition of the "Woods of Ambrose." But the reader is aware that from certain news we are little by little passing to suppositions that are not sufficiently documented.

Let us return, then, to the sources, if only to reveal that, in summarizing the holiness of Ambrose as pastor, Paulinus, in a long passage in his biography, among other things, hints at the ascetic, or more appropriately, monastic aspects of his life.[12] For example he records that "the venerable Bishop was a man of great abstinence, of many vigils and labors," and that "he weakened his body with daily fasts." In particular he usually would not take food before evening, but with a sense of moderation and out of respect for the solemn days of the ecclesial life he suspended this penance on "Saturday and Sunday or when the anniversaries of the more venerated martyrs were celebrated." The biographer recalls still other practices of Ambrose so typically monastic as his "assiduousness in prayer day and night;" also his laboriousness in writing in his own hand the works that he was composing (in a letter to Sabinus Ambrose himself states: "I have not told all to the copyist, especially at night, during which I do not wish to be a burden and inconvenience to others"),[13] and even his resistance to fatigue in ecclesiastical functions. Finally, the renunciation of his considerable family wealth which Ambrose did from the start was singularly monastic: "When he was ordained Bishop, he offered to the Church and to the poor all the gold and silver he possessed. Whatever wealth he had, he gave to the Church, having reserved the interest for his sister, not keeping anything for himself so that, henceforth… he might be able to say his desire was to follow… Christ the Lord who, though rich, made himself poor for us, so that we might be enriched by his poverty (cf. 2 Cor 8:9)."[14] Without losing anything of his exquisitely pastoral make up, Ambrose also manifests certain expressions having a monastic imprint. The expressions with which Paulinus comments on the death of the Bishop are, then, truly appropriate and are certainly not out of place: After having received the Viaticum from the hands of Honoratus of Vercelli, Ambrose "expired, taking with him the good food for the journey, so that his soul might yet be restored by virtue of that food; now he delights himself in company with the angels, with whom he was joined in earthly life, and in the company of Elijah."[15] The prophet Elijah, as Paulinus makes explicit in his next phrase, certainly recalls the blunt speech to the powerful which Ambrose had employed even in his dealings with Emperors. But we ought to add that, because he was a virgin and poor hermit who lived in the desert, Elijah is above all a perfect model of the monastic life, and surely in this sense Ambrose shared in the blessedness of that prophet. In any case that same vocation is referred to also by the "angelic life" that Paulinus asserts the Bishop to have practiced on earth and that is now revealed in heaven. Ambrose also frequently uses this expression, precisely to designate the choice of virgins who have consecrated their entire existence to God.[16]

But it is time to leave behind us the few facts concerning male monasticism to enter into the great orbit of feminine consecrated virginity, guided by the Bishop-expert on the "angelic life." It is indeed notable that Ambrose dedicated many of his works to this subject and that his teaching in this regard has left deep traces in the ecclesial tradition of subsequent centuries.

Chapter V: Guide to Monks and Consecrated Virgins

Entering this discussion we review the chronological traces present in the life of Ambrose. After having seen the Bishop, in the preceding chapter, begin his episcopal ministry in an ever deepening conflict with Arianism, it is now necessary to take up the thread of his life a bit further back, to return to that year of 377 in which he issued his first text, namely the three books *On Virgins*.

Ambrose did not break new ground. Other great Christian authors had written on consecrated virginity. Among those who influenced him most directly and most fully, I mention only the Bishops Cyprian of Carthage and Athanasius of Alexandria, and also Origen, to whom we will return to speak more fully in what follows. Jerome, that sharp denigrator of Ambrose, also took up these arguments, though in regards to this theme he expresses unexpectedly positive judgments on the Bishop of Milan. Once, writing in 381 to the virgin Eustochium, he equates Ambrose to Tertullian, to Cyprian and to Pope Damasus and he recommends reading his books *On Virgins*. On another occasion, writing in 393 or the year after to senator Pammachius, he cities certain passages from Ambrose's treatise *On Widows* and other similar themes and praises the Bishop of Milan, acknowledging that "grasping many concepts in few words, he has condensed in a brief compendium" the same contents that Jerome had amply exposed in his *Against Jovinian*.[17] We don't know whether he is speaking this way this time out of self-interest or not, using the texts of Ambrose as a shield against accusations that he had disparaged marriage in his writings; but I maintain that it may be an honest appraisal of the teaching of Ambrose regarding virginity: and Jerome says the same....

After the three books *On Virgins*, Ambrose composed, most likely in the same year 377, the treatise *On Widows* that we have just seen cited by Jerome, in which the theme of widowhood is treated as being in strict parallel with that on virginity. About a decade later, though the exact date remains uncertain, Ambrose distributed another text, *On Virginity*, of a rather composite character, in which is found the ample influence of Origen. Toward the end of his life the Bishop would return again twice to treat this subject explicitly. In

392 in Bologna, perhaps on Easter Sunday, he gave a homily for the consecration of a virgin by the name of Ambrosia, and the following year it was distributed, revised and edited, with the title of *On Instructions for Virgins*. In March of 394 in Florence he gave a talk for the dedication of a church built by a widow named Juliana: in the published text in that same year under the title of *Commendation to Virginity*, Ambrose introduces Juliana to interweave a high eulogy on virginity to her four children, three daughters and a son, concluding the homily with analogies on the same theme.

That was a considerable undertaking over time on the part of Ambrose to encourage and support consecrated virginity. Why such precocious, determined and constant attention? One asks the question exclusively on the level of utility and effect: it would have been easy early on during difficult moments for the Bishop "to find an alternative theme." Actually, the innovation introduced by him could serve to "parade the commitment of the daughters of his well-to-do parishioners in public."[18] And, in a passage in his first book of *On Virgins,* Ambrose confesses that virgins from around Piacenza and Bologna and even from Mauritania come to Milan to take the veil. Making reference especially to the young Mauritanians McLynn comments that "the exotic and decorative surroundings which they added to Ambrose's corps of attendant virgins reflect the showmanship that he brought to his Church."[19] Certainly the preaching of Ambrose regarding virginity could present itself early on as a less difficult argument than the Arian one, and Ambrose would have willingly addressed it before plunging himself into the demanding reply to Gratian and to the *homoeans* who provoked him. But the motive of convenience cannot fully explain the matter, nor can that of a "parade" be assumed to explain the positions and words of the Bishop: his writings speak in a different way. One might instead recall that, according to the succinct expression of Giulio Oggioni, "Virginity attracted the reflections of the newly baptized and new pastor as the more eye-catching and descriptive, if not the more profound, feature of Christianity."[20] But perhaps one does not get to the core of Ambrose's interest unless one locates his preaching on the theme of

Chapter V: Guide to Monks and Consecrated Virgins

virginity within a framework which he had outlined with ever greater conviction: to contribute, that is, to the healing of Roman society. It was not possible to retain the ancient convictions that had regulated it and made it grow, and thus there was a need for new stimuli, criteria, and ideals. When in a later chapter we will recall the interventions Ambrose made regarding the theme of social justice, we will find the same basis and identical motivations. And more generally, when we plummet his spiritual teaching and propose the moral criteria upon which he calls to construct the figure of the believer, in this case, even while the Bishop expresses himself in an exquisitely religious context and had therefore the aim of motivating and achieving at quite a high level, still we will recognize that the social relevance of the evangelical challenge is still present.

To return to our theme: in a context of intense decay of the institution of marriage and of a confused search for a feminine role in society, Ambrose proposes a figure of woman that, in the name of her own dignity, establishes new autonomy and a beneficial choice in life: a choice appreciated and recognized by the Church and displayed with pride before society. It is not easy to find passages of direct relevance in this regard because Ambrose was the son of his time and, in these issues, even his innovative and wisely proposed expressions appear as irredeemably "dated," bound to a context quite far removed from our own. I would like nonetheless to venture to re-appropriate certain elements from his homily for the consecration of Ambrosia, which is preserved in the book *On Instructions for Virgins*.

"Harking back to the beginning and examining the origins of things, we will discover what honor had been given to women and what grace they found, even in the wretched fragility of the human condition." Thus Ambrose, after having noted how too often the woman is unjustly accused as the cause of original sin,[21] announces the reflection he intends to develop. Reviewing, then, the biblical narration of creation and, along with the creation of man, he observes that it was not immediately praised, as was the case for the inanimate beings and for the animals. Indeed, insofar as being given freedom, he was able to be praised only "at the end," when his works appear;

because "no one, if he had not fought as he should, will be crowned." At this point Ambrose reinterprets the expression posed by God before the creation of woman: "It is not good for man to live alone" (Gn 2:18); and without connecting this to the earlier explanation of the postponed praise of man, he adds: "Therefore, without woman man has no praise; in woman he is eulogized. In fact, in saying that it is not good that man should be alone, evidently he confirms that the human species is a good thing, so that the masculine sex is juxtaposed to that of the female." On the wave of this exultation Ambrose, remembering the biblical narration of the different creations of man and woman, the one from the earth and the other from the side of Adam, proceeds: "Consider this also, that man is made from earth and mire, but woman was taken from the man. Certainly the flesh itself was mud, but man came from something unformed, whereas the woman was in reality already formed." May the reader permit me to pause for a comment: to one who knows the writings of this period, in particular certain passages from the Fathers of the Church on this argument, the explanation of Ambrose, which is stunning in the face of the habitual presentation of man as privileged, flips the argument in favor of the woman.

But let us continue our review of the text. The Bishop takes up the discourse, digressing in a curious way on the great fault of Adam and Eve. Even in this case he intends to reaffirm a favorable judgment in reference to Eve: though she yielded to evil, she had been tempted by the devil, as it were by a superior being. Adam on the other hand should well have been able to react to the word that the woman, a human being like himself, had addressed to him! More profound yet is the interpretation that Ambrose proposes regarding the word spoken by God to Eve: "I will intensify the pains of your childbearing; in pain you will bring forth children" (Gn 3:16). First of all he remembers that the woman with submissive receptivity "accepted the burden of her own condemnation": further, taking as background the Pauline expression according to which she "would be saved through motherhood" (1 Tm 2:15), he observes: "The woman battles for you with her pains and through the pain she obtains recompense; so that through children, because of whom she suffers, she is freed." Apparently the phrase seems to indicate only a necessary development of justice: from fault came condemnation, from expiation of the penalty finally comes freedom. Ambrose, however, has something more and greater on his mind. Indeed he continues: "So it is that grace (comes) from injury, health (*salus*) from weakness.... Those who have given birth in suffering also give birth to salvation (*salus*)." As the Bishop concludes, after condemnation is expiated, the woman is co-involved in the work of salvation; and rising up through the centuries and the levels of writing, in the descendants of Eve is seen all humankind right up to its fulfillment in Christ and in the Church.

So, thus renewed, for Ambrose, Eve assumes the features of the Church in its suffering, so similar to that of Christ. She thus generates children participating in this newness and salvation. Now the Bishop concludes his reflection regarding the woman, and to virgins in particular, in an absolutely pervasive light of the fullness of mystery; and in a crescendo of images he reveals them as a new Eve, and a new Sarah (the mother of Isaac), and even to the virgin Mary herself: "Come, O Eve, now at peace;... come O Eve, now such that you cannot be excluded from Paradise, but to be swiftly snatched up to heaven. Come O Eve, now Sarah, who bears sons not in pain, but in exultation; not in affliction, but with a smile: you will give birth to many Isaacs... Come therefore, O Eve, now Mary, who not only gives us the incentive for virginity, but have also borne God... who was begotten through a single virgin, but yet has called many. For this reason Mary, in the mystery of the Lord, has had this special name that means 'God of my begetting.'"[22]

I have tried to guide the reader across the meanderings of this long reflection of Ambrose. As is obvious, alongside the texts of a doctrinal character such as this one presented in the writings of the Bishop, there may also be recognized not a few passages rich in very firm precepts for the life of virgins: Ambrose does not draw up a rule, right and proper, but nevertheless offers a detailed exposition, the first in the West, with hints of various kinds, precautions to respect, attitudes to assume.[23] We might notice that he speaks of women who, taking the veil, continue to live with their families of origin, living and sharing with them on a daily basis; common life was in any case already found to be in use (at Bologna and in Rome, for example), and would be gradually introduced to Milan as well, at least through the virgins that come there from far off.

It is not easy to determine what would have been the make-up of the group of virgins in the Church of Milan. In the passage cited above, regarding the girls who came from the areas around Piacenza and Bologna and from Mauritania, the Bishop even permitted himself to joke: "You see an extraordinary thing: I teach here, and I persuade elsewhere. If this is so, I should like to teach elsewhere, in order to convince you!" Even though he had not concealed his attempts to get a hearing: "Someone might say: 'Every day he sings the praises of the virgins.' What am I supposed to do, if I sing every day the same thing and do not get any result?" But on the other hand what he adds immediately afterward ought not to be undervalued, in any case: "I know that many virgins wish to know more and that their mothers even keep them from leaving."[24] Therefore while he denounces the opposition of the parents with a clear statement — and perhaps because of this he pressed on to emphasize — with just as confident a perception, the intentions of the girls to accept their callings seriously. Then, taking up the same argument later in his treatise *On Virgins*, Ambrose turned to talk about relief from the obstacles that stood in their way: on one hand in fact he refutes and denies the accusation of having persuaded many girls, observing that with that accusation they have made him above all "to appear as one who has bought his accusers" by making him receive unearned praises; but on the other hand only that it follows that he had to confront others who confronted him in order to impede "the wedding of the girls initiated to the sacred rites and consecrated to virginity."[25] Here, then, were the virgins that Ambrose defended in the consistency and continuity of their choice. He defended still others when, at the very moment of their choosing, they were challenged by their family and forced into marriage: in the first book of *On Virgins*, in fact, he recounts that "a girl from an old noble family, even nobler now before God," had

Chapter V: Guide to Monks and Consecrated Virgins

sought refuge "before the holy altar" to find protection, thus anticipating the rite of consecration. Standing beside the Bishop the girl would have the strength to repel all the pressures of the family, giving a sign of her intention.[26]

As few or as many as there were, Ambrose offered his full instruction to the consecrated virgins of the Milanese Church which was received with great admiration even in following centuries. The Middle Ages and even the modern era have seen in the Bishop of Milan an unsurpassed master regarding the themes of monastic spirituality, especially that of women. Indeed, Ambrose knew how to construct a congenial summary, thorough even if not systematic, of all the points on virginity that could be derived from Scripture, from Origen and in general from the ancient Fathers. A veritable *summa* that, beyond the inevitably "dated" expressions and less than pleasant traits, may be appreciated in the concreteness and firmness of his suggestions and in the poetic geniality of his images, in the profundity of his theological thought and in the humane delicacy of his intuitions.

At the heart of his instruction and at the root of the virginal choice Ambrose places the figure of Christ. I would like to conclude these passages, which have presented monasticism and virginity in Milan under the guidance of Ambrose, by recalling certain brief expressions that also illustrate to the reader this fundamental aspect.[27] First of all is the identification of the One who is the author and creator of virginity: "Who are we to judge who might be its author if not the immaculate Son of God, the one whose flesh knew no corruption, he whose divinity saw no contamination?"[28] Then there is the search, following the specific characteristics that any such search must cover: it would be, in the first place, long and continuous. "Note how Christ loves to be sought and does not love idle talk…. Christ desires to be sought at length." Furthermore it must be a faithful search, with eyes wide open so as not to be deluded: "You, O virgin, only just beginning to seek, you will find him present, because it is impossible that he will come less to one who seeks him, he who is shown to those who do not seek him and is found by those who do not ask of him. While you consider and muse, he presents himself."[29] Finally, it will be an interior search, rooted and cultivated in the silence of the heart: "Seek Christ, O virgin; in good thoughts, in good works... seek him in the nights (cf. Sg 3:1), because he comes by night and knocks on the door (cf. Sg 5:2). In fact, he wants you to watch for him in every moment, he wants to find the door of your mind open."[30] The search begins at the encounter, described in the rich and most intimate image of the meeting between the Spouse and the beloved: "The soul of the just is wedded to the Word. It is that which it desires, it is that for which it longs, that for which it prays assiduously and prays without complaint; behold, it is that which may be totally turned to the Word that they may be prepared to hear the voice of him, though as one not seen. Behold the One who, with inmost perception, may be recognized by the fragrance of his divinity...."[31] There are many subjects characteristic of the spirituality of Bishop Ambrose which we will encounter again and which must be commented on adequately.

Now I wish to present just one last passage that contains the culminating conviction of all the thought and faith of Ambrose: the centrality of Christ, universal Redeemer (this, too, is a theme to which we will return!). The virgin is explained and realized only in such a context:

> We have all in Christ...
> And Christ is all for us:
> If you want to cure a wound, he is the doctor;
> If you are parched by fever, he is the spring;
> If you are oppressed by iniquity, he is justice;
> If you have need of help, he is power;
> If you fear death, he is life;
> If you desire heaven, he is the way;
> If you flee the shadows, he is light;
> If you seek food, he is nourishment.[32]

CHAPTER VI

Marcellina and Satyrus

On July 17 and September 17 the Church of Milan remembers, respectively, Saint Marcellina and Saint Satyrus, siblings of Ambrose. In the liturgical texts still used Marcellina is described as the "affectionate sister and sweet comfort to Ambrose and Satyrus," and further the "prudent virgin" who "chose to love with undivided heart the immaculate Son" of God "aspiration and crown of every virginal desire." Satyrus is, for his part, remembered as a "companion in the deeds and collaborator in the mission" of Ambrose who, "attending to the governance of the house of the Bishop, both eased and ennobled his ministry."[1] Their official cult began to be attested to in the Franco-Carolingian era and particularly in the 9th century. In this age, in fact, the Church of Milan found itself needing to defend its own prerogatives and the liturgical and cultural peculiarities typically called "Ambrosian" against external influences and the attempted reintroduction of "Romanization" pursued by the French sovereigns. In the mixed hustle and bustle of those decades, there was an attempt, in multiple ways, to elevate the figure of Saint Ambrose — unifying symbol of the city and the Church of Milan, its liturgy and its culture — consequentially, these saints were 'rediscovered' and the their cult was officially restored.[2] In any case the two siblings had not been forgotten in previous centuries. The memory of Marcellina and of Satyrus had persisted in the Milanese community, united to that more eminent of their celebrated brother.

I would like to pause now to consider what we know of them.[3] That grave moment of suffering which Ambrose and Marcellina had to face in the first months of 378 when they lost their brother Satyrus offers us an occasion. It invites us to dwell on this discrete person who is seen alongside the Bishop in the first years of his ministry. And in this unique picture of a finely cultivated fraternity we must approach Marcellina, the older sister who would become his attentive confidant during the most difficult moments in the life of the Bishop.

To present the figure of the two brothers we are assisted by the funeral homily delivered by Ambrose, brought to us as the first discourse *On the Death of his Brother*. In it, the Bishop not only speaks at length about Satyrus, obviously, but he reveals something also about his sister. A week later the Bishop delivered another homily, published as the second discourse *On the Death of his Brother*. Here, however, he develops meditations on the theme of death and resurrection without touching any further on personal matters. Besides, no mention is made of Satyrus in any other source, not even by Paulinus, who entirely ignores the brother of Ambrose. Of Marcellina, on the other hand, not only do we have the biography which has preserved precious memories, but her own brother the Bishop speaks of her on many occasions, and turns to her, especially in his letter writing.

But before entering into the heart of this narration, let me confirm the date of the death of Satyrus, which I have emphasized as the hinge of this chapter, to be fixed in the first months of the year 378. It is necessary first of all to clear the field of hypotheses recently formulated by certain scholars according to whom Satyrus may have died on the 18th of September 377 or of the following year.[4] These, noting that usually the liturgical recurrence of a saint indicates the date of his "passage" to heaven, have assumed September 18th as the date of the death of Satyrus, the day apparently reserved for him in the so-called *Martyrologium Hieronymianum,* an ancient calendar compiled in the 5th century in northern Italy. But these scholars don't take into account a curious phenomenon produced in this source and which is adequately explained by the Benedictine Monk Odilo Heiming.[5] On September 18th the *Martyrologium Hieronymianum* essentially reports the name of Satyrus under the heading "In Milan, Bishop Eustorgius and Satyrus." Further, the following day the same name is inserted in a list of Alexandrian martyrs, right after Saint Castor. But, notwithstanding the appearance, neither of the two cases is dealing with the brother of Ambrose: on the 19th because Satyrus is presented as a martyr in a group so indicated[6] and on the 18th because it is a simple duplication of Satyrus from the following day. This ambiguous notation in the *Martyrologium Hieronymianum* influenced those who, toward the 9th century, established the liturgical record of Saint Satyrus, recording the date as September 18th. The new memorial date was moved back one day so it would not coincide with that which was already the traditional memorial of Bishop Eustorgius. That is why the holy brother of Ambrose has been uninterruptedly celebrated on September 17th.

Prescinding from the day, the hypothesis that fixed the death of Satyrus as early as 375 also ought to be dismissed because, the episcopal ordination of Ambrose in 374 being accepted, the gratitude that the Bishop offered his brother for the extended and active assistance he had given him would not be justified: "You administered the household of your brother and enhanced his episcopal ministry," he declared in the funeral homily, not permitting "that I should occupy myself with personal affairs, maintaining that I should attend exclusively to the duties of my ministry."[7] The death of Satyrus, therefore, must be dated after that year. As I have already emphasized, the more likely period is the winter of 378, because in these months he would have experienced the dangerous situation about which Ambrose alludes in the funeral homily. Look how the Bishop describes him, turning to speak directly to his brother: If "you knew that right now Italy is menaced by an enemy quite near, how afflicted you would have been, as you would have lamented that all our salvation consists in the bulwark of the Alps and that the defensive wall of our honor is constructed with barricades of trees. How troubled you would have been that your own should find themselves at such a short distance from the enemy, from a corrupt and cruel enemy that has no concern for chastity or life!"[8] The enemies that press on from the far side of the Alps were most likely the Alamanni, who in those months renounced their treaties and, taking advantage of the simultaneous invasion of the Goths in the Danube region, menaced the Po Valley. It was only in May of that year that Gratian was able to conquer them in the battle of the Argentaria in Alsace.

Thus we have the precise moment in which Satyrus completed his earthly journey. From this prospective we are free to take a look at his prior life and that of his sister Marcellina, taking up again the thread with which we began. We have already seen that the sister was the oldest of the three and Satyrus the second born. It is not, however, known whether the two had already been born when the family was transferred to Trier, where we know that the youngest, Ambrose, was born, or whether Marcellina or both of the older siblings may have been born in Rome. The date of their birth also remains uncertain. We can figure that they preceded Ambrose by a few years, which is datable, as noted, to circa 340. Satyrus, therefore, born around the middle of the thirties and, dying in 378, would have been a little older than 40; Marcellina, on the other hand, born at the beginning of the thirties or a bit earlier, would have been more than 70 when she died toward the end of the century.

While Marcellina made the choice that we have already seen and took the veil at the hand of Pope Liberius, Satyrus, together with Ambrose, would have followed similar steps of study at Rome, then undertaking the career offered him at Sirmium. When Ambrose was called to Milan as governor, Satyrus too received an identical order in a province unknown to us. In this duty, his brother assures us, he showed a great sense of justice that "the provincials whom he governed... said that he was more like a father than a judge, an arbiter appreciated for kind traits, a sure interpreter of the impartiality of the law."[9] But when Ambrose became Bishop, Satyrus left his governorship and, as we have seen, rejoined his brother to serve him in the administration of his household and to personally assume the management of the family wealth. Marcellina, however, remained in Rome where, in fact, her brother found her when he returned to visit several years after his ordination and, we remember, reminded her companion of the episode of the kissing of hands. From the final pages of *On Virgins* in which Ambrose speaks of virgins and the martyr Soteris, we come to know that Marcellina was found "in the country without the company of other virgins."[10] This text seems to contradict other sources and in any case poses more than a few questions: When was

Chapter VI: Marcellina and Satyrus

Marcellina seen with a Roman companion? And when, further, was she led to a form of life of complete solitude? Where was the residence in the country of which Ambrose speaks? Was it near Rome or Milan? But perhaps Ambrose, in order to better explain the education which came to Marcellina directly from the great ancestress of the family, had exaggerated the image of her solitude; it is safe to accept that initially his sister lived for a certain time alone and that later she was united with a companion, as the tradition has it and which, furthermore, we find in the account of Paulinus. In any case we can say that in all probability Marcellina spent the greater part of her life in Rome, going to Milan only in the last years of the episcopacy of Ambrose.

The geographical distance did not entirely restrict contacts between the siblings. Ambrose maintained a strict epistolary connection with his sister and she, at least in certain particular situations, would have been present for more or less extended periods in the city. This is attested, for example, at the funeral of Satyrus. In the funeral oration Ambrose describes the profound sadness of Marcellina, her tears and her pious concentration: "Although weeping interrupted her words, she renewed them in prayer and, while she would receive some comfort from the recollection of the Scriptures, nonetheless, she balanced the desire to weep with the assiduity of her praying, weeping when no one was able to interrupt her. In that," concludes the Bishop, "I have compassion, not criticism: to cry in prayer is a sign of virtue."

Ambrose sketched Marcellina as a "holy sister, worthy of veneration for her integrity, equal" to Satyrus "in her morals, not inferior in her duties." He recalls also that sometimes arguments were generated between her and her Bishop brother, and that in those situations it was Satyrus who wisely resolved the question, without dismissing either of the two. "Desiring to make peace between them," he kept to himself "both his feelings of affection and his moderation in explaining his opinions, thus being agreeable to both and claiming the gratitude of both." Further, the bonds that linked the three were intense, and Satyrus, "mediating between the two, one a virgin, the other a Bishop, inferior to neither for the greatness of his soul," was truly unique in "reflecting the chastity of the one and the consecration of the other, not through the bonds of a vow but from the obligations derived from virtue."[11] In her virginal choice Marcellina became a model for her brother Satyrus, beyond having a positive influence on Ambrose and his preaching, as we have already noted.

Ambrose's discourse on the death of Satyrus thus spoke of Marcellina, but it is obviously rich in references to his deceased brother. Above all it sketches him alongside the Bishop, in the tranquil image of two oxen yoked to the same plow. When one of them is unfortunately taken away, observe how "the ox seeks the ox, and thinks that he lacks something, and demonstrates his tender fondness with frequent lowing." Indeed, Ambrose most passionately senses the loss of his brother because, as he records with longing melancholy, Satyrus had stood beside and had considerately protected his flank, "loving like a brother, worried like a father, considerate like an elder, respectful like a child," while the Bishop recognized that he himself was "less resistant to weariness, but profoundly loyal" to him "in love." Satyrus, his brother adds, was for him a supporter in all things: "You approved my decisions, shared my doubts, sent my cares away, cast away my sadness. You were the supporter of my actions and defender of my thoughts. Finally, you were the only one in whom my domestic concerns could find a pause and my public responsibilities find rest."[12] So, through images full of feeling, Ambrose has described for us the virtuous attitude of his deceased brother, and at the same time has revealed to us openly the tender bonds of affection which united the two.

Beyond that, Satyrus, operating in such close proximity to Ambrose, did nothing to make his brother look bad. The Bishop also tells us of this aspect in a tidal wave of memories recalling certain anecdotes that remained impressed on his mind. Because the two brothers were physically much alike, it happened that people easily mistook one for the other: "Who saw you and did not think they had seen me? How many times have I greeted people who, because they had greeted you first, said that I had already greeted them! How many told you something, convinced that they had told me!" But in this regard Ambrose harbored no concerns: "What a joy to me, what happiness this provided because I saw that they had taken one of us for the other. What a pleasant error, what a delightful mistake, what a loving deception, what a sweet intrigue!" Then, following with an extremely flattering judgment on the habitual comportment of Satyrus, he declares: "I harbored no fear from the idea of your actions or of your words. I was happy that what came from you would be attributed to me."[13]

One episode which took place in the months immediately prior to the death of Satyrus, allows us to better understand the closeness of his collaboration with his brother Bishop. It has already been highlighted that the family of Ambrose possessed wealth in Sicily and in northern Africa. Satyrus, designated administrator, used this wealth for the construction of new ecclesial edifices, at the same time verifying that these progressed with cautious prudence. "We call upon your holy soul as witness," his brother records, "that in the construction of churches I often feared not having your approval." Once, in Africa, a certain Prosperus, "following the elevation to episcopacy" of Ambrose "thought that he did not have to restore that which he had appropriated" unjustly. Satyrus, after unavoidable but fruitless negotiations that would have taken place between the two parties, wanted to go there, notwithstanding the pressures of his brother to dissuade him from such a voyage. He resolved the situation in a very evenhanded way so as to receive the appreciation of Prosperus himself. Indeed, Ambrose refers to this, turning again directly to his brother, thus "repaying every debt, without showing ingratitude for your moderation and without making fun of your modesty, but being thankful for your sense of restraint and lack of arrogance in your own efficiency." Expressing his heartfelt thanks to God for having brought Satyrus back, Ambrose recalled how he, on his trip, had to deal with a bout of illness, a sad prefiguration of that other serious ailment that would quite soon bring his earthly life to an end. Perhaps, Ambrose adds, "he was torn away from us right after his return almost as if it were only for this that his death was delayed, so that brothers could be reunited." The Bishop recalls a shipwreck, which struck Satyrus on his return, paralleling it with his imminent death that had snatched him having only arrived among them. "Returned from Africa, restored from the seas, saved from shipwreck, we supposed that you would not be torn from us so soon. But we have had to endure a worse shipwreck on land; while a shipwreck couldn't draw him to death (evaded thanks to vigorous swimming) his death is to us as a shipwreck."[14]

Before taking leave of Satyrus, I would like to propose a final aspect of that similarity between the two brothers that we have seen so incisively remarked upon in the funeral homily. Ambrose and Satyrus were in fact both patient and understanding toward their opposition, but consistent and adamant in not yielding to any compromise. Thus, in Africa Satyrus figured out how to conquer Prosperus without sharpening the differences between them, but at the same time, when it came to making the decisive choice of baptism, he was in no doubt and, like his brother, wished to be baptized only by a Catholic Bishop.

Here is the testimony given by Ambrose. Victim of a shipwreck, during a voyage not better specified, Satyrus, who had not yet been baptized, in the imminence of a disaster, "not fearing death, but in order not to leave this life without the Mystery, requested insistently of those whom he knew to be initiated, the divine sacrament of the faithful." Then, receiving the Eucharist as being all that was deemed necessary, he "bound it in a napkin, bound the napkin around his neck and thus threw himself into the sea" completely faithful: "considering it to be sufficient protection and defense, thinking he had need of no other aid." Not only that, but having regained the shore, perhaps Sardinia, he wished to receive baptism in a sign of recognition toward the One who had saved him. But when he learned that the local Bishop was not in communion with Rome because he had gone over to the schism of Lucifer of Cagliari, he refused to receive the sacrament: "He preferred to go to where he would be able to pay his debt in full… and he hurried to make that happen, as soon as he had free access to a Church. And he received the longed-for grace of God and, having received that, he kept it intact."[15] Ambrose assures us that Satyrus "kept untainted" to his death "the gifts of his holy baptism:

clean in body, purer yet in heart."[16] At the moment of his leavetaking, he wanted to be buried beside the relics of the martyr Victor, in the chapel of S. Vittore in Ciel d'oro (today annexed to the Basilica of S. Ambrogio), and Ambrose composed an epitaph for him, in which he recalled the beneficial proximity of the blood of the martyr: "Beside Uranius my brother Satyrus was granted the supreme honor of being laid to the left of the martyr. Thus are his virtues compensated, the outpouring of sacred blood bathing the remains of those nearby."[17] At the end of the 8th century or the beginning of the next, this epitaph was seen beside the tomb of Satyrus by the Irish monk Dungalus[18] who provided a copy of it. The presence of this record and the eulogistic words expressed by Ambrose in the funeral homily may have given birth to a private form of veneration which, in the 9th century expanded to the official cult that we have already mentioned.

Let us turn to Marcellina, advancing her story further so as to complete the picture of her life as well. While living in Rome, she remained in contact with her brother Bishop, who wrote to keep her updated on his actions especially in the more anxious or delicate moments of his pastoral mission. There are three letters addressed by Ambrose to his sister which have come down to us, two datable to 386 and the other to 388. Each one is dedicated to a specific episode: regarding the court battle with the Arians who had requested a basilica for themselves, referenced in *Letter* 76 written in the spring of 386; regarding the recovery of the relics of the martyrs Protasius and Gervasius, *Letter* 77, written two or three months later; regarding the controversy over the synagogue at Callinicum, the *Letter Outside the Collection,* 1, from the year 388.

We will return to these stories in the course of our narration of the life of Ambrose. Here I press on to recall the affectionate and confidential tone with which Ambrose expresses himself in these letters. In the first, for example, he attempts to calm his sister at a time when he had been made aware of her intense worry and of her having revealed to him that her sleep was disturbed by sad dreams. In the second, after an introduction with this very delicate heading: "To my lady sister, more dear to me than life and eyes, your brother,"

Ambrose confirms to Marcellina his custom to not conceal from her "anything which happens in your absence." In the last he returns again to the reason for her preoccupation, in the same opening words of the Bishop to his sister: "You are pleased to write me that your holiness is still anxious because I wrote to you that I am anxious. Thus I marvel that you have not received my letter, in which I wrote you to have peace of mind."[19] In any case, it is time to introduce some clarification. The studies of the past decades have revealed that Ambrose personally contributed to the collection of ten books of his own letters, in imitation of certain works compiled by Pliny the Younger, and that he expressly handled the publication.[20] Are we to deduce that for the Bishop the letters had above all a literary scope and were meant for distribution, and that as a consequence they do not adequately respect the facts and do not truthfully reveal his true sentiments? For the three letters in question, beyond observing that the last one is not *per se* part of the *corpus* prepared by the Bishop and that therefore only in an analogous way can these kinds of questions be applied to it, and anyway, it is admissible that, while addressing his sister, at the same time the Bishop also wanted his own interpretation of the facts to reach a broad range of other readers. But this does not impinge on their value as first hand sources and, as far as we are concerned in this context, in the conventional formality, it doesn't seem to me to reduce the human aspects that are expressed and which retain sincere displays of the soul of Ambrose.

Marcellina finally moved to Milan. Indeed, in a letter to Siagrius of Verona, datable to the last years of the life of Ambrose, Marcellina appears alongside the Bishop as his advisor in the delicate question concerning Indicia, a Veronese virgin accused of illicit relations and of infanticide.[21] After the death of her brother, Marcellina did not long survive: it is traditionally affirmed that she died under the episcopacy of Simplician, successor to Ambrose (d. 400/401). In her honor a metrical epitaph was composed, attributed by some to Simplician himself, in which the death of Marcellina is fixed at "the middle of July."[22] As with Satyrus, a certain form of private veneration would have risen around her tomb, upon which, in the 9th century, an official cult was grafted, on the date of July 17th. As a matter of fact, the placement of the memorial liturgy on a day near the middle of the month makes one suspect that it was in this way preserving the actual date of the death of the saint. The *Martyrologium Hieronymianum* is no more useful for Marcellina than for her brother Satyrus, even though in fact, on July 17th there appears in it the note "at Milan, Marcello," which may easily be imagined to be a corruption of the feminine "Marcellina," or perhaps it refers to a saint that bears essentially the same name and who is mentioned in other calendars on the 18th of July.[23] We have thus reached not only to the end of the life of Satyrus and of Marcellina, but also the point at which their memory entered, fully developed, into the cult of the Church of Milan. We are able now to take up the narrative of the life of their illustrious brother where we have left it at the moment of the death of Satyrus. But before taking leave of his two siblings, I would like to provide for the reader certain allusions to their subsequent presence in Milan, thanks to the institutions which have kept their names alive right up to the present day.

Already by the 9th century, at the time of the Archbishop Ansperto, Satyrus had the honor of having a church dedicated to him called S. Satiro in Urbe.[24] Situated in the immediate vicinity of the ancient Roman Forum and documented at least by the year 879, enlarged and dramatically restructured, it is with us yet.[25] The church was initially linked to a hospice for the poor and wayfarers and to a small monastery of eight monks, dependent on that more ancient one of S. Ambrogio founded around a century earlier by the Archbishop Peter alongside the basilica of that saint. The hospice had a brief life, while the monastery must have survived a bit longer. By the end of the 12th century, in any case, the monks also left S. Satiro, which then became a parish church. The memory of the saint remained equally fixed to the place of his sepulcher, that is, the chapel of S. Vittore in Ciel d'oro, where as we have seen Ambrose buried his brother alongside the martyr. When, at the end of the 8th century, the relics of the martyr were brought to the church of S. Vittore al Corpo, the remains of Satyrus were left in the chapel uninterruptedly preserved in their original place. Recently, around the year 1960, they were collected in a crystal urn in the crypt of the Basilica of S. Ambrogio, alongside the body of his holy brother-Bishop. Then in 1981 they were finally placed in a new urn, under the altar called "of Satyrus," in the first chapel on the right in the same Basilica Ambrosiana.

Similarly, as regards Marcellina, a church was dedicated to her name in a relatively ancient era, in Muggiano in the parish of Cesano Boscone.[26] This is attested to by Goffredo da Bussero in the 13th century. Supposedly it received the name of the sister of Ambrose because of the presence in the area of possessions belonging to the Canons of St. Ambrose; and the parochial church of Muggiano is still dedicated to her name. But later her name may have been linked to an institute of religious who, inspired by Marcellina as the teacher of her two younger brothers, wanted to dedicate themselves to the formation of children through a school and other forms of educational activity. Commonly referred to as the Marcellines, officially the Sisters of St. Marcellina,[27] they were founded in 1838 by Mons. Luigi Biraghi, Doctor of the Biblioteca Ambrosiana. The mortal remains of the sister of Ambrose, buried in the Basilica Ambrosiana, were then gathered in the crypt, near her brother. In recent centuries, in 1607 Cardinal Federico Borromeo ordered the crypt to be rebuilt and to provide a place more worthy of the relics of the saint, but nothing was done. Even the intervention of the Archbishop Benedetto Odescalchi in 1722 achieved only that the remains of Marcellina were brought up from the crypt and temporarily placed in the sacristy of the basilica. Only in 1812 were they finally placed in a new lateral altar in the Basilica Ambrosiana, up to that time dedicated to Saint Catherine, where they can still be found.

Thus both Satyrus and Marcellina have left living traces and memories of holiness in the Church that, through the centuries, has preserved the grand inheritance of their brother Ambrose!

CHAPTER VII

Aquileia: September 3, 381

"Under the consulship of the most illustrious men Siagrius and Eucherius, on the third day of September, in Aquileia, Valerian, Bishop of the city of Aquileia took up a post in the church together with the Bishops Ambrose (of Milan) and Eusebius (of Bologna)" and thirty others, all listed by name. Thus begins the *Acts* of the Council of Aquileia[1] solemnized on September 3, 381 under the presidency of the local Bishop but with the effective direction of Ambrose. At this court were present, virtually in the role of defendants, two Bishops of Illiricum: Palladius of Ratiaria and Secundus of Singidunum, both followers of the philo-Arian doctrine that we have defined as *homoeanism*. The first, furthermore, has already been noted as one who was opposed to the Bishop of Milan who refuted them in the last three chapters of his *On Faith*. Other than Ambrose, the synodal fathers would have numbered no more than 24 because that was how many Bishops were present to voice their condemnation after Ambrose himself had invited anyone of those present to express his own thought regarding Palladius. Perhaps half had come from northern Italy, the others from Africa, Gaul and Illiricum. The list of the names posted at the head of the resulting document, therefore, was merged with other prelates who, joining later, agreed with the decisions reached in the proceedings.

The Council of Aquileia, from which we have been able to select several aspects of singular interest, was the first great ecclesial enterprise of Ambrose. He was able to make it happen thanks to relationships he had established with the imperial authority: I have already described the ever improving confidence that Gratian had come to have in their relations, and all this leads one to believe that the Emperor and the Bishop, meeting at Milan in the spring of 381, would have agreed on the procedures and the aims of the impending court* at Aquileia.

Earlier, it had been organized along the lines of a general Council, even if it were discussed whether it may have been foreseen as a gathering of all the Bishops ecumenically or simply as a Council of Bishops of the West as a whole. The *Acts* have preserved the repeated complaints of Palladius regarding its reduction, in his judgment ill-conceived and unjust, from the original design. The Bishop of Ratiaria asserts, in fact, that he was ready to discuss and answer questions regarding the doctrine which he professed, but only before a court of sufficient scope as was originally intended. Let us listen to a few of his comments. Right at the beginning of the debate: "Because of your partisan efforts it has happened that the Council is neither general nor complete. In the absence of our colleague Bishops, we are unable to speak in matters of faith." Furthermore: "Where there is not the authority of a general Council, I refuse to speak." And again: "We will not respond now, but only in a general and full Council."

Finally, at the moment of his condemnation: "You have begun to make a mockery of things: you are playing around; without a Council that is also Oriental we refuse to answer."[2] As a matter of fact, from the very outset of the discussion we gather that Palladius, having met Gratian at Sirmium a year earlier, had received assurance that the Council would include Eastern Bishops, giving him some hope of receiving significant support: even if here we do not know whether this referred to prelates of the East in general or, on the theory that it was to be a Western Bishop's conference, of Bishops from the eastern part of Illiricum.* Let us take a look at the principal utterances of this part of the dialogue:

Palladius: Our Emperor Gratian ordered the Easterners to come. Do you deny that he had given this order? The Emperor himself told us he had ordered the Easterners to come.
Ambrose: Certainly he commanded it in the sense that he did not prohibit them from coming here.
Palladius: But it was your request that made it so that they would not come; under false pretenses you caused this to happen and

Chapter VII: Aquileia: September 3, 381

Ambrose: thus you have changed the Council.

Ambrose: This has nothing to do with anything; for too long now you have digressed.... (Ambrose proceeds, seeking to return the debate to the doctrinal issue, sustained in this action by the other Bishops. But Palladius returns to the question left hanging. After reading one of his memos on the argument, not recorded in the *Acts*, he comes back to the question, most likely reminding them of one of his assertions inserted in the writing).

The Bishops: When the Emperor was at Sirmium, would it have been you who brought up this matter or did he oblige you to? How do you respond to this question?

Palladius: He told me, "Go." We asked: "Are the Easterners meeting?" He said: "They are gathering." If the Easterners were not meeting, would we perhaps have not have intervened?

Ambrose: The question of the Easterners can be put aside, today I want to ask what are your convictions.... (But they continue still to debate on the way the Council was convoked; Palladius finally resumes:)

Palladius: I, thinking I was coming to a general Council, saw that my companions are not taking part; yet if they were to participate and speak according to the order received (their presence was required): but you have judged (just now), prejudicing a future Council.[3]

In the dialogue just cited Ambrose's direct responsibility is implied regarding the reconfiguration of the Council. This is not to exclude that the change of perspective may have been agreed upon at a meeting between Gratian and the Bishop which took place in the preceding spring. Indeed, it was not necessary to draw in Bishops from everywhere to verify and, as he foresaw, to condemn the two exponents of the *homoean* doctrine, now that Ambrose had convincingly and definitively clarified to the Emperor the validity of the Nicene faith. Besides, the whole of the Eastern empire had expressly aligned itself with this faith, after Theodosius had decisively embraced the faith of Nicea and had even imposed it on his subjects in an edict promulgated at Thessaloniki in February 380. Furthermore Theodosius himself, calling together a Council at Constantinople for May of that year, had made the celebration of a general Council of the Bishops of the West and East at Aquileia practically out of the question.

At the end of August the Bishops who were to participate in the Council began to gather at Aquileia. Palladius and Secundus, made wary by the absence of the Easterners and of the change that had been made, after a few days of initial contact with one or another Bishop of the Nicene group, requested in writing an informal meeting with all those present, to explain their own objections and to appeal to them for a future general Council. They did not intend to linger any longer, although they were not able to leave Aquileia without having adopted the necessary justifications. With the arrival of other Bishops of the Nicene faith, the Council would have officially begun and they would have wanted to avoid finding themselves in the unpleasant situation of having to appear before such an assembly.

Ambrose accepted the proposition, steering the gathering exactly in a direction not desired by the two *homoean* Bishops. In fact, gathering all on a pleasant morning and listening to the remonstrations of Palladius, he did not follow up on his requests. Instead, the Bishop of Milan insistently requested and finally decided to pursue a precise doctrinal debate. He demanded, in particular, that Palladius declare himself regarding the faith which Arius had once professed in the letter to Alexander of Alexandria. After a few hours of debate in which blows were not spared and which continued on without agreement or the possibility of a conclusion, Ambrose broke the deadlock by asking Palladius to sign an explicit condemnation of Arius. As expected, he firmly opposed this, not recognizing such a demand as legitimate and maintaining further that only a general Council, not such a reduced assembly, had the authority to debate questions of faith and to impose such judgments.

But the Bishop of Milan did not acknowledge that objection and with no solution in sight decided to begin a formal conciliar session. He ordered the stenographers to take notes on the oral argu-

Chapter VII: Aquileia: September 3, 381

ments of the gathering, had the imperial rescript with which Gratian had called the Bishops to Aquileia read, and summarized from the beginning the discussions conducted earlier in an informal way. This is the official part of the Council whose minutes have been preserved in the *Acts* which we have already seen.

In this dialogue, rather as an inquisitor, Ambrose was assisted by Eusebius of Bologna and Sabinus of Piacenza. One after the other they expressed the divine attributes which the wording of Arius applied in full sense only to the Father, while the Nicene doctrine applied it in the same way also to the Son. To Ambrose, that is, both the Son and the Father are identically *true God*: immortal, wise, good, powerful. For Palladius, on the other hand, consistent with the philo-Arian doctrine that he professed, while admitting that the Word is *true Son of God* immortal, wise, good, and powerful, he cannot, nonetheless, be affirmed as being of the same identity.

I offer to the reader an example of the "blow and counter-blow" of this dialogue between the deaf, in which I attempt to demonstrate the mastery of Ambrose (and of his collaborators) in leading the discussion, it may be said, with the experience and ability of an ancient Roman official, as well as the immovable and staunch *homoean* opposition of Palladius. The text here reported is taken from the beginning of the debate, where the first of the attributes indicated were examined: Is the Son also *true God*? Let us listen:

Ambrose: Do you mean to say that the Son of God is *True God*?
Palladius: When I say *True Son*, what more could I say?
Ambrose: I do not ask whether you say *True Son*, but that you say the Son of God is *True God*.
Eusebius: Christ is *True God* according to the faith of all and the Catholic profession.
Palladius: He is the *True Son* of God.
Eusebius: Indeed, we too are sons by adoption, He according to the nature of divine generation. Do you confess therefore that the *True Son* of God is *True God* according to birth and nature?
Palladius: I say that he is the *True Son* only born of God.

And after further exchanges, with reference to certain scriptural texts:

Ambrose: You are not frank in your declarations: for that reason one who does not recognize that the Son of God is *True God* should be excommunicated.

All of the Bishops: Whoever does not affirm that Christ, the Son of God is *True God* should be considered excommunicated.[4]

After having pursued the same discussion in a similar way in reference to the other divine attributes and after a final debate on the apparently philo-Arian Gospel expression "the Father is greater than I" (Jn 14:28), Ambrose moved decisively toward the final stretch, declaring solemnly: "The most clement and Christian Emperor entrusted the cause of justice to the Bishops... therefore we claim that to us is entrusted judgment regarding the interpretation of Scripture. We condemn Palladius because he has not chosen to deny the opinions of the heretic Arius and because he has negated the eternity of the Son of God and the other truths contained in the *Acts*. May he therefore be held excommunicated."[5] And everyone present confirmed, one after the other, the condemnation of Palladius.

It was then the turn of Secundus of Singidunum. Even though the *Acts* are incomplete in this final part — they are interrupted in the course of the discussion — we know that he was subjected to the same treatment as his colleague; nor were the *Acts* interested in the details, which we can easily imagine as being similar to those of Palladius.

There remains, however, the need, at this point, of a general overview of the conciliar day just described and to verify the posture assumed by Ambrose. Was the doctrinal judgment that he expressed against the two *homoean* Bishops correct? Was the procedure used in the Council acceptable? Or was there more perhaps that motivated the objections advanced by Palladius? To the first question it is not difficult to respond affirmatively, because in reality Ambrose confirmed the faith defined at Nicea and condemned two prelates who evidently refuted it. The Council of Aquileia did not debate *ex novo*

Chapter VII: Aquileia: September 3, 381

these questions of faith, but simply confirmed the correct Catholic doctrine and derived from it the judgment on the merits of the faith professed by Palladius and Secundus. There should be no objections of substance in this regard.

The question is somewhat more subtle regarding the rest. Palladius directly accuses: "Why did you insinuate yourself into the soul of the Emperor? You have acted sneakily, so that the Council would not be complete." He also suspects a falsification of the verbal record (which, on the other hand, along with his other pointed observations, in no way favoring Ambrose, are reported honestly): "I do not respond because everything I have said has not been recorded: only your words are recorded. I do not respond to you."[6] The voice of the defeated is heard even by us in a text fortunately preserved and much studied in recent years: the Council of Aquileia is unique in its brevity and for its strictly judicial aspect, and it is singular in its abundance of documentation which permits us to listen with relative completeness even to the "other side."

In fact an ancient codex in the Bibliothèque Nationale of Paris, the *Paris. lat. 8907* of the 5th century, has preserved a collection of anti-Arian texts composed not many years after 381 and also contains the *Acts* of the Council which we have consulted many times. Decades later the manuscript came into the hands of an Arian sympathizer. It was densely illustrated in the margins with writings of a *homoean* origin. A partial apologia composed by Palladius himself in the aftermath of the Council of Aquileia (and in any case in the course of the year 384) has also been traced. Certain very strong expressions speak of the totally negative judgment which the author had of Ambrose. In this biography, aiming to describe the person and the deeds of the Bishop of Milan, it is right that voice should also be given to those opposing Ambrose: therefore *audiatur et altera pars* (the other side should also be heard)… Palladius compares himself and Secundus to the apostles who were brought before the Sanhedrin and, after being flogged, were set free with the order to speak no more of the name of Jesus: "They left the presence of the Sanhedrin rejoicing that they had been found worthy to suffer dishonor for the sake of the name of Jesus" (Ac 5:41). Further, speaking of himself and of his companion in the third person, he thus reflects on Ambrose: "You have not understood that... your impudent arrogance, unbridled and excessively wicked, would have been for them, as for the apostles, a title of glory and your plot, like that of the Jews, would be the real loser.... Note that, for the rest, even in the same way that the apostles were persecuted by the Jews, they suffer persecution by you because they preach the Son of God crucified."[7] At the Council, Palladius thinks, a grave injustice had taken place, because the wicked had prevailed over the pious man. "You have not considered... that religious men cannot be judged by the evil, defenders of truth by a blasphemer, those confessing the faith by a renegade, the friend of peace by a seditionist, peaceful men by a revolutionary, the innocent by a malefactor, the faithful by a catechumen... the servants of Christ by a minister of the anti-Christ; that one who brings respect for the law and who supports a just cause cannot be judged by an adversary who is, at the same time, wickedly implicated in the process. Thus all know with absolute clarity that the process between contradictory interests demands judgment not on the part of the adversary but by a magistrate who acts freely."[8]

The judgment on Palladius did not give the possibility of a response; nor perhaps could we have expected any different reaction from one who has been suddenly stricken with a judgment without appeal. But at the same time his *Apology* leaves one to understand that Ambrose had effectively abused the situation, through the trust that he enjoyed from Gratian and of the airtight support of the Bishops, to act with intolerance and a rush to judgment that seemed ill motivated. On the other hand to interpret the Council by the standards of a legal action,* with all the comparisons that follow, is not completely correct. If the form and the outcome lead one to interpret the discussion and all that follows in this way, it remains a fact that at the core stood the pronouncements in favor of or contrary to the Catholic faith and that fundamentally what emerged was the communion or not with the Church itself. In this sense it wasn't used to conclude a disciplinary judgment against certain guilty ones, but rather to safeguard the true faith, clarifying without uncertainty those essential elements that the Catholic Bishops were bound to uphold, on pain of their separation from ecclesial communion.

But perhaps we ought to take account of another question. Already well into the Council's debate, Palladius, besides calling for a future General Council, had requested the presence of lay witnesses, and Ambrose was heard to respond that "Bishops ought to judge the laity, not the laity Bishops."[9] In the *Apology* Palladius pushes it further, launching a rather singular proposal: asking, that is, that the two contending parties should commit themselves to present their cases to the Roman Senate with their own arguments grounded on the Scriptures and that those cases by imperial order should be made known in the city through public readings and also sent to ecumenical Churches. Thus, along with the Christians, everyone would be able to be involved in the discussions, pagans and Jews included, even "the cultivators of pagan doctrine and the specialists in the ancient Law, given that the same call expressed by the Gospel and the Apostles excludes no one from a religious hearing."[10]

The appeal of Palladius, which obviously remained unheard, implies something else entirely: "That which appears significant here," indicates Lellia Cracco Ruggini, "is the conviction of the Bishop of Ratiaria that the scriptural disputes of the Illirians could find interested and competent judges from among the pagan nobility and the scholars of the Jewish community of Rome, vouching for the imperial authority itself."[11] Palladius, that is, made a practical judgment, recognizing the possibility of being supported by other perhaps not even Catholic powers in the empire (pagans and Jews), and in addition accepts as a theoretical possibility that extra-ecclesial subjects would be competent to judge in questions of faith. Ambrose, most likely seizing on a similar formulation already prior to the day of the Council and following his own project, felt the obligation to react without delay: at the practical level, to break a coalition that attempted to encircle him and so to suffocate action, and at the level of principle, to oppose whoever intended to reduce the criteria of orthodoxy of ecclesial faith to the assent which is bound to a discussion among scholars. At this point, in any case, though not trying to justify the intrigues and the excesses of the Bishop of Milan, we understand the attitude that he assumed. Regarding the faith he did not compromise and given the seriousness of the stakes being played for, the danger that menaced the Church, he pushed for a decision and an action that seemed to sweep away his adversaries without mercy and without regard.

What is left of the Council of Aquileia? Or also, taking an even broader view, what place does it hold in the history of Councils in the ancient Church? Above all there remains the condemnation of Palladius and Secundus: these were pointed out to the Emperors Gratian, Valentinian, and Theodosius in a letter that summarized the deeds and the discussions of the session of September 3, 381. At the end of the Council Fathers explicitly requested that their decision regarding the two Illirican Bishops would remain in effect. Under imperial judgment, therefore, Palladius and Secundus would have had to be referred to competent tribunals, far from their sees, and replaced with Bishops of orthodox faith.[12] In contrast to the parallel Council of Constantinople, which had gathered nearly 150 Eastern Bishops in May-July of that year and that has passed into history because of the proclamation of the full divinity of the Holy Spirit (as a consequence of being accepted as ecumenical), the court of Aquileia achieved nothing of doctrinal significance like that. With the condemnation of the two principal *homoean* exponents in the West it remained only to symbolically indicate the strong decline which was enveloping Arianism in the West, and under this profile it can be drawn to its most illustrious Eastern parallel of Constantinople, which effectively closed a contested period of Trinitarian discussions in the East. The place of the Council of Aquileia in history is located, then, at the crossroads of this turning point happily resolved which marked the path of the Church.

Besides the letter to the Emperors just mentioned, intended to explain to the recipients the process and decisions which the Council had just concluded, and a brief memo to the Bishops of the provinces of Vienne and Narbonne Prima and Secunda,[13] containing the recommendation of the condemnation of Palladius and Secundus, the

Chapter VII: Aquileia: September 3, 381

Fathers of the Council of Aquileia sent to the Emperors another letter. In it they took a position regarding the Church of Antioch, which we already know to be contested between Paulinus and Meletius, the latter having died during the Council of Constantinople. The Bishops of the region had selected a successor in the person of Flavian, without wishing to consider that the schism might be resolved by following the suggestion of Gregory of Nazianzus. He had advised that Paulinus be recognized as the leader of the Church of Antioch, being the one still alive of the two contenders, besides being warmly supported by the West. In any case the election was unanimously approved by the Council Fathers. The Bishops gathered at Aquileia, however, with Ambrose as their leader, went ahead and sent a negative judgment on this matter to the Emperors and proposed that the question should be taken up and resolved in a Council to be undertaken at Alexandria.

In analogy with this intervention, in the following months, in the name of the Italian Bishops, Ambrose also took a position in regard to the new Bishop of Constantinople. The city had finally been freed from an Arian Bishop, had been temporarily in the charge of Gregory of Nazianzus and, at his resignation during the Council, was entrusted to Nectarius, a catechumen spontaneously called to the episcopal see. Ambrose, writing only to Theodosius, Emperor of the East, broached the question of Antioch in the same terms as the other missive. As far as Constantinople was concerned, he expressed reservations on the legitimacy of the election of Nectarius, explaining above all his support for Maximus, an adventurer who had subtly managed to make himself of value to the Bishop of Milan by presenting himself to him with false credentials. Finally, Ambrose suggested the convocation of a Council this time at Rome, to seek a solution in this case.

In itself, the interest in the affairs of the East that is taken by Ambrose and the Western Bishops constitutes an extremely positive fact. We remember that Basil of Caesarea was bearer of that pressing need, though not shared by the Westerners, especially in regards to the Bishop of Milan immediately after his election. In any case, while finally manifesting those long awaited signs of response, as were pointed out in another context, Ambrose did not manage to correctly perceive the elements in play. He did not know how to use the necessary tact which he, as Bishop of the West, ought to employ for decisions taken by his Eastern confreres, so suspicious in defense of their own autonomy in the area of discipline. We can certainly believe that much by the way they asserted themselves in the last of the recorded letters: "What torments us is not, in a certain sense, a contest in regards to personal interests and ambitions; what is most bothersome is the division and the separation of the ecclesial communion,"[14] and therefore we can claim that these interventions in the area of ecumenism were motivated by an authentic desire for ecclesial unity. But for the reasons given they were not destined to produce a positive effect.

We have a clear perception of the course of events.[15] In 382, in fact, the Bishops of the two parts of the empire returned to gather in Council, the first again at Constantinople, the other at Rome under the presidency of Pope Damasus and with the always important participation of Ambrose. At the invitation to attend, formulated by the Roman Council to the Easterners in order to unite themselves to them in a common front to still unresolved problems, the Fathers of Constantinople responded with a message quite respectful in its form but, in the judgment of the commentators, laced with a subtle irony. They assured them of their desire to come, but using the words of the Psalm, they allowed themselves to note finely: "Had I but wings of a dove I would fly away and be at rest with you" (Ps 54/55:7). Besides, they added, the situation did not permit them a voyage of this nature, in that the Bishops had just returned to their sees after the troubles concerning the Arian divisions and so it was not timely to so soon leave their communities, which above all demanded an attentive and ongoing care. After having also dealt with the principal doctrinal themes, the Fathers concluded by responding to the objections formulated by the West regarding Nectarius of Constantinople and Flavian of Antioch. The first, asserted the writers, was validly elected, in the presence of the Emperor Theodosius, with the unanimous consent of that same Council of 381; Flavian had, for his part, received the nomination of the Bishops of his region, with the ap-

Chapter VII: Aquileia: September 3, 381

probation of the entire Church of Antioch. Furthermore it ought not to be forgotten that, according to the norms established at Nicea, the episcopal elections must be handled by the Bishops of the province and eventually by others especially invited: another, not very veiled signal to the Westerners that they should avoid entering into areas not of their immediate competence. To the Bishops of the Roman Council nothing was left but to take note of such a communication.[16] There is also a final letter by Ambrose to Theodosius on these themes, which can be dated to those months, if not at the same time as the Council of Rome. Ambrose now expresses himself in a different tone, with the attitude of one who is justifying himself and excusing himself for being so misunderstood. The Emperor must have responded in a resentful way to the request of the Westerners so Ambrose then explains that earlier intervention maintaining that they were moved only out of love for the unity of the Church: "We do not regret having attempted that which, not to have attempted, would have been culpable. It is often said of us that we seem to neglect good relations with those of the East and to reject their friendship." Furthermore the intention was and remained that of offering an aid to reflection, not to impose our own opinion: "We have certainly not compiled those suggestions to settle the issue but in order to provide information, and we, who have asked for a judgment, are not anticipating the verdict."[17]

Before bringing these months of intense activity on the part of Ambrose to a close it is important to present one of his writings composed in 382 and which completed the picture of the dogmatic treatises *On Faith* and *On the Holy Spirit* of which we are already aware. It deals with the book *On the Sacrament of the Incarnation of the Lord*, one of the first parts of which deals with the heresy of the Apollinarians, here discussed explicitly for the first time. In the second part he again takes up the typical Trinitarian themes already developed in preceding treatises, responding to the endless objections of his adversaries. The biographer Paulinus, who didn't write a word on the Council of Aquileia, explains instead the origin of the composition of this text, linking it anecdotally to an episode of the life of Ambrose. Indeed, he recounts that "two courtiers of the Emperor Gratian, disciples of the Arian heresy, proposed a question to the Bishop while preaching, promising that they would be present the next day in the Portiana Basilica to listen to his response. The question was in regards to the incarnation of the Lord." The next day, however, they did not present themselves at the appointed time: "They got into a carriage as if to go on a journey and left the city while the Bishop and the people went into the church expecting them." But their trip ended in a serious accident and "suddenly thrown from the coach, they died." After having complained in vain that the two should have presented themselves as they had agreed, Ambrose, "ignorant of what had befallen them and not able to wait for them any longer, went up into the pulpit and began preaching on the same question that had been proposed, saying"... and then follows the first words of *On the Sacrament of the Incarnation of the Lord*, with an explicit reference to the title of that work.[18]

In the narration of this episode I have deliberately left out the comment of Paulinus who saw in the comportment of the two courtiers a clear attitude of pride, even that of contempt for God in the person of one of his Bishops. Paulinus thus recognized in what had happened to those two almost as a consequence "of the act of arrogance" that they had committed. This is, frankly, an excessive interpretation which risks putting the entire episode in suspicion, which otherwise preserves a likely story.

On the Sacrament of the Incarnation of the Lord, therefore, as other works of the Bishop of Milan, is taken from a homily which must have extended into the actual first part of the treatise and which, on the occasion of its written dissemination, was more fully integrated with the second part, which contains the anti-Arian content. It is worth dwelling a little on the first of the two parts and on the new anti-Apollinarian theme to which it is dedicated, if only to clarify where it may have come from and what supported this new doctrine and to figure out in what sense it may have been of interest to the Arians (such as the two courtiers recorded by Paulinus).

Apollinarius of Laodicea (d. before 392), a devout Nicean who had enjoyed a friendship with Athanasius, is considered the founder

Chapter VII: Aquileia: September 3, 381

of Monophysitism, the doctrine that recognizes in Christ a single incarnate divine nature and which in consequence excludes his full human nature. At the root of it was the desire to affirm, in the Word made flesh, the fullness of sanctity and an authentic unity. To obtain this end it asserts that reason (or the superior soul) must be excluded from the humanity of Christ. In this way the divine Word was able to act reasonably through his assumed humanity and guide it reliably in the ways of holiness, having strictly bound it to itself. Paradoxically this doctrine, born in the anti-Arian context and moved by the intent to safeguard the dignity of the Word made flesh, ends by sustaining Arianism. To strictly bind the second Person of the Trinity to the "flesh" of man, was, in fact, to re-propose in another way that abasement of the Word, that of its inferiority to the Father, of which the Arian movement was champion. This is why the two courtiers of Gratian had sought to test Ambrose on this matter. But beginning with the decade of the sixties, the Apollinarian doctrine had been made an object of an ever more pressing criticism on the part of the Church. We are made to observe that "that which is not assumed, is not healed," and that therefore the Divine Word had to have assumed full humanity within which to act, in obedience to the Father, "restoring" every faculty of man: body, soul, mind, and will. The question was quite delicate, because it challenged the Monophysitism of Apollinarius without quite descending to an affirmation of a dualism that might exclude unity, because that would then confound the mystery of the incarnation of the Son of God in human nature. The most elaborate response would be formed in the following century at the Councils of Ephesus (431) and of Chalcedon (451) and further yet in the Council of Constantinople III (680/91): thus was defined the doctrine of the two natures, divine and human, sustained in the one personal *hypostasis* of Christ and it was also confirmed that the unique Lord Jesus Christ subsisted in two natural wills, divine and human, jointly coming together to our salvation.[19]

The Bishop of Milan, while offering his contribution to the issue when the anti-Apollinarian reflections were still incipient, in any case expounded on a new theme, entering that context of loving contemplation of the condescension of the divine that we have seen him express in the books of *On Faith* (which, among other things, without explicit agreement on the Apollinarian question, anticipates certain themes of *On the Sacrament of the Incarnation of the Lord*). Here is one example: Ambrose begins with an illustration taken from Psalm 18/19:6 wherein is described the sun that "rises like the spouse from his bridal chamber and, like a giant, joyfully runs its course." Christ is the spouse, and above all he is a giant in a double nature: the Bishop really loves this image, so much so that he reproduces it poetically, in the 5th strophe of the Hymn *On the Birth of the Lord* (*In Natale Domini*). Thus we read:

Procebat e thalamo suo	He steps from his nuptial chamber
Pudoris aula regia	from the royal hall of modesty
Geminate Gigas substantiae	the giant who is born of a twin nature,
Alacris ut currat viam	urged on to finish his race.[20]

But let us return to the parallel text in prose, in *On the Sacrament of the Incarnation of the Lord*: "Christ is the Son of God, eternal from the Father and born of the Virgin. The holy prophet David described him as a giant because he is one, of two shapes and a double nature, sharing divinity and flesh, 'a spouse who leaves the nuptial chamber, rejoices as a giant equipped for the road' (Ps 18:6): spouse of the soul as well as the Word, giant of the earth in order to fulfill his work in view of our good, by always being the eternal God he accepted the mysterious events of the incarnation: not divided, but one, because the one and the other reality are one, and one is in both one and the other reality, that is both in his divinity and in his flesh. Not one of the Father and the other of the Virgin, but the same person in one mode of the Father and in the other of the Virgin." And after this magisterial terminological clarification, with which Ambrose expresses both the unity of the subject and the double birth and nature of Christ, with a paired list of contrasting words, he describes in what way the one and the other natures intersect, without confusion and without mutation ("one generation not compromising the other, nor the flesh compromising the divinity"), in one divine subject: "He at

Chapter VII: Aquileia: September 3, 381

the same time suffered and did not suffer, died and did not die, was buried and was not buried, rose and did not rise, he who was raised in his own body, so that only that rose which had fallen, but it was not raised that which had not fallen."[21] An even more precise formulation was advanced in the second book of *On Faith*. Here are the core expressions: "We maintain the distinction between the divine nature and the flesh! Both refer to the only Son of God, since in the same person are found the one and the other nature; and even if it is the same one spoken of, still one doesn't speak always in the same way. Observe in him now the glory of God, now the passions of man. As God, saying the things that are of God, since he is the Word, as man, saying the things that are of man, since they are spoken in my substance."[22] Because of their anticipatory clarity and their solid orthodoxy, when the discussions on these arguments exploded in the following centuries, the texts of Bishop Ambrose were cited frequently: in Councils, in writings of theology of one and the other part, in collections of *florilegia* containing extracts of the works of the Fathers. The treatise on *On the Sacrament of the Incarnation of the Lord* was sent to the East in 431 by Bishop Martinianus of Milan and probably in those circumstances was translated into Greek; for the books *On Faith*, at least, it is documented that they circulated in Greek, as a whole or in large sections, at the Third Council of Constantinople in 680/681. To cite a brief case, even Severus of Antioch (d. 538), the Monophysite Bishop whom we have come to know as transmitter of the news regarding the patience of Ambrose toward the Arian priest, pays lively attention to the Christological reflections of the Bishop of Milan. In his treatise *Against John the Grammarian* he even takes it upon himself to comment and to interpret that which he had retained as the genuine thought of Ambrose, defending to others his explanation against the orthodox reading given by other authors for erroneously forcing the texts of the Bishop of Milan to make them support proper doctrine. Thus, proceeding this way, he verified the position of great importance that Ambrose had assumed among the Byzantine scholars, who held him to be a sure master of truth. I have already mentioned in another place the scarce interest that in these discussions the Byzantine writers attributed instead to other Fathers of the Latin Church, in particular to the great Augustine. I maintain that the exceptional fame of Ambrose in this area was due to the coincidence between the interests of the Byzantine Church in the Christological question — almost an urgent need to find valid affirmations and clarifications in the ecclesial tradition, and the singular clarity and precision, united to unquestionable orthodoxy, with which the Bishop of Milan treated the argument. In consequence, Ambrose earned for himself that fame as the doctrinally secure Father of singular testimony to the faith, which the Byzantine Church typically ascribes to his person. It is not for nothing that Joseph the Hymnist (d. 886), in the *canon*[23] in honor of the holy Bishop, expressing a judgment that recurred also elsewhere in the hymnographic compositions of the Greek-Byzantine liturgy, turns to Ambrose acclaiming: "Initiated to the full understanding of the Scriptures, as a Bishop divinely inspired, O Saint, you knew how to express with clarity to those who did not know them, truths difficult to comprehend, O father Ambrose."[24]

Chapter VIII

Roman Tradition and Christian Innovation

The year 384 witnessed the conflict between Quintus Aurelius Symmachus, prefect of the city of Rome, and Ambrose, Bishop of Milan, played out through arguments and passionate speeches. The immediate focus of the debate was the petition presented to the Emperor by Symmachus asking that the altar of Victory might be restored to the Senate and that the anti-pagan laws passed by Gratian in 382 might be abolished. But at the heart of the contest was the more crucial question about the relationship between the ancient Roman tradition, which is expressed in the *mos maiorum* (ancestral custom), and the Christian innovation that had already penetrated to the heights of society with the conversion of the Emperors themselves.

It was at this exact moment — in the months immediately preceding this conflict — that serious crises demanded the attention and preoccupied the very seat of the empire, and these directly involved Bishop Ambrose.

On August 25th, 383, at the young age of 24 years, the Emperor Gratian was assassinated. In the first months of that same year, the legions stationed in Britain, in revolt, had proclaimed as Emperor the Spanish general Magnus Maximus; and that summer they had crossed the British Channel headed in the direction of Paris. Gratian, rashly leaving from Gaul, even before having begun his frontal attack on Maximus, found himself abandoned by his own army, and, falling into a trap sprung by Andragathus, one of Maximus' generals, was barbarously murdered. Ambrose, in his *Commentary on Psalm 61*, a few years later, invoking the events that led Gratian to his death, confirms, first, that the Emperor "was stripped of everything, and was pursued by those same persons from whom he had obtained oaths of fidelity by virtue of his legitimate dynasty." This was none other than

Maximus, who had been given command of the army, thus Gratian "had not a single ally, much less a follower." Referring further to a banquet and to a betrayal, Ambrose implied that Gratian, pressed by Andragathus and delivered up by Maximus, notwithstanding the guarantees he'd received, was murdered during a banquet. This account, usually deduced to be an echo of a popular tradition originating in Milan, has today been reevaluated as substantially accurate.[1] Ambrose certainly did not underplay these events when, describing the thirst and hunger of the evildoers in that context, alludes precisely to Maximus affirming: "This was the thirst of him who, seated between the banquet plates and cups, was scheming the murder of his innocent guest at the meal, the murder of an Augustus." Returning more directly to the usurper, with crudely realistic language, Ambrose added: "Did it not occur to you, O infidel, while you were eating and preparing the carnage, weren't you able to hear the crunch of human bone under your teeth? And while you drank the wine thinking of the crime, didn't it seem to you that you were mixing in those cups the blood of an innocent person?" And so for several more paragraphs Ambrose continued to underscore a dark and expressive parallel between Maximus, deceiver and murderer, and Judas, the traitor *par excellence*.[2]

Gratian having died, Valentinian II, then about 12 years old, remained in Milan with his mother Justina, in a position of extreme weakness. The offer of peace that Maximus offered to the Augustus at Milan, was, therefore, received with relief, but this also created great apprehension, since the usurper also requested that Valentinian should be brought to him at Trier "as a son to a father." Indeed, it was evident that he had the intention of putting the boy completely within his grasp. Maximus, for his part, seeking a proper legitimization, had every interest that the young Emperor might be allied to him, not by force, but by virtue of an at least formally free choice and in any case he did not exclude the possibility of an armed intervention, in case he might not receive a positive response from Milan. In a most skillful maneuver the Milanese court chose instead to designate Ambrose as ambassador to establish a rapport of peace and also to avert or at least

Chapter VIII: Roman Tradition and Christian Innovation

delay the trip of Valentinian, or to block any immediate decision on the part of Maximus.

The Bishop himself recalled his encounter with the usurper in a letter[3] from the following year sent to Milan to the Emperor, while he was preparing to return to Trier for a second combative diplomatic visit. But let us proceed in order. Ambrose departed Milan at the end of 383; at Mainz he ran into Count Victor, sent by Maximus, who, not seeing Valentinian among the members of the corps, proceeded all the way to Milan to renew in person the invitation already noted. Ambrose, in the meantime, had reached Maximus and been received in a high level meeting, where he had to justify the absence of Valentinian: "It wasn't convenient that in the middle of winter a child with his widowed mother should cross the Alps. And without his mother would he not be exposed to the risks of a very dangerous trip in such an uncertain situation?" Further, he went on to clarify that he "was engaged in a mission to negotiate peace, not to the task of promising his arrival." The incidental nature of the excuse adopted by Ambrose is more than clear. And for precisely this reason the delusion that Maximus felt is even more imaginable in that he saw his plan fall apart. The prolongation of uncertainty over the exact moment of Valentinian's arrival, which Ambrose did not guarantee but left open the possibility that he might come the following spring, kept Maximus from having the Augustus of Milan at Trier and at the same time postponed any intervention with force into Italy. So he lost precious time and, considering the winter season that was approaching and which would have prevented any military action for several months, he saw an opportunity vanish that he would not have again. Maximus, therefore, retained the Bishop until the return of Victor, who obviously carried from Milan the desire to negotiate a common peace but without any guaranteed promise regarding the arrival of Valentinian. He let Ambrose leave, thus ratifying *de facto* a peace agreement that, while decreed without enthusiasm on the part of anyone on either side, at least froze the two contestants in their current positions. Rufinus of Aquileia summarizes sarcastically: "Valentinian, who was passing time in Italy, terrorized by the assassin of his brother and in fear of the enemy, willingly embraced, even though pretending, the peace that Maximus pretended to offer him."[4]

It is good to note, at this point, that Bishop Ambrose did not lack that sense of state and of loyalty to the Emperors that previously, in the duty of governing, he was officially required to possess and which as Bishop he continued to manifest in many ways. In the mission to Trier we see him engaged in a delicate and risky undertaking that guaranteed him a certain indubitable prestige in the eyes of the court and before the entire city, but that above all revealed in him the capacity to offer himself courageously in the service of the common good, for the defense against a usurpation and for the achievement of a difficult but achievable peace. Passing over Maximus' unreliability, his leading role in subversion and murder, nor holding against the Milan court their positions of pro-Arian sympathies that had already created serious disagreements (and others that will have been provoked by them in less than a year), nor giving any thought to personal risk or of that of the Church that found itself thus embroiled in questions of uncertain outcome, Ambrose put himself under that pressure. So it is fair to ascribe to him the same moderate and confident attitude that Paulinus had attributed to his initial decision "inasmuch as (Ambrose) understood (that which was) the will of God in his regard...."[5] The mission had thus achieved its ends: to halt the potentially military plans of the usurper and to obtain something like peace. In the following months an agreement offering more long-term relief would be established between the leaders of the Empire. Theodosius remained Augustus of the entire East. The West was, on the other hand, divided between Maximus, who held Britain, Gaul and Spain, and Valentinian, who was left the prefecture of Italy.

But toward the end of 384 Ambrose was again sent by Valentinian on a new mission, again to Maximus at Trier.[6] The official motive of the trip was a request for the mortal remains of Gratian, whom we have seen was tragically murdered. Other motives, less openly admitted, may be suspected and imagined. Perhaps the desire to learn from those near at hand what might be the status of the preparations (or accomplishments) at Trier, or also, more simply, the need to bolster the impression of a promise of Valentinian's traveling to Maximus —

Chapter VIII: Roman Tradition and Christian Innovation

the idea being floated, so to speak, but not confirmed. In the dialogue between Ambrose and the usurper, as alluded to by the Bishop in the much reviewed letter, the resentment that Maximus felt at having been so adroitly tricked emerges strongly. But it is worth the bother to hear it directly, in the Bishop's telling of the first blow of the encounter. He himself, he informs us, had come to the consistory because Maximus had refused an explicit request for a private meeting, as he would have had to do given his personal dignity and role as imperial representative. Consequently, says Ambrose, "While [Maximus] was sitting in Council, I entered. He rose to embrace me. I remained standing amidst the members of the consistory. The others began to urge me to go up to him and he invited me." And so begins the dialogue:

Ambrose: Why do you embrace one whom you do not know? If you were to know me, you would not receive me like this.

Maximus: (trying for irony, perhaps?) You are irritated, Bishop.

Ambrose: But not on account of the offense, but for the disadvantage, since I find myself in a place that is not appropriate for me.

Maximus: But even on the first assignment you entered this consistory.

Ambrose: That was not even my fault: the fault was on the part of the one who called, not of the one who responded.

Maximus: Why, then, did you come?

Ambrose: Because then I wanted to conclude a peace on the part of someone who was weaker; now I ask for one who is on a par with you.

Maximus: By what merit is he on a par with me?

Ambrose: By merit of the Omnipotent God who has preserved the reign of Valentinian II which He has given to him.

Maximus: Why, you are mocking me!

And so the dialogue, ever escalating in tone, comes to touch on that which Maximus describes as an impudent claim: "Who are you really? Had I not been kept here when you came, who would be able to oppose me and my forces?" Ambrose responded truthfully, rebutting: "Where have I confronted your legions to block your flooding into Italy? With what barricade? With what army? With what squadron? Perhaps I have blocked the Alpine pass with my body? O, would that it were in my power to do so! I would have no fear of opposing you; I would not be afraid of your accusations. With what promises have I tricked you in order to get you to accept peace?"[7] And he adds the words noted: he had come for peace and not to confirm the arrival of the Emperor. But, reading these words of Ambrose, we cannot forget how much we have already understood upon the conclusion of his first mission: the Bishop had contributed to the creation of an uncertainty that he had turned totally in favor of Valentinian and that, after at least a year of such events as these, he revealed the following consequence: Maximus had to be content with Gaul, renouncing any idea of becoming the single sovereign of the entire West.

Earlier, in complying with the reason for his mission, Ambrose presented the request on the part of Valentinian for the remains of Gratian, only achieving as a result a further heightening of the irritation of Maximus. The audience having been terminated, the Bishop did not wait for an official response. In the meantime one final event took place which Ambrose describes in this fashion: "Seeing that I had avoided all contact with the Bishops who were in communion with him or who had sealed the death of certain accused individuals of being heretics, that man [Maximus], being irritated by my attitude, ordered me to leave without delay." And the Bishop voluntarily set out on his trip, although many believed that he would not escape an ambush which Maximus might have set along the road.

The heretics (it is worth pausing for a moment on this side episode to reveal the composure of Ambrose) were Priscillianists, a rigorist group of Spanish origins, whose ideas had already been condemned at Saragosa in 380. Ambrose too had demonstrated his opposition to them, not receiving Priscillian, their leader, when he came some time back to Milan. In the summer of 384, a few months before this second mission of Ambrose, certain Priscillianists were condemned at the Council of Bordeaux. Priscillian instead had appealed to the Emperor and for this reason found himself in those months in

Chapter VIII: Roman Tradition and Christian Innovation

Trier, together with some of his followers, awaiting the process which would be unhappily concluded with his condemnation and that of his principal followers to death.

Ambrose, in his letter, refers to this situation regarding the preparation for the process. While he remained firmly against the ideas of Priscillianists, he in no way wanted to enter into communion with the Bishops who had joined at Trier in order to plead the cause against Priscillian. In fact, he could not agree to such a process being conducted under civil authority or to the violence that the Bishops were intending to use. But by not communicating with them, in a way he excommunicated them, and indirectly also condemned the Emperor. That is why, as we learn again from his account, when he tried to defend the old Bishop Hyginus of Cordova, a Priscillianist sent into exile, going "to speak in his favor with the counts (of Maximus) that they not allow an old man to be banished without a cover, without a quilt against the cold" he himself was banished.[8] Let us then leave Maximus in his consolidated power as usurper-Emperor, and keeping in mind the image of the determination and equilibrium that Ambrose had manifested, let us return to the months that passed between the two missions. In fact, during that period the dispute between Symmachus and the Bishop of Milan regarding the altar of Victory played itself out.

Let's briefly review the background.[9] The placing of the statue of Victory and of its altar at the center of the Curia Julia, the new seat of the Senate, goes back to Octavian Augustus (29 A.C.). The goddess, to whom the founder of the Empire attributed his success, thus assumed something of a role of protector over the Roman Senate, over the decisions that were made there and in general over the political life of the city and Empire. As a matter of fact the senators would have sworn their loyalty to the imperial laws before that altar. This use, and the rites connected to them, continued even when, in the 4th century, Christianity had expanded into various strata of society and the Emperors themselves began to profess Christianity. Still the majority of the Senate remained solidly bound to the ancient religion and to its customs. It was only with Constantius II, in 357, that the altar and the statue of Victory were temporarily removed; but with the coming of the Emperor Julian the Apostate and of his politics of pagan restoration it was quite quickly restored to its place.

A new removal came along in the autumn of 382, the work of the Emperor Gratian who even added legislation penalizing the pagan cult. The college of priests and the vestals lost the fiscal exemption which they had enjoyed and they saw their furnishings confiscated. For his part, furthermore, Gratian decided to do away with the title Pontifex Maximus traditionally bound to the imperial office. Notwithstanding the usual contrary claim of historians, these interventions would not have been dictated by the pressures exerted on him by Ambrose. At least the Bishop himself declared it to be so in 393 in a letter to the usurper Eugenius referring to the "goods that were confiscated" asserting, in fact that "it was not I who took the initiative when they were taken away."[10] Gratian was more probably under the influence of the Christian senators of Rome who had made strong inroads into the Milanese court, and he may have been moved by the desire to emulate Theodosius, who had earlier completed a similar renunciation of the trappings of the Pontifex Maximus and had issued severe anti-pagan laws. The petition of a pagan group in the Senate, led by Quintus Aurelius Symmachus, was not long coming, but the delegation en route to Milan was not even received by the Emperor. It had been prevented by the decisive intervention of Christian senators who had found favor with Pope Damasus. Thus Ambrose relates in the letter sent to Valentinian on the occasion of the event of 384 with which we are already familiar: "The venerable Damasus... sent me a petition signed by the Christian senators, and they were a very large number, who affirmed that they had absolutely not agreed to such a petition, nor were they in agreement with such a request by the pagans and had not given their consent; they even protested officially and privately that they would not participate in the seating of the Senate if such a decision were to be made…. I passed along this plea to the brother of your Clemency (Gratian)."[11] Hence, on the part of the pagans there had not been conceded any space.

The situation changed in 384 when the Milanese court, as we

Chapter VIII: Roman Tradition and Christian Innovation

saw, found itself in a moment of grave weakness, while, on the other hand, paganism enjoyed a particularly favorable juncture, having situated its exponents in nearly all the roles of greater prestige.[12] The following were, in fact, pagans: Bauto, *magister militum* (commander of the imperial infantry) and first minister of the Emperor Valentinian II; Rumoridius, another *magister militum* associated with Bauto; Vettius Agorius Praetextatus, *praefectus praetorio* (imperial authority in charge of one of the four prefectures into which the empire was divided) for Italy, Illiricum, and Africa; Marcian, *vicarius* (head of each of the civil dioceses into which each prefecture was subdivided) for Italy; and finally Quintus Aurelius Symmachus, elevated in those months to the *praefectus urbi* (magistrate of Senatorial rank with responsibility for maintaining order in the city of Rome).

Symmachus (340-402) is the famous Roman senator, admired and exalted for his singular capacity for oratory. We already know of the amicable contacts that he exchanged with Ambrose and with his brother Satyrus, of which we have testimony in his copious epistolary.[13] Equally relevant were the offices which he held in the public life of his time: besides *praefectus urbi* in 384, he was proconsul of Africa in 373, and in 391 he assumed the consulate together with Tatian. But his fame is bound to the defense of paganism, which he promoted on several occasions, beginning with the grand dispute with Ambrose that we are describing.

In a moment so favorable for the reprise of pagan traditions and prerogatives, Symmachus, making himself the representative of the pagan members of the Senate, presented an Appeal (*Relatio*) to Valentinian II in which he asked him to roll back the decisions of Gratian. He invited the young Emperor to assume anew the tolerant attitude that had been the position of his father Valentinian I, who had already been divinized "in his starry throne noting the tears of the priests and wondering to whom should be attributed the guilt for the violation of those customs which ought to be willingly preserved." He even suggested that he allow Gratian "to correct a decision that was not his," that is, because of the influence of Christian senators; and finally he asked him not to hesitate "to abolish those dispositions that, as one has to admit, were not the work of the prince."[14] Symmachus was well aware of the new situation created by the spread of Christianity across a large portion of the population and above all at the heart of the empire thanks to the conversion of the Emperors. He knew well, in fact, and this is confirmed in the *Relatio*, that the social and political reality of Rome, first in its republican period and now in the imperial institution, was bound up strictly with the customs of the ancestors, in particular those that are religious, finding in them their own legitimacy. He then recalled that the whole foundations would seem to need to be changed with the arrival of the Christian God, because this one, as differentiated from the other gods with which Rome had come into contact, could not be inserted into a syncretistic vision. Finally, observing that, following the pagan Emperors who "honored the rites of the fathers" there were others, more recent, who, while Christian, "did not abolish it." They, and the speaker would have been thinking of Valens and Valentinian I, were a perfect example of tolerance and had in fact suggested a solution to the serious impasse that had been created: adhering personally to Christianity while at the same time respecting the Roman tradition, they demonstrate that it is possible to distinguish between the personal religion of the Emperor and the official religion of the empire, which ought not be changed and which the Augustus, independently of his own faith, is required to conserve. Even Constans, who had indeed removed the altar of Victory, "removed nothing of the privileges of the sacred virgins, filled the colleges of priests with nobles, didn't refuse the economic means to the Roman rites" that is, he didn't carry out the other decisions imputed to Gratian so that, "even while himself followed another religion, for the empire he conserved ours."[15]

To maintain the altar of Victory, therefore, signifies not losing those values that had sustained Rome for countless centuries: "on which we swear fidelity to your laws and to your person?... That altar guarantees concord among all, that altar is a particular invitation to the loyalty of each one." On the other hand, against the demand of Christianity not to accept any religions other than its own, quite solid reasons ought to be invoked in favor of a common tolerance: "It is just

Chapter VIII: Roman Tradition and Christian Innovation

that that which all adore should be considered a single thing. We contemplate the same stars, the heaven which we have in common, the same universe which we avow: what difference does it make which doctrine each one follows in the search of truth? Before a mystery so great one cannot follow a single path."[16]

The consistory, if we look ahead, had given a sympathetic hearing to similar requests and arguments. It is worth noting that even certain Christians, when they became aware of the contents of the *Relatio*, showed a respectful sympathy for that petition. Ambrose understood the urgency of the situation and, unlike two years earlier,* wished to intervene personally, writing two letters to the Emperor. In the first he requested a copy of the *Relatio*, so as to understand its arguments; in the other, having by then received a copy of the text, he wrote a long detailed response to Symmachus, resolutely refuting his claims. In the epistolary of Ambrose, between the first and the second letter the *Relatio* of Symmachus is preserved, as if to confirm the importance in which it was held by Ambrose and as if symbolically pressed between the two decisive interventions of the Bishop. In the first of the two letters, apart from substantial observations of the content that would be more thoroughly developed in the other letter, we find certain details pointed out to Valentinian, so as to render account of the unpleasant consequences in the event that the pagan request would be accepted: First of all, the Emperor always seeks the advice of Theodosius, as is his custom "for nearly all the questions of a certain importance" (insinuation: that he ought perhaps to allow these issues to subside on their own, without reacting in the usual way?). Further, Valentinian should think about the reaction of the Bishops to his response, who would not be able "to tolerate nor feign that they do not understand" his response and find that they would practically have to excommunicate him: "You may be able to go to church with the others, but either you will not find the Bishop or he will find you in order to expel you." Finally he adds to these aspects the remonstration of Gratian whose inheritance he had betrayed: "You, who call yourself brother, have abrogated my decrees, something that he who has taken up arms against me has never done" (the insinuation here is clear: watch out for Maximus who claims to be the defender of orthodoxy!).[17]

But it is in the other letter that Ambrose offers a full reflection on the various arguments in play. I cannot guide the reader step by step along all the passages of the exposition of the Bishop; but I do not want to deprive the reader of certain more significant points, beginning with those in which one catches a spontaneously passionate response on the part of Ambrose to the claims of Symmachus. A prime example: the pagan rhetorician had begun to speak for Rome herself: "I would keep the ceremonies of our ancestors, because there is nothing in them that does not satisfy me; I will live according to my customs, because I am free. This cult has subjected the world to my laws, these rites held back Hannibal from the wall, the Senonian Gauls from the Capitoline" (in a famous assault which tradition links to the episode of the Capitoline geese). Ambrose responded with magisterial derision, demanding where might the gods have been when Hannibal advanced "victorious right up to the walls of the city" and regarding the Senoni, still more acerbically he asks: "What can be said of the Senoni, whom the rest of the Roman army could not resist, while they were penetrating the interior of the Capitoline, if a frightened honking goose had not betrayed their presence? Behold what protectors the Roman temples had! Where was Jove? Perhaps he spoke by means of a goose?"[18] In this case, the Bishop explains with a loose interpretation of the facts, Rome was saved not by false and ineffectual rites but by the valor of Camillus, by the sacrifice of Attilius Regulus, by the heroism of Scipio Africanus.

Another example: Symmachus had insinuated his suspicion that the anti-pagan measures of Gratian may have been derived from "all the dregs of the Roman people" and thus "a general famine followed; and a blight which disappointed the expectation of all the provinces." The cause was not natural because "it was sacrilege that caused the vintage to wither." Ambrose had a good laugh in rebutting, again with irony, that the gods were tardily vindicated because already "for a great many years the privileges of the temple had been abolished," and further, if the gods were truly offended, why after a year of scarci-

Chapter VIII: Roman Tradition and Christian Innovation

ty were there not more priests assigned to the task so that in the present year "the country people" could look forward to "marveling at their own harvest?" And finally, if we expand our perspective, it can be noted that during the year of famine there were many provinces that produced abundant harvests.[19] But perhaps neither Symmachus nor Ambrose believed the evidence for this kind of argument!

In fact, the key points were two: the one more practical, and the other that goes to the root of the whole discussion. In the first case, we might ask how consistent paganism was and whether Symmachus might not have erred through excess when he presented the pagan religion as a still vibrant reality, because, in effect, paganism no longer had a significant social impact. In the past it may have been important in the daily life of ancient Rome and the military operations of the Republican era, but among the people of the time it had been substituted by the mystery cults, because in them the people wished to seek refuge and to find relief from the struggles of life and in the face of sadness and death. Ultimately, moreover, the ancient religion was ever more marginalized by the spread of Christianity. Especially in the cities, in the late 4th century it really only remained in the form of traditional customs. Symmachus and the remaining senatorial nobility not yet converted to Christianity were sincerely bound to those rites and those usages, so intimately connected with the history of Rome.

But Ambrose was tireless in his reply, highlighting the fictitious character and minority status of that tradition. The Roman rhetorician, for example, had asked to maintain the privileges and the subsidies of the vestals, the seven virgins who tended the sacred fire in the temple of Vesta; Ambrose was able to show how that position had become formalized and devoid of content; the parallel with the virginity cultivated within Christianity was explosive: "Open the eyes of your mind and body, observe this flock which is an example of modesty, this people which is a model of purity, this assembly of virginity." The same may be said for the priests. In this practical aspect the battle of Ambrose advances in the direction of history and draws into evidence that all could affirm: the ancient Roman cult was by this time near death, sustained by a few senators and a small group of priests and vestals: it was not right that the state should continue to give it its support with their subsidies. It is unseemly to insist on matters of ideal principles, how much less when the issues are merely matters of interest. It is interesting that Ambrose nobly and scornfully wanted to hold himself aloof: "I have brought this out," that is the injustice of subsidies no longer justified in parallel with the Christian virgins and priests who do not receive them, "not to lament, but that they know that I do not lament; I prefer, in fact, that we have less wealth and more grace from God!"[20]

There remains, in any case, the other key point:[21] by abandoning the ancient pagan religion, is that not, in the end, to betray Rome by renouncing the ancient tradition? Even though neither Symmachus nor Ambrose intend to conclude such a refutation, it remains significant that, in the entire discussion, as in the trail of successive years, Ambrose never wishes to offend his adversary: not only because of their common senatorial origins and friendship dating back a long way, but more substantially for the complete fidelity they share for the political, military and civil traditions of Rome. It is not for nothing that we have read a passage in which the Bishop exalts the virtue of the citizens and heroes who had defended and restored the greatness of Rome: Camillus, Attilius, Scipio..., etc. To this subject Ambrose introduces a clarifying intuition: fidelity to Rome, to its traditions and its customs, does not imply a necessary acceptance of its religion. As a matter of fact, this was not authentic Roman tradition insofar as the Romans had agreed with other people foreign to those traditions and those values. Ambrose, impersonating the voice of Rome, declares, "With the barbarians I have only this in common: to have not known God up to now." But finally the awareness of truth is disclosed, and hence "it is not a shame to learn something better."[22] Therefore the ancient rites should not be preserved, because the greatness and security of Rome were not dependent upon them. Ambrose consents to a universal law which states that "All is progressing toward improvement" and he sees this also applied in the evolution of creation, in the progress of human labor, in the growth of a baby

Chapter VIII: Roman Tradition and Christian Innovation

toward adulthood. Consequently he observes: "Even the first stages of the earth, as those of all things, vaccilated so that they might follow the ancient worship of a faith experienced." One ought therefore to pay attention to the time of month and to patiently wait the day of harvest. But this moment has finally arrived: the season of faith, the harvest of grace "finally is spread among the people following which were exhausted the beliefs that had dominated in preceding ages; for good reason the truth is preferred to a good law."[23] Ambrose does not listen to the proposals for tolerance offered by Symmachus because these risk conveying a relativism unacceptable to Christianity. Rather, he replies on the basis of that which was closest to his heart, viz., the continuity of Rome's traditions, assuring that these which had made Rome great through the ages remain in all of their force, adding that that tradition is not broken but rather will continue and will be perfected in Christianity which, with its truth, will finally complete the attestation of the betterment that Rome carries in itself to the end of the ages.

This is Ambrose's thought on paganism and Roman tradition. Toward the end of his life he reappraised his reflections on these arguments, in a form more complete and thus definitive, in the discourse *On the Death of Theodosius*. But we will return to it later. Here we ought to at least pick up the sequence of facts, to signal that Valentinian listened to Ambrose and left in force the laws decreed by Gratian. Perhaps, as has been observed,[24] this was a victory of limited value: perhaps the Emperor did not wish to insult the Bishop in a period of such delicacy in his relations with Maximus. In any case, a deep sense remains that at the root of this episode is something that is beyond the contingencies of the moment and also beyond the powers that will come to be attributed to Ambrose. The subsequent events confirm the trajectory by now well initiated: in 389/390 Symmachus renewed the same request to Theodosius and in 391 to Valentinian, always without a different result. The pagan cause did achieve a momentary success in 393 under the usurper Eugenius. He in fact sided with the delegation of senators lead by Flavian, cousin of Symmachus, and allowed the nearly total abolition of the norms of Gratian; but with the victory of Theodosius over the usurper in September of the following year, everything returned to the way it was previously, and that same Flavian killed himself in order not to fall into the hands of the Emperor. It was the end of the ancient pagan religion.

We have noted the action of Ambrose first against Arianism, now against paganism. It is very important to remember that the battles of the Bishop, including those in reference to Judaism of which we will wish to speak further in subsequent chapters, do not assume the aspect of personal attacks on individuals. At the end of these passages I think the true significance may be presented in an episode that confirms that comportment of Ambrose: it is preserved by Sozomen in his *History of the Church* and was collected at the time of the Emperor Gratian. The Bishop here figures as an intercessor in favor of a pagan who was condemned to death for having offended the Emperor, describing him as "unworthy of his father," most likely because the offender, reacting to the interventions of Gratian against paganism, had thrown in his face the abandonment of that neutrality that had distinguished Valentinian I. "Ambrose, then" recounts Sozomen, "while the perpetrator was led out to torture, was received at the imperial palace to intercede in his behalf." Gratian, however, was amusing himself by watching the action of the hunt while "none of his functionaries dared to enter the palace to inform him, making the excuse that he was not available at the moment." The Bishop, therefore, made a show of leaving; "but he secretly went through the door that was used to bring in the beasts. So he entered together with the hunters; and he did not stop nor did he withdraw from Gratian and those who were following him until he had extracted from the Emperor a sentence of salvation, with which he could guarantee the liberation of the one who was being led to death."[25]

We understand therefore why, at the death of Ambrose, both pagans and Jews, as is testified in the biography of Paulinus, remembered the deceased with respect, and were moved to attend the funeral.[26]

CHAPTER IX

A Contested Basilica and a People Bound to Their Bishop

Readers certainly remember Auxentius, the philo-Arian Bishop who had preceded Ambrose. Now, again in Milan, we encounter another Auxentius, the deposed Bishop of Durostorum (Silistria in Romania, toward the mouth of the Danube). He is also known by the name of Mercurinus; and it remains uncertain whether one or the other name might be original to him or whether, as Ambrose asserts,[1] the appellative Auxentius was added so as to invoke and emulate the old *homoean* Bishop, either a truly singular coincidence or an undoubtedly eloquent choice.

Mercurinus Auxentius[2] had been a disciple of the philo-Arian Ulfilas (311-c.383), the famous evangelist to the Goths noted for his combative attitude against the adversaries of Arianism. From him the Bishop of Durostorum had assumed the *homoean* faith and a strong missionary sense. In recognition of his death he had dedicated a panegyric, reaching us in the marginal gloss of the codex *Paris. Lat. 8907,* already noted by us for having passed down to us the *Acts* of the Council of Aquileia and the *Apology* of Palladius. In 384 Auxentius, deposed from his see following the anti-Arian instructions of Theodosius, had come to Milan, most likely summoned by Justina, the mother of Valentinian II, whom we have had reason to know for her Arian sympathies. Gratian dead and freed from the immediate fear of Maximus, she wanted to revive the *homoean* community of the city. This Arian group, which we saw active in Milan in the years preceding the Council of Aquileia, certainly did not vanish after that event but maintained a real vitality thanks again to the presence of Justina. The renewed request for a basilica for the Arian cult, which will soon be insistently refused by Bishop Ambrose, will not emerge without basis.

We do not have detailed information concerning the activities of Mercurinus Auxentius in Milan. Ambrose, in a homily delivered in those months but later inserted into the *Commentary on the Gospel of Luke*, offers us a pointed description, though without naming him, inspiring him to apply to him the Gospel expression: "Guard against false prophets who come to you dressed in sheep's clothing, but inside are rapacious wolves. They will be known by their fruits" (Mt 7:15-16); Auxentius "is dressed like a lamb, but he acts like a predator; outside he is a sheep, inside he is a wolf with no limits to his rapine; prowling around about at night, his limbs frozen by the chill of Scythia" (the steppe region near which Durostorum is located), "he is bloodthirsty, seeking to devour. Does he not resemble a wolf that is only satiated by consuming human blood, and has no other desire than to satisfy his own furor with the demise of the believing population?" Continuing to develop the image of a rapacious wolf, Ambrose recalls the philo-Arian preaching of Auxentius: "He who howls, but does not teach, because he has denied the author of the Word, and with his sacrilegious discourses he strides about proclaiming with a savage voice, because he does not recognize in the Lord Jesus the judge of eternal life."[3]

But what effect did the preaching of this Arian Bishop have? Did he only have the ear of the Court, or did his "missionary" activity in Milan gain adherents? In the first book of *On the Duties of the Clergy*, Ambrose himself refers to one like him, a person whom he had not admitted to the clergy "because his comportment was quite unsuitable,"[4] who later revealed far more serious deficiencies in that "he denied the faith at the time of the Arian attacks." It is not difficult to imagine that his switch may have been caused or at least encouraged by the preaching of Auxentius. Another indication: in 386 Ambrose accused the Arian Bishop of the fact that, "in your opinion, they ought to re-baptize the faithful already baptized in the name of the Trinity" in the bosom of the Catholic Church.[5] Therefore, most likely cases of that sort had arisen. Finally, and thus we reintroduce ourselves to the most intense events of these years, it is significant that Justina renewed, first in 385 and again the following year, her

Chapter IX: A Contested Basilica and a People Bound to Their Bishop

request to have a basilica for the Arian community of Milan. The principal motive, to validate the *homoean* presence in the city against the Bishop, would have been connected to the necessity of having a church in which to celebrate during the Easter vigil, at the time of the Christian rites of initiation.

Before starting this narrative, I would like to first present the context in which these events are placed. Ambrose, as we will see, will have to sustain serious attacks by the court and he will find himself surrounded by the imperial machine. All the same, he will not appear alone. In fact we are able to attest that the Milanese in those turbulent situations wanted to form a body around their Bishop, peacefully uniting themselves to him in a full and firm solidarity. The relationships of fidelity and esteem that had been created in the days of his election to the Milanese seat were not only undiminished by the impact of subsequent events, but were even elevated and intensified.

In 381, on order of Gratian, the basilica that Justina had obtained after his arrival in Milan some two years earlier was released. In the spring of 385 the Court renewed the request, in order to provide a church for Auxentius on the occasion of the approaching Easter. Ambrose was summoned before the consistory and, as he himself recalled a year later in his *Discourse Against Auxentius* he was certainly not "intimidated by the imperial residence" nor did he lose heart perceiving that the Emperor wanted to take a basilica away from the Catholics for the Arian cult. In any case, he found a decisive buttress, the first in a long series, in his faithful. In fact, Ambrose declares "the people, knowing that I had been called to the palace, caused such an eruption with unstoppable force that when the military count went with a light troop to put the crowd to flight, they all presented themselves ready to be killed for faith in Christ." The Court then pleaded with Ambrose to placate the people. This he did, giving them his word "that no one would take over the basilica belonging to the Church." Thus concluded the first attempt, leaving a very understandable residue of dissatisfaction on the part of the Court which dismissed the Bishop. "While they might have requested my good offices as a favor, nonetheless they were resentful of me because the people had gone to the imperial palace." Ambrose had acted.⁶

The Court, therefore, would have to prepare a more thorough strategy. Upon his return to Milan toward the end of the year, after a residence of several months at Aquileia, on January 23, 386, Valentinian issued a law. With it he prepared the groundwork for a new order of seizure, while immediately lending support to the missionary activity of Auxentius at Milan. The Arian Bishop would have been the inspiration. Once again, Ambrose, in his *Discourse Against Auxentius*,⁷ came to believe that those arrangements would have had to be "written by his hand and dictated by his mouth." The law⁸ granted freedom to the cult and to the congregations of those who professed the faith proclaimed at the Council of Rimini in 359 and at that of Constantinople the following year, that is, to the followers of the *homoean* doctrine. Conversely it commands the exile and penalty of death to whoever may dare to oppose the imperial edict, making them guilty of treason.

The historian Rufinus has preserved for us a noble example of the moral law connected with the promulgation of this decree. He records the fact that Benevolus, the imperial functionary charged to draw up the decree, refused to complete a deed so contrary to his own faith, declaring himself "unable to pronounce disrespectful words and to speak against God." To the offer of advancement in rank if he would give in, he responded that he would prefer coherence with his own conscience and, "saying that, threw his belt at the feet of the one who had commanded these impious actions."⁹ Thus another person, with personal sacrifice, had taken the side of Ambrose! It is nice to find Benevolus a few years later as a revered member of the church in Brescia. The Bishop Gaudentius, passing along fifteen of his homilies, laid out a eulogy to his faith and of his exemplary life and, recalling the episode of 386, remembers that Benevolus "without hesitation" had scorned "to exchange for the glory of God both the dignity of a promised promotion and earthly ambition and worldly glory."¹⁰ Before taking up the description of the events it is opportune to supply a brief introduction to the three ecclesial buildings about which we will be speaking in the following narration. We find first

Chapter IX: A Contested Basilica and a People Bound to Their Bishop

of all the Basilica Portiana, which Ambrose indicates as being located outside the walls and which might correspond to the church seized at the time of Gratian; it has still not been identified through an excess of attributions; in the course of this century it has been identified, at one time or another, with S. Vittore al Corpo, with S. Eustorgio, and with S. Lorenzo. Nor can it be said that a clarifying link with any of these has been found. The other two buildings, however, were inside the walls, joined one to the other and thus near the house of the Bishop. Back then, as in medieval times, both would have functioned as the cathedral church. Ambrose indicates that much on the basis of their more or less recent origin. The more ancient of the constructions was the Basilica Antica (*basilica vetus*), named S. Maria Maggiore in its high medieval reconstruction. Located in the area where the Duomo now rises, it was oriented along the apse of the current building, while being much smaller in dimension. It had its own baptistery, called S. Stefano alle Fonti, whose baptismal font was discovered under the northern baptistery of the Duomo itself. The other basilica was the Nuova (*basilica nova*), which in the Constantinian era was constructed in front of the Antica and which later would have assumed the title of S. Tecla: the remains have been rediscovered in the area in front of the current Duomo. This later basilica, of five naves, was larger than the earlier one. Ambrose defines it as the "major" by comparison with the other one which he called the "minor." The Basilica Nuova also had its own baptistery, entitled S. Giovanni alle Fonti. Constructed in octagonal form by Ambrose himself, its foundations have been rediscovered in the area of the churchyard of the Duomo.[11] Since the laws had been promulgated, and therefore Ambrose was at least formally threatened if he would not retreat from his intransigent position, the events took on an increasingly urgent pace.[12] Already in February, or a bit later at the beginning of March, the Court returned to request the Basilica Portiana. These doings were revealed by Ambrose himself in his *Discourse Against Auxentius* which he very likely delivered orally himself in the Basilica Portiana, and in *Epistle 75a* (*to Valentinian*) written in those same turbulent times. These, in summary, are the events: Dalmatius, tribune and secretary of the consistory, came to Ambrose and invited the Bishop to a debate that was to be held at the palace in the presence of the Emperor. Dalmatius informed him that Auxentius had already selected judges and begged Ambrose to do as much. But Ambrose did not comply with the request. A Bishop could not accept such a confrontation, he rebutted in a letter to the Emperor. It was enough, in any case, to reconsider the law emanating from Valentinian I in which he had recognized that "in a cause regarding the faith or ecclesiastical dignity there must be judges who are not inferior in grade nor found to be in a contrary juridical situation." Ambrose confirmed all this in a question: "When have you heard, most clement Emperor, that in a matter of faith the laity may judge a Bishop?" On the other hand, in light of the law that had come out the preceding January, how would it be possible to carry out equal justice? The judges would necessarily in fact have had to follow the injunctions, or otherwise, in the case of opposition, they would have incurred serious punishment in prohibiting them: "I, therefore, having summed up, would have to expose the person either to apostasy (against the right Catholic faith) or to be condemned!" Without doubt, then, that law must be abolished.[13]

In the *Discourse Against Auxentius* Ambrose reconfirms his refusal to be judged by the laity, and he positions his refusal in the broader and deeper context of the relationship between the Church and the Emperors. Let us read his expressions, keeping in front of us the questions that were then and subsequently are posited regarding his attitude and his thought: Had the Bishop perhaps assumed an attitude of insubordination before the constituted authority? Was he making a duty bound defense of the autonomy of the Church or, partly in reaction to an earlier illegal usurpation of power by the Empire itself, does he now go to the opposite extreme? Look at his words, which take their cue from noted phrases of the Gospel: "Render unto Caesar that which is Caesar's and to God that which is God's (Mt 22:21): "The tribute belongs to Caesar and ought not be denied; the Church belongs to God, and it certainly must not be handed over to Caesar, because the temple of God cannot be obliged by the laws of Caesar." Following on this point is the more demanding expression,

Chapter IX: A Contested Basilica and a People Bound to Their Bishop

anticipated by a reaffirmation of that loyalty which we already appreciate in Ambrose: "No one can deny that this has been said with honor for the sovereign. What is more respectful than to affirm that the Emperor is a son of the Church? The Emperor is, in fact, within the Church, not above it: a good Emperor asks for aid to the Church, he does not refuse it. All of this, which we say with humility, so too do we express with firmness."[14]

The Bishop then requests that he only be guaranteed autonomy in religious questions, even if, as has been made clear, "this vindication of autonomy… was profoundly new and seemed inadmissible to the profane authority, such that it collided with a tradition as ancient as Rome itself. It is undeniable that, in a State that did not know the separation between the civil power and the religious power, the spiritual authority that the Bishop claims over the Emperor seems a heavy obligation, and he effectively posits that duty, on the freedom of the decision of the latter." Even when Ambrose asserts that the Emperor is *inside* the Church "this does not imply in any way a protection of the Church concerning political actions, even if the imprecise definition of the boundary between the two powers in the Roman state justifies reciprocal interference, based on the balance of power at the moment."[15] At this point we cannot delve into these reflections more deeply, since we are already bound to take them up again in commenting on the discourse *On the Death of Theodosius*.

After the encounter with Dalmatius, the situation must have intensified. For a few days after Ambrose delivered the *Discourse Against Auxentius*, the Church was surrounded by soldiers "drawn up all around it" with "a clamor of arms." The faithful maintained their guard "for many days and nights without closing their eyes." In the confusion and tension of those moments the paradox was again demonstrated of a surveillance which, meant to be constant and complete, had instead left open several breaches: "You are bothered because you have found two open doors that you say were left wide open by a blind man, while returning to his own dwelling." And again: "Two days ago or so, as you well remember, was it not discovered also that on the left side of the basilica an entrance remained accessible that you believed to be closed and blocked?" And he commented: "The Lord has not neglected the surveillance of his mercy... therefore cease your worrying, because what will be is what Christ commands, and he expedites what will come to pass."[16]

One can imagine that the Court had no desire to impose the death penalty, or even that of exile, on Bishop Ambrose. In any case, a situation like that strained the strategy of both sides; testing the limits gave the impression that some such resolution may have been imminent. Let us review the expressions that describe this state of things. It was suggested that the Bishop should leave the city in a voluntary exile. Nevertheless, he had declared to the faithful: "I will never abandon you of my own free will; but I will not resist the use of force. I will worry, I will weep, I will lament: even against armies, against soldiers, against the Goths, my tears are my weapons; such as these are the defenses of a Bishop. In any other way I cannot and I ought not resist." Paulinus, recalling this detail to us, recounts that Justina "promised positions and various other dignities to anyone who would kidnap" the Bishop "from the church and lead him into exile." A certain Euthymius is mentioned, who had acquired "a house near the church" and who had positioned "a cart in order to more easily kidnap him, bundle him on the cart and take him into exile." But this came to nothing, and moreover, a year later Euthymius suffered the exile that he had prepared for the Bishop (experiencing the magnanimous aid of the Bishop in that sad turn of events...). Death, too, seemed to be near, and surely it was to this possibility that Ambrose declared before the assembly of the faithful: "There is no reason for anyone to fear, my most beloved brothers; I know in fact that whatever affliction I may have to suffer, I will suffer it for Christ," and referring to scripture: "I have read that I ought not to fear those who are able to kill the body (cf. Mt 10:28), and I have heard him who said: 'Whoever would lose his life for me, will find it' (Mt 10:39)." Regardless, he did not avoid making a virulent attack on Auxentius because, if the philo-Arian laws had been inspired by him, then all that Ambrose had to suffer was his responsibility: "Many have said that assassins have been sent out, and that the death penalty has been

Chapter IX: A Contested Basilica and a People Bound to Their Bishop

decreed. I do not fear those threats; I will not leave this place. In what place could I go where everything will not be full of suffering and tears, when it is commanded that in all the churches the Catholic Bishops are to be hunted down, to be struck by the sword if they offer resistance…? And these orders have been written by the hand and spoken by the mouth of a Bishop…."[17]

After these moments of extreme emotional tension, the battle would continue along other lines. With the approach of Easter the one and the other side perceived that they were entering the final stretch. Ambrose informs us in detail about these final events in a letter to Marcellina which, significantly, begins with recalling certain "dreams" that "did not leave in peace" his sister and that she had communicated this to him in one of her recent letters.[18] At this point the Bishop recounted what had happened day by day; and so we too can follow the narration beginning on the Friday before Holy Week.

Friday, March 27, 386. The counts of the consistory came to Ambrose requesting him to surrender the Basilica Nuova instead of the Portiana, which seems momentarily no longer to be an object of the contention. Thus, with this psychological move the Court raises the ante. In any case the Bishop responds negatively.

Saturday, March 28. As the Bishop enters the church, most likely the Basilica Antica, the people applaud him. As is predictable, the counts return to request the Portiana: the *praefectus praetorio* comes in person to attempt to convince him. But this time it is the people who protest, and again it comes to nothing.

(Palm) Sunday, March 29. This Sunday, Ambrose, as was his habit, explains and consigns the symbol of faith (the Creed) to the catechumens who were to receive baptism on the coming Easter.[19] This part of the rite was celebrated in the baptistery, either that of S. Giovanni or that of S. Stefano, and he is made aware that *decani* (officials of an inferior rank), have entered the Portiana, and were installing imperial banners. Thus, with such an unequivocal, if moderate, sign, they prepared the church for the coming of the Emperor, arranged the place in the basilica where he would participate in the celebrations and in consequence of which he would have reserved

the church for the Arian cult. A little later, during the celebration of the Mass, Ambrose had to intervene again: he is told that an Arian priest, by the name of Castulus, risked being lynched by the Catholics. Deeply disturbed and fearful that it all might end in serious violence, the Bishop demanded that they liberate him.

Holy Monday, 30 March (or perhaps already on the afternoon of the Sunday). A tax of "200 pounds of gold" was imposed on the merchants to be paid "within 3 days." The merchants reacted with the same solidarity toward the Bishop that we have already found in Benevolus and by all the people in the spring of 385: "They responded that they would have given as much or even double, if requested, in order to preserve their faith. The jails," the Bishop adds with obvious exaggeration, "were full of merchants."[20]

Holy Tuesday, March 31. Negotiations continue between the Bishop and the Court, which sent counts and tribunes to speed up the delivery of the Portiana Basilica. The arguments from the discussion already dealt with in the *Discourse Against Auxentius* and in the letter to Valentinian are taken up again. If, according to the emissaries of the Court, "the Emperor used his own law, because all was in his power," Ambrose responded that that law had value for those things that pertained to Ambrose personally, although he considered his wealth already as the property of the poor, but he confirmed that "that which belongs to God was not subject to imperial authority." He added that he was ready for anything, as regarded his person: even as far as going to prison and to face death. When, during these debates, he became aware "that soldiers were ordered to occupy the basilica," who intended to surround the Basilica Portiana, Ambrose worried that it not come to violence and, to the demand of the counts and of the tribunes that he "control the people," he confirmed that he had no desire to excite the people, but that to calm them was not entirely in his power, but "was in the hands of God." After their discussion, Ambrose remained all that day in the Basilica Antica. In the evening he returned to his house to sleep because, as he pointed out to his sister, "if someone wanted to arrest me, they would find me ready."[21]

Holy Wednesday, April 1. A day fraught with events that touch

Chapter IX: A Contested Basilica and a People Bound to Their Bishop

on all three basilicas: a circumstantial description of the facts is not easy, because Ambrose is not explicit in identifying, moment by moment, which church was in question but, taken by emotion and trusting that his sister already knew much, he uses generic expressions.[22] As on the day before, the Bishop remained in the Basilica Antica. At the Portiana the blockade was taken up again: it seems that the soldiers were ordered to act as police, so that the Emperor would be able to go himself for the liturgical rites and not encounter confrontations or disturbances. These same soldiers, who knew Ambrose, had perhaps informed the Emperor that he was certainly free to exit the palace but that "they would remain at their posts, if he was seen in the company of Catholics; otherwise they would move over to the side of the assembly called there by Ambrose." They were, that is, ready to maintain order only if the Emperor came to the Portiana and only if he would celebrate a Catholic rite, open to all the orthodox faithful. And it wasn't just words: while Ambrose celebrated in the Basilica Antica and was proclaiming the readings, the soldiers began to trickle in. It was another unexpected turn of events: "On seeing them the women were upset; one rushed outside." But the soldiers weren't trying to upset them, because their intent was much simpler: they knew that the Bishop had ordered them to be excommunicated (if they intended to continue the occupation), so they came to him, and as they repeated to everyone, "to pray, not to fight." Even in the Portiana they demanded the presence of the Bishop; and surely in the Basilica Nuova many faithful were gathered, more numerous than was usual, and these asked for a reader to lead them in prayer.[23] Ambrose, however, remained in the Basilica Antica and began to preach the homily to the people, in which he recalled the discussions of the past several days, about which they already knew, and he fought valiantly against the intrigues of Justina, even comparing her to the queen Jezebel, who had persecuted the prophet Elijah, and to Herodias, who had caused the murder of John the Baptist....

Let us pause for a moment in order to make a point in this weaving together of the facts. The people, as they had some seven years earlier, were mobilized, demonstrating their full solidarity with the Bishop against the Court. Further, gathering together with him in the Basilica Antica, and perhaps because of the constriction of this building, they spilled over into the Nuova also, and they requested the presence of a reader there. In the Portiana, finally, instead of Arians (none of whom "dared to appear in public,"[24] according to Ambrose), Catholics had entered and requested that the Bishop come to offer the proper celebration in the contested church. Ambrose, however, did not respond to their request because the philo-Arian laws were in force. Any false step in that direction could be interpreted as explicit opposition to the imperial edict and would thus become a weapon in the hands of his adversaries. They needed to remain strong and together, but not overdo it because the potential risk was really quite real. Through it all, while the Bishop was preaching, he was informed that at the Portiana the imperial banners had been put aside; furthermore, the basilica was full of people who renewed the invitation for him to come to them. Still Ambrose didn't budge; he did, however, send priests.

The reaction was immediate: while he was concluding the homily, full of joy at the news he had received, a secretary arrived from the Court. In a secluded place he asked the Bishop a question which was at the same time an accusation: "Why have you intervened to act against the imperial will?" And to the surprise of Ambrose, who said that he knew of no reason for such a serious reaction, the other one replied: "Why have you sent priests into the basilica? I want to know if you are a tyrant, in order to know how to respond against you." The Bishop justified himself, explaining the facts as we already know them. Regarding the accusation of tyranny, he rather suggested that the Emperor "not create for himself a real tyrant." In this way he brought Maximus to mind, inviting Valentinian not to forget the mission he fulfilled in Trier precisely in defense of the Court and in a veiled way invited him to be prudent. Could it follow that Maximus, who posed as the protector of Catholicism, might seize the pretext of these events against a Catholic Bishop to intervene and descend to occupy Italy? Ambrose was quite the prophet, as we will soon see.

The situation was extremely tense because, beyond the signs of

Chapter IX: A Contested Basilica and a People Bound to Their Bishop

an apparent breakdown of order being verified at the Portiana (the imperial banners had been torn down by a group of teenagers playing!) he surmised that the Court, forgetting the rest, were now concentrating all their force directly against the Bishop. That evening, in fact, he wasn't able to go home "because soldiers were on guard all around the basilica." Thus he passed the night in prayer with the faithful, repeating the experience he had lived through at the time of the *Discourse Against Auxentius*.[25]

Holy Thursday, April 2. The last day, finally! Another homily by Ambrose, another interruption and more news that arrives unexpectedly: "The Emperor has ordered the soldiers to leave the basilica. Furthermore whatever they had confiscated from the merchants following the condemnation was to be given back to them." Justina and Valentinian and the whole Court had thus definitively capitulated. Had they been led to that decision during the night because of an unexpected suggestion on the part of Theodosius? It may be, but we know nothing for sure. Maximus, however, did intervene: indeed, there is a letter from him addressed to Valentinian and attributable precisely to these days. In it the tyrant regrets having heard that at Milan, because of new Imperial edicts, "violence was done against Catholic churches and that the Bishops were being besieged in their basilicas." About this Maximus, professing to write in good faith, prays that his young colleague desist from such behavior.[26] And it certainly wasn't possible to ignore his suggestion.... In the deliberations of the Court the strong solidarity of the people who had remained faithful to the Bishop and who had tightly surrounded him for a whole week up to the last night, would also have to be taken into consideration. In the end, Ambrose confides to his sister, the people were able to explode in united exultation: "How great, then, was the joy of all the people, the cheering of the crowds, the thanksgiving!" Even the soldiers were caught up in everyone's joy, "competing with one another to bring the news and, rushing toward the altars, they kissed them in a sign of peace."[27]

Concluding the letter to his sister, Ambrose seems to nurture again that uncertainty over the immediate future and to a possible "final blow" of the Court, so humiliated by these events. But we will see that after two months, when the Bishop recovers the remains of the martyrs Protasius and Gervasius, there will be no shadow over his security.

A final aspect of the genial "rule" (*regia*) conducted by Ambrose in those days of tension still remains to be described. He tried to keep alive the regard of the people, to guide them in prayer, to make them see the unity and the bondedness of that assembly, to sustain their morale and reinforce their convictions. Very simply he tried to pass long hours of the day and night together with them. Paulinus of Milan noted that in those events "for the first time in the Milanese Church the antiphonic singing of the psalms and vigils were introduced and began to be celebrated; these liturgical uses persist to this day not only in that Church, but in nearly all of the provinces of the West." Augustine, providing the same news in his *Confessions*, explains that they took up those innovations "so that the people would not collapse from the affliction of boredom."[28] What was the intention of the Bishop? Above all, he taught them to sing the psalms in an antiphonic form, that is, the assembly was divided into two choirs entrusting to each one alternatively one verse after the other. Further, he had them sing the hymns, which we know to have been composed by Ambrose himself. Finally regarding the watches, i.e., the "vigils" in prayer that were spread out through the entire night and that were appropriate in a monastic environment, beyond inventing them, he had them arranged in an adaptation for the participation of the people. All were thus able to experience them actively and take part reciprocally in song and prayer.

But central were the hymns[29] to which those same Arians made their own contribution. In the *Discourse Against Auxentius* Ambrose had in fact declared with subtle irony: "They say that the people are enchanted by the incantations of my hymns. Quite so: I do not deny it. They weave a great magical spell (*carmen*); nothing is more powerful. What, indeed, is more powerful than the confession of the Trinity, which the people sing every day with a single voice? As if it were a competition they all want to proclaim their faith. Everyone has been

Chapter IX: A Contested Basilica and a People Bound to Their Bishop

taught to praise, in verse, the Father, the Son, and the Holy Spirit. They have therefore all become masters, those who only recently were disciples."[30] The Bishop attests to the convinced and impassioned engagement of the people in the singing of his hymns, and he explains it by playing on the double significance of the Latin word *carmen*, which may mean both "incantation" and "song, hymn-like poem."

The hymns, so precious in those tumultuous situations, retain a broader pastoral value. They were, in the plan of the Bishop, a weighty instrument of teaching and catechesis which render "masters those who only recently were disciples" and which, therefore, gave even to the faithful who would never be experts at following the tortuous paths of theological discourse the ability to use appropriate and persuasive words. In the West Hilary of Poitiers had already composed a few hymns, but his attempts did not produce good results because of the complex form of those poems and because of the ponderousness of their content.

Ambrose is, then, the true founder of Western hymnology. The hymns that can be attributed to him with confidence or with a good likelihood are a little more than a dozen.[31] They had a very wide distribution in Spain, then in Switzerland, in Germany, in France, in England, etc. Furthermore, because of this use, they were imitated more and more to the point that the term "Ambrosian" was finally adopted to designate those liturgical hymns that were composed on the model of those of the Bishop of Milan. Thus began the happy insertion of the hymns of Ambrose into the liturgy. Indeed, they are intended to accompany the different moments of the day in which liturgical prayer is raised (hymn for the Office of Night Prayer, at Sunrise, at the Third hour, for Vespers), or perhaps to introduce one to the mysteries of the liturgical year (Christmas, Epiphany, Easter), or again to enliven the celebration of the principal apostles (Saints Peter and Paul or Saint John the Evangelist), of the martyrs of the universal Church (Saint Lawrence, Saint Agnes) and the martyrs of the local Milanese tradition (Saints Victor and Felix, Protasius and Gervasius).

There arises, at any rate, the question of why these hymns are so precious. There is no single response apart from recalling the positive aspects already indicated. One element that should not be overlooked, it seems to me, is appropriately suggested by Jacques Fontaine when, in his study dedicated to the prose and the poetry in the literary production of the Bishop of Milan, he asks whether if "one of the greatest originality" in the writings of Ambrose could be found "in the fact that this *singer of hymns* wrote in verse without forgetting that he preached in prose, and that this *sacred orator* spoke without being able to escape a profound and natural tendency toward the poetic form where his literary genius found its highest expression." As a consequence these hymns, to dwell in particular on them, being intimately linked to the simplicity of his discourses in prose, appear free of formalistic rigidity: in them, Jacques Fontaine again indicates, are realized the axiom that true poetry makes a joke of poetry[32] and it is experienced as "under the discipline of a fixed simple form and almost without defect," "the highest virtue of prose and poetry is harmonization without dissonance." In conclusion: this "paradoxical harmony is not the only explanation possible for the lasting success of the Ambrosian hymn across the sixteen centuries that separate us from their creation. But it is perhaps one of the more illuminating traits of his literary originality."[33]

The reader might want an example. Even so, it is not easy to offer one because every translation and every comment loses much of the freshness and geniality of the style of the Bishop. In any case I would like to suggest the hymn *Aeterne Rerum Conditor,* taken from the Evening Office. It is less theological than others, at least at first glance, and completely built around the lively image of the rooster, which appears from the beginning to the end. The rooster symbolizes the last phase of the night, the awakening with his song, anticipating the light of day (in the second strophe, with a bold substitution from auditory effect in the visual, the song creates "light" for the wayfarer). The rooster signals the coming day and announces activity and solace, and invites one to awaken to the light, to assume anew one's own commitments, to shake oneself from every interior torpor and to embrace life with a good spirit. It is the signal that the night is ended;

Chapter IX: A Contested Basilica and a People Bound to Their Bishop

the rooster, then, is the symbol and the reminder to come out of the dark, which not even the Apostle Peter knew how to avoid. But he, after having denied, heard the rooster crow and "went out and wept bitterly" (Lk 22:62). In this dynamic the song of the rooster recalls the look that Jesus gave to the penitent apostle, and suggests to the faithful a loving invocation around which one's praying turns and which, at another time, Ambrose, developing this same image, expressed in this fashion: "Guard us as well, Lord Jesus, so that we too might recognize our errors, that we might wash away our fault with the tears of remorse, that we might deserve pardon for our sins."[34]

Aeterne rerum conditor	Oh eternal Creator of all
Noctem diemque qui regis	who rules the night and day
Et temporum das tempora,	and divides the seasons
Ut alluves fastidium,	to relieve uneasiness
Praeco diei iam sonat,	the herald now sounds the day
Noctis profundae peruigil	watchful in the depths of night
Nocturna lux viantibus	nocturnal light for travelers
A nocte noctem segregans.	Dividing night from night
Hoc excitatus Lucifer,	Through it Lucifer* aroused
Solute polum caligine:	the pole loosed from the dark:
Hoc omnis errorum chorus	Through it the hordes all error
Vias nocendi deserit.	and hurtful ways forsake
Hoc nauta vires colligit	Through it the Sailor binds his strength
Pontique mitescunt freta;	And the tumult of the sea subsides
Hoc ipse petra ecclesiae	Through it even the Rock** of the Church
Canente culpam diluit.	Dissolves his guilt in that crowing
Surgamus ergo strenue:	Let us rise up, then, with vigor
Gallus iacentes excitat	the Crow arouses the drowsy
Et somnolentos increpat,	And rebukes the late-sleepers
Gallus negantes arguit.	the Cock reproves the deniers
Gallo canente spes redid,	the Cock crowing Hope returns
Aegris salus refunditur,	health is restored to the sick
Mucro latronis conditur,	the Blade of the bandit is sheathed
Lapsis fides revertitur.	Among the lapsed faith is returned

Jesu, labantes respice	Jesus, attend to the waverers
Et nos videndo corrige:	And straighten we living ones
Si respicis, lapsus cadunt	if you attend, faults fall away
Fletuque culpa soluitur.	And with tears sins are dissolved
Tu lux refulge sensibus	You, Light, shine on the senses
Mentisque somnum discute,	and dispel sleep from minds
Te nostra vox primum sonet	of You first may our voice sing
Et vota soluamus tibi[35]	and may we unbind our prayer to You

We have finally arrived at the close of this chapter, so full of tensions and harmony, a beautiful image of the people who enter the church and sing and pray, like the sea and the murmur of the waves and their breaking on the shore; "The sea is... incentive to devotion for faithful and devoted people, such that the song of their psalms competes with the whisper of the waves that sweetly break on the beach and the islands applaud with the quiet choir of their holy ripples echoing the hymns of the faithful. How can I describe completely all the beauty of the sea as if it were contemplating the Creator? What else is the song of the wave if not a kind of song of the people? So often the Church is rightly compared to the sea when the people enter as into a current: from the first there is no turning back the waves of all those being thrown up, further, while the faithful pray in chorus, thundering like the flowing of waves, it is that the song of men, of women, of innocent children, in the guise of the resounding roar of the waves, that makes an echo in the response of the psalms."[36]

CHAPTER X

"Because I Don't Deserve to be a Martyr, I Have Acquired These Martyrs for You"

Protasius and Gervasius, Vitalis and Agricola, Nazarius and Celsus: all are martyrs who owe their cult and their remembrance to Ambrose. But other men and women who have testified to their faith with their lives also populate the writings of the Bishop of Milan. We already know his ancestor Soteris; we can add Nabor and Felix, together with Victor; further, Agnes, Tecla, Theodora of Alexandria and Pelagia of Antioch; the Roman martyrs Lawrence and Sebastian whom Ambrose asserts were originally Milanese.

The Bishop of Milan manifests a particular veneration for the martyrs and develops a profound understanding of their value and their role in the community of believers.[1] In the martyrs, as Ambrose teaches the faithful, the action of Christ continues. They re-present the work of salvation and extend in history his life and his conduct, his choices and his dedication to the Father, right up to their passion and death. Not only did they follow Christ as faithful disciples, but they also "put before all the faithful that perfect example in defending the faith and in giving good proof of it." Thus everyone, even in time of peace, learning from the martyrs, are called to give testimony, conquering those persecutors who attack from inside and who "without returning to the threat of the sword, often crush the human spirit, those which defeat the soul of the believers more with temptations than with threats."[2] From the martyrs one may learn to adhere to the true faith without being overcome by heresy. One may learn to confront those temptations that attack faith and virtue putting the believer to the test. In this sense "martyrdom is the demonstration of perfect love, which alone cancels all sins; anyone who wishes to escape the death of sin must engage in a kind of bloodless martyrdom." At the end of the battle one thus receives the crown of victory since death becomes the prize of one's life. In this way one would confirm the expression of the Psalm, "Precious in the eyes of the Lord is the death of his holy ones" (Ps 115/116:15). Finally, Ambrose writes that martyrdom, as the total offering of oneself to God, resembles consecrated virginity, with which it has close similarity. For this reason Ernst Dassmann, from whom I have condensed this picture of the teaching of Ambrose on martyrdom, recalling in one sweeping glance the concerns and the pastoral care of the Bishop, observes: The Church is called to be "holy not only in theological theory, but also precisely in its concrete aspect and in daily reality," thus "those who guarantee that the holy Church remains the bride across time 'with neither stain nor wrinkle' (Eph 5:27), are none other than the martyrs and those who retain the spirit of the martyrs, beginning with the virgins, the authentic brides of Christ."

It is in this context of deep reflection and vigilant pastoral action that the rediscovery by Ambrose of certain martyrs is to be placed as is the translation of their remains, notwithstanding contrary imperial legislation, to worthier or more respectful locations. These interventions had various immediate reverberations: first of all, that of the Bishop Vittricius of Rouen (d. before 409), who around 395 received from Ambrose the relics of the martyrs Protasius and Gervasius, and of Agricola and of Nazarius. In one of his homilies Vittricius underlined the importance of the gifts he had received; and in a sign of recognition, sent a text, elaborated on as the treatise on *The Praise of the Saints,* to Bishop Ambrose.[3] In those years Paulinus of Nola, too, who had a strong relationship of affection and esteem for the Bishop of Milan, received from Milan relics of the martyr Nazarius, commemorating the event in a song of his own composition in 403.[4] So too, in the first years of the century, Gaudentius of Brescia, in his *Discourse on the Dedication Day of the Basilica of the Assembly of the Saints,* listed, among the relics deposited in the church, those of Protasius and Gervasius and Nazarius. These saints, the prelate notes, a few years ago or so in the city of Milan, condescended to reveal themselves to the holy Bishop Ambrose. The reliquary preserved in Brescia

Chapter X: "Because I Don't Deserve to be a Martyr..."

is "the blood collected as powder," and Gaudentius insists that he did not wish to ask for more because, once having the blood, he possessed "the witness of the saint."[5] But it is time to turn to Ambrose to see him at work discovering and translating the remains of the martyrs. In chronological order: the recovery of the remains of Protasius and Gervasius took place in Milan in June of 386, a few weeks after the conclusion of the battle with the court; the participation of Ambrose in the discovery of the martyrs Vitalis and Agricola in Bologna took place in the summer of 393, in the presence of Eustacius, Bishop of the city; finally the recovery of the remains of Nazarius and Celsus, again at Milan, took place in 395.[6] So, to begin with the first episode regarding the martyrs Protasius and Gervasius, in the last days of spring in 386 Milan was called to live a new intense experience which once again gathered the people around their Bishop. This time, however, not in a climate of tension and to defend themselves from unjustified requests, but rather to participate cordially in a joyous event, a sign of the restored ecclesial trust. In four days they accomplished both the recovery and the translation, from Wednesday the 17th to Saturday the 20th of June, as Ambrose recalled, recounting the events of this case in a letter to his sister Marcellina.

At the beginning of the letter, the Bishop, referring to the basilica which he himself named the "Ambrosian," today the church of Sant'Ambrogio where the rediscovered relics of the martyrs would be transferred, records that, though not quite completely built, it was already consecrated to the cult. The people, in any case, had insistently expressed to the Bishop their request that he would also dedicate that new basilica as had been done "for that of the Porta Romana," by placing in it the relics of the martyrs. Ambrose had simply responded that he was ready to do so, providing he was able to find such relics.[7] This brief dialogue makes us aware of a beautiful ecclesial innovation, a practice encouraged by Ambrose in those decades, according to which a church ought to be consecrated with the deposition of the relics of martyrs under the altar. On the altar, indeed, the sacrifice of Christ, the memorial of his death and resurrection, is offered. In the crypt, instead, the martyrs were symbolically placed, because they, as we have already heard, had faithfully emulated the experience of Christ. After having participated in the Eucharist during their lives, they have at last fulfilled it in their own flesh, in imitation of Christ and with his help. Ambrose confirmed this doctrine in the course of a few days, from the moment in which he deposited the relics of Protasius and Gervasius under the altar of the Ambrosian Basilica: "These triumphal victims approach the place where Christ is the sacrificial offering. But he, who died for all, is on the altar; these, who are redeemed by his passion, remain under the altar."[8] Ernst Dassmann comments insightfully: "The intent of Ambrose is not in putting 'the altar in an ever more strict alignment to the cult of the martyrs' (J.P. Kirsch), but in joining that cult to that of the Eucharist. It isn't that the relics give a higher significance to the altar, but that the altar integrates the relics in a fully significant veneration. The intentions of Ambrose are correctly understood by means of a similar interpretation, because in the veneration of the remains of Gervasius and Protasius we do not see in action a fanatic for the cult of martyrs, but a Bishop pastor of souls, who is enough of a theologian to realize that he has to demonstrate the way for a meaningful insertion of the devotion of the martyrs into the liturgical-sacramental life of the community."[9]

Ambrose showed us, in addition to the Old, the New, and the Portiana Basilicas referred to in the previous chapter, two new cult buildings. One of the new buildings is the Basilica Ambrosiana[10] which the Bishop had only recently completed. It is located at the Porta Vercellina, next to the chapel of S. Vittore in Ciel d'oro where Ambrose had placed his brother Satyrus' remains. The Bishop had considered it as the location for his own sepulcher. To this day the mortal remains of the holy Bishop are preserved in the crypt between the martyrs Protasius and Gervasius. The other is the basilica now called that of the Porta Romana[11] which Ambrose also had built, the first church in the West to be constructed on a cruciform plan, located along the Via Porticata (now the Corso di Porta Romana) — the solemn street decorated with parallel colonnades which, at the Porta Romana ushered into the city whoever came to the ancient capital

Chapter X: "Because I Don't Deserve to be a Martyr..."

of the Empire. The basilica was dedicated on the 9th of May of an unknown year, with the deposition under the altar of the relics of the Apostles (in fact, these were the martyrs to whom the faithful had alluded in making their request to the Bishop). The *Martyrologium Hieronymianum* in fact, recalls, on that date, the dedication of the basilica of the Apostles at Porta Romana and at its entrance the relics of the Apostles John, Andrew, and Thomas.[12] We see that, toward the end of the life of Ambrose, this basilica received the remains of Saint Nazarius, also assuming the name of this martyr (S. Nazaro).

Ambrose had, thus, promised the faithful that, if he was able to find them, he would consecrate the Basilica Ambrosiana with the relics of martyrs. Events moved quickly in that direction. Nearby, in the place where today the station of the Polizia di Stato in Piazza S. Ambrogio is found, there was a basilica dedicated to the saints Nabor and Felix. These too were martyrs. As Ambrose recounts in a beautiful passage from the *Commentary on the Gospel of Luke* and in a hymn dedicated to them and to their companion Victor,[13] these three were soldiers, originally from Mauritania, but stationed in Milan. With the rise of persecution, most likely that ordered by the Emperor Diocletian at the beginning of the 4th century, they suffered capital punishment at Lodi. A few decades later their remains, initially interred in the city in which they had been martyred, were carried in triumph to Milan, plausibly during the episcopacy of Maternus, the seventh Bishop of that city, who exercised his ministry during the first half of the 4th century. Victor was placed in a chapel we already know about, that of S. Vittore in Ciel d'oro; Nabor and Felix went to the basilica dedicated to them. The two martyrs "were venerated by a great many devotees," records Paulinus, and many drew near to "the gates that protected the sepulchers from any possible profanation," without knowing that they were walking on holy ground wherein were sheltered other Christian saints![14]

Ambrose set right to the task. Here is the account that he gave to Marcellina: "It pierced me with the ardor of a premonition. The Lord gave me the grace. Notwithstanding the fact that the cleric himself showed a certain fear, they excavated the ground in the area before the gates of the saints Felix and Nabor. Finding probable indications… the holy martyrs began to emerge because while we remained in silence, the bone of one forearm was picked up and deposited near the place of the holy sepulcher. We found two men of extraordinary stature, as they were in ancient times. All of the bones were intact; there was a great deal of blood." Moreover the Bishop added that "the head was cut off from the trunk," a sign of the violent death that the two suffered. The martyrs were discovered on June 17th. That day and the following an immense crowd of people came together.[15] Then, after incensing the bones, as the evening of the 18th approached, they were carried into the Basilica Fausta, a sacred building, perhaps a little chapel which must have been nearby but which is impossible to identify. Throughout the night vigil was kept in prayer: the Bishop and the people had already had a prolonged experience but in quite other circumstances! The following day, Friday, June 19th, the bones were transferred into the Basilica Ambrosiana. Finally, on Saturday the 20th the holy relics were placed under the altar, in a location that Ambrose had prepared for his own sepulcher: "I chose this place for myself," he had revealed to the people the previous day in a homily, "because it is proper that a Bishop ought to rest where he was accustomed to offer the sacrifice; but to these holy victims I yield the right-hand side: this place is owed to the martyrs."[16]

Ambrose also transcribed for his sister two homilies given on the Friday and Saturday on the occasion of the translation and deposition of the martyrs. And it is in the first of the two discourses that the Bishop introduces the name of the two martyrs, Protasius and Gervasius, without, however, explaining where he had gotten this information: From a scroll found beside their bodies? From inscriptions found on the site (*in situ*)? Or perhaps from the memory of the elderly who "now… come claiming to having heard in the past the names of these martyrs and of having read the funeral inscriptions"? Rest assured that the memory of the martyrs was neglected and that until then Milan was unable to rejoice in its own martyrs. Nabor and Felix, along with Victor, were not Milanese nor had they endured their passion in Milan: "sterile of martyrs," the city "had stolen those

Chapter X: "Because I Don't Deserve to be a Martyr..."

of others."[17] Nor was there preserved any news regarding the period in which Protasius and Gervasius had given testimony to their faith, whether toward the middle of the 3rd century during the persecution of Decius and Valerian or at the beginning of the following century at the time of Diocletian. Thinking, in any case, of the elderly who perhaps vaguely remembered having heard some talk, between the two hypotheses, that with the more recent dating seems to me most likely.

Ambrose noted the exceptional nature of the moment and the divine benevolence in which he felt himself to be bathed: "While this may be a gift of God, in any case I cannot deny the grace which the Lord Jesus has conferred at times on my episcopacy; because I do not deserve to be a martyr, I have acquired these martyrs for you." The Bishop had not deserved to become a martyr… in this expression we relive the battle recently concluded with the Court. We also understand how, in the discovery of the martyrs, he read a confirmation of divine protection: in Protasius and Gervasius he found his beloved defenders, understood properly, defenders who in their non-violence were without doubt preferable to soldiers in arms posted at the presidio of the basilica. "I give you thanks, Lord Jesus, because you have raised up for us spirits as powerful as these holy martyrs, in a moment in which your Church felt the need of more efficacious protection. Let all know what kind of defenders I seek, capable of defending me but incapable of offending. Such defenders I desire, such soldiers I have with me; not soldiers of this world, but soldiers of Christ… I hope that these defend also those who envy me. Let them come, therefore, and let them see my body guards: of such arms as these I do not deny being surrounded."[18]

Indeed, the Arians did come, but not with good intentions. They came because they were annoyed by the surge of the crowd toward the martyrs and Ambrose, to accuse as deceptive all these goings on and to suggest skepticism about a discovery that, with an ostensibly suspect timing, after the confrontations of the preceding weeks, conferred on the Bishop quite a solemn reputation. Ambrose, to attest to the authenticity of the discovered relics, noted the many miracles, healings, and freeings of persons possessed, which had accompanied the recovery and the translation of the relics. He paused in particular to describe the prodigy of a blind man named Severus, a butcher who had regained his sight after contact with those bones and for the rest of his days as a sign of his perpetual recognition, wished to offer his services in the Basilica Ambrosiana. Ambrose also recalls this episode in his *Hymn XIII* (*On the Discovery of Saints Protasius and Gervasius*). It is also recorded with care both by his biographer Paulinus and Augustine. The Bishop of Hippo, who was in Milan during this time, speaks of them in his *Confessions* and in his sermon *On the Birth of the Martyrs Protasius and Gervasius*. In this latter testimony, datable to around the year 425, he reports the event regarding Severus thus: "So then, I too was witness to the great glory of the martyrs. I was present, being in Milan, and came to know of the prodigies that had taken place by which God declared precious the death of both of your saints... A blind man, well known to the whole town, received his sight: he pleaded that if he were led there he would return without a guide. We have not heard that he was dead: perhaps he is still alive. He vowed to spend the rest of his life in service in that same basilica where their bodies were deposited. We feel a great joy for the man who was to see; we left him who was to serve."[19]

There remains, in any case, the insinuation of the Arians, which, in its most critical form, was this: had Ambrose invented the discovery? Or at least, how had he decided to dig in front of the gates of the basilica of Nabor and Felix? Must we admit a "revelation" from on high, beyond our control, and therefore suspend every other proof? In the first lines of the letter to Marcellina, Ambrose told us of "a burning premonition" that "pierced" him: that is, it was a "presentiment." Paulinus and Augustine, on the other hand, refer to a supernatural intervention: for the biographer it was the saints who had "revealed themselves to the Bishop," while the latter says Ambrose was given a "vision" or a "dream."[20] But if Ambrose is more believable with his moderate expression, how are we to interpret it? How was this "presentiment" produced in him? We bear in mind that the zone of the Porta Vercellina was and is noted as an area of ancient sepulchers, including Christian, and that the place of the Basilica of Nabor and

Chapter X: "Because I Don't Deserve to be a Martyr…"

Felix in particular could lead one to imagine the presence of other martyrs. Moreover it cannot be excluded that the vague memories of the elderly, of whom the Bishop speaks in his letter, might have already come to his ears. The decision to excavate may have been born in him from the memory of these clues and why exclude them, even if a possible interior illumination added strength to the initial intuition? And from the presentiment one may go on to the excavation and all the rest that follows as we have already noted.

Let's go back to the Arians. Wondering about their annoyed reaction, Ambrose asked himself whether it might not derive from jealousy in their dealings with him. He observed, in any case, that the prodigies had not come about because of his work or in his name. Might he then have deduced that the Arians "nurtured jealousy for the holy martyrs"? But if this is so, the conclusion would be extremely serious, because in this way the Arians would "demonstrate that the martyrs were of a faith different from their own: otherwise, they would not be jealous of their works." The Arians, that is, by refusing to believe in the prodigies accomplished by the work of the martyrs, place themselves in a position apart from the martyrs and their faith: that faith which, moreover, is validated by the tradition of the Fathers and the testimony of the martyrs is shared by the Catholic community.[21] Gervasius and Protasius, therefore, are raised up to defend the Catholic faith of the Bishop and of the city. For Ambrose this was self-evident and for the Arians it represents a humiliating defeat, now definitively irremediable. Also because they cannot deny that the Bishop had, masterfully, exploited the entire episode to his advantage and, as Angelo Paredi sarcastically remarked, with "a masterpiece of political psychology" had known how to capture the attention of the faithful showing them "that God was on their side."[22] We do not perceive, at the conclusion of these events, any further evidence of the relevance of the Arians in Milan: no source gives us any sign of their presence!

After Protasius and Gervasius the other two pairs of martyrs arrived: Vitalis and Agricola, Nazarius and Celsus. The discovery of the relics of the first two took place at Bologna in the summer of 393:

during these months Ambrose had left Milan in order to avoid meeting the usurper Eugenius, whose pro-pagan actions he had reproved. He chose Bologna as his first stop on his self-imposed exile. Following that he may have reached Faenza and finally, from March to July of 394, Florence. In this last city, as we have seen, he celebrated the dedication of a church erected by the widow Juliana and, analogous to what he had done in the Ambrosian Basilica with the remains of Protasius and Gervasius, he deposited under the altar of the new church certain relics of the martyr Agricola which he had brought with him from Bologna.[23] In his discourse entitled *Exhortation to Virginity* delivered for the occasion, the Bishop recalled the discovery that had been made a few months earlier at Bologna. At that event Ambrose had accompanied the Bishop of the city, whom we can positively identify as Eustacius, successor of that Eusebius who had participated in the Council of Aquileia. Of the two martyrs discovered, Ambrose knew — it is not noted on the basis of which sources — that Vitalis had been the servant of Agricola and that he received the palm of martyrdom before his patron: equal in regard to the faith, "each competed with the other to benefit each other. Agricola first set Vitalis free, Vitalis summoned Agricola to himself." The persecutors had in fact postponed the martyrdom of Agricola out of respect for his mild temperament, which made him amenable even to his enemies; but they were, more than anything else, false friends: "They wanted to terrorize the patron by torturing his servant. Christ had transformed this plan into a grace, such that the martyrdom of the servant became an invitation to the patron." Agricola, in fact, did not yield and, apparently not being a Roman citizen, received the punishment of crucifixion. Of Vitalis we know nothing other than the torture he had had to endure. Of neither is noted in which persecution they testified to the faith. It is probable that Agricola and Vitalis, or perhaps only Agricola, were originally Jewish. Ambrose records, in fact, that the martyrs "were buried in a Jewish place, among their graves," and that at the moment of their exhumation they became the crown even of the Jews.[24]

As for the last two martyrs, Nazarius and Celsus, we return to

Chapter X: "Because I Don't Deserve to be a Martyr…"

Milan in the final period of the life of Ambrose. Our only source regarding this is the biographer Paulinus,[25] who attests to being witness to the discovery and who locates this episode in the months following the death of the Emperor Theodosius (January 17, 395). First, the Bishop had found "in a cemetery zone outside the city" along the Via Porticata, the body of Nazarius, preserved in a marvelous way, with "his blood still so fresh, almost like it was on the day of his death and his head, which had been cut off by the impious, quite whole and uncorrupted with hair and beard, that seemed to be washed and situated in the sepulcher on the same day that it had been exhumed." The relics of the martyrs were then brought into the Basilica of the Apostles, which, as we have noted, was already in existence in 386. For that occasion Ambrose composed an epigraph in which he claimed to have built that temple and to have consecrated "it to the Lord with the title of the Apostles and with the gift of their relics," further adding, regarding the newly discovered martyrs, that their relics were located in the apse: "At the head of the temple was Nazarius, of the virtuous life, and the ground is elevated over the martyr's remains; at the curve of the apse where the cross raises its sacred head, there the temple has its beginning and Nazarius the place of his rest."[26] From then on the basilica has preserved both titles, and today is officially labeled as the *Basilica dei Santi Apostoli e Nazaro Magno*. After the exhumation of Nazarius, in the same area of the cemetery, Ambrose also discovered the martyr Celsus, whom, in any case, he wished to leave *in situ*. Not far from the other basilica there eventually arose first a chapel and later a church which carried the name of *Celso* in which his relics were kept.[27]

As with Protasius and Gervasius, so too regarding the two newly discovered ones specific records are lacking. In any case, there also remain certain memories of them: indeed, the custodians of the place reveal having received from the fathers "the assignment for all of their generations and descendants to never abandon that place where such great treasures reposed." Similarly the date of their martyrdom seems to be located, as with the other two martyrs, at the beginning of the 4th century during the persecution of Diocletian.

All of these martyrs were crowned by Ambrose, who had discovered them. Thanks to him the two Milanese groups, Protasius and Gervasius and Nazarius and Celsus, immediately became cult objects in the city. Vitalis and Agricola, on the other hand, by deducing the date, entered into the official cult of the city of Milan only in the 9th century, during the same Franco-Carolingian period in which the cult of the two siblings of Ambrose had also been initiated at the official level.

The celebration of the martyrs had always raised the necessity of knowing the details of the life and in particular the testimony which they gave with their death. Ambrose loved to satisfy this understandable desire of his faithful and, when the tradition offered him information on this or that martyr, he willingly told the people the details which he had learned, details often fascinating and full of edification, even if somewhat already enriched with hagiographic elements that are not historically verifiable. In his *Hymn XI: For Saint Agnes*, for example, he marvelously sketched this martyr called to testify for the faith while still a teenager and he dwelt on her firmness and serenity. Where the adults were afraid, she found the courage of faith, and from the security of her house she moved fearlessly toward that altar where the persecutors were intending to force her to sacrifice to the gods:

Prodire quis nuptum putet	It would seem that she were going to her wedding
Sic laeta uultu ducitur,	walking with such a radiant face
Novas viro ferens opes,	bearing unusual riches to her spouse
Dotata censu sanguinis	blood her gifts and dowry.

Further the Bishop imagined her at the moment she refused to burn incense on the pagan altar; going even further, she challenged those present to strike her, so that her blood would extinguish the fire of those braziers. Finally, Agnes was executed. And with incomparable delicacy the hymn writer emphasizes for us the dignity of her demeanor and composed tranquility, as if it were an immolation ritual. And it was observed: "Everything is marvelously described by

Chapter X: "Because I Don't Deserve to be a Martyr..."

a poet who is visibly taken by her person, and he shows himself fascinated particularly by one of such tender age, of a pure and strong faith, of a decency so lively that it transcends death." Here are the expressions of Ambrose:

Percussa quam pompam tulit!	Struck, she fearlessly maintained her noble bearing
Nam veste se totam tegens	with careful modesty,
Curam pudoris praestitit,	she drew her clothes about her
Ne quis retectam cerneret.	against any and all prying glances.
In morte vivebat pudor	In death modesty lived
Vultumque texerat manu	and covered her face with her hand
Terram genu flexo petit	she seeks the ground with bended knee
Lapsu verecundo cadens[28]	falling with a modest slip.

Of the martyrs whom he brought to Milan Ambrose was unable to recount a single episode. We already know that he had known nothing either of Protasius and Gervasius or of Nazarius and Celsus. To fill the lacuna a legend subsequently arose, often taking for itself a shield behind the name of Ambrose himself. It was not unusual, in fact, to attribute certain writings to him, as if guaranteeing them with his own name. These, with love and imagination, created and recounted the life and the passion of the martyrs.[29] For example, the *Letter on the Rediscovery of Gervasius and Protasius,* composed in the region of Ravenna at the end of the 5th century or the beginning of the next, is attributed to Ambrose.[30] It unites the story of the two Milanese martyrs with that of Vitalis of Ravenna (a fusion of the martyr with another having the same name discovered at Bologna), of his wife Valeria, and of Ursicinus, a martyr of Pannonia who was, rather, a doctor of Ligurian origins operating in Ravenna and who was arrested and decapitated at the outbreak of persecution. Vitalis and Valeria are represented as the parents of Gervasius and Protasius, who, at the same time are understood to be twin brothers. Vitalis, originally from Milan, suffered martyrdom at Ravenna, was thrown into a ditch and covered with dirt and stones. Valeria, on the other hand, returned to Milan from Ravenna where she had sought in vain to obtain the body of her husband. Along the road she suffered mortal blows from pagans and reached the city only to die. Gervasius and Protasius, then, being made orphans, sold the family goods and withdrew to Milan for ten years in prayer. But when Count Astasius arrived in the city as the leader of a military campaign against the Marcomanni, they were denounced as Christians. Upon their refusal to bless the expedition with a pagan sacrifice, they were martyred: Gervasius first, under the blows of a whip, then Protasius who was decapitated.

This is linked, without, however, any attribution, to another legendary account which unites the four martyrs discovered by Ambrose at Milan and which is transmitted in an ample series of revisions, both in Latin and in Greek, of which the earliest nucleus was formed in central Italy in the 5th and 6th centuries.[31] The tale is situated at the time of Nero and constructed around the principal deeds of the martyr Nazarius. He, a native of Rome, was baptized by Pope Linus and set out wandering through various cities of Italy preaching the Gospel. He arrived in Milan ten years later, where he found in prison Protasius and Gervasius who had been arrested for their faith by a magistrate named Anolinus who, in any case — as he himself affirms, had not dared to interrogate them with torture, knowing them to be noblemen of senatorial rank. Anolinus himself was therefore resigned to imprison them, because at least they wouldn't be able to proclaim the word of the Gospel. Nazarius, after having encouraged them, was thrown out by Anolinus and resumed his wandering. Entering Cimiez, today a neighborhood in the modern city of Nice in France, he received from the hands of a noble woman of the city her son Celsus, still a child, who from that moment became his inseparable companion. The two, following other trips and journeys, were persecuted and hunted by Nero and his functionaries, imprisoned and finally thrown into the sea so that they might be drowned. They were miraculously saved and landed at Genoa. From here they entered Milan, where Nazarius again met Protasius and Gervasius. But his wanderings were not yet finished. Anolinus, having become aware

Chapter X: "Because I Don't Deserve to be a Martyr..."

that Nazarius was in the city, remanded him to exile in a carriage, in the meantime writing to Nero to inform him of what was happening. Celsus, however, remained at Milan, entrusted to the care of a believing woman. The Emperor then decided to order the death penalty for the four protagonists of the legend. In the meantime Nazarius, having returned from preaching at Rome, was still a long way off. He then reappeared in Milan where, reunited with Celsus, he was arrested along with him. Thus the four martyrs were decapitated. A certain Cerealius provided for their burial while a certain philosopher of unknown name composed a biography of the martyrs, which was buried alongside their remains. Finally, concludes the narration, at the right moment the Lord revealed the saints "to Ambrose, the most blessed Bishop of Milan... he came with the people to the place which had been indicated by the grace (of the Lord); he sought and found the saints as treasures resting in three coffins, along with the little Celsus" (who did not require his own coffin).

The reader should not be surprised if the details of one legend do not match those of another. Nor should one pretend to find a precise logic or adequate motivation for each of the episodes. For the rest, certain elements came to be inserted to explain this or that topographical detail. The death of the holy Valeria in Milan, for example, seems to recall the presence of a church dedicated to her in the city near the Basilica Ambrosiana and which, in its origin, was probably a chapel dedicated to the family of the Valeri. The reference to Ravenna, in the first legend, is motivated by the espousal of the cult of the Milanese martyrs in that new seat, following the transference of the capital from Milan to Ravenna. The book written by the philosopher, in the second legend, allows one to imagine from whence the stories of the martyrs might have been united: precisely by the notes recounted by a contemporary.... Further, several details are a simple repetition of commonplace elements used in many similar stories: Nero is the anti-Christian Emperor *par excellence*, the name of the magistrate Anolinus is derived from the Acts of the African Martyrs, and so on.

We notice that Ambrose had created a sober narrative which we can now appreciate better and which the tradition does not seem to have maintained. And we shouldn't cease to marvel at the numerous echoes of him and of his actions which we find in quite disparate contexts: even in polar opposite traditions and in various legendary creations. Above all, thanks to Ambrose, the cult of the martyrs remains vivid before our eyes along with their testimony to life with which "they precede all believers with such a perfect example in the preservation of the faith and in giving good witness."[32]

CHAPTER XI

Augustine, Son of the Church of Milan

Jacobus de Voragine (1228/30-1298), in a famous account of the lives of the saints entitled *The Golden Legends*, describing the baptism conferred by Ambrose on Augustine during the Easter vigil of 387 (the night between April 24 and 25), inserts into the narration a touching anecdote. The retelling in the vulgarized 13th century Tuscan accurately renders the original Latin of the hagiography in this way: "As the time of Easter drew near, Augustine… received holy baptism. Thus, the story goes, *santo Ambruogio** said: '*Te Deum laudamus.*' And Augustine replied: '*Te Dominum confitemur.*' And so alternating, the one speaking the one verse, the other the other, this hymn was put together and they sang it to the end."[1] The original nucleus of the episode reproduced by Jacobus de Voragine appeared for the first time a little after the middle of the 9th century, in a treatise on *The Predestination of God and Free Will* by Hincmar of Reims (d. 882). Around the year 1100 it is found in the *History of Milan* by Landolfo Seniore and, a few decades later, in the *Mirror of the Church* by Honorius of Autun (12th century).[2] The anecdote also inspired artists who, in the miniatures of manuscripts and in paintings of every genre, showing the baptism of Augustine, began uniting the scene with the first verses of the *Te Deum*.[3] The episode is not historically supportable and, although until this century the attribution of the ancient hymn to Ambrose was largely accepted, in recent decades it has been reattributed to Bishop Niceta of Remesiana who lived around the year 400, while most recently its author is considered anonymous.[4] But let us get back to Augustine, to the meeting between Ambrose and this restless rhetorician from Africa, to his conversion and, to the point, to his baptism. Our principal source is the protagonist himself, in the re-evocation that he made around ten years later in *The Confessions*.

We have the story from the moment he arrived at Milan, coming from an unhappy experience in Rome: an experience aggravated by the excuses that the students came up with for not paying the inexperienced teacher, but above all Augustine had been marginalized by the skepticism into which he had fallen, disappointed by his earlier religious experiences.

One may, in any case, comment with pleasure on the providential turn of events which, in the autumn of 384 facilitated the coming of Augustine to the place of his conversion. Indeed, it was the city prefect (*praefectus urbi*) Symmachus whom we have seen in those months passionately, but in vain, interested in obtaining a renewal of ancient pagan traditions, who received from Milan "the request for a teacher of rhetoric for that city, with the offer, also, to travel by State carriage."[5] Augustine, then, profited from the good offices of the Manicheans with whom he was in contact at Rome, and it was they who had recommended him to the magistrate. Symmachus was encouraged to choose Augustine for his anti-Catholic stance as well: a sort of pay-back that Symmachus allowed himself against Ambrose, after the humbling he had recently received. Thus the pagan managed to send a non-believer to the place where he would find the way to his conversion!

Augustine arrived in Milan during the last months of 384 and on the 1st of January of the following year he delivered the solemn address for the beginning of the consulate of a friend of Symmachus, the pagan Bauto whom we have come to know as the *magister militum* and first minister of the Emperor Valentinian II. Indeed the task of the professor of rhetoric in the capital, Milan, involved the important and wide-ranging duty of giving the official panegyrics for the consul of the year and for all imperial anniversaries. On November 22 of that year Augustine would have delivered the discourse for the 10th anniversary of the reign of Valentinian II. At the level of a ritual to be fulfilled, a courtesy visit to the Bishop of the city would certainly have to be included.[6] Augustine took the occasion, in the passage of *The Confessions* from which we are drawing, to express his own judgment on "Bishop Ambrose, noted the whole world over, as one of the best,

Chapter XI: Augustine, Son of the Church of Milan

and a devoted servant" of God; and that is all that he recounts of that meeting. Reading the description, we search to understand what kind of rapport was established between the two in that moment, at the same time being wary regarding other questions that have frequently been posed regarding the contacts between Ambrose and Augustine: that is, whether they understood one another or if they remained mutually distant and never spoke in a serious way, and what might have been the influence of the Bishop on the conversion of the African rhetorician. Let us listen to what Augustine himself says: "That man of God listened to me as a father and accepted my visit properly as a Bishop (*satis episcopaliter*). I was immediately drawn to love him. First of all, certainly not as a master of truth, since I had no experience of finding that inside Your Church, but rather as a person who showed me kindness." How then did Ambrose comport himself? Ambrose might have been expected to be cold or indifferent because he knew that this newly arrived individual had been picked by Symmachus with the intent of being spiteful. Nonetheless, the formal visit left Augustine with the impression of a kind welcome. In fact, Ambrose applied toward him those paternal mannerisms and gentleness which, in his episcopal ministry, he reserved for everyone. We do not sense, in any case, that they had connected with familiarity or confidence; as a matter of fact, the expression used by the author is eloquent, "*satis episcopaliter*" (which we can also translate as "he conducted himself as a perfect Bishop," or "impeccably in an episcopal style"). Indeed, he is saying that Ambrose chose not to make his visitor feel uncomfortable or ill at ease, as any Bishop at least ought to know how to do even if he had no particular motives to be welcoming to his guest.

And what about Augustine? The love that he affirms to have nurtured for Ambrose from the very beginning is more about respect than familiarity, more about admiration than closeness. The attention to Ambrose, even to participate assiduously in his public instructions, was not given out of interest for the Christian contents of his preaching, of which Augustine himself had already heard for a long time, but much more for his admiration for the eloquence of the Bishop. This appreciation was accompanied by a verification of the oratorical ability of the Bishop and it was that which led him to articulate a critical judgment: "I wanted to ascertain for myself whether his eloquence deserved the fame which it enjoyed, or whether it might not be superior or inferior... the sophistication of his word delighted me. It was more learned, but less light-hearted and endearing than that of Faustus."[7]

And after that first approach what type of rapport was created between the rhetorician Augustine and the Bishop Ambrose? Augustine is searching; he needed to return to the "port" he had left. At Milan, his spiritual journey[8] would undergo the fits and the starts that would shortly conduct him to his final landing place. After having navigated "for a long time" with fixed gaze "on the stars that set in the ocean and that lead one astray," at Milan Augustine was finally able to recognize "the polar star" to which he entrusted himself.[9] The "star," without excluding others who had positively influenced him in his quest, is principally Ambrose. This is what Augustine himself intends to convey in the text which we are following, the dialogue *On Happiness*, composed in these months. It reaches the identical conclusion of the explicit and appreciated judgments that he will explain a few decades later. In 413 (or the following year), after having recalled in his *Letter to Paulina* the opinion of Ambrose on the theme of the vision of God, he will confess: "Above all through his mouth the Lord freed me from error and through his ministry accorded me the grace of baptism which saved me." Thus, for Augustine, Ambrose was "the one who planted and the one who watered" (cf. 1 Cor 3:7); and in 421, introducing the citation of certain texts of Ambrose in the first book *Against Julian*, he will present the Bishop as "an excellent steward of God," venerated by him "as a father," and he will add: "He has given birth to me in Christ Jesus with the Gospel (cf. 1 Cor 4:15), and as minister of Christ he has washed me with the bath of rebirth. I speak of holy Ambrose, in whom I myself have experienced the grace, the constancy, the deeds, the threats to the Catholic faith, in his works and in his discourses, and of whom together with me the whole Roman world does not hesitate to celebrate in praise."[10]

When Augustine thinks back on Ambrose, the central refer-

Chapter XI: Augustine, Son of the Church of Milan

ence is that of the baptism received from him and, together with it, the rapport that the Bishop offered to his journey of conversion shines through clearly. Although between the two there was never a sustained intimacy, nonetheless we can deduce their reciprocal relationship was one of confidence and friendship: they were quite different people and found themselves placed in objectively different situations. Ambrose, by then well into his 40's, had already been Bishop of the capital city of the Empire for 10 years; he came, moreover, from a senatorial family and was therefore a member of the Roman aristocracy. Augustine, on the other hand, barely 30 years old, a professor with a promising future which had yet to be realized, was moreover a foreigner of the Berber race, from the southern periphery of the Empire. Further, with a view that embraces both the present (of Ambrose) and the future (of Augustine): the one who had been a governor of the Empire was now in the episcopal ministry in which he found himself expressing, in a renewed and perfected form and in the service of the Church, the ancient skill of guiding people; the other in his conversion left every attachment to the "passions" of his past, and had first of all chosen to become a monk and a contemplative, a man of reflection and study. Only gradually was he "pressed" into pastoral service, to which he would give himself with irrepressible dedication.

The consequence of such differences is easily imaginable. Augustine needed to find someone who would listen to him, who could discuss with him his countless problems, who might suggest to him, item by item, clues to aid his intellectual search, and stimuli for his moral conversion. This man was Simplician, not Ambrose. We have already encountered this elderly priest, and we understand how he was the most skilled individual for such delicate duties which required time and patience, openness to private encounters and personal explanations in an atmosphere and tone of great confidence. *The Confesssions* themselves document the openness of Simplician in dealings with Augustine.[11] When, on the other hand, he went to Ambrose, we remember, he found the Bishop completely absorbed in study and did not dare to disturb him. Thus, Augustine signaled in summary, Ambrose "was unaware of my storms and the ravines into which I risked falling. It was not possible for me to ask him what I wanted to ask in the way I wanted. The masses of business people, whom he succored in distress, interposed themselves between me and his ears, between me and his mouth.... It was not really possible for me to ask that saintly oracle, that is his heart, about that which was oppressing me, but only about things he might have been able to listen to in a hurry."[12] In commenting on this scene, Giacomo Biffi amusingly observed: "Ambrose, then, did not have the time, but perhaps neither did he have much of a desire to be occupied in the intricate speculations and in the spiritual tumults of this complicated intellectual, capable of the most subtle dialectical acrobatics and incapable of letting himself just live in a just and dignified way.... A man like Augustine would have presumed to take up whole days in patient conceptual arguments and of miniscule philosophical analyses, and a man with the temperament of Ambrose certainly would not have had either the means nor the taste to launch himself in that enterprise." And why, it being difficult to enter into Ambrose's study, didn't Augustine manage to make himself known to him? We can intuit that that may have been due to the profound concentration of the Bishop. And might we now add this other interpretation that the illustrious scholar gave to the episode? "I don't want to think badly, but it seems to me, not that the Bishop may not have noticed the visitor; but that he did not wish to encourage him."[13] The explanation is, if it is true, a bit mischievous, but for all that, is it less likely?

With the arrival of Monica, the mother of Augustine, in the summer of 385, the possibility of a stronger relationship was created. Monica became a faithful frequenter of the rites and gatherings of the Milanese community: "running to the church, where she hung on the lips of Ambrose... she loved that man 'as an angel of God' (Gal 4:14)" and drew close to the Bishop to recommend her son to him: "She loved him for my salvation," Augustine later remembered, and added: "Further, he loved my mother on account of her very religious life." The Bishop in any case still did not enter into a discourse with Augustine: "Often, encountering me, he couldn't keep himself from lavishing praise and offering me congratulations for having such a mother," passing over other more personal and complicated matters.[14] And even when, at the end of his journey toward conversion, Augustine wrote to Ambrose to inform him of his "past errors" and of his "present intentions" to receive the grace of baptism, and wanted suggestions from the Bishop on texts of Sacred Scripture with which he might prepare himself for that happy event, the understanding wasn't complete. Ambrose, with advice in reality not very well thought out and largely inappropriate, "prescribed" reading the prophet Isaiah; but Augustine confessed that, finding the beginning incomprehensible and "supposing that rest would have been the same," chose to leave the reading for a more propitious moment.[15]

This being the case, how was it possible for Augustine to affirm the influence of Ambrose on his return to the faith? Why did he preserve that sentiment of recognition that we have identified in irrefutable passages? The response relies on a very important and at the same time very simple claim: Augustine, who did not enter into contact with Ambrose in a personally significant way, had still met him in his episcopal ministry and specifically within his community, in the faithful whose vitality we have seen in the episodes narrated before and whom we have admired as ready and solidly beside their Bishop. He met by chance a Church of intense Christian life[16] which offered itself as a concrete and positive witness to the experience of faith: a testimony that manifested itself to the rhetorician searching in the proclamation of the Word, in the liturgical celebration, in the sharing and friendship among the members of the community, in the ascetic commitment which gave vigor to greater works. The expression of Augustine is marvelous: "I saw the whole Church, and in it one going one way, another in another." I cite again the comment of Giacomo Biffi: "Augustine met by chance the 'whole' Church; inside this 'wholeness' it offered its members diverse paths, each according to his gift.... Of this wholeness he was little by little fascinated and persuaded; by contact with this 'wholeness' he sensed little by little that every difficulty disappeared and he disentangled himself from every internal complication."[17] In this context the various aspects that contributed to the conversion of Augustine can be put into proper perspective. First of all, his frequenting the Sunday church assembly, listening to the preaching of the Bishop and coming to receive from it the contents as well, with the happy consequence of his testifying "that even your theses were defensible and... that it wasn't a fearful thing to uphold the Catholic faith." From Ambrose he came to understand that the Catholic interpretation of the Scriptures was not something uncultured as he had been inculcated to believe by the Manicheans, and he began to perceive the spiritual nature of God and of the soul; thus he came to the decision to "remain as a catechumen in the Catholic Church..., in expectation that the light of certainty might arise, toward which he might direct his path."[18] Augustine met the Bishop in his ecclesial preaching, and through him he developed personal contacts with members of the Milanese Christian community, not only with Simplician but especially with that Neo-Platonist circle that we have seen to rise around him.[19] To Augustine it presented itself as a Church enriched by varied attributes and even the capacity for a dignified cultural commitment: an experience certainly captivating for the questing rhetorician.

Even the events of the battle with the Court [concerning the Arian use of a basilica], right up to the solemn rediscovery of the relics of the martyrs, entered fully into his progressive awareness of the reality of the Church. Augustine still remembered the flock of the faithful which "kept vigil every night in the church, ready to die with their Bishop"; again he saw his mother Monica living by prayer "in her zeal being in first place at these vigils"; he recalls his own participation and that of his friends: "We ourselves, who may still have been cold to the warmth of Your Spirit*, were nonetheless aroused by the anxiety of the whole city."[20] Augustine experienced a courageous and solidly committed Church, without compromise in proclaiming orthodox faith, a Church cheered by those songs and hymns that spoke of a union between words and intentions; the taste for prayer, hope in overcoming even the most serious and painful situations.

Augustine's hard interior work, substantiated by all these testimonies, finally brought him to the "port" of conversion. In August of that year, 386, he submitted his resignation from teaching, wrote to

Chapter XI: Augustine, Son of the Church of Milan

Ambrose to inform him of his choice, and with certain friends, withdrew himself to Cassiciacum,[21] to a villa left to his use by Verecondus, where he remained until the beginning of the following year. The retreat of those months and the discussions that animated them, recalled in five *dialogues*,[22] were seen by Augustine and his companions as moments of philosophical reflection of a Christian character: reflections, that is, which drew on Platonic and Neo-Platonic roots, but which were necessarily complemented by references to Christian revelation and redemption which the philosophers were neither able to nor wanted to reach. In that way Augustine prepared himself for baptism, joining to those conversations the reading of Sacred Scripture, prayer, the search for that ascetic-contemplative lifestyle that would be significantly concretized in his experience at Tagaste once he had returned to Africa following his baptism.

The only thing left was to enroll as one of the *competentes,* that is, the aspirants to baptism who were then approaching the final stage of their preparation. As was the custom in the Church of Milan, Augustine would have to undergo this ritual, signing the request in his own hand on the day of Epiphany, January 6 of 387. With him were inscribed his son Adeodatus, then 15 years old, and Alipius, friend and "brother of the heart" of Augustine. For that date, therefore, they would have had to return to Milan. And during the Easter vigil, on the night between the 24th and 25th of April, he would have received baptism by Bishop Ambrose. Augustine is dispassionate in recalling the rite: "We were baptized, and thus was the restlessness of my past life dispelled." But the following lets us to know the state of his soul better: "During those days I was not content to consider with wonderful pleasure your profound design for the salvation of the human species. How many tears were spilt listening to the accents of your hymns and canticles (cf. Eph 5:19), that resounded sweetly in your Church! What passionate emotions: those accents flowed into my ears and the truth was expressed in my heart, exciting there a warm feeling of piety. The tears that flowed made me well."[23] These references to the ecclesial community, to the beauty of the liturgy, to the hymns are not, of course, surprising.

Some days later Augustine left to return to Africa, passing through Rome. We know that at Ostia his mother passed away and that in this crisis he found comfort in recalling to mind the hymn Ambrose composed for the evening liturgy.[24] The memory of the Bishop remained strong: we earlier saw the beautiful and grateful expressions that he dedicated to him in his writings; and we shouldn't forget that it was his passionate desire that Paulinus undertake the writing of his biography. We might add also the theological influence of Ambrose that flowed into the theological reflections of Augustine. Researchers in this regard have yet to spell this out in an adequate way, but interesting discoveries and confirmations in this regard are not in any case lacking. Indeed, several intuitions and emphases, present in an unsystematic form in the preaching of Ambrose, can be rediscovered later elaborated upon and restated according to the thought of Augustine, beginning with the theme of grace which remains fundamental in his reflections.[25] But let us return anew to his baptism to imagine Augustine in that solemn celebration, together with the other catechumens who descended into the baptistery to receive from Ambrose the sacrament of Christian regeneration; to picture him earlier as a diligent listener to the catecheses[26] which the Bishop proposed to the *competentes* throughout the time of Lent; and finally to imagine those present during the week following Easter when he offered to the baptized a series of mystogogical homilies as a clarification so to speak of the mysteries they had received. These catecheses of Ambrose on Christian initiation are, in fact, commented upon and in large part even preserved. For the Lenten ones let us content ourselves with the mention that the Bishop makes at the beginning of his post-Easter preaching: "Every day we dealt with moral questions when we read the history of the Patriarchs and even more the Proverbs so that, formed and instructed by these you might become accustomed to enter into the way of our fathers and to follow their path obeying the divine precepts until, renewed through baptism, you might observe the way of life that befits those who have been purified."[27] To the moral contents the dogmatic should also be added. Their instruction reached its culmination in the rite of the *tra-*

Chapter XI: Augustine, Son of the Church of Milan

ditio symboli (the transmission of the Creed) that the Bishop carried out during the Eucharistic celebration on the Sunday before Easter. At the end of the liturgy of the Word, he gave the Creed — symbol of ecclesial faith, to the *competentes* and explained it in detail so they would know the fundamental truths of the Christian faith. One of these catecheses is found in the small treatise *The Explanation of the Creed*. It sets forth the initial expression through which the Bishop foretells what he intends to reveal: "Now is the time and the day when we transmit the symbol, the symbol that is a spiritual seal, the symbol that is the meditation of our heart and which is an ever present defense. Without doubt it is our heart's treasure." The concluding invitation is also very interesting: in submitting to the discipline of the mystery one is obliged not to reveal to the uninitiated the most profound truths of the faith. Ambrose asks his listeners not to copy the Creed, which should, rather, remain a secret. How ought one to behave then? In this regard, there is transcribed in a small treatise a lively dialogue, whether imagined or real we do not know, which I reproduce here in its own intensity:

Questioner: But what ought one to do?
Ambrose: Commit it to memory.
Questioner: How can it be remembered, if not by writing?
Ambrose: You can remember it better if you don't write it.
Questioner: How is that so?
Ambrose: Pay attention! The one who writes doesn't go over it meditating on it every day, because he doesn't worry, thinking he will be able to re-read it. However, the one who does not write it is afraid of forgetting it and goes over it every day.[28]

How would Augustine have heard such suggestions? Would he have smiled, remembering his own teaching experience? Or would he have once again admired the Church and its consummate pedagogy?

Then the great Vigil with the rites of baptism that the Bishop would have celebrated in the baptistery of S. Giovanni alle Fonti. We have already become familiar with this sacred edifice constructed by Ambrose himself. When, 13 years earlier, the governor Ambrose had agreed to be baptized by a Catholic Bishop, he would have received the sacrament of regeneration in the only baptistery then existing, that of S. Stefano alle Fonte, which we also encountered earlier. In 387, on the other hand, it is most likely that the new one would have been constructed, dedicated to St. John, bigger than the older one and in an octagonal form. The inscription which the Bishop had inscribed *in loco* is still preserved and is found in a codex of the Apostolic Vatican Library, the *Pal. Lat. 833*: in perfect continuation with the older one. Today it is relocated in that same baptistery which can be visited in the remains that have come down to us under the piazza of the Duomo of Milan. In the first diptych of the inscription we find initially a confirmation of the eight-sided plan of the building, just as it still appears: each side with its own apse, and the baptismal vessel itself also in octagonal form:

> This temple with eight apses was erected for the use of the saints;
> And eight-sided is the font, worthy of the gift conferred in it.

The number eight is not accidental because it carries profound resonance: Ambrose introduces us to it in two distinct sequences upon which we need to comment soon. Here, however, I prefer to transcribe the rest of the inscription, which over all results globally to having been composed in eight diptychs, which was predictable.... With it we return again to the theme of the pardon of sins connected to those receiving baptism, to the innocence and holiness which it introduces and encourages, and to the efficacy of the sacrament:

> It was only right that on this number the royal hall of sacred baptism, where the true salvation is given back to the people, rises,
> In the light Christ who, risen, opens the gates of death and raises corpses from their tombs;

Chapter XI: Augustine, Son of the Church of Milan

Who dissolves the stain of sin from confessed sinners washing them in waves that clearly flow.

How many chose to abandon the shameful crimes of their life, who bathe their hearts and keep their souls pure.

They come here willingly; even if overwhelmed by darkness, they come boldly: and will leave whiter than snow.

The saints rush here; no one is holy without experiencing these waters: in them is the rule and plan of God,

and the glory of justice. What can be more divine than this which in a very short time dissolves the fault of a people?[29]

Why then the number eight? From the moment that Jesus rose on "the first day after the Sabbath" (Lk 24:1; Jn 20:1), and the Sabbath is both the seventh day of creation and of the week, thus it is that the day on which he rose is precisely the eighth, the day of the definitive accomplishment of salvation, the day of new life and of eternity. Symbolically the number eight recalls the resurrected life that is given to the baptized because in baptism they have died with Christ, with him they are buried and with him they are raised from the dead. It recalls the eternal day of God and of that eternal life to which the faithful are introduced on the other side of death. It is probable that Ambrose, while constructing the baptistery, would have also had in mind the mausoleum of Maximinian constructed in an octagonal form in the western fringe of the city.[30] In any case that edifice was designed to keep alive the memory of a famous deceased person; the baptistery that copied the ground plan, on the other hand, assured those who entered it, being immersed in its waters, of rising truly to a new life and of acquiring the pledge of future resurrection.

Let us return to the focus of the Christian symbolism.[31] The baptismal font of S. Giovanni alle Fonti had a relatively shallow basin; and it is evident that in Milan, in contrast with Africa where the candidates entered on foot into the baptismal font, immersion would have been in a horizontal form. Those being baptized would have been aided in lying down in the font, almost as if letting themselves be buried in that spiritual tomb, turned and symbolically drowned in the water, and then re-emerging risen. For this Ambrose says that the aspect of the font "corresponds in a certain way to the form of a tomb" and that in it, "after having professed our faith in the Father and in the Son and in the Holy Spirit, we are welcomed and immersed and we emerge, that is, we arise"; and when he describes to the newly baptized the rite of the triple interrogation and baptismal immersion, he recalls them explicitly: "You have been questioned... You have responded: "I believe" and you are immersed in the font, that is you have been buried." Once again he explains: "As Christ died, so too you have tasted death; as Christ died to sin and lives for God, so also you, through the sacrament of baptism, ought to be dead to temptation to sin and to be restored through the grace of Christ. It is a death, not in the reality of a physical death, but in a likeness. When you emerge from the font, take on the resemblance of your death and of your burial, receive the sacrament of your cross, because Christ was put on the cross and his body was pierced by nails. You are crucified with him, you are joined to Christ; you have been attached by the nails of our Lord Jesus Christ so that the devil cannot tear you away from him. Though the weakness of human nature would want to keep you far from him, the nails of Christ will hold you fast."[32]

Thus we have listened to a full treatise of a mystagogical catechesis; we have also heard the theme of baptism for the forgiveness of sins reechoed, and we have also listened to the underlying themes which we know Ambrose so enjoyed, of the condescension of Christ for humankind, of his humiliation for us, and of the nearness and grace that one is able to experience as "attached" to Christ by the nails of his cross. The catecheses of the week after Easter have been transmitted in two works of Bishop Ambrose: one comprised of six homilies *On the Sacraments,* from which are taken passages just cited, the other consisted of a treatise *On the Mysteries.* Some critics have shown doubts as to the authorship of *On the Sacraments,* which reveal a style unusual for Ambrose. But I have already hinted that, in the judgment of the majority of scholars, this diversity is quite explainable. The first treatise that we have has, in fact, transmitted his preachings just as they came from the mouth of the Bishop, taken down directly in text by stenographers: their style cannot therefore be compared to that of his other writings which were carefully revised by the Bishop. In the treatise *On the Mysteries* we have, then, a writing of the Bishop in the standard accuracy of revision. Thus are indicated all the writings which the Bishop has left us which directly concern the Christian catechesis of initiation.

The last two of these, describing in its entirety the celebration of the Vigil, following the baptism, go on to speak also of the Eucharistic celebration which completed the Easter rites. About this, too, we want to recover the teaching of the Bishop. Still drawing from the homily *On the Sacraments*, Ambrose repeats again and again: "You have come to the altar… you have come to the altar," as if to emphasize the new and unfamiliar situation of the baptized, now able to receive the gift distributed from the altar. For Ambrose the highest significance of that gift was to be proclaimed forcefully, that the bread is the body of Christ: "You may say: 'It's my usual daily bread.' Before the sacramental word this bread is bread; when the consecration intervenes the bread becomes the flesh of Christ." In what sense? "It is the word of Christ that makes this a sacrament," that efficacious word "by means of which all things are made. The Lord commanded; the heavens were made; the Lord commanded, the land was made; the Lord commanded, the seas were made; the Lord commanded; all creatures were born. You see therefore how efficacious is the word of Christ." In conclusion: "Following the consecration I say to you that it is by then the body of Christ. He has spoken, and it is done; he commanded, and it was created."[33] In another passage from the same homily, commenting on the *Our Father*, taking up the invocation "Give us this day our daily bread," Ambrose returns to speak about the Eucharist, identified in the bread invoked by the prayer, and gives certain hints that, rather than being addressed to the neo-baptized, are intended to shake up the Christian community as though they had become lazy in their Eucharistic piety: "If the bread is daily, why do you receive it only after a year? Receive every day that which is useful to you every day! Live in a way of being worthy to receive it every day!... You hear repeated that every time the sacrifice is offered, the death of the Lord is announced, the resurrection of the Lord, the ascension of the Lord and the remission of sins, and still you do not receive every day this bread of life?" He adds, "If you had a wound, you would look for some medicine." The wound of man is that he is inclined to sin; he has precisely the need every day of this "celestial and venerable sacrament" that fortifies him. Receiving the Eucharist, adds Ambrose, every "today" becomes a day signed and enfolded in the resurrection of Christ. In fact, as in the Psalm, interpreted as being messianic, the Father says to the risen Christ, reborn to a new life: "You are my Son, today I have begotten you" (Ps 2:7), so it is too that the believer who receives the Eucharist becomes assured of the presence and the grace of the Resurrected One: "If you receive every day, for you every day is this day. If today Christ is yours, he rises through you another day... the 'today' is when Christ rises."[34]

And beyond these passages and these teachings we can imagine Augustine convinced by the preacher and confirmed in the faith he finally rediscovered. He had definitively returned to the "port," guided by the "polar star" of Bishop Ambrose and ever more fascinated by the Milanese Church. Now, through baptism received in that Church by the hands of that Bishop, he has become his son. Augustine would be reminded of the doctrine he received, and in one exchange of gratitude the Church of Milan would continue to speak "of happy memory of him for having generated in him to the life of grace."[35]

CHAPTER XII

Anti-Semitism?

On the 1st of March, 1162, Fredrick Barbarossa entered victoriously into Milan and humbled the city by tearing down its walls and gates. But within a few years the Milanese were able to provide for the reconstruction, giving an unequivocal signal of the will toward rebirth that inspired it. So in 1171, when the Porta Romana was erected, among the bas-reliefs with which it was decorated, one was set in place that illustrated Bishop Ambrose in the act of dispersing the "Arians:"[1] indeed, this was instructively written above the line of thirteen people who preceded the Bishop. By then the appellative "Arian" generically indicated all heretics and enemies of the city, regardless of the era to which they belonged; so even the Emperor Fredrick was depicted in the line of those Arians construed as enemies of Milan.

But it isn't a case of Arians only. One inscription, placed in the cornice that carries the bas-reliefs above it, singled out the Jews, who were the objects of this charge of Ambrose: *"Ambrosius coelebs judeis abstulit aedes."* It means that Ambrose, Bishop and therefore "celebrated," had removed "the Jews from their homes," sending them into exile. It isn't hard to grasp the motive behind this new attribution: it is derived from that anti-Semitic mentality that had arrived in the medieval West and that the Milanese unfortunately thought to be able to attribute also to their great Bishop.

In any case this was not the first instance. Already three centuries earlier an anonymous biography of the saint entitled *Life and Deeds of Saint Ambrose* traced the ascetic practices of the Bishop, specifying the strength of his "inflexible soul," "in respect to which it seems difficult to find among mortals a man so prudent as to always and in every case avoid having any relations with Jews and heretics as this most holy man who so detested the enemies of the Catholic religion that not only would he not sit at table with them, but would not, even in passing, exchange a greeting with them."[2] The author of this text, which was probably written in the second half of the 9th century, while being appreciated for his excellent historical citations and his diligent reference to the sources, here has falsified the historic truth, which is that Ambrose had enjoyed the esteem of the pagans and Jews, at least on occasion of his death, as I have already indicated.[3] Perhaps the anonymous author was erroneously inspired by a homily of Maximus of Turin which, as a matter of fact, also circulated under the name of Ambrose. In this the preacher exhorts that "we ought to avoid not only the company of pagans, but also that of the Jews, because even conversation with them is a serious contamination"; and he continues pointing out the dangers the Jews represent, "because the more they manage to prevail the more impudent they become," ultimately recalling their responsibility in the condemnation of Jesus.[4]

In the 9th century, and again in the 12th, in an ever more widespread context of anti-Semitism, an image of Ambrose as hostile to the Jews came into being. And so it is very important to be able to clearly reconstruct the attitude and thought of the Bishop in his dealings with the Jewish world beginning with the destruction of the synagogue of Callinicum by the Christians of that city in 388.

Before entering into the argument it is first necessary to briefly recall the thread of political events which we left off at the eve of the second mission of Ambrose to Maximus at Trier at the end of 384. By now the empire was officially reorganized, with the confirmation of Theodosius as governor of the East and the division of the West between Maximus and Valentinian II. After three years of stability, in May of 387, just after the Easter that had witnessed the baptism of Augustine, Adeodatus and Alipius, the situation was shaken by a new crime perpetrated by Maximus, which may be attributed to the weakness of his colleague in the West. Presenting himself as the defender of the Catholic faith against the pro-Arian sympathies of the court, he invaded Italy and occupied Milan. Valentinian sought refuge in Illyria, Thessalonica, in an area subject to the rule of the Augustus

Chapter XII: Anti-Semitism?

of the East, placing himself under the protection of Theodosius. It seems that the latter was initially uncertain about how to confront the situation. Only after a year was it decided to move against Maximus. In the meantime he had married Galla, the daughter of Justina, thereby creating a familial connection that allowed him to justify his intervention in favor of the Milanese Court; moreover, during these months Valentinian had renounced *homoeanism*, thus avoiding any contradiction the Catholic Theodosius may have felt coming to the aid of an Arian Emperor against an avowedly Catholic usurper. It was all decided in the span of a few months. On August 28, 388, at Aquileia, Maximus was killed by the vanguard of Theodosius, and by the next October they were able to enter victoriously into Milan.

We don't know what position Ambrose may have assumed in facing Maximus during his occupation of the city. We note, however, his concern when finally, after the departure of the usurper, further bloodshed against his supporters was avoided. It is they, in fact, who seem to be referred to in the expressions that Ambrose offers to Theodosius in a letter sent shortly after these events, concerning the matter of Callinicum, in which Ambrose declares himself to be in debt to the Emperor because, at his suggestion, "a great many" were liberated "from exile, from prison, from pain of death" in a merciful manner.[5] Theodosius now acted as the effective head of the whole empire. He ruled the Eastern part directly, although nominally he had named his son Arcadius as lord, though he was only eleven years old. As for the other part, while Valentinian preserved the title and the rights of the Augustus of the West, he was already exercising his role under the protection of his more powerful colleague. Ambrose may have already had dealings with this other Emperor, well known for his having acted in favor of Catholicism in the East in the first years of his rule, but in regards to this, he could not forget the confusion and misunderstandings born in the aftermath of the Council of Aquileia.

The Church historian, Sozomen, has preserved an anecdote[6] that in its sobriety seems historically grounded and dated to the first few months that Theodosius was in Milan. The account precisely points out the careful attention that Ambrose paid to appropriate protocol in initiating contacts between himself and the new Emperor. We come, thus, to understand that the Bishop, most likely following the ceremonials used in Constantinople, established that the place of the Emperor in church ought to be in front of the assembly of the faithful, but not in the sanctuary, because this place ought to be reserved exclusively for the ministers of the altar. He therefore made this clear to the Emperor who must have given his consent. Theodoret of Cyrus, recalling and dramatizing the episode, locates the explanation Ambrose gave to Theodosius as taking place during a celebration of the Eucharist and draws out the narration in a second scene, located at Constantinople. Thus he imagines the Emperor comporting himself according to Ambrose's norms even in that seat (Constantinople) and then explaining to Nectarius of Constantinople, who was surprised at this new disposition, of his having learned "with difficulty the difference between the Emperor and the Bishop." In fact only with difficulty had he been able to find "a master of truth." This dialogue appears excessively artificial. Theodosius supposedly concluded: "Now I now that Ambrose is the only Bishop worthy of that name!" But this is historically unlikely though it did indicate the preoccupation Ambrose had, in those first moments of meeting with Theodosius, to clarify the difference between their places and roles: that there should be no interference by the Emperors in ecclesiastical affairs. An analogous intent probably also moved the Bishop in the goings on concerning the synagogue of Callinicum, which I am about to explain even if, in this case, and perhaps lacking a complete understanding, Ambrose went too far.

At the origin of the "Callinicum case" were two episodes of intransigence for which the Christians were responsible. In the summer of 388 they had torched places of prayer and worship of other religious confessions. The more serious action, the only one for which we can confirm the involvement of Ambrose, was that of the synagogue of Callinicum, an isolated center on the Euphrates, north of Mesopotamia (today, near Raqqah, Syria). Given the close relationship with the Emperor through the *Comes Orientis* (magistrate in charge of the civil dioceses of the East), that grave deed was carried out by the local community, instigated by the Bishop of the city. The other event is less easily locatable but one might suppose that it took place not far from Callinicum. It consisted of the burning, on the part of certain monks, of a meeting place of the Valentinians. These, as already noted, were among the most important groups of gnostics, that large religious movement which developed concurrently with Christianity in the first and second centuries and which offered salvation transmitted through a revealer-savior and guaranteed it by participation in esoteric traditions.[7] The monks, in any case, blocked by the Valentinians from finishing their procession on the occasion of the feast of the Maccabean martyrs (August 1), responded to this provocation by torching their place of cultic worship.[8]

The response of Theodosius underscored the sense of respect that ought to be guaranteed to any religious expression. He commanded that proceedings begin immediately against those responsible for both and further, that the Bishop ought to supply whatever was necessary to reconstruct the destroyed synagogue to its former state. In a letter to the Emperor in December of that year Ambrose made it clear that he wanted to intervene. The letter was sent from Aquileia, where he had most likely gone at the death of Bishop Valerian, whom we recall presided over the Council held in that city on September 3, 381. Indeed, Valerian had passed away on November 26th and Ambrose may have been able to assist in the nomination of his successor, in the person of Cromatius. In this letter, Ambrose assures the Emperor that he wanted to address him candidly because, he explains, it is important for an Emperor to be able to count on the frankness of those with whom he is surrounded. "Silence," even from a Bishop, would be "displeasing; pleasing, his freedom to speak." The Emperor will be able to turn to his advantage the frankness of Ambrose. "I do this for love of you, to render you a service, out of desire to secure your salvation" assures Ambrose; and he adds that, in any case, he wishes to avoid the fault of silence or of dissembling: "I prefer that you judge me rude rather than useless and unworthy."[9] What does he request so frankly? What request, so difficult and wholly impertinent, could ever make the Bishop approach the Emperor? We remain puzzled:

the Emperor, according to the suggestion of Ambrose, should hold back from every kind of punishment or fine for the deeds at Callinicum. In fact, Ambrose asks what should the Bishop of that city do? Should he become "traitor or martyr"? Should he pay to reconstruct the synagogue and thus become a traitor to the faith; or should he perhaps oppose the injunction, and in this case be prepared to suffer martyrdom? The argumentation is, without doubt, forced. But in the confrontation between the Church and Synagogue, Ambrose goes even further: "Should the place that houses Jewish incredulity be rebuilt with the spoils of the Church? And the patrimony acquired by Christians with the protection of Christ be transferred to the temples of the impious? ... Perhaps the Jews should place this inscription on the façade of their synagogue: 'Temple of impiety constructed with the spoils of the Christians.'" Judaism is, then, unbelieving and impious, and not deserving of any aid, either legal or physical: expressions as heavy as lead. He goes on: If they should win, what might follow? Does the Emperor thus intend to give them such satisfaction... to give "this celebration to the synagogue and this grief to the Church? The Jewish people will add this solemnity to their festival days.... They will rank it among other festivals to signal their having achieved a triumph over the people of God."[10] Here the rhetoric is forced and has gone too far and this explains in part the formal exaggeration of his words; but we are not able to follow the Bishop in these obdurate inferences. Nor are the indications that he introduces in reference to violent analogies repeatedly imputed to the Jews in their confrontations with the Christian Church able to justify such judgments.

In any case we should not gloss over the fact that, in the same letter, Ambrose reminds the Emperor that he wants to deal with the ecclesial realities, respecting the autonomy which they claim. We know the importance of this conviction to Ambrose, which, in any case, ought to be understood as similar to and parallel to the interventions of civil authority in defense of the public order. Let us review the invitation of Ambrose to Theodosius to listen to the Bishops: "If you consult your counts in matters of finance, how much more just is it that, in matters of religion, you consult the Bishops of the Lord?"[11]

Chapter XII: Anti-Semitism?

In other words, Ambrose asks that [the proceedings should not be left in the hands of the Emperor and the civil power.] If such interventions have consequences in relation to the Bishops or of Christians, these are the responsibility of the Church, which will verify and respond according to its specific criteria and which will be able also to severely reprimand the Bishop, remembering that, against the Jews, one ought to use the force of persuasion rather than the violence of intimidation. The Emperor, in any case, should refrain from punishing or making any decision. And we draw from this a very important interpretive criteria, viz., the anti-Jewish polemic expressed by Ambrose in this letter, so indefensible to our modern sensibilities, does not, in any case, constitute the core of his reflections and of his convictions, but is only an instrumental feature of emphasis to reach the other principal aim.

    The letter did not bear the fruit hoped for, or at least not fully. It is likely that the Emperor, fulfilling the order to reconstruct the synagogue, simply put the burden of the expense no longer on the Bishop but on the entire city. Returning to Milan, Ambrose wanted to raise the question again on the occasion of a liturgical celebration in which the Emperor participated and which we are able to situate toward the end of 388. The Bishop describes their falling out in a letter, as we have seen him do in similar cases. In this instance the letter was to his sister Marcellina sent at the same time as was the other message addressed to the Emperor which we have seen. The content of the letter to Marcellina summarizes the transcription of the homily delivered by Ambrose during that celebration and the communication of a brief but decisive dialogue that was exchanged between Ambrose and Theodosius just before beginning the Eucharistic ritual. In the homily, Ambrose set the stage for the request that he intended to renew with the Emperor. Repeating the motif, already developed in the letter, that the Bishop "should not be afraid to denounce disagreeable acts... since his demands, even if, for a time, they seem to be somewhat bitter" in the end are revealed to be truly profitable. He comments further on the Gospel passage of the sinful woman who, in the house of Simon the Pharisee, washes the feet of Jesus bathing them with her tears, drying them with her hair, kissing them and anointing them with the perfumed oil: thus Jesus assures her that, for such love, her many sins are forgiven (cf. Lk 7:36-50). This pardon, assures the Bishop, is conceded by Christ to his own, and it is experienced in the Church, to return to the remarks of Ambrose, by "the one who has the water and the tears of penance" in contrast to Simon the Pharisee who represents Judaism, "does not believe in Christ" and therefore "has no tears" and all of the other gifts offered by Jesus.[12]

Ambrose presses the point remarking on the gratuity of this pardon and the parallel responsibility to pardon others in turn. And we, in reading this, already imagine the invitation that Ambrose will place before the Emperor, namely, to pardon the Christians of Callinicum. Indeed the rest of the parable of the condemned debtor who does not make the same gesture toward the one who owes a small sum teaches the same thing. Ambrose thus pleads: "Let us remit a little, because we have been forgiven much more; and let us understand that we will be that much more pleasing to God the more we forgive." A similar lesson can be derived from another Gospel passage, that of the pardoned sinful woman. It would seem to be fair to allegorically identify the "feet" cared for with such affection by the woman, with the "little ones" of whom Jesus speaks in the Gospel when he affirms "Each time you have done these things for only one of these little friends of mine, you have done it for me" (Mt 25:40). It is only right to repay the immense love received, as does the pardoned woman, taking care of those little ones: "He who loves even the least of my holy people kisses these feet; the one who treats the poorest of the poor with meekness also anoints these feet with ointment. In these ways the Lord Jesus claims to be honored." By now it is clear, even to the Emperor: the little ones, the Christians of Callinicum, must be treated gently, given pardon. Thus Ambrose turns directly to Theodosius: "Pour water on the feet" of Christ "and kiss them in a way not only to free those who are trapped in sin, but also to benevolently bestow pardon on them in the interest of concord and to return serenity to them for the sake of peace…. Whoever honors these least ones acts in such a way that their pardon makes the angels rejoice, just as a single sinner who repents gladdens the apostles and brings joy to the prophets (cf. Lk 15:10)." In conclusion: "Inasmuch as all this is necessary, protect the whole body of the Lord Jesus that he might protect your reign with his heavenly benevolence."[13]

At the conclusion of the homily Ambrose approaches the Emperor: a dialogue is initiated that we are able to imagine was only perceived by the people but clearly grasped by those nearby. Here, then, is the exchange, as we are able to reconstruct it from the Bishop's letter to Marcellina:

Theodosius: Clearly, you were speaking about me.
Ambrose: I merely dealt with an argument that I thought might be useful to you.
Theodosius: (referring first to the payment already condemned by the Bishop, then to the monks who had torched the temple of the Valentinians, the punishment for which it appears had never been retracted) In reality my decision to have the Bishop make restitution for the synagogue was perhaps too severe, but it has been modified. The monks commit many misdeeds.

At this point Timasius, commander of the cavalry and the infantry, intervenes assailing the monks. Ambrose does not rise to the provocation: "I deal with the Emperor as is suitable because I know that he fears God; with you, on the other hand, who speak too harshly, I must deal in a different manner"... in other words by ignoring him!

The Bishop turns back to Theodosius and brings the conversation to a firm conclusion in order to obtain from him total immunity for the Christians as well as a withdrawal of the state from any intervention to aid the Jews: "Act so that I may be able to offer the sacrifice for you without any worry. Calm my soul."

And since the Emperor took his own place in church without in any way expressing a clear agreement to the Bishop's request, Ambrose remained beside him, on his feet, demonstrating his intent to obtain something more explicit and not subject to reconsideration. It was not enough that Theodosius assured him that there would be a modification of the decisions soon; the Bishop insisted because any inquest could be annulled and any pretext for tormenting the Christians with some such vexation might be taken to the *Comes Orientis*. The Emperor promised this as well. But he was not finished yet! Twice Ambrose declares to him: "I trust your word"; and only when Theodosius finally replied: "Have faith!" did he mount the altar and resume the Eucharistic celebration.[14] "That day Ambrose demanded too much and his subsequent victory was not positive for those who honor and love him," observes Gérard Nauroy citing Pierre de Labriolle.[15] I have already personally suggested that, beyond the excessive demands of Ambrose, should be read his desire in this episode to defend the autonomy of the Church in a period of history that correctly sought to redirect relationships with the Emperors. In fact, the abuses and various interventions of Constantius of unhappy memory should not be forgotten.... And these measures of Ambrose must have worked because similar situations were not repeated in the future. As Lellia Cracco Ruggini has explained, the "inflexible opposition of Ambrose to any punitive measure whatsoever on the part of the Emperor" ought to be understood also as "a warning — wisely measured in its severity — with which Ambrose wished, like a great politician, to rebuild the relationships between Church and Empire right after the passing of Valentinian II, of Justina, and of the 'usurper' Maximus, in a moment in which the 'pious' Theodosius still pretended to be able to continue the earlier religious policy of neutrality and equidistance." And too, let us remember that in these years, as we find from referencing the Council of Aquileia, the Bishop had to stand up to a certain encirclement made up of the three minority religions, Arians, pagans and Jews, which had united against the Catholic Church. His reaction, then, is commensurate with the complexity of the situation and the danger that threatened the Church.[16] But there remains no better comment than the significant silence that Ambrose himself reserved for the "Callinicum Case" in his discourse *On the Death of Theodosius*. In that work, indeed, he recalled many episodes in the life of the Emperor and of his relations with Ambrose, even his penance

Chapter XII: Anti-Semitism?

after the massacre at Thessalonica, but he does not choose to return to this "victory." Perhaps he was no longer very proud of it....

But the moment has come to pay attention to the more general question: what was the relationship between Ambrose and Judaism?[17] To enumerate the diverse aspects: how does he read the Hebrew Scriptures, the books of the Old Testament? How does he judge the repudiation of Christ on the part of the Jewish people as a whole? How did he relate to contemporary Jews?[18] The reader will understand the delicacy of these questions and the importance of adequately differentiating the arguments in responding.

First, a word regarding his abundant use of the Old Testament: these are the Scriptures that had prepared for the coming of the Messiah, and Ambrose amply comments on them. In the preceding chapter we learned of the Easter catechesis on the books of Genesis and Proverbs, but it is enough to look over the titles of his commentaries and of his other works to appreciate how important such texts are in his preaching: we find the *Explanation of 12 Psalms* and that very ample *Commentary on Psalm 118*, the detailed explanation of the *Six Days of Creation* and the small treatise *On Paradise;* further there are the titles with the names of *On Cain and Abel, On Noah,* the three great patriarchs (*On Abraham, On Isaac or the Soul, On Jacob and the Good Life*) and on the just man *Joseph,* and David (*Apology for David, Second Apology for David*) and of still others. Ambrose comments on the Old Testament in an allegorical way, so that, in the most profound meaning of these texts, the word that had already announced the coming Christ might emerge. But we can return to this in a subsequent chapter.

Here, my first point is that the Hebrew revelation passed down from the Old Testament is valued by Ambrose as the initial stage of the three levels through which is channeled knowledge of the divine word: these stages are those of the *shadow,* the *imagination,* and the *truth.*[19] For Ambrose, and in general for the patristic teaching of that time, there exists a first level of consciousness, typical of the Jewish world, that takes the name *shadow,* because the Jews are given a shadowy vision of reality; a still imperfect consciousness, out of focus and not sufficiently detailed, needing to be perfected by the coming of the revelation of Christ, but already open to this successive development. The second level of consciousness follows, the *imagination*, which is proper to Christians in their lived condition. And finally, on the approach to death, the consciousness of full and total *truth*: one who knows according to the *image* already delights in the Light of Christ and sees reality in this new Light; but the vision without shadow or limit will be given only in the eschatological encounter. The Bishop frequently describes this passage from one to the other level of consciousness: first of all the overcoming of the *shadow* that is accomplished thanks to one's awareness of Christ, and then the other that, according to the Pauline expression, will permit one to see, no longer "as in a mirror" but "face to face" (1 Cor 13:12). But Ambrose gives credit also to the Judaic phase: in fact, he records in a passage of the second discourse *On the Death of his Brother* that "all is of Christ and all is in Christ" and now "we see future goods as in an *image*," it remains always true that of those goods "we have seen a shadow in the Law." Thus, if "the Law has been given by means of Moses" (Jn 1:17), the Bishop recalls that "the *shadow* was given by means of a man," that is Moses, and "the prefiguration by means of the Law"; even though one must hasten to add — and how can it be otherwise? — that only "by means of Jesus (comes) the truth."[20] Here we arrive at the decisive point: since the Jewish people refused to accept the Christ, they remained on the threshold of salvation and are excluded, from the moment that salvation is now unavoidably bound to the acceptance of Jesus, Messiah, Son of God. Ambrose does not deny the good merits, still valid, of the Jews: in his *Explanation of Psalm 1*, he recalls that "certain among the Jews have chastity, much diligence and attention to the reading of the Scriptures." But, alluding to that fig tree on which Jesus found only leaf and without fruit (Mt 21:19), he judges that they "are without fruit and they twist and turn like leaves."[21] Again, writing to Horontianus, echoing the teaching of the Apostle Paul, the Old Testament Law has fulfilled its mandate to teach: it is joined to faith in Christ, and with it, freedom. "We leave aside the works of slavery," concludes the Bishop; "we possess the grace of freedom; we abandon the shadow and follow the sun: we abandon the Jewish rites!"[22]

In this sense the accusation of incredulity and impiety that we have found in the letter to Theodosius and that recur frequently in the writings of Ambrose makes sense. If the Jews were called to await the coming of the Messiah but they missed the appointment, they are now outside the true faith. "O senseless Jews" — Ambrose says to them in his *Commentary on the Gospel of Luke* — "Do you not believe that he has already come; even though you see, you do not believe that he has come, of whom you say he still must come!" And in another passage he describes them as "progeny of the Devil" because, notwithstanding the fact that they may be descendants of the elect, they are now found as "descendants of sin."[23] Furthermore, just as many times, even before the first coming of Christ they were shown to be reluctant to follow the mission assigned them by God, so now they have maintained the same attitude, filled to overflowing. I do not want to bore the reader illustrating more than is necessary texts that jar our sensibilities, but it is necessary to recall one more, the treatise on *On the Six Days of Creation* where Ambrose describes "the inconstant whims" of the leopard, easily recognizable "by its variegated pelt": in the same way "the Jewish people, depicted in variously changing shadows, turbulent and voluble in their unfaithful mind and soul, are no longer able to maintain the grace of a wholesome proposition or to return to an emendation and correction, since they are clothed once and for all as a ferocious beauty."[24]

What are we to make of these texts? What judgment can we express? Lellia Cracco Ruggini, reframing the question briefly and checking the medieval literature on Ambrose already indicated at the beginning of this chapter, frees the Bishop completely from the accusation of anti-Semitism: "The medieval fame of Ambrose as a 'scourge' of the Milanese Jews — more than of the Arians — appears completely unjustified, a late and novel fruit — post 9th century — of a tradition going back to the 'political' episode of the "Callinicum Case" and preserving only a hint of historicity in the obscure notion of a link between the Arians and the Jews effectively existing in those years."²⁵ Anyone aware of the writings of the Fathers of the Church is ready to second that judgment. Not because the errors of the others justify or excuse the weakness of Ambrose, but out of a more objective motivation.²⁶ Invectives and polemics are frequent in the writings of the ancient Christian authors, against the Jews as against the pagans and the heretics. And they are also made against Christians when they need to be reprimanded or reproached. And we don't suspect malice or preconceived judgments in these confrontations! The use of such categorical and generalized harsh expressions does not derive from animosity or in any case do not have their primary origin in such. It is above all a literary genre with which the most serious questions were dealt, in particular those in which the truth or falsehood of a choice was in play: adhesion to the faith or the refutation of it; habitually behaving in the right way or acting in another dangerously deviant manner. In other words: the invective which appears to vent malice and rage in dealing with the erring is really only a literary expression used in the battle with error and the juxtaposition of opposing positions.

The more than legitimate desire of Ambrose is that all come to know Christ and believe in him. Since 4th century Judaism exercised a strong effort at conversion among the ranks of the Christians, the Bishop in his preaching felt compelled to rebut and block their influence. But above all he proclaims clearly the truth of Christ, warning of the curse on those who still reject it, and he imagines a possible approach to Christianity even on the part of those Jews who were his contemporaries. He does not think that this would be an easy thing, but possible and certainly desirable! In his treatise *On Noah* the Bishop goes out of his way above all to reveal the obduracy of the Jews in rejecting the Christian faith, because "even though it is the water of celestial doctrine, even though it is drink in abundance, they think that they ought not imbibe it." Even when the priest appears in the city square to proclaim the word in their presence, "exhorting and recalling examples from divine Scripture… they plug their ears so as not to be, in spite of themselves, washed in the water and sprinkled in the dew of the divine word." However at this point he also describes a happy case of belief: "But there are those who have believed, who have run to the fountain, who ask insistently to be instructed, who ardently desire to have the Gospel preached to them and are never satiated by drinking without interruption. In such a way they aspire to have their thirst quenched at that font of wisdom that previously they sought to avoid at any cost."[27] In the *Commentary on the Gospel of Luke* we find an interesting passage on the method to be followed in evangelization. Ambrose first describes how to introduce the faith to pagans, then looks at the Jews, and finally explains how to instruct a catechumen already in possession of the faith. The Bishop thus considers the Jews as also destined to the invitation that the Church offers to all the non-baptized. The text is therefore quite positive, both as a sign of the faith that the Bishop has placed in them and as an indication of the inspiration that Ambrose received as an evangelist; thus the valid aspects of Judaism, which he wants to elevate by highlighting them, emerges. Here is the text nearly in its entirety.

Ambrose exhibits above all the method used by the Apostles. "When they revealed the truth to the Jews, they said that he is the Christ, the one promised to us in the sayings of the prophets: but they don't yet call him the Son of God, appealing to his own authority, as a man approved by God, a just man, a man raised from the dead, a man expected, of whom it was said in prophecy: 'You are my son, this day I have begotten you' (Ps 2:7)." In the same way today's evangelist should conduct himself, beginning with the Old Testament texts which for a long time have been held as trustworthy by the Jews: "You too have recourse to the authority of the words of God for the truth that causes you to believe, and to see that his coming was promised by the voice of the prophets. Teach further with precision that the resurrection was well known already long before through the testimony of the Scriptures, and not in a general way common to the rest of humanity." Ambrose suggests, that is, that they present the prophetic word which pre-announced the resurrection of the Messiah, thus interpreting the biblical expression, "He did not allow his Holy One to undergo corruption" (Ps 15/16:10). The evangelist thus comes to prove that he who has "conquered the limits of the human condition must therefore be considered more on a par with God than with man."²⁸ Once the Jew who has come to the recognition of Christ risen and Son of God the path to a more detailed catechesis is opened. In this passage Ambrose is certainly insightful in imagining the convergence between the Christian faith and that of Judaism, but above all he shows again how great was his desire to make known also to the ancient people of the covenant the Messiah promised and come.

For the rest, all are placed under the sign of mercy: Christians and Jews together. Again in the *Commentary on the Gospel of Luke*, recalling the beautiful evangelical image of the Father who "causes his sun to rise on the bad and the good and the rain to fall on the just and the unjust alike" (Mt 5:45), Ambrose comments: "The goodness of God has no limits... the Lord waters the Jewish people with the rain of the prophets and shines on them with the rays of the eternal sun, even if they don't deserve it; but since they remain soaked in the dew of the world, the Church of God was made to enter into celestial light." Do the Jews, then, remain excluded? Is God perhaps partial? Let us leave it to the Bishop to conclude: The Church has entered into the light but "by covenant also those who have joined the faith have been given the privilege of mercy."²⁹ Thus St. Paul the Apostle assures us: "God has consigned all to disobedience so that he may show mercy to all!" (Rm 11:32).

CHAPTER XIII

An Effective Aid to Social Life

Occasionally and with undeniable skill, Ambrose uses irony and sarcasm.[1] We have a very lively example of this in a passage from *Elijah and the Fast*, a small treatise distributed toward the end of the 380's,[2] dedicated to the theme of intemperance (in particular drunkenness and avarice) and of fasting. This is a "tasteful pamphlet of worthy artistic prose," as Franco Gori convincingly indicates, "for the humor of the situation and also for its colorful language reminiscent of Plautus," in which "Ambrose presents a scene dominated by confusion: here he describes the frantic preparation for a banquet, the race to the market of a cunning and dishonest servant, the anxiety of the master who doesn't know where to find the money for the shopping, a disorder in the kitchen beyond description, the agitation and hard work of the cook and the servants."[3] Let's read the story. It begins with the image of a "servant busy shopping," already at work early in the morning. "Before dawn he knocks on other people's doors, as if war was breaking out, and wakes those who are sleeping. They see him distraught and out of breath. They ask him the reason for such agitation. 'My master,' he says, 'is throwing a feast and is looking to see where he can buy better wine, procure a thicker sow's womb,[4] a more tender liver, a fatter pheasant, fresher fish.' Running this way and that, when he found it all, he made a big scene disturbing the master who had fallen asleep, exaggerating the prices." And here he lays out a gross contradiction between the master, who does not trust the servant and barters down the cost, and the servant, who praises the products he had acquired in order to raise the price and cause expenses to go up: "If the price of the fish alarms the master, the servant affirms that he could find no better anywhere, or rather, there is no more to be found. 'Yesterday,' he says, 'there was bad weather, today a storm; it is only with difficulty that I managed to find this one, which was hidden. There are many flocking to the market. If you send it back, another will pay more for it and then what will you offer for your meal? This wine is of a famous vintage, these oysters were fished in that place.' Thus for each and every product a price is proposed. Between the servant who is an accomplished shopper and the host who is throwing the banquet a kind of auction takes place. The devastated host sells his patrimony and keeps asking whose fault it is that his disposable wealth is diminished."

After the purchase comes the preparation of the meal: "He runs to the kitchen, creates an enormous chaos, and a great confusion results. The whole staff is upset, cursing because he won't let them catch their breath. 'Let the cook rest once in a while!' 'The right hand of the wine pourer is frozen: his hands and feet are numb from the cold!' He handles cold water with which he washes the pavement: they wash the floors soaked in wine and covered in fish bones. Many hurt themselves running around!"

The banquet is finally underway and already the host wishes it were over. Here are the final pen strokes of Ambrose. "During the festivities the clamor of the guests and the crying of the beaten servants rise up. If by chance something goes wrong, the friends laugh: you become angry. Finally a little silence reigns in the house bringing to an end the confusion of those who were running to and fro, along with the cries of the animals being slain; all are freed from the smoke and the smell of half-burnt food. It does not seem like a kitchen, but rather a place of torture; you would think that a battle had been fought there, not a meal prepared: with everything swimming in blood."[5]

Bishop Ambrose, as indicated in the chapter dedicated to consecrated virginity, wanted to contribute to the healing of the society of his time: introducing a level of evangelical teaching to the ancient Roman tradition in decadence. He intended to infuse a new basis for the reconstruction of a social fabric in obvious decay. The piece just narrated, a grotesque mockery of wealth and of the social norms from which it is derived, must be situated within a larger framework. So,

Chapter XIII: An Effective Aid to Social Life

toward the end of the decade of the 380's the Bishop dedicated to this theme, not only *Elijah and the Fast,* already noted, but also two other pamphlets entitled *On Naboth* and *On Tobias.* Most likely in these months he also developed the same argument in the third book of *On the Duties of the Clergy.* This is the famous collection of norms for Christian life that Ambrose composed, inspired by the treatise of Cicero having the same name (*De Officiis*) and which, finally completed around 389, he offered to the entire ecclesial community and especially to his clergy.[6] Furthermore the general unrest was aggravated by the agricultural situation in Italy during those decades and the recent famine triggered by the invasion of Maximus in 387. With the inevitable trail of speculations and abuses, of suffering and privations, the attention of Ambrose was focused on social topics. In this chapter I wish to recall the teaching of the Bishop on this question and his subsequent action; beginning with these writings, written at the same time as, or shortly after, the events at Callinicum.

In all of these the intent to expose the degradation of society, with the injustices and inequalities that distinguish it, emerges as does the undertaking at the same time of his proposal of a strong moral teaching for those who might wish to react to such a situation. In particular the Bishop leaves the impression of the harshness with which he regards wealth, recognizing in it — or more precisely in avarice, in the avidity and excesses that accompany it — the cause of this disastrous situation. In his little treatise *On Naboth* this teaching appears in a decisively effective form: the humble Jew Naboth, as is recorded in 1 Kings 21, fell victim to King Ahab who, aided by his wife Jezebel, in order to take possession of his vineyard caused him to perish miserably. Commenting on the episode, Ambrose offers affirmations that seem to exclude the legitimacy of private property itself: "The land was created as a common good for everyone, for the rich and for the poor: why, oh you rich, do you arrogate to yourselves an exclusive right to the land?" And again, "(When helping one in need) you do not give of your own to the poor man, but give him what is his own; in fact the common property, which was given for the use of all, you have appropriated for your own. The land is for all, not for the rich, but those who use it are few in number compared to those who do not use it. Therefore (when aiding one in need) you restore what is owed him and do not lavish on him what is not his due."[7] It is worth pausing a moment over these expressions which have provoked the most varied and extreme interpretations of the thought of Ambrose.[8] The Bishop has no interest in posing theoretical questions. He sees the situation that is right under the eyes of everyone, that is, the growth of an unproductive countryside falling into the hands of a few rich people and the flight to the city and into misery of many small landowners, and notes the consequence that the property held by the rich, since it is a cause of the most serious and unacceptable injustice, takes on the clear features of an abuse. This is why really defending those small landowners is essentially a condemnation of the exorbitant and unacceptable manner which it assumes in the rich. Moreover the social doctrine of the patristic era is aware that the goods of the earth are destined by God for people to enjoy. Therefore even the rich man, who possesses it in greater quantity than others, is only its administrator, not its master. It is not licit, therefore, for one to maintain an exclusive possession of goods as if they were his own; and if he refuses to share them, he should know that he has put himself in strict contrast with the Gospel doctrine of universal brotherhood.

The rich landowner, therefore, cannot rest easily and in peace with himself to the detriment of others. Also because, despite appearances, he is suffocated by anxiety: dissatisfied with all he possesses he is fearful that the injustices by means of which he has acquired his many goods may be revealed; while on the other hand the situation of the just, of the small landowners or those who have the least, is full of serenity, because they are free and without worry or remorse. Ambrose, again in his small treatise *Naboth* notes: "Each well-off man is still poor, because he is convinced that he lacks something that is possessed by others. He desires everything in the world, he whose longing the whole world could not satisfy. He is afraid of being exposed, as happened to King Ahab who, before the prophet Elijah, had to admit: 'Have you found me out, my enemy?' (1 K 21:20)." The Bishop comments: "He is found to be a sinner when his iniquity

Chapter XIII: An Effective Aid to Social Life

is laid bare. The just man instead can say: 'You have tried me by fire, but find in me no malice' (Ps 16/17:3)"; and the conclusion follows: "Wealth imprisons, poverty sets one free."

What, then, does the Bishop have to say to those captivated by riches? First of all, he admonishes them harshly: "You are slaves, oh rich ones, and your servitude is miserable because you are slaves of error, slaves of desire, slaves of avarice that cannot be satisfied. It is like an insatiable vortex, which becomes increasingly more voracious when it swallows the things thrown into it." Then he asks them to prefer an equitable redistribution of the goods, putting them at the disposal of everyone, sharing them, that is, with those in need. Ambrose uses the image of a well, frequently employed by the Fathers to teach the necessary circulation of riches: "If nothing is ever drawn from it, the well is easily polluted through stagnant immobility and through degrading abandonment; if, on the other hand, it is used, its waters appear clear and pleasing to drink." The same happens with accumulated riches: "dusty when amassed, resplendent when used" for the aid of the neighbor; "But if they are left unused, they are useless."[9]

Accumulated riches: in his third book *On the Duties of the Clergy* the Bishop condemns those who possess it who, at the time of the narration, are withdrawing from the market huge amounts of wheat, thus artificially provoking a real and serious crisis which was moreover made worse by the precarious agricultural situation of which he had already spoken, that is, what had been amassed was resold at an inflated price, speculating on the situation of need which it had caused. Ambrose reports that they excused themselves with a bold self-justification that they dared to advance: "I plowed (says the farmer) with great commitment, I seeded without rest, I cultivated with every diligence, I harvested the good fruits, these I have placed away with much care, these I have faithfully preserved, these I have watched over with the necessary precautions. Now, in a time of famine, I sell them, succoring the hungry. Where is the fraud, now at a time when many would fall into danger if they had nothing to buy? Perhaps industry is called a crime? Or perhaps diligence can be criticized? Should forethought be censured?" But the judge is equally unyielding. "Why do you make a fraud of the industry of nature? Why do you deny people the use of the produce destined for public use? Why do you long for a crisis?... You greedily await the lack of crops, the lack of food, you groan over the abundance of farm products, weep for the general fertility, you lament the full granaries, you anxiously anticipate when the produce might become scarcer, the fruits more limited.... Then you rejoice at having sold your harvest; on the misery of others you have heaped up your fortune." For Ambrose this is a genuine and real "rape or usury." He therefore concludes: "You commit usury by hiding the harvest; like an auctioneer you sell to the highest bidder. What motivates you to wish on everyone that famine will increase in the future, that there will be no grain left, that next year will be even less productive? How is it that the common misfortune is for you a gain?"[10]

The call to desist from such exploitation was thus formulated without compromise and solidly anchored to the more general principles of social justice. Ambrose targeted the needs of the common good, and apart from that he reacts against the various modes in which we have seen injustices present themselves: inequalities of the more general type, speculations of the market, exploitation of recurring scarcity to their own advantage or even of their own provocation. We can add those investments that, making interest rates rise, created unsustainable situations of debt without any solution. And in this regard Ambrose expresses a total condemnation including, in his judgment, every pretext towards charging interest, which in fact assumed the form of usury and exploitation. This is based on evidence from the teaching of the Old Testament and at the core of the thought of the Fathers.[11] To this theme is dedicated the small treatise *On Tobias*, in which Ambrose, referencing the narration of the biblical book of the same name and recalling the gratuitous loan offered by Tobias's father to his distant relative Gabael, develops the theme of loan for interest.

Certain passages merit being cited, in which the irony and sarcasm that we have already appreciated in the prose of the Bishop returns. Here they are used to deride the pretense of those who only offer a loan when they see looming a substantial possibility of profit: "When a man, constrained by necessity or anxiety to ransom their own family which the barbarians sell as captives, begins to beg, immediately the rich man turns his attention elsewhere, does not recognize him who pleads, his very nature is not moved to pity by the humility of his supplicant... swears he has no money, that, rather, he too is looking for a borrower to provide for his own needs. But, as soon as mention is made of usury or betting the usurer, forgetting his pride, smiles and embraces with a kiss the man whom he had before said he did not recognize, boasting of an almost fatherly affection for him; he calls him son in virtue of a hereditary love; he forbids him to cry. 'We'll find out whether there is any money in the house; for you I will divide the family silver which is the work of an artist. It would be a real shame. What lender could repay the value of such crafted objects? But for a friend I have no fear of suffering a loss. I will remake it when you have repaid me.' And so, even before giving, he hurries to reclaim, and in summary, he who bids another to come to him for help, collects interest." He even goes so far as to sequester the dead, seizing them as collateral and denying them burial!

Ambrose also recalls these excesses in another passage from a small treatise which seems to repeat the expressions he used when he was still governor and perhaps also in the exercise of the *episcopalis audientia*, the episcopal tribunal about which I will speak later on. Thus he comments: "I readily consented that they could keep the (defunct) debtor so that the debt holder might be freed more speedily." Further, he refers to a discourse that he gave to usurers, which is completely steeped in derision and enriched by certain ridiculous details: "Keep him as your prisoner and, so that he will not flee, take him to your house, close him in your bedroom.... I will not stop you from keeping your pledge.... Now truly the one you have brought to court has lost his rights as a citizen. All the same you have incarcerated him ever more strictly, fearful that he will not notice the harshness of your chains. The debtor is already hardened and unbending and no longer feels shame. There is one thing that you most certainly do not have to worry about any more: that he might ask you for food!"[12]

The time has come to move on to describe the actions of Ambrose himself, to recognize how he put into practice in the first person his use of goods, openly and freely, which he was proposing to others. I have already mentioned that Ambrose, when made Bishop, had renounced all of his family property, giving it to the Church and to the poor and reserving only the benefice for his sister Marcellina.[13] Similarly he took on himself the administration of the wealth of the Church. He made this extremely courageous and highly significant decision in the aftermath of the defeat of Hadrianopolis (August 9, 378). To come to the aid of several prisoners fallen into the hands of the enemy and to procure the huge sums necessary to ransom them, as he himself records in the second book of *On the Duties of the Clergy*, to achieve these aims he did not hesitate to smash the sacred vessels and sell the precious metal thus gained. He was harshly criticized for that choice, which would have appeared blasphemous and irreverent; the Arians in particular reacted, who — Ambrose interprets — "were not so much displeased with the deed, as much as they wanted to find a reason to criticize" him. He boldly replied "that it was much better for the Lord to save the soul than gold." In fact, he added, "the Church possesses gold, not to preserve it, but to distribute it, to offer succor in necessity." The Bishop is convinced that, if the Church does not behave in this way, it would be exposed to reproach from the Lord: 'Why have you permitted that so many poor would die of hunger? It is certain that you have the gold; you have the ability to offer them food. Why are so many prisoners put up for sale and, not being rescued, killed by the enemy? It would be better that you had saved living vessels rather than vessels of metal!" Nor could there be objection if he removed the ornaments offered to the sacred temple, because the same Lord would have responded that "the sacraments do not require gold, nor does that which is not purchased with gold acquire value by means of gold."

At this point the Bishop finds himself leveling the road ahead for the development of a rich theological symbolism: the redemption of the prisoners of Hadrianopolis reminds him of another great

Chapter XIII: An Effective Aid to Social Life

redemption, that of "the remission of sins" brought to pass through the blood of Christ; and the love of Christ, mysteriously and efficaciously present in the sacred vessels in the sacrament of the Eucharist is prolonged in the gesture which breaks open those vessels out of love for those in need. Here is the lively expression of the Bishop: "The embellishment of the sacrament brought about the ransom of the prisoners; but truly precious are the vessels that liberate the soul from death. The true treasure of the Lord is that which achieves what his sacred blood has achieved. Here (without any doubt) the chalice of the blood of the Lord is indicated, when with the one (the chalice) and with the other (the blood) he redeems, thus the chalice rescues from the enemy those whom the blood has rescued from sin." Ambrose, admired and well known for this virtuous and completely new use of riches, exclaims: "How beautiful it would be if it were said that when the Church redeems masses of prisoners: 'It has rescued Christ!' Behold the gold that is worthy of praise, behold the useful gold, behold the gold of Christ that frees from death, behold the gold by means of which is rescued purity, is preserved chastity!" And in a marvelous summary: "I know that the blood of Christ poured into gold not only tints it red, but also with the gift of redemption the virtue of divine charity leaves its mark."

With this Ambrose has led from the reference point of social justice to the heart of Christian charity. In conclusion he adds the irreproachable personal correctness required of those who work in that context: "It is necessary that this undertaking be fulfilled with sincere faith and wise foresight. Certainly, if one derived personal advantage, he would commit a sin; but if he distributed the profit to the poor, rescued a prisoner, he would be doing a work of mercy." Thus, Ambrose recalls and concludes that in this case as when it may be necessary to construct new churches or acquire spaces for the burial of Christians, "it is licit to break, melt down, and sell the vessels of the Church, even if they are already consecrated."[14] Alongside acts of charity, constructing sacred buildings is likewise a precious service to the community. But let us return to his works of charity and assistance. We have heard from Augustine about the "multitudes of businessmen whom he helped in their distress" and who interposed themselves between him and the Bishop. Because of the flood of visitors with free access to the Bishop's house, there were left to Ambrose precious few instances "in which he was not occupied with someone."[15] Of the hints that we find in his writings, in particular in the second book of *On the Duties of the Clergy*,[16] we can imagine the Bishop overseeing, personally or by means of his deacons, the daily distribution of bread to the poor, giving assistance to the sick and welcoming foreigners. He would aid with sensitivity those who may have fallen from a position in which they were better off and who were ashamed to manifest their poverty in public. He facilitated the matrimony of orphaned youths, supplying them with a dowry, and defended the property of widows against profiteers.

With what spirit did Ambrose complete and teach others to perform these acts of charity? In a beautiful passage from the *Commentary on Psalm 118*, listing the works of mercy one by one, the Bishop presents himself in joint participation with Christ, with him who, in his poured out blood, is the origin of all charity, of the Eucharist, and of the vessels broken for the needy. In fact he seeks to be, in solidarity with Christ, "the one who consoles with sentiments of sympathy another who is mourning; who does not refuse his services to another who finds himself in jail; who goes to a sickbed... to relieve with thoughtful assistance the suffering of one who is ill, to console with a kind word one whose spirit is dejected; who clothes the naked, and feeds the hungry." This spirit of mercy, nestled in the charity of Christ, also became the spirit of union and of fraternity with people of every social class in the single ecclesial Body. Giving weight to the verse of the psalm: "I am the friend of all those who fear You" (Ps 118/119:63), Ambrose presents us a model of the believer, animated by true charity, "in solidarity with the Body of Christ, which is the Church." This man "even if rich, noble, healthy, strong, cultured, cannot say to the poor, the humble, the sick, the weak, and the uneducated: 'You are not of my family'." He in fact "knows that those within the Church who seem weak, poor, uncultured, even sinners, have greater need of consideration and ought to be sustained with an

Chapter XIII: An Effective Aid to Social Life

even greater support," and so therefore, "demonstrates compassion more than annoyance, towards such people."[17] This charity is therefore animated by the universal sense that, within the context of the Church, one is to be open without limit to all those in need.

At the same time, in order to not frustrate oneself in confusing and ineffectual approaches, the work of charity ought to be organized in a prudent way and with well verified interventions: we sense a long and direct experience that dictated the norms that Ambrose enjoins on others in the second book of *On the Duties of the Clergy* and which are intended to teach a sincere, and therefore more profitable approach, in the administration of charity. These I repeat at length because of the common sense attitude that permeates these teachings and also because of the clarity with which they are expressed. "Priests," the Bishop teaches, should use good judgment "in distributing alms not for show, but for the sake of justice (also) because in nothing else is there shown greater greed than in begging." His observation has perennial validity.... Here is an illustration: "They seem to be healthy, vagabonds by profession who want to seize the subsidies of the poor and to use up all available supplies. Not content with a little — demanding ever more, they seek to obtain satisfaction of their requests by walking around in old clothes and lying about their family situation, to compel the alms to be forthcoming. If anyone puts faith in them, in the batting of an eye, they will easily carry off the savings meant for the future needs of the poor." It is necessary, rather, to give something to all the needy and not leave space to the swindler, such that "we must not lack a sense of humanity and true necessity must not be forsaken." Then follows the suggestion to get appropriate verification: Document what can be affirmed about whoever claims to have serious debt or to have just been robbed. "It is not enough to offer our ears to listen to those who plead with us, but we must also open our eyes to evaluate the real need. The one giving aid with discernment must give greater weight to need than to the voice of the poor. While it may be inevitable, on the other hand, that the persistence of the one who cries the loudest may exhort more, that does not mean always giving in to the impudent."

Such prudence even attracts the esteem of the bystanders and their generous contributions: "The more people see you helping others the more they will love you. I know that many priests, the more they gave, had that much more in abundance, because to each one who knows how to give generously as required by his office, means are provided, certain that his charity will reach the poor." Ambrose observes, without danger of contradiction, that the one who makes an offering does not want it to be squandered; furthermore he will have no faith in the one who dispenses it in an extravagant or miserly way, but will condemn both, whether "he squanders excessively the fruits of the work of others" or "he keeps stashed away" those goods without employing them for the poor for whom he had offered them.[18] Also to perform works of charity and organize their realization is a delicate undertaking requiring intelligence and competence along with those profound motives and Christian spirit about which the Bishop had spoken in other passages.

Ambrose had to confront other situations in the context of the so-called *episcopalis audientia*,[19] that is of the specific jurisdictional role recognized by imperial laws, by means of which the Bishops resolved controversies between the laity in matters of private law. This was an activity that required not a little expense of time and effort and which, on the other hand, was requested, and not only by Christians, for the efficiency and the principled affability of the episcopal tribunals, in comparison with the red tape, cost and also the corruption that characterized the civil courts.

One letter, preserved in the epistolary of Ambrose and addressed to a Bishop of an unknown see by the name of Marcellus, describes for us a case of *episcopalis audientia* which he judged and which is worth the effort to look at more closely. Marcellus had made a donation to his widowed sister of an estate he owned. To guarantee its security, he had also established that, when she might leave it, it would pass to the Church. Their brother Lietus, a person of consular rank, having felt himself unjustly excluded and defrauded by the liberality of his brother blindly accused him before the prefect of the praetorium. He had expected a quick and definitive sentence,

Chapter XIII: An Effective Aid to Social Life

when the defense for its part requested an extension in order to transfer the case to the episcopal tribunal of Ambrose. Each one "scolded one another mutually" saying that, in executing the inquest, "there should be transparency as to which party carried more support by law and justice" and joining their lively desire "that the prefect ought not to judge the cause of a Bishop." The quarrel had reached levels of depressive harshness and the question was shown to be most intricate: "The judgment was doubtful, the law was controversial, and the interventions of both parties were multiple, leaving the supplicants full of resentment," Ambrose recalls. He stated further that a generic process, whatever might be the final judgment, would end with the discontent of both the one and the other parties. Above all, it would have contributed to mutual misunderstanding, leaving in its wake serious "rancor, which for upright people is always a loss," and drawing it out further would have caused unsupportable expenses for both parties. He could not avoid the request that had been presented to him: it would have been a gesture of cowardice before an obvious and serious need. With consummate competence he wanted, nevertheless, to confront the cause not in the juridical forum, but within the structure of arbitration which would permit him to eliminate bitterness from the debate and to bring about an intervention with a definite resolution. Having obtained acceptance of his mediation on the part of both parties, he assumed as "a policy" that "no one would win and all might be victorious." In what sense? Marcellus himself suggested that his sister should have the possession and enjoyment of one part of the estate during her natural life and that on her death all would pass to the brother Lietus; however, because Lietus feared possible damage to the property during his sister's administration, "he decided that Lietus… might take the land and each year pay a determined quantity of the harvest of wine and oil" to his sister.

In any event Ambrose concludes commenting to Marcellus his arbiter's solution: "You have all won: Lietus, because he obtained the exclusive right that he had not had before; your sister, because she will enjoy the annual produce at least without litigation, or contest. No one in any case has won more completely, more gloriously, than you who, while you wanted to confirm your generosity toward your sister, you have addressed both, enabling both siblings to participate." Marcellus could have objected: had he not given too much to his brother? And hadn't he lost to the Church a donation that would certainly have been useful? The beautiful and peaceful conclusion of Ambrose is notable. Speaking with a colleague, the Bishop feels it appropriate to refer, beyond the strict criteria of justice, to more exquisitely evangelical principles: "Nothing is lost to the Church which it yields to family bonds. Charity, in fact, is not a loss, but a profit for Christ.... The process reveals itself in conformity with the style of the Apostle," that is according to the teaching of Paul who advises suffering injustice rather than battling over the concerns of this world (1 Cor 6:4-7). "Previously we were saddened that you would have sued; the dispute has helped you to bring your life into conformity with the precept of the Apostle." And as for the Church, Ambrose assures Marcellus, it "dispenses your abundant fruits: it enjoys the fruits of your doctrine, the tribute of your life, the fecundity obtained by means of the waters of your teachings. Rich in these offerings, it does not seek temporal goods, because it possesses eternal goods," and moreover it has received from its Bishop an exquisite testimony of charity and brotherhood.[20] "Torn from the tribunal and the magistrate," as he had confessed at the beginning of the tract *On the Duties of the Clergy*,[21] Ambrose in his episcopal ministry in any case had not ceased working for justice, though now with new zest and more radical depth as a minister of the Church.

CHAPTER XIV

"I Have Loved This Man"

Upon the death of Theodosius, on the 17th of January 395, in the funeral oration given on the 25th of February — forty days after his passing — Ambrose remembered an event that had taken place five years earlier when the Emperor had ordered an unjust massacre at Thessalonica. The Bishop, with a deep pastoral sense and delicate discretion, had called him to an appropriate penance. The recollection of Ambrose is full of yearning, as for a lost person in his care, as for one sincerely loved. Alluding to that sad episode, beyond the serious error he had committed, Ambrose saw in Theodosius a model of humility and an example of a sincere penitential journey. Matching his phrases to the cadence of psalmic expression, he repeats: "I have loved... I have loved...."[1] Here is how he expresses himself: "'I have loved' (Ps 114/116:1) this merciful man, humble even in the exercise of his imperial power, blessed with a pure heart and a meek soul.... 'I have loved' this man who preferred an individual who reproved him to one who praised him. Dispensing with all royal regalia, which he usually wore, publicly bemoaning his sin in the Church, a sin which he had committed in part unwittingly due to the deception of others, he pleaded for pardon with lamentation and tears. The Emperor was not shamed by that which would make a private citizen blush, that is, to make public penance, and afterwards not a day passed in which he did not grieve his own error.... 'I have loved' this man who, even when he was being released from the flesh, was worried more about the condition of the Churches than for his own illness.... This one 'I have loved,' and I am confident that the Lord hears 'the voice of my prayer' (Ps 114/116:1), with which I accompany his soul."[2]

Even while recognizing in these words a certain well intended exaggeration, appropriate to the literary style of the homily, we cannot help but notice that it is in glaring contrast to what is found in the *vulgata* [popular] story of the penance imposed by Ambrose on Theodosius, as it has been passed down in innumerable artistic representations[3] and repeated in the *History of the Church* by Theodoret of Cyrus, Bishop and Byzantine historian of the 5th century. Here we read that, informed of the massacre, "when the Emperor came to Milan and, as was his habit, wished to enter into the sacred temple," Ambrose "imposed himself before the entrance, in order to deny access to the atrium of the temple." Instead, he engaged in a long discourse of reproof, concluding with the injunction: "Go from here if you do not want to add new iniquities to those which you have already committed, but accept the bonds of penance... which lead to a cure and procure health." The Emperor, Theodoret continues, "returned to the imperial palace amidst tears and groans." For the next eight months, until the arrival of Christmas, he still "remained sitting in his palace, groaning and shedding rivers of tears." What are we to make of this?

Rufinus, *magister officiorum* (administrator of the imperial palace), inserts himself as something like an intermediary from Theodosius to the Bishop, assuring the former that he could persuade the latter to loosen the bonds of penance. The Emperor, convinced with some effort of the possible success of such a mission, commanded Rufinus to go to Ambrose. Not only that, adds the historian, "but he himself, misled by hope, followed him at a brief distance, confident in Rufinus' promises." The scene, then, is tense: Ambrose advises Rufinus that the Emperor would not be allowed to enter the church. Informed of this by Rufinus, Theodosius, who was already in the middle of the piazza, wants desperately to go to the Bishop, declaring himself ready to receive his just reproofs. "Reaching the sacred walls, he did not enter the holy temple but, approaching the Bishop in the reception room, immediately pleaded with him that he might remove his penitential chains." A surreal dialogue is engendered in which the humble and acquiescent submissiveness of Theodosius is contrasted with the unrestrainable and impassioned harshness of the Bishop. In the end, having fulfilled the demands of the Bishop and been released from his penance, "the most faithful Emperor dared to enter the holy

Chapter XIV: "I Have Loved This Man"

temple, but not standing upright on his feet did he plead with the Lord, nor throwing himself on his knees, but remaining prone on the ground. With his hands he tore at his hair and struck his chest, and with tears that soaked the ground, he pleaded to obtain pardon."

At this point Theodoret imagines the solemn Eucharist wherein the Bishop crowns the readmission of the pardoned penitent. It is precisely during this celebration where he places the episode, which we have seen having taken place some years earlier, of Theodosius distancing himself from the altar at this celebration. The Emperor supposedly accepted this added lesson declaring to Ambrose: "I am grateful to you, even for this treatment."[4]

Let's be frank: whoever wants to know either Ambrose or Theodosius from this narration would only be misled. For the rest, the entire reconstruction by Theodoret, in the caricature to which he subjects his characters, is annoyingly forced and psychologically inadmissible. The Byzantine Bishop, who wrote a half century after these events and who is constrained to bear the tyranny of the homonymous Emperor Theodosius II, has transferred to this narration a desire for revenge for the abuses which he suffered, and he wanted to sketch an ideal relationship, in his judgment, between Bishop and Emperor, in which the ecclesial authority might earn its proper autonomy separated from imperial power.

But how did the facts unfold? Let us proceed in order. In the spring or summer of 390, at Thessalonica, a popular revolt led to the murder of Butheric, *magister militum* of Illyrium, who was the chief of a troop of barbarians billeted in the city. A jockey, well loved by the people in the circus games, had been arrested for immoral behavior; the crowd, stirred up, attacked Butheric and, after having stoned him, dragged his corpse through the streets of the city. Theodosius, made aware of the serious assault, with notable impetuosity, ordered a disproportionate and terrible punishment: "For more than two hours the city was abandoned to the massacre" attests Paulinus, "and a great many innocent people were murdered." Rufinus imagines that the punitive action took place in the circus, where the people might have been invited in order to help with the track. At that point the troops, suddenly pouring in, were supposed to have encircled the crowd; then, not distinguishing from among those present, they began a massacre.[5] And we might well believe him; or perhaps, as has been suggested,[6] to suspect that the historian, through error, had transferred to the moment of punishment what had rather happened in the popular uprising in which Butheric was murdered: the people bringing themselves to the circus and wary of the absence of the jockey required for the spectacle, had reacted in a violent manner as we know. But it is right not to get excessively absorbed by these inquiries and turn rather to the substance of the events, with their great numbers of dead and with the horrifying butcher of so many innocents; adding only that later historians were not able to claim credit for whoever, with obvious exaggeration, elevated the number of the murdered to seven thousand (Theodoret) or as many as fifteen thousand (John Malalas)!

From Ambrose we have heard that Theodosius had made that choice "in part unwittingly, due to the deception of others" and perhaps we might add that the vindictive action, entrusted to the very soldiers of Butheric, had gotten out of hand, involving more people than those who were intended.[7] Paulinus hints at "secret contacts between the high officials of the empire," because of whom, though the Emperor accepted it at first, the attempt to suspend the action as suggested by Ambrose was rendered vain.[8] Certainly Theodosius, always concerned to neutralize the influences of the Bishop on the Emperor, by his own impetuosity let himself be taken in and influenced by his Councilors. For this reason the news attested to by Ambrose is all the more probable, according to which Theodosius, returning to his senses, wished "to revoke the order, if only it weren't too late."[9] But he didn't succeed in his attempt and the massacre was carried out!

Such a sin should not be passed over in silence, nor could the Emperor, being a Christian, be exonerated from the penance imposed on those guilty of such a grave crime. On the other side of the picture, throughout those months relations between the Bishop and the Emperor were not easy, as Ambrose had used undue pressure in his confrontation with Theodosius concerning the synagogue of Callinicum, if not also for other reasons. Historians, anyway, find an indication

Chapter XIV: "I Have Loved This Man"

of the coolness that had insinuated itself between the two in certain laws, less favorable to the Church, coming from the Emperor in those same months. In any case, a sense of justice, and even more a need to not hesitate in the face of his own pastoral responsibility, required Ambrose to intervene. This Bishop himself indicates to us that, when the news of the massacre arrived at Milan, there had gathered in the city a "synod for the arrival of Bishops from Gaul. There was no one who was not saddened, no one who underestimated the gravity of the situation." It could not be admitted that the action of the Emperor "should be absolved through communion with Ambrose. In fact, hatred for this sin would have grown even greater had no one asserted that reconciliation with our God was absolutely indispensible."[10] What to do? Because the Emperor was en route to Milan, Ambrose chose to distance himself from the city to avoid meeting him upon his entrance. Instead he sent him a private letter, written in his own hand, from which we have recovered the information already referenced, in which he delicately but firmly proposes to Theodosius the necessity of penance.

This letter is a masterpiece of discretion and pastoral sensitivity. After having recalled in the opening lines the tensions that stood between himself and the Emperor, as I have indicated, Ambrose prepares the recipient of his letter for the reprimand that he intends to deliver. He begins to describe his temperament. "You have an impetuous nature," he says: a character that turns to mercy if one assists it in calming down, but which flares up with excess if one excites it. "This impetuous character of yours," he explains (and having thought of the unjust severity that he had used with Theodosius in the affair of Callinicum), "I have preferred to bring to your attention in secret for your reflection rather than to provoke you, perhaps, through my public intervention." As to why the Bishop had distanced himself from Milan, he offers the excuse of his own state of health which in truth, was not good. What follows [in the letter] is the recollection of the events of Thessalonica, "the likes of which are unequaled." Then follows the tentative conclusions of Ambrose to convince him, and the judgment expressed by the Bishops gathered together with Ambrose who, we know, already knew the content. The moment was arriving to ask Theodosius to submit to the penance for the serious sin he had committed. Once a great king, David, had agreed to complete a similar gesture of humility, the Bishop recalls, and "by that act of humility became more pleasing to God" because "we ought not marvel that men sin, but it is a thing that deserves reproof if one does not realize the error, if one is not humble before God."[11]

And now what? Here is the invitation which stands at the heart of the letter which is worth citing in full: "I have written you this not to upset you, but so that the examples of kings might instruct you to remove this sin from your reign; and remove it by humbling your soul before God. You are a man and temptation has come to you: conquer it. The sin is not removed except through tears and penance.... I advise, I pray, I exhort, I admonish, because I am grieved that you, who were an unparalleled example of piety... are not saddened by [the deaths of so many] innocents. Even as you have struggled with great success, even as you have earned praise for other enterprises, all the same the culmination of your work was always a religious feeling. The devil was jealous of you because of this which was your most excellent quality. Conquer him, while you still have the means of doing so.... I have no reason to be hostile toward you, but I am afraid for I dare not offer the sacrifice if you would like to take part." You must be reconciled to God in order to be able to receive the Eucharist anew. And after having rebuked him again for not having been able to stop the massacre, he concludes by affectionately recalling Gratian, a child of Theodosius who had died as a baby, and his other children: "I love you, I esteem you, I accompany you with prayer." And, immediately afterward, he offers a heartfelt request: "If you believe, listen to what I have suggested; if, I repeat, you believe, recognize the truth in what I say; if you do not believe, excuse my way of acting in which I stand on the side of God."[12] The letter is truly restrained: Ambrose avoided including it in his epistolary which we know he himself had prepared for circulation; nor was it known to Paulinus, to whom we owe instead the circulation and diffusion of the first group of letters left outside the collection, among which we do not, in any case,

Chapter XIV: "I Have Loved This Man"

find included this letter to Theodosius. It was, rather, part of a second group of letters outside the collection, noted neither by Paulinus nor by Rufinus nor by the other ancient historians of the Church, but most likely kept apart, in Milan, and only revealed subsequently. This confidential letter to Theodosius was cited for the first time, in a large excerpt, around the year 860, by Hincmar of Reims.[13] With this calculated intervention, at once full both of respect and firmness, the Bishop then asked the Emperor, as a person of faith caught in a grave sin, to submit himself to ecclesial penance. By whom was he treated? Ambrose himself discusses it[14] in a treatise which he had finished just a few months earlier, entitled aptly *On Penance*. The author refuted the rigorist doctrine, supported by Novatian, which excluded any possibility to pardon anyone who, after baptism, committed serious sins. Even as he described the penitential rite, he prescribed it as a public gesture to be completed before the ecclesial community. The treatise looked at three capital sins: idolatry, homicide, and adultery, each brought into relief by the other and, because of their gravity, were able to be received only once in a lifetime. By norm the penitent began by realizing his own fault and then presenting himself to the Bishop to be joined to the order of penitents and thus complete the established penitential exercises. But in such a rare case, as was that of Theodosius, it may have been left to the Bishop to take the first step towards the guilty one. Nevertheless, in either situation it depended on the interested party to embrace the prescribed way of penance.

It involved, in any case, the exclusion from the Eucharist of whoever would be readmitted until the end of the penitential journey as a sign of the return to ecclesial communion. Added to this was a series of other acts, such as remaining in a place reserved for penitents during the celebrations, recommending himself with incessant pleas for the prayers of the community, personally dedicating himself with great fervor to prayer, fasting, and other mortifications, and finally assuming a humble and demure attitude. Ambrose doesn't conceal the sternness of this penitential practice: as a matter of fact he holds it up in his teaching. Thus, for example, as he explains in a passage full of passion but that still leaves the impression of a decisively demanding request: "I desire that the guilty one hoping for pardon would ask for it with tears, plead for it with sighs, beg for it with the weeping of all the people, imploring that he be pardoned. After communion which will have been postponed a second and a third time, if he believes that his pleadings were tepid, he will increase his tears, returning repeatedly, awakening greater compassion." And he, like the sinner in the Gospel who washed the feet of Jesus, bathing them with her tears (Lk 7:36-50), "wiped them with her hair, covering them with kisses and anointing them with oil" did not stop until Jesus was able to say to her: "Your many sins are forgiven because you have loved much (Lk 7:47)." In another passage the Bishop completes the picture: "You need to renounce the world, you need even to agree to sleep less than what nature demands; sleep ought to be broken up with weeping, interrupted with sighs, divided with prayers; you need to live in such a way as to die to your normal way of living."[15]

Even Theodosius, even in the particular situation on account of the position he held, had to take on such penance and assume certain acts as just described. Rufinus records that he "acknowledged his own fault and, tearfully admitting his sin, fulfilled the public penance in view of the whole Church and to that aim, discarding all regal pomp, patiently observed the time that was prescribed for him." As to the rest, Ambrose, in comments already cited from the discourse *On the Death of Theodosius*, described the Emperor who, having taken off his royal regalia, "bemoaned his sin publicly in the Church..., and with cries and tears pleaded for pardon." Further, as I have already noted, "He, the Emperor, was not shamed by that of which private citizens may be shamed, that is, to make a public penance." Even Augustine adds: "Hit by ecclesial discipline (Theodosius) performed penance with such commitment that the people who were praying for him were sadder to see the humiliation of his imperial majesty than they feared knowing that it was their fault that he suffered this indignity."[16]

Yet Ambrose, firm in demanding the prescribed penance, approached the penitent with respect and understanding, with a feeling and a mercy that he had learned from his Master. We remember yet

Chapter XIV: "I Have Loved This Man"

that beautiful prayer he offered to Christ the Lord: "Every time I treat one who has fallen, let me show compassion and not to arrogantly reproach them, but to groan and weep, so that, as often as I weep for another, I weep for myself." In the Gospel the subtle parable of the Samaritan is recounted in which the Samaritan stopped to assist an injured man after the priest and the Levite had passed on neglecting him; Jesus related this in response to the question that had been posed to him by a doctor of the law: "Who is my neighbor?" (Lk 10:29-37). Ambrose comments on the parable as a counter to the rigorism of the Novatians who denied "the hope of pardon." The Samaritan, on the other hand, whom we immediately identify as Jesus, is the one who assists the sinner, "not leaving without assistance the man whom the brigands had abandoned half dead: he... places the wounded man on his own pack animal, upon which he transported all of his sins. Thus," adds the Bishop, making reference to another well-known parable, "the Shepherd does not neglect the lost sheep." The Novatians refuse to accept the sinner as their neighbor. They pass by, like the priest and the Levite. You, Ambrose says to them, "do not offer hospitality to the one for whom Christ has paid two coins and to whom he has commanded you to be neighbor that it might be easier for you to have mercy on him." Then he added a formulaic phrase of formidable theological gravity and deep human subtlety: "Your true neighbor is not the one who is bound to you by a like nature, but the one whom mercy has intimately united to you!"[17]

The Bishop also comments on the episode of Lazarus raised from the dead and assures that Christ will come to the sinner, as he had gone to the tomb of one who was dead, and share the tears and emotions of whoever begs him that his brother might be restored to life. Similarly, he recalls the parable of the prodigal son and identifies him with the sinner who confesses his own sin and toward whom the father runs to give him the kiss of reconciliation and the sign of the Holy Spirit and the invitation to celebrate again the Easter of the Lord.[18] In the *Commentary on Psalm 118* he takes up again, more carefully, the parable of the sheep that was lost and found. In a passage that becomes an invocation and expression of the fidelity toward the One who pardons: "Come, Lord Jesus, seek out your servant, seek out your weary lamb... your sheep has gone wandering while you delay, while you focus on yours on the mountain. Leave your ninety-nine sheep and come in search of the one who has wandered off. Come without dogs, come without crude wage earners, come without mercenaries.... Come without helpers and intermediaries, because I have been waiting so long for your coming.... Come, but without a club: with love, rather, and with an attitude of clemency.... Seek me, find me, lift me, carry me. You have the power to find whatever you seek. You agree to take upon yourself whoever you have found, to bear on your shoulders what you have taken up. The weight of mercy is not loathsome to you; the burden of justice is not a bother to you.... Come, Lord, because you alone can cause a wandering sheep to turn back, without saddening those whom you had left behind because even those rejoice in the return of the sinner. Come to work salvation on the earth, joy in heaven.... Carry me on [the shoulders of] the cross, which is salvation for the errant, in which alone is found rest for the one who is tired, in which alone the man who dies finds life."[19]

Theodosius would have known this sermon; and we might imagine that the themes it offered may have sounded in his ears on various occasions. In the silence of the sources, we cannot know in any case how he had reacted to the letter of Ambrose. There is noted, however, a law which Theodosius issued from Verona on August 18, 390 in which is established that every decree of condemnation to death ought to be executed only after 30 days so that, Rufinus explains, "the possibility of a gesture of mercy might not be inhibited or, if the circumstances call for it, a reconsideration."[20] In this law it is possible to catch the first signal by which Theodosius wishes Ambrose to understand that he is truly penitent. Before the end of November the Emperor returned to Milan and, if we accept the chronology of Theodoret, was able to be reconciled and readmitted to full ecclesial communion on the feast of the Nativity.

The length of his penance, because the situation was so exceptional, was necessarily a bit brief, reduced to only a few months. Besides it wouldn't have been set according to a fixed period but would have been decided by the Bishop in reference to the gravity of the fault or on the basis of other circumstances. Moreover, for the choice of when to celebrate the reconciliation, it must have been worked out in an unusual way: normally, in fact, the readmission of sinners would have been on Holy Thursday, the day on which, to borrow the beautiful expression of Ambrose, "the Lord surrendered himself for us, him in whom the Church remits the penance."[21] It doesn't seem necessary to question Theodoret's news by transferring the long awaited pardon to several months later, to the following Easter. As is the case with other penitents at the completion of their penitential journey, so also, with the imposition of hands by the Bishop and with the prayers of petition that accompanied that gesture, Theodosius was absolved and reconciled by the grace of the Spirit.

Paralleling this event with the episode of two years earlier, when Ambrose had imposed his will regarding the question of Callinicum, Gerard Nauroy comments: "This second victory achieved by Ambrose over Theodosius is not subject to any criticism; the loftiness, but also the humility of the step taken by Ambrose, who had refused to take revenge on the Emperor who had 'marginalized' him after Callinicum, the new definition of episcopal duties before the great of this world, the idea that even the Emperors are subject to the laws of morality and here on earth must render account for their acts to God (and thus to the Bishop, God's earthly representative), these are the powerful lessons of this episode."[22] What might we say conclusively regarding the relations between the State and the Church as we see it slowly being shaped by the attitudes assumed by the Bishop in his dealings with the Emperors? We have already recognized that Ambrose nourished a passionate sense of the State and of its dignity and that he assumed an attitude of loyalty toward it, respecting its authority and teaching his faithful to do the same. At the same time he claimed a new autonomy for the Church, formulated strictly lest it succumb to illegal encroachments on its turf, but which in any case had to guarantee the Bishop's freedom to express judgments of the moral order, with the consequent practical denunciation as deemed appropriate to formulate. On the other the novelty of the presence, as a guide of the State and of Emperors who were Christian and who therefore were recognized as full members of the Church, must be added. It is in this context that we have been interested in the penance of Theodosius. This was an exceptional episode and above all innovative in the imperial practices of the time that for all practical purposes had resulted in identifying the law with the very will of the sovereign and therefore did not recognize any institution whatsoever that set itself at any distance from the Emperor in order to recall him to moral behavior. It certainly required the fortitude of a Bishop like Ambrose to convince an Emperor to submit himself as a humble penitent; even if it may be before the divine power that offered him his pardon. In this sense Angelo Paredi observes that, in that case, "for the first time in history, a monarch admitted publicly to being under the eternal law of justice, and a Bishop claimed for himself the right to judge and to absolve even Kings."[23] Thus was reclaimed that freedom which the most authentic tradition of Rome, of ancient Republican stamp, had sought in order to counter the ever encroaching imperial despotism. When Ambrose, in his *On the Death of Theodosius*, offers to the penitent Emperor the confident and affectionate eulogy that we heard at the beginning of this chapter, he presupposed and confirmed, according to Marta Sordi, the happy and necessary "coexistence between loyal acceptance of a supreme power and the preservation on the part of the subjects of a *libertas* (freedom) that held them as *cives* (citizens)," because it is precisely this "political ideal that Ambrose had theorized in his writings and had envisioned in his stance before the imperial power."[24]

In that discourse, almost a manifesto of the Bishop regarding the criteria and the values that ought to rule the now Christian empire, we find the solution to an earlier question: Now that the Emperors had embraced the Christian faith, what does it mean to administer power? How ought they to function from within this new horizon? The response directs us to his final point where Ambrose introduces into the discourse, apparently unexpectedly, the story of the discovery of the cross of Jesus by Helen, the mother of the Emperor Constantine. The story, which appears here for the first time in the

Chapter XIV: "I Have Loved This Man"

Christian tradition, is only offered as an example. He wishes above all to introduce a reflection on the nature of imperial power and to demonstrate how the victory of the cross had caused a renewed vitality of that power. Ambrose begins at the very beginning (and we don't pretend that his story respects the criteria of critical historiography): Helen, an old innkeeper, who "preferred to be deemed trash in order to gain Christ" and whom "Christ raised from dungheap to Empress" went to Jerusalem to search on Golgotha for the cross of the Lord; thus digging in the dirt, she saw appear three crosses, and thanks to the inscription hung on one of these, was able to identify that as the one on which Jesus died; and "she adored him who, named in the inscription, had been hung on that wood." Here the Bishop prepares us for a solemn gesture made by Helen, describing her as "happy in heart but cautious in her step," initially uncertain about what to do but then struck by such a bolt of truth that she can be compared to the Virgin Mary herself. Indeed, Ambrose assures us, she "achieved the seat of truth. The wood glowed and grace shone, so, given that Christ had already visited the woman Mary, the Spirit visited Helen. She was taught that which a woman is not able to understand and led her on a way that no mortal would be able to understand."[25] What was accomplished by such elevation? "Seek the nails with which Christ was crucified, and you will find them. Offer a nail to be made into a bit, insert another into a diadem." Operating in this way, with the symbolism that that choice indicated, she was brought to save the empire. As "Mary had been visited in order to free Eve," so "Helen had been visited in order that the Emperors might be saved." She gave both objects to her son Constantine: Constantine used them, claims the Bishop, "to transmit the faith to his successors." What is the meaning of the two symbols? The nail in the crown symbolizes the "guiding rudder" (through the double meaning of the term *clavus* meaning both nail and rudder) which is to mean that the cross is placed on the head of the sovereigns. These had indeed received the faith and therefore in regards to them the rudder of the cross "governs the entire world and covers the forehead of the princes, that they, who once were in the habit of persecuting, might proclaim the faith." Even the sovereigns have therefore recognized him who was killed: they have believed and so are redeemed.

Consequently, and here we see the significance of this other symbol, the power ought to be used as a service: the nail is transformed into a bit so that "it might rein in the arrogance of Emperors and suppress the wantonness of tyranny which, as with horses, encourages the eagerness to please." The Neros and the Caligulas did not have this check, and their wickedness stands before the eyes of everyone. Helen, however, Ambrose notes, with her symbolic gesture seems "to speak through divine inspiration to the Emperors: 'Don't be like the horse or mule.' Rather close 'their jaws with bit and muzzle' (Ps 31/32:9), because they must first recognize their responsibilities to govern, to rule their subjects." This comparison of sovereigns with animals needing to be domesticated is amusing, or perhaps tremendously serious, because it recalls that without that, then "power abandoned itself without restraint to vice and, like beasts, the rulers contaminated themselves in rampant lust and ignored God." Now, on the other hand, it is the symbol of the nail in the bit that is intended to confirm "it was the cross of the Lord that had reined them in and had recalled them from the fall into impiety; it raised their eyes so that they search the heavens for Christ. Thus they have dropped the muzzle of disbelief and have accepted the bit of devotion and faith, following him who said: 'Take my yoke upon you; my yoke, indeed, is sweet and my burden light' (Mt 11:29-30)."[26] Faith, accepted by the Emperors, has thus led them to assume power in the form of service, which Jesus, King Crucified and Risen Lord, had modeled. He is their font and their foundation.

The imperial dignity and authority, Ambrose pointed out, had lost nothing by the adherence of sovereigns to the Christian faith. Thus the administration of power is shown to be renewed and "redeemed." If at one time Emperors were encouraged to guard themselves against a creeping despotism and to adequately respect the freedom of their subjects, they now choose to understand power ultimately and fundamentally as service, assuming an elevated moral significance rooted in a profound religious context.

CHAPTER XV

In the Service of the Word

At the conclusion of his treatise *On the Six Days of Creation* Ambrose dedicates a brief but intense reflection to the rest that God allows himself on the Seventh Day, the day after the creation of man. "It is now time to put an end to our discourse," he confides to his listeners and readers, "because the sixth day is finished and so is concluded the creation of the world with that masterpiece: man who exercises dominion over all living beings and is thus the culmination of the universe and the supreme beauty of all created beings." The Bishop is enthusiastic about man, of the perfection with which God has enveloped him; and he continues: "Truly we ought to maintain a reverent silence, so that the Lord *might rest* from every work in the world. So that he *might rest* moreover in the intimacy of man that he *might rest* in his mind and in his thought; in fact he made man with the capacity for reason, to imitate him, emulating him in virtue, yearning for celestial graces.... I give thanks to the Lord our God who has created a work so marvelous in which to find his rest." Thus man is admired for his natural characteristics of intelligence and free will and for his receptivity to the gift of God, to the "celestial graces." We can follow the text: God, Ambrose observes, "created the heavens, and I do not read that he rested; he created the land, and I do not read that he rested; he created the sun, the moon, the stars, and I do not read that even then he rested; but I read that he created man and that *at this point he rested, having a being to whom to remit sins.* Perhaps even then the mystery of the future passion of the Lord was foreshadowed in revealing that Christ would rest in man, he who predestined for himself a human body for the redemption of man."[1]

One cannot escape the intense, almost abstruse, profundity of this passage, in which is recalled the theme of the remission of sins, already developed in the last chapter. Inos Biffi correctly indicates that we have here one of Ambrose's "more characteristic points and one of the higher motives behind his originality," and he observes acutely: "It is as if to say that God, by some mysterious and miraculous design, the reasons for which belong to his unfathomable secret, when he decided to create, wanted, as an ultimate and finished prerogative, to express himself through his mercy. He creates man in order to be merciful." Let us understand this well: here the Bishop does not teach that God "creates man sinful or flawed," but he introduces, rather, the idea that "the passion of the Lord, the repose of Christ in redemptive death, represents the sense of creation, prefigured in the repose of God at the end of the six days." The "repose" of Jesus on the cross was thus already prefigured and foreshadowed in the repose of God on the seventh day! Thus is highlighted the unitary vision that the plan of God assumes in the eyes of Ambrose: the redemption completed by Christ is not a contingent or chance choice, coming as an afterthought, but "The Man-God Redeemer… is the very end of creation, through a choice by which he dodges every rationally and thoroughly comprehensible logic."[2]

With this passage of marvelous theological significance we have confronted one of Ambrose's principal treatises dedicated to providing a detailed exegesis of *On the Six Days of Creation*, that is, of the biblical writings of creation transmitted in the first chapter of Genesis. We already know that the Bishop laid out the nine homilies of commentary, once delivering two in a single day, in the course of Holy Week of 386 (that is at the same time as the battle for the basilicas) or of some year shortly afterwards.[3] Beyond that, in the last years of the 80's the literary productivity of Ambrose was quite vast. It is enough to recall the great *Commentary on the Gospel of Luke*, which was produced toward the end of 389 or in the following year, 390, which we took up in describing the penance of Theodosius. In this present chapter, taking cue from this and other exegetical works of the Bishop, which form the mainstay of these years but which are spread across the entire course of his life, I would like to aid the reader in drawing nearer to "the service of the Word," which Ambrose took

Chapter XV: In the Service of the Word

on for the sake of his people. Already, in fact, we have recognized significant aspects of his pastoral action: we have seen him guide the catechumens to the sacraments of Christian initiation, sustain the penitents in the journey that leads to reconciliation and to pardon, teach and lead the faithful in lives of justice and love. But at the heart of all this stood that nourishment which Ambrose guaranteed to his faithful with his preaching of the Scriptures.[4]

The Biblical word, the Bishop is convinced, is a spiritual food that sustains the believer, a necessary and most rich nourishment, provided that one has the patience and the constancy to "ruminate" on it in a prolonged meditation. We find this conviction expressed in a passage from the treatise *On Cain and Abel* in which Ambrose exhorts his listeners thus: "Let us procure for our minds this food that, ground and refined by long meditation, may be for the heart of man like celestial manna: food that we have not received already ground and refined without having to do anything. For that reason we must grind and refine the word of the celestial Scriptures, applying ourselves with all our soul and all our heart, so that in the end the essence of this spiritual food is distributed to all the veins of the soul."[5] The biblical books to which the Bishop dedicates most of his attention are Genesis, Song of Songs, the Psalms, and the Gospel of Luke. But even in regard to these books he does not typically undertake a systematic exegesis. Besides, we know that his writings derive from oral preaching, and in consequence they retain characteristics of extemporaneousness, reworked but not removed from the revision done in view of the final publication. Even in the *Commentary on Psalm 118*, so methodical in interpreting one after the other of the 176 verses of the psalm, the explanation is intertwined with a commentary on certain passages of the Song of Songs; and the *Commentary on the Gospel of Luke*, which is presented as a great general commentary, is not preoccupied too much with providing accurate and complete explanations for the entire Gospel, but certain passages are left out of the whole, inserting certain other passages omitted by Luke but inferable from the other evangelists. Even the Song of Songs, a biblical book strongly present in the spirit of Ambrose especially from the middle of the 80's on,[6] while commenting on large sections of it in some of his other writings (especially in the treatise *On Isaac or the Soul* and, as we have seen, in the *Commentary on Psalm 118*) nevertheless only finds a continuous exposition in another author of the first half of the 12th century, William of Saint-Thierry, who in his *Commentary on the Song of Songs drawn from the writings of St. Ambrose,* diligently reunited all the references of the Bishop to this book.[7]

Regarding the different exegetical senses available to adopt in the study of the sacred text, Ambrose does not use a precise and consistent terminology. It is noted that the Fathers, and before them, the Jewish Philo of Alexandria, convinced that the meaning of the Scriptures is not exhausted in that which is apparent at a first reading, prepared an interpretive schema at many levels. Origen, in particular, proposed to take the Scriptures in a literal sense, a moral sense, and an allegorical-mystical sense. In the first of these he remained fixed to the immediate sense of the text; with the moral sense he took up the biblical passage as if it were a school of existential behavior; with the allegorical-mystical sense he sought the mystery of Christ and of the Church in the analyzed passages, recalling in the images and the biblical episodes an anticipatory sign or "type" of that mystery: this last level of the reading was also called the "typological" sense.

Ambrose was aware of this tripartite schema, by then already classic and made reference to it in not a few of his programmed writings. Still, the exegetical practices habitually followed by him seem rather constructed on an interpretive schema of two senses of reading,[8] with the omission, that is, of the first level of the tripartite schema. In his *Commentary on Psalm 118* the Bishop symbolically identifies those two senses with the eyes of the Church: "one that sees the mystic realities and one the moral," because, he explains, "the holy Church is not only in possession of moral discipline, but also teaches the secrets of the celestial mystery." Indeed he elaborates on this and in his instruction proposes to the faithful two types of discourse. The first explicitly concerns moral realities, the other the mystical.

Ambrose describes them in detail in another passage of his *Commentary on Psalm 118* where he explains the verse of the Song of

Chapter XV: In the Service of the Word

Songs in which the spouse expresses his joy at entering the garden of love and being a guest at his own table, and exclaims: "I have eaten my bread with my honey, I have drunk my wine with my milk" (Sg 5:1). Here Ambrose has symbolically illustrated for us the two discourses that the Church lavishes on believers like food and drink. The first discourse, the moral one, is symbolized by honey for food and milk for drink; the other, the mystical discourse, is set forth in the images of bread and wine. More to the point and analyzing first of all the two foods of bread and honey, it is understood that "ethical discourse is persuasive, pleasant and more loving," likening it to honey; "this is appropriate because the exposition of moral principles is made by touching, as with a caress, the interiority of the spirit and to sweeten with agreeable condescension the heart, made bitter with fever, that is with remorse for sins committed." Conversely "mystical discourse is like bread that restores a man's strength, as if with it the word nourishes more strongly." Furthermore, regarding quenching thirst, the figure of milk indicates the lucidity and the simplicity of discourse, similar to the smoothness and persuasiveness indicated in the symbol of honey. The wine, instead, makes one think of a discourse that produces inebriation: obviously the Bishop loves to make clear (here, as in other places) not to be inebriated by something but by the "sober inebriation of the Spirit." This is a characteristic theme in the spirituality of Ambrose, to which we will return again: here the Bishop teaches that this "good inebriation produces a kind of ecstasy" that at the same time "transports the spirit to a better and more pleasant zone." If it says in a psalm that God visited the earth and it inebriated Him (cf. Ps 71/72:6), it indicates that the wine, that is to say the mystical discourse already identified with Christ-Word of God itself, "inebriated the veins... of the soul, or of the spirit with divine preaching and aroused a passion for diverse virtues and perfumed the fruits of the faith and a pure religiosity."[9]

The Church, therefore, with the simple (milk) and persuasive (honey) language of "moral" discourse introduces to the faith and to a suitable behavior whoever is found in ignorance or error. The more robust preaching in the "mystic" discourse further commits the baptized to a mature asceticism (bread) and leads them to a living encounter with Christ-Divine Word (wine). Likewise, and thus we return to the interpretive levels of Scripture, in reading the sacred texts which animate every ecclesial teaching, both kinds of discourse must emerge. And this is how Ambrose does it when commenting on the biblical text. Presupposing the liturgical proclamation in front of the assembly, and hence keeping in mind the immediate and literal significance of the text already noted and discounted, he passes directly to take from the passage in question, first of all the moral reality, then that of the mystical, with the typological reference to the mystery of Christ and of the Church.

I would like to propose an example, taking it from the treatise *On Joseph*, where Ambrose comments on the sad experience of this biblical personage, sold by his brothers to Midianite merchants, led into slavery in Egypt and bought by the Egyptian Potiphar. In this case, uncharacteristically, mystic realities emerge first. Joseph, sold and consigned to merchants and then to Egypt, is the image of Christ; he too was consigned and sold for the salvation of humanity. The prophet Isaiah, the Bishop continues, said that men were sold for their sins (cf. Is 50:1). Therefore humanity had to be ransomed from the price of sin and freed from its consequent slavery. Christ, who assumes the human condition without, however, allowing himself to be bound by the price of sin, was able to accomplish this ransom, and thus "he redeemed with his blood those who had been sold by their own sins." We, in fact, were not permitted to leave the slavery of sin because a debt remained to be paid and a chain to be loosened. "He took it upon himself for us, to drive this slavery from the world, to restore the freedom of paradise, in order to bestow a new grace with the honor of his participation." This, then, is the mystic, exquisitely typological interpretation.

The moral explanation follows: the Lord, Ambrose elucidates, "by means of Joseph, gave comfort to those who were in slavery; he offered them instruction so that they might learn that even in the basest conditions the conduct of one's life may be superior and that no situation is deprived of virtue." The required condition is that they know themselves, "namely that it is the body which is subject to slavery, not the soul, and that many humble slaves are even freer than their owners; though reduced to slavery, they can decide to abstain from servile works." Moreover, the Bishop adds citing the words of the Gospel, "whoever commits sin is a slave to sin" (Jn 8:34). Hence the rich man is a slave, as we have already seen in another passage of Ambrose, because "he sold himself as if at an auction for minimal monetary profit." The lustful one is a slave, who in the ardor of his desire "is burdened with every dread robbing him of sleep: to obtain that one woman which he desires, he becomes slave of all." On the contrary "anyone in the condition of slavery is always free who is not captivated by affection, is not held by the chains of desire, nor bound by the chains of guilt. He is secure who faces the present and is not terrified by the future."[10] We are not to compare this patristic mode of commenting on the Scriptures with the criteria of modern historical-critical exegesis. Ambrose, and the Fathers in general, certainly lacked the rich instruments that today permit us to know and to investigate with greater relevance the biblical text and its redactional history. But their conviction remains emblematic and essential that the sacred text may be a carrier of a message about faith and about the moral behavior of the believers; and that therefore the probing of the biblical word ought to be directed toward such depth and in such a direction. Under this profile Ambrose and the Fathers are very powerful and relevant teachers.

They are even more so for the basic affirmation of the centrality of the Scriptures, to which they are passionately dedicated. For Ambrose the word "ruminated" upon personally enters into all of his preaching and on the whole of his pastoral action. For him, Gérard Nauroy recalls, "the exegesis is not a particular type," but much more "the substance of all the literary types used by a Christian pastor. His own commentary is not only on the Scripture," such that a biblical passage is brought to light thanks to expressions drawn from other scriptural texts, "but it is adapted to all the situations of life, to all of the discourses required of a Bishop: funeral orations of Emperors or exhortations in praise of virginity." In fact, "for Ambrose exegesis is a fundamental way of thinking rather than a method or a category of artistic composition: everywhere required and everywhere present, not merely that he might include it in a particular literary category."[11] In many writings of the Bishop the constant presence of the Scriptures makes itself evident visibly by the continuous linking together of citations which follow one another and connect as in an ingenious structure, clustered like grapes. Frequently, in fact, alongside one text another emerges as if attracted, drawn by an identical word or a similar image, and then others still in this same fashion, in a more or less sustained chain. But it still occurs that one or the other of these linked passages might contain, besides the element that had caused it to be joined to the preceding passage, also a new element to which is connected the next passage, which thus begins the development of a self-generation; and nothing prohibits that at a certain point one returns to the original text or image in order to set off again with other developments in other directions. Thus may be born a web of interlaced references and multiple connections which, to a less expert reader, will appear as an indecipherable complex, almost an inescapable labyrinth. It may even constitute a provocation and a challenge, even an emotional involvement, to those who have familiarity with the sacred text, and they may let themselves be captivated by Ambrose's genial construction. In a later chapter (ch. 17) the reader will find interesting examples based on a famous passage of the Song of Songs (1:3: "Your name spoken is a perfume which spreads") and on the image of perfume to which it is joined. But the diffuse presence of the Scriptures does not stop here. Ambrose not only passes from citation to citation with agility and with surprising imagination; his language, trained to the reading and "rumination" of the Biblical word, is enriched by numerous allusions, sometimes clearly perceptible, other times identifiable only with difficulty. The Bishop reveals here, as is precisely indicated again by Gérard Nauroy, an "intimate incorporation of the Scripture to the style proper to the Christian preacher. He now 'speaks the Bible,' no longer with the juxtaposition of citations now from various styles, but in a synthetic discourse, eminently allusive, 'mystically,' as is the Biblical Word itself."[12]

Chapter XV: In the Service of the Word

Thus Ambrose "serves the Word" and offers to the Church his lavish exegetical undertaking. In any case many may pose a question, honest and radical at the same time: what did the people understand of this preaching, composed of scriptural commentaries, filled with citations and allusions, profoundly imbued by the Biblical word? Could they manage to understand it? Could they really follow him in the meanderings of his discourse? We can proceed in stages, beginning with the collection of the instructions on preaching that the Bishop gave to his priests in a passage in *On the Duties of the Clergy*. What he taught others certainly constituted his conviction; and he himself will be careful to personally put into practice his own instructions. The treatment of the arguments of the doctrinal or moral content, Ambrose explains, "doesn't always have to be the same, but takes its points from the *lectio* (the daily readings of the Scriptures in the liturgy) and developed as we are able. It shouldn't be too wordy or truncated immediately, in order to not leave a sense of boredom or indicate negligence and carelessness. The style should be spontaneous, simple, transparent and clear, thoughtful and dignified, without affected elegance, but always pleasing."[13] We already know that for Ambrose every sermon ought to start with the Biblical text. We have also noted that homilies should be of balanced length, neither too long nor excessively brief. Do we have other information in this regard? Once, at the end of the eighth homily of *Six Days of Creation*, he confesses to being himself more drawn out than he ought, until the rooster crows: but perhaps this chronological allusion is more symbolic than real and served the Bishop to introduce the model of the Apostle Peter, who at the crowing of the rooster repented the denial he had committed and thus to allude to the forgiveness of sins, if called for in the course of the preaching.[14] On the other hand, because of a chronic illness to which we will return to speak, the Bishop had to be very careful and not strain his voice. At times he was forced to interrupt his talks to catch his breath, and in any case was not able to carry on beyond a certain point in his speaking. Augustine already indicated to us that Ambrose, when he studied, read without pronouncing the words, the point being that he had "to rest his voice, which was easily exhausted."¹⁵ The people, furthermore, sensed that the Bishop held them close at heart and that he worried about them with passionate preoccupation. In a homily in the *Commentary on the Gospel of Luke* Ambrose thus confided: "How many even of these present will fall by the wayside even after these words... would that there be only one and not many!" And at the same time he did not draw back from the optimism that characterized him. All, even the errant ones and those far off, would be able to hear with emotion another of his expressions, also found in the *Commentary on the Gospel of Luke*: "See how good God is, and how ready to pardon sinners...; it is one of the greatest graces of the Lord, that even those who have denied him acknowledge it." The Bishop offered these consoling words in his commentary concerning the events surrounding Zechariah, father of John the Baptist, who for his incredulity was made mute, but at the birth of his son had his voice restored by the Holy Spirit and he was even able to prophetically sing a praise to God (cf. Lk 1:67). Ambrose continued to exhort: "No one therefore should lose faith; no one should despair of divine recompense, even those reproached by their old sins. God knows how to change his opinion if you know how to emend your fault."¹⁶

Ambrose's listeners therefore would have been well disposed toward him in their dealings with him. They came to hear his sermons every Sunday and on other important occasions in the life of the community. For the most part they did not directly approach the sacred text, because they did not possess the texts for reading and often were unable to read. Listening, nevertheless, to the Word proclaimed in the liturgy and through this oral communication they came to understand it in an ever more profound way. Here is the key to resolving the question which we posed. It is true, in fact, that Ambrose's biblical explanation required an exceptional ability for listening; but it is just as certain that the Bishop did not intend to speak only to the elite or to select listeners of a superior cultural class. He knew himself to be, and he wanted to be, father to all, and to all of his children he loved to explain and to teach the Scriptures, and he gave each one of them what they wanted in order to understand. And so with his Sun-

Chapter XV: In the Service of the Word

day homilies, week after week, little by little he would have created in the faithful that biblical and Christian awareness and formation that made them familiar with and able to comprehend the allusions and connections that energized the talks of Ambrose. The Bishop, like every wise interpreter, knew that he had to adapt his words to his listeners' level of comprehension, and so he made a point of reading the sacred Word to them, commenting on it according to the interpretive senses indicated, thus with simplicity introducing them to a knowledge of the mysteries.

So, beyond the impression that is frequently created in the modern reader, Ambrose would have explained things in a manner comprehensible to the public. When in the treatise *On Isaac or the Soul*, he speaks of the good sense and of attention that a real master uses in dealing with his listeners, especially the weaker ones, he is not far from describing himself. This master, the Bishop explains, "should be expert in speech and knowledge, yet descending to the level of knowledge of those who do not understand. And it helps to use simple and everyday language that they can understand! Therefore, anyone among his listeners who is of keener intelligence and can easily follow along challenges the master and he rouses them. Seeing people like that, he calls on them for they enable the teacher to pause over humbler and more basic questions. In the end, the rest are even able to follow."[17] The process, moreover, is analogous to that followed by Ambrose in composing his hymns: these are full of theology and biblical allusions, but this aspect does not hinder their comprehension nor impede the assembly from being enchanted and singing them with gusto. On the contrary, those contents, in the hymns as in the homilies, rightly consist in an object of lively interest, feeding the passion of the listener and encouraging comprehension.

Before concluding, I would like to take up again certain citations from his treatise *On the Six Days of Creation* with which this chapter began. In this writing Ambrose, going over the various stages of creation, was pleased to describe with refined taste this or that natural fact, or a particular aspect of the vegetable or animal world. Here is a beautiful example from the third day: when God says, "Let the earth bring forth vegetation, every kind of plant that bears seed" (Gn 1:11) Ambrose imagines a field in flower, and he approaches it full of wonder: "But what a spectacle is the meadow in full bloom, what fragrance, what an attraction, what a delight for the farmers!" Then he enters into detail, making use of the rhetorical figure of omission. "Why describe the violets with their deep purple color, the white lilies, the vermillion roses, the fields now tinted in gold, now variously painted, now covered with saffron yellow flowers, in which you do not know which gives you greater pleasure, the sight of the flowers or their penetrating fragrance? The eyes graze over this pleasing vision while the fragrance spreads far and wide filling us with its sweet exhalation." Concerning 'fragrance', as I have already indicated, we will return to it again because from its symbolism the Bishop constructs a very rich spiritual teaching. Instead, our passage continues with the citation of the psalm verse, placed on the lips of that same Creator and which in the Latin of Ambrose reads: "The beauty of the field belongs to me" (Ps 49/50.11). "It belongs to him," the Bishop comments, "because he himself fashioned it: indeed, what other craftsman would be able to express such great beauty in his creatures one by one?" In the preceding list he named the lilies; Jesus too recommended that they be observed to grasp with what care the Father makes them grow. The Bishop expresses this in a most delicate description: "'Consider the lilies of the field' (Mt 6:28), how white their petals, how close one to another, how from the bottom to the top they grow in a manner that reproduces the form of a goblet, how inside they almost seem to glow like gold which, defended on all sides by the protection of its petals, is not exposed to any harm." Jesus had good reason, concludes Ambrose, in affirming that "neither Solomon, in all his glory, is arrayed like one of these" (Mt 6:29). In fact, "If one might pick this flower and pluck its petals, what craftsman's hand would be able to reshape it in the form of the lily? No one would be able to imitate nature with such perfection as to presume to reconstruct this flower!"[18]

As with the meadows, we want to take a look at the sea, as Ambrose invites us. Commenting on the fifth day of creation, we witness a vision more luminous yet. After having spoken amply about fish

Chapter XV: In the Service of the Word

and having made a special mention of the great whales, the Bishop admires the corals, the pinne and the murex from which purple is extracted. The pinne are particular bivalve mollusks that secrete filaments which, coagulating on contact with water, are used by the animal to fix it to a host. Ambrose makes reference to them describing them with wonder as "golden wool" that he says is produced by the sea itself: he makes a point of talking about those filaments which are collected and woven into a soft cloth of a golden brown color, otherwise called marine silk or "byssus." At this point the Bishop is seized with enthusiasm and exclaims: "What enchantment of the meadows or what offerings from the garden can equal the tint of the sky colored sea? It may be true that the flowers of the fields have a golden glow, and the glory of gold flashes in sea-wool, while these quickly fade, this itself lasts for a long while." And since one comparison attracts another, notice the next image: "The white lilies in the garden stand out in the distance; on the boats the white of the sails stands out; there a sweet odor wafts, here the wind." He then passes to a more utilitarian observation, but immediately discovers curious and frivolous aspects as well: "What usefulness do petals have? On ships, rather, how much commerce! The lilies bring pleasure to the sense of smell; the sail, human survival. Add to this flying fish, dolphin's games, the sound of flutes with their hoarse murmur; add to this the ships that rapidly approach the beach or depart from it."[19] At the resumption of this same discourse following a brief pause for rest, the Bishop, passing to the description of the flying creatures, would conclude with the expression that we all know: "I have no fear that in following the flights of birds boredom would overtake us… or that someone might fall asleep in the course of the exposition.…"[20] We can well believe him: it was not easy to be distracted listening to him!

CHAPTER XVI

Concern for the Churches

The activities of Ambrose cannot be restricted to the city of Milan alone. We have seen him occupied with quite a broad range of religious questions and political problems. As regards his interventions in the ecclesiastical arena, he manifested that "concern for all the churches" which animated the Apostle Paul (2 Cor 11:28) and which the biographer Paulinus did not hesitate to attribute to the Bishop of Milan.[1] Because of this Ambrose made several trips, including some quite far from his see. For example, around 376 he went to Sirmium for the election of the new Bishop of that city. In September of 381 he guided the famous Council against Palladius and Secundus at Aquileia. The following year he went to Rome for another meeting under the chairmanship of Pope Damasus. And following that, the Bishop was kept busy in many other important trips. In this chapter, pursuing the narrative up to the death of Theodosius, we come across two of his trips in particular: one to Capua, at the beginning of 392, to preside at a Council; the other to Bologna, Faenza and Florence in the spring of 393 until the following summer, in order to avoid running into the usurper Eugenius in Milan.

The period that we are addressing is dense with political events which both involve and influence the actions of Ambrose. Therefore, before focusing our attention on the trips of the Bishop and on his teaching in these years, it is appropriate to go over those events, beginning with the spring of 392 when, on May 15, Valentinian II died. There were serious conflicts in these months between the Emperor and the count Arbogastes, a Frankish general whom Theodosius had placed beside the young Emperor after the reconquest of the West against Maximus. Valentinian, only 20 years old, wanted to free himself from the influence of Arbogastes and make himself more autonomous. From Vienne, to which he had been transferred from Trier, he pressed for a visit from Ambrose, expressing his desire to receive baptism from him and at the same time also wanting some "guarantee" of his "good faith toward the count." In his discourse *On the Death of Valentinian* Ambrose confesses that, without presuming on his own ability, with kindness and zeal he had sought "to bring peace and good harmony" between the Emperor and his general, and that in any case, "if the count would not bend," he would remain on Valentinian's side.[2] Thus, after some uncertainty due to the false announcement of the imminent arrival of the Emperor in Milan, the Bishop left. But at the moment he crossed the Alps he was informed of the death of the one whom he had finally gone to visit. A rumor was spread that Valentinian had committed suicide but, while not being able to establish if or in what way Arbogastes himself may have been the instigator, Ambrose always remained convinced that he had been the victim of homicide.

In the following months the situation remained confused. The body of the Emperor was transferred to Milan. Ambrose waited for instructions from Theodosius before proceeding with the burial. But only toward the end of June did Theodosius write to the Bishop, giving certain instructions regarding the funeral; and Ambrose gained nothing by responding to him anxiously and by asking for further instructions. In the end, on a Sunday in August in 392, in the presence of his sisters and the Milanese people, the solemn funeral of Valentinian was celebrated. Already in a letter to Theodosius, the Bishop, recalling the pro-Arian past of the deceased, even if it was inappropriate to exonerate him of responsibility for those actions, maintained that he did so "not to remember old wrongs, but to give testimony to his conversion." Turning to Theodosius and recalling the influence which the Emperor had had on the conversion of Valentinian he added: "His first position was due to others; his own, rather, was this that, influenced by you, he maintained it to such a point that it excluded the influence of his mother."[3] In his talk Ambrose, along with his other virtues, again praised the Emperor's ability to correct himself and he sums up: "We admit that we ought to be sad because

Chapter XVI: Concern for the Churches

he died while still young, but we ought to rejoice because he left us a veteran in the service of virtue." While also recalling the humble episodes of his life, which we already know, he remembers above all that Valentinian was finally welcomed into the Divine dwelling place.

In regards to this proposition the Bishop knew that the Emperor had not received the sacrament of Christian initiation, but he asks him not to be saddened by this fact because, he explains, on the part of an individual only "the intention, the request to receive" the sacrament is required. And Valentinian, a little before his death "had expressed this desire; did he not have the grace which he had insistently requested? And since he had requested it, he received it." Just as the martyrs who were still only catechumens "are baptized by their blood" so Valentinian "was baptized by his devotion and by his will." Later on, describing Gratian who welcomes his stepbrother into heaven, Ambrose imagines Gratian turning to Valentinian saying: "No one else but Christ has illuminated you with spiritual grace; he has baptized you, because you lacked any human intervention."[4] In the light of faith even the sad tragedy of Valentinian's death is transfigured; and the ancient wrongs which the Bishop had suffered at the hands of the deceased are sincerely forgotten and completely overcome in a vision of peace.

With the death of Valentinian, unfortunately, a period of further upheaval was opened. On August 22, 392, Arbogastes proclaimed Eugenius the Emperor. Due to the "wait-and-see" attitude of Theodosius, who did not clarify his political approach toward the new ruler, and through the fastidious rapprochement of Eugenius toward pagan customs, Ambrose had no desire to have any contact with him and, as he records in the letter which he wrote later while away from Milan, he responded to neither of two missives which he had been sent. Only "when reasons for ministry arose" would he intervene "in the interest of those who were anxious about their fate" because of the intervening political change.[4] In the end, to avoid meeting Eugenius in the city in the spring and summer of 393, Ambrose left Milan for a long voluntary exile in Bologna, Faenza, and Florence. In the meantime, to explain his decision, he sent Eugenius the letter already cited, in which he threw in his face the fact that he had made gifts to the exponents of paganism; thus Eugenius, for having refused to intervene against laws favoring paganism, had demonstrated a dangerous concession in these regards, after these had already been denied consistently by Gratian, by Theodosius, and by Valentinian II.

Because of this Ambrose left Milan in order not to violate his "fear of the Lord," which alone inspired his actions. "I offend no one," he clarified, "if I prefer God to everyone and, confiding in him, I do not fear to say to you Emperors what is in my capacity to say, that is, what I feel." Thus he wished to speak frankly to Eugenius. In fact he had chosen exile, a form of removal which would allow him not to be subjected to pressures of any sort, precisely to demonstrate his own opposition to the compromise which Eugenius had made. He added that this was not a personal contest: "To one to whom I have shown deference in the intimacy of my heart when he was a private person, why would I not show deference to him once he had become Emperor?" But one must not betray the essential: "You, who expect to have our respect, allow us to render our respects to him whom you wish to acknowledge as protector of your Empire."[5] The exile of Ambrose must have lasted until the beginning of August of the following year. Reentering Milan, he brought with him from Florence, as many commentators suggest,[6] that Paulinus who would remain at his side as a faithful secretary and from whom we have heard many times as his diligent biographer. In the meantime the situation evolved: Theodosius had decided to attack Eugenius, who had, in turn, left Milan to confront Theodosius in the open field. The battle was fought on the river Frigidus (today, Vipacco, a tributary of the Isonzo, in Slovenia), on the 5th and 6th of September, 394. Eugenius was defeated and killed by the army of Theodosius, while Arbogastes committed suicide. In the letter which the Bishop sent to the victor by the hand of the deacon Felix, he interceded with Theodosius, as he had after the defeat of Maximus, "in favor of those who, requesting mercy, have sought refuge in the Church."[7] This missive was preceded by another in which Ambrose rejoiced with the Emperor for the victory and praised him for having requested a celebration of thanksgiving

Chapter XVI: Concern for the Churches

to God: "Other Emperors, when conquering, construct triumphal arches and other trophies; your Clemency prepares a sacrifice to the Lord in his honor and desires that through the Bishops an offering and a giving of thanks will be fulfilled." He further describes the ritual gesture that was completed: "I carried the letter of your Piety to the altar with me and placed it there; I held it in my hand while offering the sacrifice, so that through my voice your faith might speak and the august text might assume the function of a priestly offering." Even this letter ends with a mention to pardon "above all those who remain guilty in your sight."[8] Thus is confirmed, alongside the other characteristics of Ambrose, his delicate and considerate compassion toward those unhappy ones whom every war leaves behind.

On the 17th of January, 395, as we know, Theodosius passed away leaving his two young sons, Arcadius and Honorarius, to guide the Empire. In his *On the Death of Theodosius* delivered on the 25th of February, Ambrose recommended the two young Augustii to the general Stilicho,[9] who had assumed the burden of regent, and to the faithful support of the army. And, as we have already assessed, he underscored the Christian principles that now must govern the empire, while with great affection he recalled the figure of the departed Emperor. He concluded by adding to it the memory of Gratian, both now "no longer protected by the arms of soldiers, but by their merits, dressed not in purple vestments, but in the mantle of glory." And if Theodosius, as the Scriptures affirm, "had borne a heavy yoke from his youth" (Lm 3:27), nonetheless "even if he had lived here amidst trials, there he is in peace." Now his body will be transferred to Constantinople. Ambrose felt compelled to add "surrounded by the army in full array." He returns now "more powerful and more glorious because he is escorted by bands of angels and is accompanied by a throng of saints." Truly blessed is Constantinople, which receives "a citizen of paradise and which in the august residence where his body will be buried," safeguards "an inhabitant of the celestial city."[10] In these years, then, and in the course of these events, Ambrose embarked on the two trips already indicated. Let us begin with the one which he undertook in 392, thus prior to the death of Valentinian, when he went to Capua to participate in a Council that was held in that city.[11] Ambrose convoked a court to intervene once again in the Antiochene schism. As we recall, together with the Bishops of the Council of Aquileia, Ambrose had defended Paulinus who was the legitimate Bishop of Antioch against the newly elected Flavian. Now he summoned to Capua both the latter and — Paulinus being dead by now — his successor Evagrius, whom we had seen many years earlier at Milan while still a layperson, in opposition to Auxentius. But Evagrius had gathered around himself a very small number of faithful, while Flavian governed practically the entire Antiochean Church and was better known than virtually any other Oriental Bishop. Flavian, moreover, having obtained from the Emperor a rescript which authorized his absence, was not present at Capua and so the efforts of Ambrose were in vain, which would have otherwise sufficed to defer the whole business to the Bishop of Alexandria, Theophilus, so that he might complete a thorough investigation and judge it on its merits. But, as with his intervention of 381, the impression remains that Ambrose was not very effective in that affair which was already resolved for all practical purposes.

In any case, the last expression of the letter with which Ambrose explained the matter to Theophilus is significant: "We maintain that our holy brother, the Bishop of the Church of Rome, ought to be informed, so that presuming that you pronounce a judgment which would not be in any way unwelcome to him…; in a way that we too…, well knowing that a resolution of your decisions has been approved by the Church of Rome, will happily rejoice in the results of such a request."[12] Siricius at the time was the Bishop of Rome, and that same Siricius will establish relations of full communion with Flavian in 398, immediately following the death of Ambrose. We might note the respect which the Bishop of Milan demonstrated for Roman authority: his interventions on a universal level do not express an equivocation in his dealings with that See, but were above all conceived in consonance with it and in dutiful respect to its prerogative.

At Capua Bonosus was also discussed. He was a Bishop from Illiricum who went about denying the perpetual virginity of Mary.

Chapter XVI: Concern for the Churches

Because, according to certain evidence, the See of Bonosus was in Serdica (today, Sofia in Bulgaria) or Naisso (today, Niš in Serbia), it was not within the jurisdiction of the Council and the Fathers did not consider themselves in the right to take a position against him, but requested that Anisius of Thessalonica complete a full investigation and provide evidence. Nonetheless Ambrose did not abstain from confronting the doctrinal question which Bonosus raised. During a Council held in Milan, possibly at mid-year in 392,[13] he wanted to send a letter to Anisius, from which we have taken the news just expressed,[14] in which he proposed again the doctrine of the virginity of Mary even following childbirth. The letter, written in the name of the Council but added for us to the epistolary of Ambrose, is also attributable to him for its content. In fact, regarding the virginity of Mary even after the birth of Christ, Ambrose added one of his typical arguments[15] that hinges on the words spoken by Jesus on the cross to his mother and the Apostle John, in which, closing his earthly sojourn, he entrusts Mary to the beloved disciple (cf. Jn 19:26-27).

Commentators, arguing that Joseph was already dead, see in this gesture, above all, the compassionate attention of the dying Jesus toward his mother, that she might not be left alone after the events of the crucifixion. Ambrose, however, maintained that the marriage between Mary and Joseph was in appearance only and not real. Thus it could serve as the basis for defending the mystery of the virginal birth from any scandal. Ambrose thought that at the death of her son she could have been entrusted to John. From that moment the marriage had served its purpose. The Bishop defends this singular interpretation in other compositions as well but we cannot count it among the authentic justifications that support the virginity of Mary. These exercises, while pausing on them, do allow us to approach a parallel and nearly contemporaneous text wherein Ambrose, returning to the argument, develops a fascinating image of the Virgin Mary.

It is treated in a passage entitled *The Education of a Virgin,* which we already know to have been derived from a homily delivered at Bologna in 392 for the vows of the virgin Ambrosia and distributed the following year in the same city. In this passage Ambrose, alluding again to the error of Bonosus, recalls the episode of Christ on the cross according to the interpretation already referred to and, commenting on the gesture of the disciple who "from that moment took" Mary "into his home" (Jn 19:27), concludes with the rhetorical question: "With whom might the virgin be allowed to live, if not with him who, being heir of the son, knew that he was the protector of her virginal integrity?" Mary is thus imagined at the foot of the cross and Ambrose further pauses to contemplate that scene, to intuit the profound values that animate it, beginning with virginity, here but presented, with correct intuition, as the virtue which roots itself in the strength of Mary: "The mother stands before the cross, and while men flee, she bravely remains. Consider whether the mother of Jesus could have lost all shame, she who did not lose courage." But Ambrose presses to underline the participation of Mary in the mystery of Christ: she in fact "observed with pious eyes the wounds of her son, through which she saw the future redemption of all. She stood, not disgraced by the spectacle in which she had no fear of the killers. The son hung on the cross; the mother offered herself to the persecutors...; knowing that her son had died for all, she was ready in case her death might add something to the welfare of all. But the passion of Christ was in no need of aid."[16] Alongside the Marian theme, Ambrose also developed that of virginal consecration. In the first months of 393, before leaving for Bologna, he called a Council at Milan to take a position against Jovinian. He, a monk operating in Rome, had wanted to react to the exaggerated affirmations of Jerome, which, by defending consecrated virginity, went so far as to detract from the dignity of matrimony. But to defend matrimony, Jovinian went to the opposite extreme of contesting the specific values of monastic life, negating the particular merits associated with the choice of virginal consecration and effectively declaring that abstaining is no different from not abstaining. At the beginning of 393 Pope Siricius called his own priests together in a synod and officially took the position against this doctrine and against the negative influence which it had among monks and virgins.

Ambrose, on receiving the encyclical letter of the Roman

Chapter XVI: Concern for the Churches

Council containing the condemnation of Jovinian and eight of his companions, immediately called a synod participated in by eight Bishops under his guidance and a priest representing the Bishop of Modena. The concluding letter from this Milanese tribunal, signed by the Council Fathers and sent to the Pope, beyond confirming the condemnation of Jovinian and his companions, made reference to their doctrine, paralleling it to "a howling savage" and describing it as "having no love for virginity nor chastity as a state of life, a desire to confuse everything indiscriminately, to do away with a hierarchy among diverse rewards and to introduce a certain kind of poverty as a celestial recompense." Instead, the letter adds, Christ himself "chose virginity for himself, as a special gift, and demonstrated the virtue of purity manifesting in his own person that which he had chosen in his mother."[17]

We are already aware of the motives that render consecrated virginity full of significance and value in the eyes of Ambrose. Here, rather, we continue to review his attention to this theme in places to which he travelled as an exile from Milan in those long months. Returning to Bologna, as we have already recalled, Ambrose distributed the writing entitled *The Education of a Virgin*; we remember too that at Bologna he assisted in the discovery of the remains of the martyrs Agricola and Vitalis. He then moved on to Faenza, where he received an invitation to go to Florence. He would have willingly consented because, as Luigi Franco Pizzolato rightly indicates, "the Florentine invitation summarized that theme around which the spirituality and pastorality of Ambrose revolved at the time: that of martyrdom, of the consecration of widows and virgins, and of ecclesiastical service."[18] In fact, as we know, Ambrose was called to Florence by Juliana, a consecrated widow who, with her own money, dedicated a basilica very likely to the martyr Lawrence. And Ambrose, for his part, brought with him relics of Agricola, pausing to remember, during the celebration, the two Bolognese martyrs and the recent recovery of their remains. Moreover, diverse expressions of consecration to the service of the Church were expressed in the family of Juliana, all singularly bound by the bonds of kinship: the ministry of priesthood by the son,

Lawrence, who would have completed his own service in the church about to be dedicated; the virginal consecration of three daughters, who were ready to receive the veil; and of widowhood in that same Juliana, recently deprived of a husband and completely dedicated to the service of God and of the Church.

In the homily delivered on the occasion, distributed with the title *Exhortation to Virginity*, Ambrose pulls these themes together and deepens them, and in a moving prayer he concludes by taking up the fundamental point, first establishing a parallel between the consecration of the Church to God and that personal consecration of virgins, then between the Eucharistic sacrifice that he celebrated in the temple and that of the daughters of Juliana who offered themselves to God in their virginal life. Let us listen: "Now I entreat you, O Lord, preside over this house daily, over these altars which today are dedicated to you, over these spiritual stones, which are consecrated to you as a living temple; and listen in your divine mercy to the prayer that your servants offer you in this place. May every sacrifice that will be offered to you in this temple with pure faith and devoted concern be for you as a fragrance of holiness. And while looking upon that victim of salvation, through whom the sin of this world is cancelled, turn your attention also to these victims of devoted chastity and protect them with your incessant help. May such victims so pleasing to Christ the Lord, become for you a delicate perfume; and make them worthy to preserve entire and pure their spirit, their soul, and their body without complaint until that day of our Lord Jesus Christ."[19] In this context it merits mention that the monastic choice had matured in those months by a person of a noble and rich senatorial family, Paulinus of Nola, concerning whose conversion Ambrose had influenced in significant measure.[20] Paulinus, in fact, writing in 395 or in the following year, to Alipius, a friend of Augustine, with sincere gratitude referred to Ambrose with the appellative "Father," and even while recording his having received baptism from the hands of Delfinus of Bordeaux and his priestly ordination from Lampius of Barcelona, recognized his having "always been nourished in the faith by the benevolence of Ambrose" and to have been "sustained by him to this day in priestly orders." The Bishop of Milan, he adds, "wanted to claim me as a member of his clergy, in such a way that, despite living far apart I might be considered his priest."[21] The priestly ordination was conferred in 394, when he was still living in Spain; there Paulinus together with his wife Terasia, had matured his choice of undivided adhesion to the Gospel which led him to sell his enormous wealth and to go to Nola to undertake an ascetic lifestyle with his wife and other confreres.

The gesture of Paulinus in renouncing his wealth gave rise to a powerful scandal, of which we have a prelude in a letter of Ambrose to the Bishop Sabinus of Piacenza. Ambrose, first of all, describes the event as he knew it: Paulinus "sold both his own belongings and those of his wife, and he himself adopted, in conformity with his faith, a tenor of life such that he left the money he had put together for the care of the poor and made himself poor, as one relieved of a serious burden, bid adieu to house, country, even his own kin to serve God with greater commitment." The Bishop then went on to indicate the mighty outburst and violent reaction which all of this caused among members of the Roman aristocracy: "When important men heard this news, what did they say? 'A member of an illustrious family, a descendent of a line so eminent, so blessed by nature, provided with such eloquence, to have abandoned the senate, to have broken the succession of his noble estate: it is something that cannot be tolerated!' They might shake their heads and lift their eyebrows were one of them to become a follower of the cult of Isis, but if a Christian were to change clothes in order to practice our holy religion in a more perfect way they call this a shameful crime."[22] But neither the gossip of the conformists nor the doctrine of Jovinian and his companions could curb the choice of these new ascetics. As for the rest, the reactions of their mothers did not impede the young people who listened to the preaching of Ambrose from joyously fulfilling their virginal consecration.

But let us turn again to Florence where Ambrose had dedicated the church constructed by the widow Juliana. A later tradition recounts that while there he would have met Zanobius, yet a priest, and that upon his recommendation the Florentine community would have chosen that prominent priest as their Bishop.[23] The biographer Paulinus, in any case, though he wrote the *Life of Ambrose* while Zanobius was actually exercising the episcopacy in Florence,[24] does not attest to such a meeting. In any case this story reminds one of the numerous episcopal ordinations carried out by Ambrose in many places, sometimes even quite distant from his own See; and, more generally, we are drawn back to his interventions across a wide range, in more complex ecclesiastical affairs, which clearly show his pastoral concern. Thus the Bishop of Milan broadened his perview all the way to Illiricum, to Constantinople, and to Antioch; and he involved yet other various Sees in his actions: that of Alexandria, after the Council of Capua; and the Churches of Africa and of Gaul at the Council of Aquileia.

But Ambrose paid his special attention to the churches closer to Milan. In those years, in fact, he created the institution of the "Metropolitan" in a form appropriate also in the West.[25] It partners, that is, the ecclesial life in the province (or "metropolis") with a primary see of greater profile, whose Bishop assumed something of a particular dignity and the authority of a "Metropolitan" in his dealings with the provincial churches. At Milan this reality would have had its first known manifestation with the episcopacy of Ambrose, again thanks to the exceptional personality of the Bishop and the importance acquired by the city as an imperial residence. The territory over which Ambrose exercised the authority of a Metropolitan spread beyond the confines of the civil province of Emilia-Liguria — encompassing today's regions of Lombardia, Emilia-Romagna, Piemonte and Liguria — and came to cover a good part of other provinces in the civil dioceses of northern Italy. In this geographical area, therefore, more directly subject to the pastoral concern of Ambrose, his actions were quite intensive. It suffices to recall, by way of example, the Bishops whom he provided for many of those churches by electing and ordaining them.

A few months before his death, as we will see in one of the next chapters, Ambrose resolved the difficult succession in the See of Vercelli, where Honoratus would be elected; and he even went to Pavia for the nomination of Bishop Profuturus. Furthermore, according to a testimony of the 9th century attributed to Ramperto di Brescia, Ambrose had also ordained Dominatorus, the third Bishop of Bergamo.[26] In the case of Brescia, however, it is the same Gaudentius, successor of Philastrius, who attests to being consecrated by Ambrose, it is believed around 390. This is referred to in his *Discourse Offered on the First Day of Ordination*: it was his "blessed father Ambrose" who, together with other Bishops, urged him by sending letters to the Orient, where Gaudentius was found at the moment of his election, to urgently recall him home: "letters of such precise import that I really could not have resisted any further without damning my soul, since I would have been denied the communion of salvation even by the Bishops of the East, had I not promised to return among you."

Further, the new Bishop, confessing his own inadequacy to comment on the sacred texts, said he wanted to ask "our common father Ambrose" to intervene personally "to irrigate your hearts with the mysteries of the divine Scriptures;" and he assured: "He will speak through the Holy Spirit, of which he is full, and from the center of his being (*ventre**) rivers of living waters will flow and, as the successor to the apostle Peter, he will be the mouthpiece of all the Bishops who surround him," in the same way that Peter at Caesarea confessed Jesus to be the "Son of the Living God" (Mk 16:16).[27] Here Gaudentius, with a pairing which at first reading seems rash but certainly efficacious, without otherwise confusing the dignity of Ambrose with that of the Bishop of Rome, intended rather to parallel the profession of Peter who, first from among the apostles, had confessed Christ the Son of God with the teaching of Ambrose who, in a preeminent position among his confrere Bishops, had preached and defended the doctrine of the divinity of Christ against the Arians.[28] Como too owed the ordination of one of its Bishops to Ambrose: in this case, as a matter of fact, Ambrose founded the Church of Como by sending Felix[29] as its first prelate. His ordination, as Ambrose explicitly indicates in a letter addressed to him, was on the 1st of November, very likely in the year 386. That missive also contained the invitation, which

Ambrose transmitted to Felix on the part of Bassianus of Lodi and whose affirmative response he vouched for, to participate together at Lodi at the dedication of a basilica in honor of the apostles. The extremely cordial tone that Ambrose assumes in dealing with Felix indicates a warm friendship between the two. Notice how full of subtle wit are the words of Ambrose: "I therefore made a promise in your name, since you too would do the same for me: I promised him, never doubting myself that it would be kept; I presume in fact that you will come, because you ought to come. My promise does not oblige anything more of you than your own usual mode of acting, because it is your norm to do what is proper. I report this to you, though, as one who knows your soul that I have not been rash in promising this, in assuming a commitment on behalf of a brother. Come, then, so as not to embarrass two Bishops: you, because you have not come, and me, because I have promised such so lightly."

Even at the beginning of this communique Ambrose shows a sincere openness, full of confidence, toward the letter's recipient: "Though physically indisposed, still when I read the words dictated from your heart in unison with mine, I received no small aid to regaining my health, restored, that is to say, by the thought behind your kind words and, at the same time, because you let me know that tomorrow, a solemn day for both of us, was the day on which you took the helm as high priest." Indeed, it was on the 1st of November when Ambrose had ordained Felix Bishop.[30] Equally well-known is the card that Ambrose sent to him in thanksgiving for the extraordinarily large truffles that Felix had sent him. Ambrose, in any case, reproached Felix because he had substituted with that gift a visit that he had promised: "A welcome gift, not in such a way as to suppress my legitimate complaint, because for a long time now without good reason you have not visited those of us who love you." Certainly the fact that Felix felt obliged to excuse himself with such a gift ought to be appreciated! But Ambrose wanted something else entirely: "In the future, then, don't make excuses; in fact, although these excuses of yours give me some advantages you make a bad impression, or rather you cause me to make one if you believe that you can compensate your absence with presents or buy me with gifts."[31] Letters and cards full of good humor, indicating cordial understanding and pure confidence: Ambrose knew how to cultivate friendship. In any case, he never forgot that even in these simple and informal contacts, he revitalized his care for the pastoral life. In the letter containing the invitation to go to Lodi, Ambrose prompted Felix to dedicate himself generously to ministry. You, he recalls, "fight the good fight" for Christ (cf. 1 Tm 1:18), "for him you guard what has been entrusted to your care (cf. 1 Tm 6:20)… when he has seen that you are a good administrator, he will give you the *many* in exchange for the *few*; and such will be for me the sweetest fruit, because it will be a confirmation of my judgment concerning you, the ordination that you have received 'through the imposition of my hands' (2 Tm 1:6) and with the blessing of the name of the Lord Jesus, will not be criticized. Accomplish your ministry (cf. 2 Tm 4:5), so that you will find recompense on that day, and I in you and you in me will find rest." And if in the city of Como the response to his preaching has been generous and many have turned to the faith but they still lack workers for the harvest because "it is difficult to find people to help," there is still no need to despair. "This is an old story," Ambrose observes, "because the Lord is able to summon workers to his harvest (cf. Mt 9:37-38). Certainly from among the decurions of Como (officers in command of ten men in the army of ancient Rome and/or members of a municipal senate who ran the local government) many have already begun to believe in your Master and have heard the word of God through your instruction. But he who has provided the faithful, will also provide the helpers." It is noted that such an outcome will achieve, among other things, a surge of helpers "so that your need to apologize for seldom coming to see me will be removed, and I shall more often have the oft-repeated favor of your company!"[32]

Thus, in a context of abundant optimism and subtle irony, the profound concern for the Churches which animated Ambrose is inserted in his passionate taste for friendship, "that most beautiful reality of all things on earth," to use his expression in the treatise *On the Duties of the Clergy*. Because in friendship, the Bishop continues, you experience the consolation of "having a person to whom you can open your heart, with whom you can share your secrets, with whom you can confide the intimacy of your heart"; and thus you are able "to count on a faithful person who in times of happiness rejoices with you, in sadness suffers with you, and in persecution counsels you."[33]

CHAPTER XVII

Effusive Fragrance and Sober Inebriation

The Song of Songs, a Book of the Bible of limited scope but quite original in its content, passes before the reader a fascinating sequence of hymns in which a married couple reveal their mutual love, their passionate feelings, their intense desire to be together, the missed encounters and the uninterrupted search for the beloved. Ambrose, we know, commented extensively on this book to inspire the reader, and beginning in the years 385-7 he made ample reference to it as had, a century earlier, Origen of Alexandria. Jerome, whom we know often lashed out in his judgments and who in the second phase of his life had heavily attacked the thought of the Alexandrian, in his *Prologue* to the translation of his *Homilies on the Song of Songs,* gravely affirms that: "Origen, who in other books surpasses all others, in the Song of Songs surpasses himself."[1] Following Origen and in fact applying his norms of the criteria for reading the sacred word, Ambrose, in the archaic hymns of love of the Song, searches for the mystical sense wherein they speak of Christ and his mysteries. Thus, in the two spouses, he looks with a view to reveal the entire economy of salvation, the marriage between Christ and his Church and, on the personal level, the union of the soul with God. It is significant that the two principal spiritual works of the Bishop, the *Commentary on Psalm 118* and the treatise *On Isaac or the Soul* are pointedly devoted to develop first the one and then the other of these aspects. Similarly, I would like to dwell on the essential elements of the spiritual teaching of Ambrose, emphasizing in particular these two works which a recent theory proposes were collected in the years 395 and 396,[2] that is, in the months following the death of Theodosius.

Before entering into this theme, however, I would like to discuss certain examples of the commentary that Ambrose made on a brief text of the Song of Songs. It has to do with an expression spoken by the wife in the prologue of the book, the one where, dwelling on the beloved in a passionate soliloquy, after having confessed her urgent desire to be able to explore the sweetness of love, she pauses to admire her beloved and the fragrance* of the perfumes in which he is enveloped and exclaims: "Your name spoken is an effusive perfume" (Sg 1:3).[3] The perfume, with the correlative image of aroma, of a sweet fragrance, of the oil and unguents that give off a fragrance, of flowers that spread their pleasing effulgence,* recur other times in the Song of Songs: especially in the continuation of that verse where the wife, in the name of her companions, exclaims: "We will follow after you, running, following the fragrance of your clothes" (Sg 1:4). Further along we find the two lovers who express the pleasure of their meeting with the expression: "My nard gives forth its fragrance" (Sg 1:12). And another time the wife, rising to open the portal to her beloved, describes herself with hand and fingers immersed in the myrrh which is "dripping from my fingers... on the fittings of the lock" (Sg 5:5); and the references are still more numerous. Following the principle of the "clustering" of citations, Ambrose collects and intersperses biblical references between them. Thus he collects and surrounds this first group with other passages from Scripture, forming a rich reference base for commenting.

Here we find, first of all, the Gospel episode of the sinful woman who washes the feet of Jesus in the house of the Pharisee Simon and pours perfumed oil on them (cf. Lk 7:36-50). From the Apostle Paul, Ambrose cites the significant text of the Second Letter to the Corinthians, in which the perfume is seen as a symbol of the evangelization of the people by the disciples and of the different reception with which they were received. Indeed, God, the Apostle explains, "manifests through us the perfume of the knowledge of him in every place"; and as a consequence, "we are before God the fragrance of Christ among those who are being saved and among those who are perishing; to the latter an odor of death that leads to death and for the others an aroma of life that leads to life" (2 Cor 2:14-16). Also the expression according to which Christ "humbled himself making

Chapter XVII: Effusive Fragrance and Sober Inebriation

himself obedient to death, even death on a cross," a fragment of an ancient Christian hymn inserted by Paul into his Letter to the Philippians (2:8), is remembered by the Bishop in this context: the Latin word used to indicate the humiliation of Christ (*exinaniuit semetipsum*) is, in fact the same that the Song of Songs employs to describe the effusion of the perfume (*unguentum exinantium*); which is to say that the perfume which is poured out in great quantity is the image of Christ who has annihilated himself, divested himself of his divine glory, "poured forth" himself out of love.

But let us hear what Ambrose has to say, following as a fundamental thread the long commentary on the evangelical episode of the anointing of Jesus by the sinful woman which the Bishop proposes in his *Commentary on the Gospel of Luke*. That sinful woman, Ambrose states, beginning his explanation, "had in herself the image of a far greater woman, that is, the soul and also the Church, descended to the earth at last to reunite around herself people with his good odor." Another woman is also presented in the Gospels who, at Bethany, anointed on the head of Jesus with an alabaster jar of oil (cf. Mt 26:6-13). The Bishop recognizes that these are two distinct episodes, but he suggests that we see, symbolically, in the two different gestures, a union, the chronological evolution of the spiritual life, from the situation of the sin of the woman who washes the feet of Jesus to the more perfect woman who anoints his head. This last one "starts at the head of Christ... spreads the odor of his merits." In her is realized the Pauline expression: "We are, for God, the good odor of Christ." And it is true, comments Ambrose, that "the life of the just, giving off a good odor, honors God." Thus at the beginning of his reflection is illustrated what will be the conclusion of the journey, when the disciples manifest in their comportment "the fragrance of a good life in their right actions."

But it is necessary to return to the first phase, in which one is still a sinner, to understand where one gets the perfume, and in what way it is received and grasped, and further, how it is diffused. The Gospel narrative confirms that the sinful woman had the ointment with her. She obviously approached Jesus to receive pardon and to change her life; for this reason she does not stop kissing his feet, "knowing of no other way of speaking than wisely, knowing of no other way of loving than justly, knowing of no other way of kissing than purely; knowing of no other way of kissing than modestly." How is it that the sinful woman had perfume with her? Because, the Bishop clarifies, she is the image of the Church, and the Church "assumes the figure of the sinful woman from the moment that Christ himself assumes the aspect of a sinner." The Church, therefore, does not possess the perfume of itself, but receives it from him who has pardoned her, making himself akin to sin, forgiving it, and heaping the sinner with blessings: "To us is given the Son of the Virgin… to us is given Emmanuel, God With Us, to us is given the cross, death and resurrection of the Lord. If Christ has suffered for all, all the same he has suffered in a special way for us because he suffered the passion for the Church." A debt of gratitude results as Ambrose explains with high lyricism: "Since there is nothing that we are able to worthily give in exchange to God — in fact what could we give in exchange for the afflictions suffered by the body that the Lord assumed, what in exchange for the wounds, what in exchange for the cross, his death, the tomb? Woe to me if I do not give love!… Therefore, let us give him love in payment for our debt, charity for blessing, recognition for this richness; he loves the more who has been forgiven more." All of this, then, will have to be made concrete by a precise attitude in response, which will be explained in more detail further on. But here we are above all drawn to grasp the origin of this perfume that has inundated humanity, namely the immolation that Christ makes of himself: "He offered his death for the poor," Ambrose judges.[4]

But in what sense is this perfume the symbol of Christ? A passage from the treatise *On Virgins* may facilitate a reply. Here Ambrose comments on the words of the wife in the Song of Songs who, rising in the night to open to her beloved, has her hands dripping myrrh on the fittings of the lock to open the portal (cf. Sg 5:5). This myrrh, the Bishop explains, is "the perfect fragrance of faith" because "this is the perfume that the soul gives off when it begins to open to Christ." The soul, in fact, believes in him who "has annihilated himself in order to pour out his perfume upon you." It is superfluous to note that here Ambrose alludes to both the "perfume that is poured out" in the Song of Songs and to Christ who "has poured himself out" in the Letter to the Philippians. This comparison is developed in detail: the one who believes "first receives the perfume of the burial of the Lord and believes that his flesh has not experienced corruption nor has it decayed due to the odor of death, but has risen strewn with the perfume of that eternal and always lush flower. How could he whose name is 'ointment that is poured out' become corrupt, even if only in the flesh?" Christ, therefore, is perfume because he is the life that pours itself out; in his burial he did not experience corruption and from death he has triumphed in the resurrection. This perfume, one must clarify in order to complete the picture, from eternity in which "he was with the Father and in the Father," descended to earth. The outpouring is really, first of all, the incarnation of the Word, and further the Word manifest among the people. "This perfume is poured out on the Jews and was collected by the pagans: it was poured out in Judea and gave fragrance to all the earth. By this ointment Mary was anointed and as a virgin she conceived, as a virgin she brought forth the good odor, the Son of God." From that day the perfume has not ceased to be present: "Every day this perfume is poured out and it will never cease." And believers, such as the virgins who are the recipients of this treatise, have to draw near to be filled with this perfume.[5] What, then, will life be like for those who let themselves be bathed in this perfume? They will certainly have faith, as has been indicated in the passage already cited; and above all they will unite themselves to the offering of Christ in an attitude of generous charity. For the rest, Ambrose observes in continuing his commentary on the episode of the sinful woman in the *Commentary on the Gospel of Luke,* "The Lord accepts, not an ointment, but love; he invites faith, he judges humility." Hence the Bishop exhorts: "And you, if you desire grace, grow in love; pour out upon the body of Christ your faith in the resurrection, the perfume of the Church, the ointment of a common charity. Making progress in that way, you will give to the poor." We return thus to that final conclusion which was already indicated in the first line of the passage: whosoever responds in faith and love is precisely the Church, and believers are so in their life of obedience to the Gospel because, as Ambrose recalls — obviously alluding to the passage from the Second Letter to the Corinthians — "we are the perfume of his body."

But, if it is really of the makeup of perfume to diffuse itself out and give of itself, it will also make itself the gift and the propagation of the word it has received. In his concluding passage, the Bishop borrows expressive allusions from the Pauline epistles: "When one gathers the flowers of genuine faith and proclaims Jesus Christ crucified, then the ointment of his faith spreads throughout the whole Church... the whole house begins to smell of the passion of the Lord, begins to smell of death, begins to smell of resurrection, and thus, whoever joins with the holy people is able to say: 'Far be it for me to boast except in the cross of our Lord Jesus Christ' (Gal 6:14). Breathe its fragrance, spread the ointment of his body so long as one is able to say with faith — O that even I could say: 'The world has been crucified to me' (ibid.). The world is crucified to those who do not love riches, to those who do not love worldly honors, to those who do not love what belongs to them but what belongs to Jesus Christ, to those who do not love visible things but rather those that are invisible, to those who are not eager to live but who hurry to die to be with Christ.... This is what it means to take up the cross and follow Christ, such that we also die along with him and with him we are buried together until we are able to exhale the perfume of the ointment that this woman poured out for his burial. It is not an ointment of little value if by its means the name of Christ is spread everywhere. For such a reason it has been said even in a prophetic sense: 'Your name is a spreading perfume' (Sg 1:3)."[6]

In the symbolism of perfume Ambrose finds an expression of the figure of the divine Word that is made human and which pours itself over humanity in the incarnation, spreading himself completely in the passion and on the cross: a perfume of life that in the tomb does not suffer the mortal odor of corruption and in the resurrection manifests the fragrance of immortality. This perfume is communicated to the Church and her disciples thanks to the promulgation of the Gospel and by means of the sacraments: through baptism, as Ambrose assures us in the treatise *On the Sacraments*, recalling the famous Pauline expression, "You indeed are also the good odor of Christ, indeed in you there is no stain of sin, no odor of fault of any grave sin"; and in *On the Mysteries* citing the Song of Songs, he exclaims: "How many souls who loved you, Lord Jesus, are raised up today to new life, saying: 'Draw us behind yourself, we rush following the scent of your clothes' (Sg 1:4), to inhale the scent of the resurrection."[7] Thus the baptized, free of sin and reborn to new life, are taken in to the Eucharistic banquet, tasting the sober inebriation of the Spirit (another image that Ambrose derives from the Song of Songs which will be commented on a bit later). The symbolism of the perfume is completed with the posture required of the disciple, thanks to which he too is permeated with Christ's fragrance: with faith, he truly believes in Christ who is our "effusion," and with the love that unites him to this gift with which Christ has "spread" all of himself in love for the poor and in the further announcement of the Gospel.

Finally we move on to the two key works in the spirituality of Ambrose, yet without abandoning immediately the rich symbolism of perfume. Indeed, in the principal text, *Commentary on Psalm 118* we are confronted with it again. Here we get a phrase full of fantasy and of a fascinating depth, still based on that image. The Bishop is commenting on certain expressions of the Song of Songs in which he speaks of the nard that gives forth its fragrance and of the vineyards of Engedi (cf. Sg 1:12-14). This geographic name permits him to speak of the oozing balsam, a plant which, as far as he knew, was native to that place. The oozing balsam, he explains, is "a tree that, if it is pierced, emits an unguent…. If the tree is not cut, there is neither perfume nor fragrance; when, on the other hand, it is punctured by a skilled hand, it sheds a tear." What are we to make of this singularly symbolic tree? "Christ," the Bishop replies. We are to think specifically of Christ transfixed on the cross by the lance of the soldier: Jesus, in fact, "hanging on the cross, on that tree of temptation, sheds tears over the people in order to wash them of their sins, and from the bowels of his mercy he pours forth ointment saying: 'Father, forgive them because they do not know what they do' (Lk 23:34). So then, hung on that tree, pierced by a lance and even shedding blood and water sweeter than any ointment, a victim acceptable to God spreads the perfume of sanctification over the whole world."

The image of this generous effusion, full of efficacy, is even further amplified: "Thus Jesus, transfixed, pours forth the fragrance of the pardon of sins and redemption. In fact, in becoming man from the Word which he was, he confined himself, and though he was rich he became poor thus enriching us out of his misery; he was powerful yet appeared as one despised, so much so that Herod mocked and derided him; he was able to shake the earth, and still he remained attached to that tree; he could close the heavens in the shadow of darkness and hang the world on a cross, and still he was crucified; he bowed his head, and the Word exited; he became nothing (*exinanitus*!), and yet he filled everything." This is, in the end, the "marvelous exchange" between the divinity and humanity, with the divinity that descends and the humanity that ascends and receives an advantage unheard of and undeserved. Obviously Ambrose thinks that the humanity of Christ is, in itself and thanks to itself, involved in this "exchange." For all humans "God descends, the human being is lifted up; the Word became flesh in order that flesh could reclaim the throne of the Word at the right hand of God; a terrible sore from which an ointment yet flowed." In sum, recalling the expression of another passage in the same *Commentary*: "Christ, fastened to the tree, pours out the good fragrance of redemption upon the world."[8]

And so it is in the *Commentary on Psalm 118*, where Ambrose presents to us the characteristics with which we are now familiar: a taste for the word of Scripture, the poetry to be found in images, the depth and complexity of thought. I have already hinted at the date of this writing, born from a series of homilies preached Sunday after Sunday probably in the second half of 395 and in the first weeks of the following year.[9] The Bishop, as the title of the piece suggests, had commented on Psalm 118 (119), dedicating a homily to each of the 22 eight-line strophes of which this psalm is composed; but Ambrose

Chapter XVII: Effusive Fragrance and Sober Inebriation

also found a way to interweave many passages from the Song of Songs into the principal thread of his explanation. Enough has been said of this biblical book at the beginning of the chapter. Psalm 118, on the other hand, we recall, consists of a prolonged meditation on the Divine Law, revealed by God to his people. The Psalmist expresses his total dedication to the Word of God, his desire to understand it better and to follow it in sincere and loving obedience. In bringing together the two biblical books, Ambrose emphasizes the respective identity of each one as well as their reciprocal connection.

If, therefore, in its most immediate approach, the psalm serves to repeat the moral doctrine, and, conversely, the Song of Songs opens up to the contemplation of the mystical theme of the encounter with God, the union of each aspect with the other permits him to avoid partiality and contrast. As Luigi Franco Pizzolato has observed, "The infiltration of the Song" into his *Commentary on Psalm 118* "serves to reveal the mystical basis and goal of its moral perspective" and, moreover, suggests that one should not seal the psalm off in a purely legalistic perspective, since, from the other point of view, by having drawn the Song itself to the psalm preserves it from the abstraction of the Law and from the pure intellectuality of the mystical doctrine proposed by Ambrose. Thus the two biblical books "maintain between themselves a relationship of opening taken with respect of the one to the other: Psalm 118 is the carrier of a morality already fulfilled in the mystic encounter; the Song traces the unified mystique in the spousal encounter, preparing for it with the discipline of a virtuous life. Thus it seems that the Song is introduced into the *Commentary on Psalm 118* to make much more explicit the mystical perspective that the morality of Psalm 118, as every morality is truly founded, necessarily presumes."[10] The *Commentary on Psalm 118,* as I have hinted, reinterprets all of this in the global experience of the history of salvation. It is, therefore, the Church that must be the conduit for the transmission of the commandments and of the physical and spiritual practices and therefore be the guide toward the mystic encounter, just as the wife is led to union with her divine Spouse. In another writing, however, the treatise *On Isaac or the Soul,* Ambrose, always following the track of the Song of Songs, proposes the same teaching but on the individual level: so, to be called to run that race and to reach the happy finish line of the meeting, this time it is the soul — that is, each believer in his or her own personal experience. The Bishop expressly declares this to be his intent in the passage that we read in the first pages of the treatise. Regarding an expression in the Song of Songs, concerning which he supplies the commentary, indeed Ambrose observes that "some relate" this text "to the Church and to the people of God"; as for himself, he explains, he intends to propose a different interpretation: "Of this mystery I have spoken frequently in other texts, above all in the *Commentary on Psalm 118,* in which my interpretation is that of speaking of the soul."[11] This phrase confirms, among other things, the chronological succession of the two writings and therefore suggests the connection with his treatise *On Isaac or the Soul* at the end of 396.[12]

But how does Ambrose describe this journey, the drawing near, the preparation, the encounter? It is, in fact, by drawing parallels to similar explanations that we are able to arrive at an understanding of the spiritual teaching of the Bishop. In the treatise *On Isaac or the Soul* an outline is proposed and spelled out in four steps that mark out the access of the soul to God.[13] We can reproduce these in quick succession. At the *first* stage the soul discovers, in the depths of its being, the divine reality that has already been impressed there. From there is enkindled the desire for the divine Word and the soul finds its satisfaction in the kiss of the Spouse and in union with him: "He kisses me with the kisses of his mouth" it says in the words of the Song of Songs (1:2). We then come to the *second* stage, in which the soul begins to be aware of itself and cognizant of its darkness; in the Song of Songs, in fact, is confided "do not stare at me because I am dark" (1:6). Thus the dangers arise which may cool the union and lead to the loss of the Word; for this reason many invitations are sent to the soul until it finally realizes its own original beauty, detaches itself from its passions, denies itself and chooses to give its life to the Lord. The *third* stage, as a result, is totally dedicated to a long and engaging passage of ascent and purification.

Chapter XVII: Effusive Fragrance and Sober Inebriation

But it is with the *fourth* and final stage that the soul arrives at the level at which it rediscovers the Word its Spouse and unites with him forever. Thus this encounter is understood as described by Ambrose with the symbols of the table of plenty and the nuptial bed. The table symbolizes the fullness of awareness: at this point the Bishop cites the Song of Songs in which the Spouse says to her beloved: "I would lead you and bring you in" (8:2) and he comments: "If one opens the door to him, the Word will enter and dine (cf. Rv 3:20). Thus the bride takes the Word inside herself, that she might be instructed." The nuptial bed conversely indicates the fullness of love. Citing another verse in the Song of Songs: "Who is this coming up from the desert, leaning on her lover?" (8:5), Ambrose contemplates the bride in a total intimacy with the Word and comments: "In this passage she rises up leaning upon the Word of God. In truth the more perfect ones lean on Christ, just as John had reposed on the chest of Christ. And so she either reclined on Christ or leaned on him or at the very least, since we have been speaking of a wedding, was by now consigned to the right of Christ and was led by her spouse to the nuptial bed."[14]

These are the four stages proposed by the Bishop, with the summit being the fullness of awareness and union in love. The goal is very high and fascinating and includes a vision of God and an intimacy with him which only symbols succeed in perceiving. Moreover, as Ernst Dassmann, carefully studying the spirituality of Ambrose, notes[15] the Bishop does not maintain that along one's temporal life the person can be led to an ecstatic mystical vision, but reserves that for the eternal life in heaven: not because of a sense of weakness or incapacity, but on account of the vital perception of the concreteness and the naturalness of human life, even there where it is led to experience the higher gifts of grace. Beyond that, Ambrose, with the practical optimism that sets him apart, does not lose himself in the vain search or anxiety for such experiences, but recognizes above all the "higher forms of encounter with God in the word and in the sacraments of the Church, forms which in fact do not lack the reality even if they are deprived of the ecstatic character." In other words, the Bishop offers a catechesis on the "normalcy" of the Christian life, a spiritual project for the entire community of the baptized, intimately bound to the "instrumentality" of the Church. The disciple, in fact, experiences God in listening to the word and in participating in the sacraments through which he conquers death and sin and is introduced to the divine mysteries. Moreover it corresponds to the gift of grace by means of an ethical obligation which remains at the root of every nobler spiritual goal. Even more, to cite directly the expression of Ernst Dassmann, "From this moral element, which Ambrosian spirituality also fully preserves in the writings on the Song of Songs, the mystical-ethical characteristics are attenuated. These, in certain parts, confer a particular splendor to the description, and so the sentimentality of the spirituality inspired by the Song of Songs is soberly controlled. Because he avoids placing the encounter with God exclusively in the sphere of mystical-ecstatic experience, it becomes a task, a goal achievable by all, and not the experience of a few."

We may take up again this spiritual approach of Ambrose, at once modest and embracing, "normal" in his expressions and loaded with profound resonance, in the oxymoron of "sober inebriation," which recurs frequently in the writings of the Bishop. We want to approach it as it is presented in *Splendor Paternae Gloriae*, a hymn designated for the morning Office, placing it in context in order to better understand this other highly poetic composition of the Bishop. Ambrose begins with an invocation to Christ:

Splendor paternae gloriae	Splendor of the Father's Glory
De luce lucem proferens	Emanating light from light
Lux lucis et fons luminis	Light of Light and font of Light
Dies dierum inluminans	Day illuminating days
Uerusque sol inlabere	True Sun descending
Micans nitore perpeti	sparkling in perennial brilliance
Iubarque sancti spiritus	the radiance of the Holy Spirit
Infunde nostri sensibus	echoing in our hearts[16]

While we admire the sparks of light that emanate from these two strophes, we remember how fundamental the figure of Jesus[17] is for Ambrose. In the Bishop's homilies we have time and time again considered the union of Christ with man entirely within the mystery of the incarnation, his presence at the heart of the virginal choice, his redemption already prefigured in the origins of the world and after which creation and the entire history of salvation are finally united. For this reason keeping his gaze on Christ the Lord dominates and guides the prayer and spirituality of Ambrose. "Christ stands at the center of Ambrosian spirituality," Ernst Dassmann affirms again: before all and above all, the practical moral interest of Ambrose is to contemplate the life and activity of Jesus and, as a result, to follow and imitate him, "in lively communion of destiny with the Lord, by imitating him, to obtain a participation in Christ." Thus there is tension between the glorious Christ and glorious mystical union with him.[18]

In the hymn, in prayerful contemplation of Christ, the Bishop turns to the Father, petitioning for the day that is dawning and, always in an attitude of prayer, describes the plan of God for the daily life of the person. The Father is well disposed toward the faithful who invoke him: he defends them from Evil, he makes them strong in deed, and they consent to live in his grace. In the next strophe, the sixth, Ambrose returns to speak of Christ and, finally, of the "sober inebriation," in order to close with a review on the day, lived virtuously in each of its parts, and on the Word who reveals himself as the fullness of dawn. Let us listen, then, to the sixth strophe:

Christusque nobis sit cibus	May Christ be our food
Potusque noster sit fides:	and Faith be our drink;
Laeti bibamus sobriam	happily may we drink the sober
Ebrietatem spiritus	inebriation of the Spirit[19]

The reference to food and drink tells us that Christ is the nourishment of faith, sustaining the life of the person, and is also a reminder of that tangible sustenance and intimate union which the faithful receive in the Eucharist. Onto this theme is grafted that of the "sober inebriation," the most beautiful prize that the Holy Spirit gives to those who have welcomed Christ into their life. The strict connection between the Eucharist and inebriation is also found in his treatise *On the Sacraments*, in the passage in which Ambrose comments on the expression of the Song of Songs concerning bread and honey, and the wine and the milk offered at the banquet table of the groom. We are familiar with these images because the Bishop already introduced them to explain his criterion for reading the Scriptures; now we understand that this text concludes with an invitation: "Eat, my brothers, and get drunk" (Sg 5:1). The bread, Ambrose teaches, is that of the Eucharist, a bread in which "there is no bitterness, but every sweetness." The wine recalls a joy that "cannot be contaminated by the stain of any sin" because, the Bishop assures, turning directly to his listeners, "Every time you drink, you receive remission of sins and you are inebriated by the Spirit." Thus surfaces the image of inebriation suggested in the Song of Songs, immediately integrated with the invitation of the Apostle Paul: "Do not get drunk on wine…, but be filled with the Spirit" (Eph 5:18). Finally, the comment follows: "Whoever is drunk on wine, reels and staggers; whoever is inebriated in the Spirit is rooted in Christ. Thus it is an excellent inebriation, because it produces sobriety of the mind."[20]

Among the numerous other pages on this theme we have chosen one more, an exquisite passage from the *Commentary on Psalm 1* in which inebriation is recalled in the careful assimilation of Scripture. The text begins with an invitation to draw on the Old Testament in order to pass sequentially to the New, according to the balanced relationship that we have already come to know: "Drink first of the Old Testament, in order to then drink of the New Testament. If you do not drink of the first, you will not be able to drink of the second. Drink the first to assuage your thirst; drink the second to achieve satiety. In the Old Testament there is affliction, in the New there is happiness." In fact, just as the devil deceived Adam "with fraudulent food," Christ now, "has rescued everyone with the food of salvation." Even more, if Moses in the desert caused water to spring up from the rock, it is Jesus who now gives that thirst-quenching drink. Then, those who drank were satisfied; now they drink and remain

Chapter XVII: Effusive Fragrance and Sober Inebriation

inebriated. The explanation follows: "Good is that inebriation which strengthens the step of a sober mind! Good is the inebriation that irrigates the land of eternal life!" Thus one must draw from the one and the other Testament because, according to the mystical sense, in both, one drinks Christ. The reader therefore allows himself to be overcome by the exhortation:

Drink Christ, for he is the life;
Drink Christ, for he is the rock that showers water;
Drink Christ, for he is the fountain of life;
Drink Christ, who is the river whose currents cheer the city of God;
Drink Christ, who is our peace.

Let us now take note of this very concrete appeal: "Drink Christ, in order to drink his discourse! His discourse is the Old Testament; his discourse is the New Testament. The divine Scripture ought to be drunk daily, the divine Scripture to be devoured daily, so that the sweetness of the eternal word may descend into the veins of the mind and into the energies of the soul."[21] This inebriation therefore is truly sobriety because it is anchored in the reading of Scripture, in receiving the sacraments, and, as we have already emphasized, in searching for the will of God in obedience to the commandments and in imitation of Christ. That which leaves us pleasantly impressed, in the "sober inebriation of the Spirit" taught by Ambrose, consists in being fascinated, not by dreams that intoxicate through ingenious and fantastic illusions, but by reality and in its more genuine actualizations that are realized in the Church and in its members and in their experiences.

CHAPTER XVIII

The "Encounter"

"The ordination of the Bishop of the Church of Pavia having been taken care of, Ambrose fell ill." Thus Paulinus introduces news of the infirmity which, keeping the Bishop "confined to his bed" "for a great many days,"[1] would lead to his death on April 4, 397. To tell the truth, it was not the first episode of illness that Ambrose had to suffer. Already in the letter to Felix of Como we heard him confide to his disciple of being "physically indisposed," and Augustine, too, recorded the Bishop's weakness of voice to explain his reading the texts silently.[2] For this last aspect we have explicit confirmation on the part of Ambrose who, while delivering his homily, confessed to not having the energy to continue preaching. At the end of the first discourse *On the Sacraments*, for example, he proposes a motive for the interruption, besides the time already spent, to "the weakness" of his voice, and he hopes that he will be able to take it up again the next day "if the Lord will give me the ability and the time to speak." In the *Second Apology for David*, on the other hand, taking up again the discourse left in suspense from the day before, he indicates having interrupted it because, "either through limitation of intelligence or through weakness of voice," he had lacked the strength "to complete the whole discourse in a single day."[3] But it was not just a question of his voice: more often the Bishop suffered episodes of illness that kept him in bed for long periods of time. Already in 378, while accompanying Satyrus to a burial, he prematurely left on account of illness. In his first discourse *On the Death of his Brother* addressing him directly, he confessed: "A little while ago, being oppressed by a serious illness (and if possible, may it be the last!), I regretted that you could not be by my bedside and, sharing with our holy sister the fulfillment of my desire, namely that you would close my eyes with your finger at the moment of death." In 383 we find a second testimony, inserted by Ambrose into a letter sent to the Thessalonians on the occasion of the death of their Bishop Acolius: "One day, when he came to Italy," Ambrose recounts, "since I had come down with an illness, I was unable to go meet him, so he came to visit me." In 390, writing the famous private letter to Theodosius following the massacre at Thessalonica, the Bishop advised him to adopt as the official motive for his absence from Milan a "physical illness," one that was "really serious."[4]

To this information can be added elements of notable interest deducible from the skeleton of Ambrose[5] conserved in the Milanese basilica that bears his name. From an analysis of these remains experts have argued that the Bishop suffered from chronic arthritis of the spinal column to which they theorize they would have to attribute the sharp pains that sometimes confined Ambrose to his bed. This illness, in its normal progression, gradually leads to a stiffening of one's body, because of which in the end one's more limited motions are made only with extreme suffering. To such affliction are also sometimes joined that rheumatism of the pharynx, to which Ambrose could also attest and that we have seen caused him no slight fatigue in preaching. Those that are afflicted with this malady, it may be noted, in every case, maintain a relatively normal life, though having to battle against the pains of quite notable intensity. In this sense the intense activity of the Bishop can be understood which is evident to us in all the years of his episcopal service. The experts complete their observations, speculating on the cause of the death of Ambrose: since the progression of chronic arthritis finally produces limitations and irregularities in respiration, his death is interpreted as most likely due to a cardio-respiratory deficiency.

This picture of Ambrose's illness puts in even clearer light his industriousness that knew no rest until the end. Truly he did not spare himself or let himself be dissuaded by the suffering that he might have had to endure.

We have thus come to the final months in the life of the Bishop; and we owe to Paulinus the description of many episodes relating to these moments. At the top of the list is the recovery of the remains of

Chapter XVIII: The "Encounter"

the martyrs Nazarius and Celsus, of whose story we are already aware and which took place after the death of Theodosius, most likely in 395. Certain anecdotes follow: one regards a certain Cresconius who had sought refuge in a church but on the way to the altar, notwithstanding the attempt of the Bishop and clerics who were there to defend him, was removed by brute force on the part of the soldiers sent to arrest him. In the amphitheatre at that time a wild animal spectacle was going on, and these soldiers, having completed the task they had been given, went there to assist at the performance. But while they were giving a report to the proper authorities about the task completed, the leopards, Paulinus recounts, being freed at just that moment, "with a quick leap, got up to the place where they were posted… and left them horribly mangled." General Stilicho, who had authorized the incursion into the church, impressed by the event, "immediately did penance, and for many days was disposed to support the wishes of the Bishop."[6] "We won't attempt to separate the truth from the legend in this pious account," Gérard Nauroy wisely suggests.[7]

Equally anecdotal and frankly a bit naïve is the story immediately following. Ambrose, the biographer says, was going to the imperial palace; he had with him Theoduleus, one of his secretaries who would later become Bishop of Modena. He, "seeing someone trip and fall to the ground, laughed at the fallen man." The Bishop then, paraphrasing a text of St. Paul, said to Theoduleus: "You who are standing, take care that you don't fall" (cf. 1 Cor 10:12). And (should we expect any different outcome?) "At such words, immediately the one who had laughed at the fall of another, suffered the same thing himself."[8]

More significant, however, are two other pieces of information that we gather, again from Paulinus. The first comes from the Marcomanni, a distant Germanic tribe that dwelt in the region between the Elbe and the Oder: indeed, rumors of the fame of Ambrose had reached this people and through this news the path was opened to receive the Gospel. Fritigil, their queen, had come to know "of the fame of a holy man from the words of a Christian from Italy who happened to be among them," and hence "believing in Christ, through whom she had recognized in Ambrose a (faithful) servant," she sent ambassadors to request from the Bishop a text with which she could be instructed in the Catholic religion. Paulinus knew of the "splendid letter in the form of a catechism" with which Ambrose responded and in which, confirming once again his own loyalty in dealing with the empire, he added to Fritigil the suggestion to "convince her spouse to maintain peace with the Romans." Everything worked out for the best, according to the wishes of the Bishop; and Fritigil decided to crown her adhesion to the faith and to peace with the empire by coming to Milan to meet Ambrose, reaching there, however, after the Bishop had already died.[9]

The other episode, specifically located "a few months before Ambrose was confined to his bed," is included among the testimonies told by the biographer to demonstrate the familiarity of the Bishop with the supernatural world. Ambrose was dictating, for the definitive text, his *Explanation of the 12 Psalms, Psalm 43*; Paulinus was acting as stenographer. "At one point," he recounts "a tiny flame, in the guise of a shield, wound itself around his head and, little by little, it entered his mouth, as if entering its own home. After this his face became like snow; then his appearance regained its usual aspect." On the suggestion of the deacon Castus, Paulinus interpreted that marvelous event as a sign of the Holy Spirit who descended on Ambrose.[10]

Certainly the vision describes to us an experience of the biographer and to him we leave the responsibility of how it is attested; in any case we can substantially accept the hint that he gave us, with anecdotes and various kinds of experiences, to consider the indubitable spiritual elevation of the Bishop. Anyway, it remains the case that the *Explanation of the 12 Psalms, Psalm 43* is interrupted at the explanation of verse 25, without proceeding to the final two verses of the psalm. In any case, Ambrose wished to conclude with a strong call to "remain in the Lord and not be distanced from him."[11] Along these lines, Francesco Braschi comments: "Although, then, the *explanation* is objectively unfinished... we may yet grasp the affirmed necessity of remaining united to the Lord not only from the most profound passage of Psalm 43, but, further, that this is also the most suitable leave

Chapter XVIII: The "Encounter"

taking of a man and a Bishop of the caliber of Ambrose."[12]

I have already mentioned the responsibility as a metropolitan invested in Ambrose; and we have seen that before his final illness he was in Pavia to assist with the election of the Bishop Profuturus. In the months immediately preceding he would have completed a similar mission to Vercelli as well, for the nomination of Honoratus as Bishop of that church.[13] In 396, in fact, the see of Vercelli had been vacant for many months after the death of the Bishop Limenius and it did not appear that there was any positive conclusion in sight. In particular, strong dissent and conflicts were sown in the community by the two monks, Sarmationes and Barbazianus, supporters of the doctrine of Jovinian, whom we have seen condemned at Rome and Milan at the beginning of 393. Writing a long letter to the Vercellians with the intent of resolving the situation, Ambrose called the two monks "men full of chatter," for whom "there is no merit in abstinence, no consideration of frugality, or of virginity; for them all things are esteemed at the same level; those are crazy who mortify their bodies with fasts and who subject themselves to the spirit."[14] The teaching of Ambrose recalled them to the authentic teaching of the Church of Vercelli, begun by its first Bishop Eusebius. We remember how he had favored a form of communal life among the members of the clergy, joined together in priestly ministry and monastic life. And we shouldn't forget that Ambrose himself was also possibly the inspiration behind this experiment in the Milanese context. The new Bishop, Ambrose maintained, would have to confirm that tradition, reflecting it in himself, alongside genuine priestly characteristics and the values of the monastic experience.

The letter, in any case, did not have the hoped for consequence and Ambrose, despite the burden of an illness that had gotten worse, wanted to go in person to Vercelli. The *Life of Gaudentius of Novara* speaks of this trip. A hagiographic writing difficult to date, in any case, it contains a nucleus certainly fixing it in the seventh and eighth centuries.[15] The *Life* attempts to reconcile the stories of the protagonist, dedicating only one passing mention to the coming of Ambrose to Vercelli, which, while brief, does indeed appear to be plausible. The Bishop "had come," it explains, "because of some discord in the heart of the people. After having enlightened the whole city like the rays of the sun, he left an enduring concord and peace." Nothing more: but we can reason that he managed to elect a worthy cleric, Honoratus to be precise, who among other things in his youth would have been made a cleric by Eusebius, experiencing communal life under his guidance. The new Bishop therefore reproduced the characteristics of the best priestly and monastic tradition of the city.

But the *Life of Gaudentius* presents us with another episode following that one, historically less supportable[16] and yet fascinating in the serenity of its narrative. It was intended to show another aspect of the metropolitical action of Ambrose, connecting it to the foundation of the episcopal see of Novara. Thus the hagiography continues: "Returning then swiftly to his own see and passing the night at Novara (Ambrose) hurried along the way to reach a certain place: he thus dispensed himself from paying a visit to his blessed friend (Gaudentius), saying to his companions: 'We should have paid a visit to the most reverend Gaudentius, but it is already evening.' With these words he continued on the way. But not much further on Ambrose's horse halted unexpectedly, nor could he manage to make it go on any further. He applied the whip and spur, but the horse remained frozen as if terrified by a deadly precipice. Worn out by whipping it, he was suddenly enlightened by the divine Spirit, and coming to himself as was his habit, he said: 'We're not permitted to pursue the trip we had undertaken until we have visited the blessed Gaudentius.' This said, he immediately started to go back, returning to the city and on his own went willingly where before he had not wanted to go." Then follows, at this point, an emotional meeting, with a dialogue in which the two holy men competed with one another in reciprocally prophesying their own future: "As soon as the blessed Gaudentius, through divine inspiration, knew of the arrival of a eminent personage, he went out to meet him. That one for his part, seeing him, embraced him warmly; he kissed him and, revealing to him a secret as if through a reproach, told him: 'I see that you will be Bishop.' (Gaudentius) then, seeing the future through that same grace, with serene face which was habitual

Chapter XVIII: The "Encounter"

for him, far from contradicting him, replied to him saying: 'Yes, but I will be consecrated by another.'"[17] Obviously such "prophecies" are not revealed in vain...; and traditionally it is known that Simplician, the successor of Ambrose, was the one who consecrated Gaudentius as the first Bishop of Novara.

We are thus brought to 397 and the final episodes in the life of the Bishop, for which we return to draw on his faithful biographer Paulinus. When Stilicho noticed that the illness was getting worse, and anticipating the worst, he sent an official delegation to bid Ambrose "to request the Lord to prolong his life." The response of the Bishop is famous: "I have not lived among you in such a way as to be ashamed of living; but I have no fear of death, because we have a good Lord." Possidius, in his *Life of Augustine*, assures us that the Bishop of Hippo, "by then already old and admired, praised the precision and equilibrium" of these words: "It needs to be understood in fact that (Ambrose) had said: 'nor do I fear to die, because we have a good Lord.' He did not believe that he had prefaced it with 'I have not lived in such a way that I am ashamed to live among you' through excessive faith in his stainless conduct."[18] As a matter of fact, the response of Ambrose, in the two parts of which it is composed, expresses the Bishop's most profound convictions. The spiritual thought of Ambrose certainly runs through that aspect of concreteness and of human undertaking which is reflected in the first phrase, but it is no less rooted in his prevailing and superabundant gratitude for the divine gift. For this reason the Bishop, in all humility and faith, declares that he is not afraid of death, "because we have a good Lord."

Not for nothing in his *Explanation of the 12 Psalms, Psalm 43*, dictated in those last weeks, do we find certain pregnant expressions that confirm this conviction, which Ambrose drew clearly from the teachings of the Apostle Paul. In fact, he advised that one ought not trust "presumptuously on one's own arm, that is, on one's own capacity for action, but on the grace of God, believing that it is not works that justify, but the faith at one's disposal," as he had affirmed earlier, "the gifts of the generosity of God are more abundant than are the wages of human toil." Later he confirms: "Human salvation therefore is the result of the will of God, not of one's own ability to act. God has preferred that one should seek salvation with faith more than with works, so that no one may boast of their own deeds, thus falling into sin. Rather the one who glories in the Lord obtains the benefit of mercy and avoids the sin of presumption."[19] With these strong and cheerful thoughts the Bishop prepared himself for the "encounter." His collaborators had already discussed the probable successor, naming that Simplician who had such a great role in having aided in the preparation of Ambrose himself. Paulinus recounts that the Bishop, while for a long time the little group around him stood quietly debating the problem "as if participating in the discussion… approving exclaimed three times: Old, yes, but good;"[20] and so made them to understand that Simplician was advanced in years, but still in good health and therefore capable of managing the duties of episcopal ministry. The suggestion of Ambrose was heard and Simplician was elected to succeed him.

With the worsening of his illness, Bassianus of Lodi and Honoratus of Vercelli came to Milan. A few days before the death of Ambrose, according to a testimony of the Bishop of Lodi and related by Paulinus, "in the place where he lay… while engaged in prayer" together with Bassianus, "he saw the Lord Jesus come to him and smile at him": a discrete sign, almost a symbol, of that continuous presence of Christ in the life and in the preaching of Ambrose that now revealed a definitive encounter with him. Honoratus then administered the holy Viaticum. The evening of Holy Thursday (April 3), notes Paulinus, Honoratus had gone upstairs to rest while Ambrose from five that afternoon remained rapt in prayer "with his arms open in the form of a cross" as if awaiting death which, by now, was imminent. In the room where he had retired, Honoratus suddenly heard someone calling him "three times in a voice that told him: 'Get up quickly, because he is dying.' The Bishop of Vercelli then descended, took to the dying man the body of the Lord; and as he had received and swallowed it, he expired taking with him the good viaticum."[21] It was in the first hours of Holy Saturday, April 4, 397.

The biographer was aware of and documents the events that fol-

Chapter XVIII: The "Encounter"

lowed: the accommodation of the mortal remains of the Bishop, still before dawn, in the Basilica Nuova, where he remained on view the whole of the Easter vigil the following night; the "visions" of those who were baptized, who "coming from the font, saying that he was seated on the cathedra placed in the apse, while others pointed him out to their fathers and their mothers in the act of getting up from there"; the transfer of his body into the Basilica Ambrosiana, where he was buried, with the participation of a huge flock of people too numerous to count preceded by the crowd of newly baptized; the cure of some possessed persons, and the act of some present who, as they did with the martyrs, "threw their handkerchiefs and cinctures so that his holy body might be touched in some way."[22]

Paulinus has thus presented to us the protagonist of his biography assigning him the glory attributed to the martyrs, but, while recognizing and attesting to the crossing of the finishing line of the holy Bishop, he stops at the threshold of the "encounter," without being able to describe it. Ambrose, in any case, had prepared his faithful for this moment many times, indicating and explaining the Scriptures; he had even composed a tract with the title: *On a Good Death*. Speaking to others, he in that way already announced that which he himself was prepared to experience. Already in the second discourse *On the Death of his Brother*, reflecting on the separation of Satyrus from this life and to the encounter that he would have with the world above, Ambrose observed: "The soul then ought already to tend toward the divine assembly reserved for the saints above"; and directing his discourse specifically to Jesus, the goal and center of this encounter, he exclaimed: "The soul ought to see also your nuptial feast, Jesus, in which your bride, no longer subject to this world but joined to the Spirit, is led from earth to heaven, while the universal joy is poured out in song... it ought to see the nuptial bed bedecked in linen, roses, lilies, crowns. With what else are the nuptials also decorated: with the bruises of confessors, the blood of martyrs, the lilies of virgins, the crowns of priests?" And after having recalled that "the holy David wanted more than anyone else to contemplate this vision perfectly," he entrusted himself to the words of the psalm: "One grace I have asked of the Lord, this I will seek: to live in the house of the Lord all the days of my life and to see the sweetness of the Lord" (Ps 26/27:4); and he concludes: "It is beautiful to believe this, it is a joy to hope in it, certainly it is not wrong to have believed it, but it is a grace to have hoped in it."[23]

The encounter, then, taking nothing from the centrality of the relationship with Christ, is enlarged to encompass also an aspect of assembly. One passage from the treatise *On Virgins*, nearly copying the text just cited, offers another description in which a panoramic imagination of vast scale is united to an expressive tone still more personalized and warm. Here Ambrose contemplates the virgins who, at the end of their life, are presented by the Mother of God to Jesus and by these to the Father. He begins with an exclamation: "How many virgins will meet her [Mary]! How many, embracing her, will she bring to the Lord saying: 'These have kept with immaculate innocence the bed of my son, the nuptial bed!'" He imagines further that Jesus, recommending them to the Father, using the expressions of the prayer preserved in chapter 17 of the Gospel of John, will say in fact: "'Holy Father, these are those whom I have kept for you (cf. Jn 17:11), on whom the Son of man has placed his head to rest (cf. Mt 8:20). I ask that where I am they may also be (cf. Jn 17:24). But not for themselves alone must they be able, since they have never lived for themselves alone: this one redeems her parents, that one her brothers. Just Father, the world has not known you, but these have known me and they do not wish to know the world.' What a triumph that will be, what great happiness for the cheering angels, for the fact that they deserve to live in heaven with the one who lived a celestial life in the world! Thus everyone will exult saying: 'And I will go to the altar of my God, to God who gives joy to my youth' (Ps 42/43:4). 'I will offer to God a sacrifice of praise and present to the Most High my vows' (Ps 49/50:14)."[24] I have spoken of the treatise *On the Good Death*, a writing dated to the second half of the episcopacy of Ambrose, maybe toward the end of his life.[25] There the Bishop proposes a meditation on death, that is, on the moment in which "we end the course the responsibilities of this life: namely, the separation of the soul from the body."[26] The reflection, enriched by undeniable Neo-Platonic influences, while being very cultivated from a literary point of view, nonetheless contains arguments from a philosophical background that arouse little attention. In his final part however, in a passage full of poetry and animated by the great affection which Ambrose nurtured for the figure of Jesus, we find a refined and admirable description of the final encounter of the person with Christ, our life. The Bishop, in his preaching to the faithful, revealed to them and also to us the meaning of one's own death.

The passage begins with a decisive declamation: "Since the just have this remuneration, to see the face of God and 'that light which illuminates every man' (Jn 1:9), let us dedicate ourselves from this moment to a precise obligation: that is, that our soul may approach our God, that our prayer may approach God, that our desires may draw us to him, that we might never be separated from him. And even while we are on earth, meditating, reading, and studying, we must be united to God, we must come to know him as we are able: in fact, we know him only in part because here all is imperfect. There everything will be perfect; here we are infants, there we will be strong. 'Now we see indistinctly as in a mirror, there, however we will see face to face' (1 Cor 13:12). Then with face unveiled we will be permitted to contemplate the glory of God (cf. 2 Cor 3:18)."

We need, then, to concentrate on the goal, directing ourselves toward the Lord Jesus and there to reach the assembly of the saints: "Confident in that reality, let us bravely direct ourselves toward Jesus our redeemer, bravely let us direct ourselves toward the Council of the patriarchs, bravely let us depart to go to our father Abraham when the destined day arrives, bravely let us go toward the assembly of the saints and the reunion of the just. Yes, we will go to our fathers... We will go to those who repose in the reign of God together with Abraham, Isaac, and Jacob because, invited to the meal, excuses are not allowed. We will go there where the paradise of delights is to be found, there where Adam, who fell among the thieves, no longer has any reason to weep over his wounds, there where even the thief himself will rejoice at having entered to take part in the celestial reign....

We will go there where the Lord Jesus has prepared a home for his poor servants (cf. Jn 14:2-3), that we might also be where he is: for so he has willed."

For the rest, Ambrose observes, "the will of Christ already is accomplished. He also shows the way and the place, saying: 'You know were I am going, and you know the way' (Jn 14:4). The place is at the Father's side, the way is Christ." And repeating in all its fullness the assertion of Jesus: "I am the way, the truth and the life" (Jn 14:6), the Bishop urges: "Therefore let us enter through this *way*, let us cling firmly to the *truth*, let us follow the *life*. The *way* is that which leads, the *truth* is that which gives confidence, and the *life* is that which is given by his means."

Jesus prayed for this, Ambrose records, taking up anew the solemn prayer of Jesus preserved in the Gospel of John; and in particular he cites the expression, "Father, I would that where I am they also may be with me, that they may see my glory that you gave me" (Jn 17:24). Further, with simplicity, he opens himself to the invocation: "We follow you, Lord Jesus, but summon us, so that we might follow you: without you no one can rise. You indeed are the way, the truth, the life, the possibility, the faith, the prize. Gather your own: you are the *way*; confirm them: you are the *truth*; enliven them: you are the *life*." The Bishop asks to be able to see "the good things of the Lord in the land of the living" (Ps 26/27:13), to be filled with the wealth of his house (cf. Ps 64/65:5) and finally to find flung wide open before him that divine wealth "in whom we live and move and have our being" (Ac 17:28). In this wealth, he assures us, "are found pure peace, immortal light, perpetual grace, that pious inheritance and carefree tranquility of souls, not subject to death but freed from death, there where there are no tears, no weeping (how could there be any weeping, where there is no sin?), there where your saints are freed from errors and preoccupations..., where there is the land of the living."

The great good desired, in fact, is life; and this highest good is Christ himself. Thus the prayer is transformed anew into a warm conclusion to his discourse: "Let us hurry on toward the life...! Let us seek the Living One!" This quest reminds us of the one under-

Chapter XVIII: The "Encounter"

taken by the women and the apostles on Easter morning, and causes Ambrose to recall the invitation to search no further among the dead for him who lives (cf. Lk 24:5) because he has already risen to the Father (cf. Jn 20:17). And joining the expressions of the prologue of the Gospel of John to the images of the Gospel accounts of the post-resurrection appearances he concludes: "We seek him, therefore, there where John sought and found him. He sought him 'in the beginning' (Jn 1:1), and he found him who lives among the living, the Son with the Father (cf. ibid). We must seek him to the end of time and embrace his feet and adore him, because he says also to us: 'Do not fear' (Mt 28:10), which is to say: Do not fear the sins of this age, do not fear the iniquity of the world, do not fear the onrush of bodily passions: I am the remission of sins. Do not fear the darkness: I am the light. Do not fear death: I am the life. Those who come to me 'will never see death' (Jn 8:51)."[27]

CHAPTER XIX

Saint Ambrose

In the last years of the 6th century Gregory of Tours, who was Bishop of that see from 573 to 594, in his book on *The Virtues of Martin*, speaks also of Ambrose, attesting that "the flowers of his eloquence" spread their perfume "over the whole Church." He tells in particular that one Sunday, during the celebration of the Eucharist, the Bishop dozed off during the first reading (a passage from a prophetic text). As a consequence, they weren't able to begin the proclamation of the second reading, a passage from an epistle of St. Paul, since Ambrose had instituted the practice that "the lector, presenting himself with the book, must not take the initiative of reading before the holy *nutu* (inclination of the head) had approved his doing so with its signal." Those present, not wishing to disturb the Bishop, waited for two or three hours, but finally "they woke him, saying: 'How the time passes. The Bishop must order the lector to read the sacred text, since the people are already very tired.' But Ambrose called for calm and revealed how much, through a divine miracle, he was allowed to see and to accomplish during his sleep: 'Know,' he said, 'that my brother Bishop Martin left his earthly body and I was paying homage at his funeral; and, after having finished the liturgical service according to custom, having been awakened by you, it was not in my power to finish some of the verses of the psalm.'" Gregory's narration concludes with the witty observation that those present, "stupefied and in awe, noted the day and the hour" of the episode, and "began to diligently look for" information in this regard which, once examined, could only confirm the details of Ambrose's story![1]

We, on the other hand, with a simple chronological observation, are able to ascertain that the legend narrated by Gregory of Tours has transposed the date: Ambrose would not have been able to participate at the funeral of Martin thanks to the miraculous bi-location with which he may have been graced, because Martin left this earth on the 8th of November 397, by which time Ambrose had already been dead a few months. In any case the story is truly amusing and it signals a time when the figure of the Bishop of Milan had entered into the memory and cult of many Christian communities, even in far off regions.

At Milan, Ambrose was immediately taken as a patron; the first datable testimony was, in fact, in a letter written earlier than that one just cited, sent in 551 or the following year to Nicetius of Trier, Bishop of the city that had given birth to Ambrose. The sender, a certain Florian, who lived in a monastery of the diocese of Milan, asked Nicetius to petition "my most holy confessor Ambrose, who protects me as his special servant, to assist me as his fellow citizen and save me from danger as one who was brought up in his family." At the end of the century, moreover, in the month of September, 600, a letter of Pope Gregory the Great designates Deusdedit, the new Bishop of Milan as "Vicar of Saint Ambrose" and addressing himself to the priests, deacons, and other members of the clergy to whom the letter was sent, he characterizes them as "acolytes in the service of Saint Ambrose." For Gregory, therefore, the great Bishop was still present to protect his Church.[2]

But the memory of Ambrose, together with the cult in his honor and the invocation of him as patron over the community that had been his, must have developed spontaneously as a protraction of celebrations that, already during the Bishop's life, had annually recalled the anniversary of his elevation. We know of a passionate and intimate homily from December 7, 385, when he referred to his congregation as a parent might and even identified all of them, each one, as his children.[3] At his death it would have been natural to continue that remembrance, transforming it into a cult, appreciating the Bishop who never ceased protecting his city and his Church.[4] From this date on, then, without interruption, Ambrose was celebrated; and already not long after his death there was composed a liturgical formula for the Mass celebrating him on that anniversary. Further, in the 9th century in the Franco-Carolingian era, the commemoration of two more anniversaries were added: the remembrance of his baptism and that of his death. The first was celebrated on the date of the anniversary, November 30 together with the feast of the Apostle Andrew. His death was commemorated on the Thursday after Easter, perhaps to align it with the solemn office that it is believed took place in the Ambrosian Basilica with the procession of Bishops from nearby churches, precisely on the Thursdays following Easter. These innovations aligned themselves, as we recall, to the introduction of the cult of the siblings of Ambrose, Marcellina and Satyrus, and of the martyrs Vitalis and Agricola, whose remains he had found and they were therefore inserted in the response that the Church of Milan wished to give to the attempted "Romanization" promoted by the Frankish kings.

The memory of Saint Ambrose remained, in any case, bound, principally, to December 7 and around this recurrence one of the most popular of the Milanese feasts developed, which consisted of a rich and expressive group of religious celebrations and civil events. In the Middle Ages, in fact, on this day one of the four general markets was held, with a great influx of peoples[5] and a solemn liturgical celebration involving the Archbishop and the clergy of Santa Maria Maggiore going in procession to the Basilica of S. Ambrogio, in which the mortal remains of the Bishop were venerated along with those of the martyrs Protasius and Gervasius. The Archbishop, pausing at the atrium of the church, before entering for the rite in the Mass, blessed twelve skins of wine, together with bread and meat, to be distributed to the poor. In the Basilica the three saints rested in two tombs side by side, located parallel to the main aisle of the building. In one were the remains of Ambrose, in the other those of the two martyrs.

In the 9th century and thereafter in concurrence with the renewed attention to the figure of Ambrose, under the episcopacy of Angilberto II (824-859) a worthier systemization of their remains took place. They were, in fact, brought together in a porphyry sarcophagus, and placed obliquely over the original tombs. Above the urn was the famous golden altar decorated in those years by Volvinius and a group of artists under his guidance. From the altar, by means of a little window, the faithful were allowed a view of the underlying sepulcher and could venerate the saints who were resting there.

A thousand years later, on January 13, 1864, during the work to shore up and restore the Basilica, a sarcophagus was recovered with three bodies in it, one beside the other (Ambrose to the left of the martyrs) and under it were two empty tombs. After official identification, completed on August 8, 1871, the three skeletons were identified: the smallest one, belonging to a man 1 meter 63 centimeters tall (5 feet 3 inches), was Ambrose, while the other two, each around 1 meter 80 centimeters tall (5 feet 11 inches), were the two martyrs. It wasn't for nothing that Ambrose, at the moment of rediscovering Protasius and Gervasius, had described them as "men of extraordinary stature, as were men of ancient times."[6] In the mosaic in S. Vittore in Ciel d'oro, the two martyrs are shown having much greater stature relative to that of the Bishop. The skeleton of Ambrose, moreover, reveals a groove of about three millimeters corresponding to the right eye, perfectly equivalent to the lowering of that same eye discernible in the image of the mosaic.[7] A few years later, in 1874, it was desired to celebrate the anniversary of the episcopal election of Ambrose with a solemn exposition in the Cathedral with those relics which had happily been found. The Milanese showed all of their esteem for their patron despite the polemical interpretation of the recovery of the saints endorsed by the radical press and the whipped up danger of disorder induced the public officials to prohibit the planned processions. Nevertheless, following the transfer of the remains to the Duomo during the night between the 11th and 12th of May, these became an object of veneration by an extraordinary number of people when, on the following 15th they were newly taken to the Basilica of S. Ambrogio. During the night of May 15, in fact, recounts Ennio Apeciti, based on the abundant documentation of that period, "in the expectation of the moment, the Piazza del Duomo was flooded with the devout and, for fear of riots, by undercover guards. At 2:30 a.m. the doors of the Duomo were opened and the urns brought forth," covered by a dark waxed cloth, "and followed by certain members of the metropolitan Chapter and Archbishop Calabiana. In the dark of night the piazza rapidly began to be lit up from the candles that certain faithful had brought and distributed among all those present, calculated at several thousand. These formed a spontaneous and long procession: at the head the bodies of the saints, followed by the small entourage of Calabiana, and behind, by a disjointed line of dim lights which snaked along, from which rose the subdued sounds of prayer. Joining the crowd at the basilica the youth of the homonymous club intoned the *Te Deum*, which was taken up by the people. With this triumphal hymn, the remains of the three saints reentered their basilica. Calabiana celebrated the Mass, accompanied by the song of the people and all awaited the dawn: only then did the crowd begin to slowly melt away, to yield their place to the pilgrims, who continued uninterruptedly for more than a month."[8] The understanding between the Milanese and their Bishop, begun in the very moment of his election and continued constantly after his death, expressed itself with as much esteem and devotion fifteen centuries later....

But let us return to the more ancient testimonies of this "understanding," to catch the stages of an ever growing connection between the Bishop Ambrose on the one side and the Church and the city of Milan on the other. We already know of the ecclesial reaction to the "Romanizing" impositions of the Carolingian period in the 9th century, with a strong reminder of the figure of Ambrose. But even earlier, in 792, Alcuin, Councilor to Charlemagne, in a brief but still significant expression, showed that he perceived the particular link that united the city with Ambrose, and the protection that it was convinced it received from him. In his *Life of St. Willibrord* he observes, indeed, that "Milan, a one-time imperial city, enjoyed St. Ambrose as its defender."[9] The stories that stretch through the centuries confirming this idealized involvement between the Bishop and the city are numerous. These typically play on the legendary tales of events in which the city of Milan risked grave threat of war, invasions, or internecine battles: in all of these cases, it is related, Ambrose intervened to intimidate those who imperiled its liberty by defending it against enemies, by protecting whoever sincerely battled for its good. Here is just one example among many in which the legendary transfiguration does not even permit one to correctly identify the era and the protagonists of the story. It treats, in fact, of an episode attributed to the Merovingian king Theodobert I (504-547) in the archives of the Malaspina family, and to Lamberto of Spoleto, king of Italy (892-898), in the *History of Milan* by Landolfo Seniore, composed toward the end of the 11th or the beginning of the following century. But even in this other source Lamberto is located in the 6th century, during the time of Bishop Honorarius.

We will follow the narration of Landolfo Seniore: Lamberto, he tells us, treacherously entered Milan after having vainly besieged the city for ten years. "Full of demoniacal furor, he unsheathed his swords, contrary to every human sensibility, and executed a vast massacre of citizens, little ones and the aged, the young and babies." He razed the palaces, the towers and the fortifications. "In this massacre," Landolfo continues, "Saint Ambrose, seeing that the city and its citizens were gravely oppressed by such pillage and destruction, during the night of Saint Severus," that is, the night before February 1, "appeared personally to the wicked Lamberto saying: 'Oh enemy of God and men, denier of God and worthy of damnation and death, you unjustly destroy the city and its fortifications which I have blessed and consecrated to the honor of God and the usefulness of the Christians who dwell here! Like a pagan you have murdered the people whom God had redeemed with his precious blood hanging on a cross. Know, then, that neither you nor your earthly heirs have long to govern, and that you will die like a dog in an infamous death.'"

I won't recount in detail the subsequent curses that fell on Lamberto who, in a vendetta, was killed with a razor sharp thorn plunged into his heart while he was sleeping.[10] I only note that the more that popular credulity created fantastic descriptions to demonstrate the irreplaceable defense of the city guaranteed by Ambrose, the less likely these fantastical images fit his true features. When, further, among the factions of the Visconti family battling for possession of the Milanese seigniory, on February 21, 1339 at Parabiago, Luchino defeated Lodrisio who had come against him at the head of a group of Germans, and the Milanese saw in Luchino the defender of their civil

Chapter XIX: Saint Ambrose

liberty and in his enemy an outcast in league with foreigners. Once again they sensed that they had been saved by Ambrose who, according to the Dominican Galvano Fiamma, had appeared, "in white vestments and with a whip in his hand," and "struck the enemies that were seizing victory." But because of his intervention "their forces waned and they were defeated. In the city a procession was formed of clergy and religious that snaked its way to S. Ambrogio."[11] By then the story was that the Bishop had entered the battle, grasping the whip and maneuvering on horseback as were the other combatants: from then on and for many centuries the use of his image in this fashion was widely diffused,[12] while immediately there was organized a feast of the so-called "Saint Ambrose of the Victory" to commemorate that event, and at Parabiago was set the first stone of a church that was to be dedicated as a reminder for ages to come of the battle fought by the Bishop in favor of his people.

The whip, in any case, had already been attributed to Ambrose at least a few centuries earlier: it is seen used against the Arians in the bass-relief already noted, set as a decoration on the Porta Romana in 1171.[13] As for the bas-relief of the 11th century, which is found in the atrium of the Basilica of S. Ambrogio and according to some ought to be considered a first attestation, it seems, rather, that he holds a club with a pinecone and a fluttering ribbon and this would seem to indicate, then, simply the temporal power of the Bishop: very relevant at that time.[14] For the rest, a trace of this image may be provided by expressions that Ambrose had himself used in his discourse *Against Auxentius*. Recalling the Gospel episode of the expulsion of the merchants from the temple, the Bishop contrasts Jesus, who "threw them out of the temple with a whip" to Mercurinus [Auxentius] who wanted to distance the faithful from the Church "with an ax"; because "the Lord, motivated by respect [for the house of God], scattered the sacrilegious with a whip; the wicked one, on the other hand, persecuted devoted persons with iron."[15]

Perhaps the introduction of this image came only in the 11th century, that has bequeathed us that first figurative testimony. At that time the Patarini family and their adversaries clashed in Milan.

Those on one side were supporters of the ecclesiastical reform promised by Gregory VII; the other side was hostile to this in the name of local tradition. It seems that the former, imagining that Ambrose would support them in their just cause, portrayed him with a whip in his hand, ready to correct the clergy who did not wish to adjust to the reforming norms of the Pope, just as Jesus had done in the temple and, implicitly, as Ambrose had imitated him in "throwing out" the Arians.

The mutual assimilation between Milan and Ambrose, as it progressed, rendered the two respective attributes, "Milanese" and "Ambrosian," practically interchangeable. If the first proofs of such a use go back to the 9th century, we owe to the anti-Patarini, who felt offended in those matters that they considered to be legitimate local autonomies, in the 11th century, the renewed recalling of Ambrose and the consequent intensification of the use of the adjective "Ambrosian," attributed to the Church and its institutions, to the city of Milan and to her multiple expressions and realities. "Saint Ambrose," Enrico Cattaneo concludes, with a comprehensive perspective that extends to the present day, "is present on every page of the history of the Church of Milan and also to a great extent of the history of its citizens. His name has given rise to an adjective, 'Ambrosian,' which, in rare cases, is joined to 'Church' thus designating a local Church, and it is joined to many other terms to designate the characteristic marks of the citizens and even to the products of Milan."[16]

Even the particular rite which characterizes the Church of Milan has assumed the name "Ambrosian," just as, by the 11th century, there began to appear liturgical books whose titles bear the specification: "According to Ambrosian use."[17] In this case the expression might even be seen to imply that the Milanese liturgy was effectively instituted by Ambrose. Moreover, already by the end of the 7th century an abbot of the monastery of S. Martino in Rome, a certain John, named Ambrose in a list of saints by whose authority certain local churches were referenced in order to claim their own liturgical tradition, differing from the Roman.[18] The case of Ambrose is obviously that of the Church of Milan, which had attached its own liturgical specificity to the great Bishop. In any case a correct presentation of the facts excludes any that indicate Ambrose as the institutor of the rite that bears his name. Rather, to borrow the measured expressions of Marco Navoni: "He picked up and extended ritual practices from his predecessors, introducing certain novelties which contrast with the liturgical tradition of Rome taken as a model; in certain instances he defended the autonomy of a local tradition; above all he inserted his own liturgical ministry into a unique pastoral, catechetical, and doctrinal activity, which established him as one of the principal Bishops and doctors of the ancient Church."[19] And from this undoubted involvement of his was born the reference to him in the liturgical tradition which came to be developed in those centuries at Milan and that has continued to characterize the Milanese Church.

All the same, bound to the rite, to the Church, and to the city of Milan, the figure of the Bishop expanded to an ecclesial presence with universal scope. And it was not only because Ambrose was entered into the liturgical calendar of the Church of the West and the East that he became known and venerated in many different cultures, in the Syrian, Armenian, and Georgian regions, or those of the Greeks and Slavs. In the Byzantine East[20] Ambrose emerged, as we recall, as a Father of the Church, witness of an authentic faith and mastery of sound doctrine. But certain episodes in his life are even described in the historiographic and chronological tradition of the East, in particular by three writers who added to the *History of the Church* begun by Eusebius of Caesarea: Socrates Scholasticus and those already noted, Sozomen and Theodoret of Cyrus. In their *Histories*, alongside the story of the episcopal election of Ambrose and his battle against Justina, the intervention that he carried out against Theodosius after the massacre of Thessalonica is particularly remembered. Unfortunately the account dramatized by Theodoret regarding this last episode leaves a false impression in all subsequent narratives. His influence reached all the way to the West, thanks to the *Tripartite History*: a compilation and Latin translation of the *History of the Church* by Socrates, Sozomen, and Theodoret, which was composed in the 6th century by the monk Epiphanius and by Cassiodorus, the chancellor to Theodoric and the founder of the monastery at Vivarium.

Indeed, the *Tripartite History* knew the broadest diffusion and therefore contributed to make known the figure of Ambrose in the manner described; and even the anonymous biography composed in the Milanese region in the second half of the 9th century and which we know under the title of *The Life and Merits of St. Ambrose*, has borrowed heavily from the *Tripartite History*. Thus, whoever wishes to scan the numerous pictorial images of Saint Ambrose will find a notable section dedicated to this subject. Ambrose is made to appear as imperious and severe, firm in his decision making, red in the face (sometimes, however, less flushed and even apparently serene), with his arms stiffened in front of him as if to throw out the Emperor who advances timorously, or with an upraised hand to admonish him. Theodosius, for his part, seems to fall back before the posture of the Bishop and to humbly beg pardon, but more often he seems to argue about something or even to confront Ambrose angrily and with violence. The ambiguity of the representations tells us something about the psychological contradictions that we already noted in the account of Theodoret. It pleased us to find at least one canvas, painted in 1745 by Pierre Subleyras, in which the absolution of Theodosius from his sin and his readmission to the Church is, in contrast, depicted in an atmosphere of ease and of suffused religiosity.[21] But by means of this partial and even deviant historiographic tradition, however, there is, especially among the Byzantines, a recognition in Ambrose of a certain frankness of word and action, the *parrhesia* of the Greeks, with which the Bishop confidently fulfilled his ministry in the capital city with courage and dignity in his dealings with the Emperors.

Focusing more strictly on the West, we must not forget, among the historiographic sources which spread awareness of Ambrose, the biography written by Paulinus which has permitted us to apprehend many episodes and features of the Bishop's life. It a relatively brief *vita* and so intentionally incomplete; it is also of modest literary value. In it, nonetheless, the author, according to the authoritative judgment of Christine Mohrmann, with stories of notable historical importance or with curious anecdotes, intended above all to provide "a portrait of Bishop Ambrose, to illustrate the role that he had played in the life of the Church in strict relationship with the political life of the period."[22] And we can confirm that he correctly understood Ambrose's profile. It would be enough to review the many episodes already noted, significantly inserted by Paulinus in his biography such as: the action of Ambrose against Milanese Arianism and his defense of right doctrine, his opposition to attempts to restore paganism, the assumption of delicate missions in service of the imperial court, his commitment to raise the prestige of the Church against imperial power, his concern for all the Churches.

To mention Paulinus is to recall other aspects of the presence of Ambrose in the West, above all his assumption of the typical figure of pastor. The *Life of Ambrose* is, in fact, the first biography dedicated specifically to a Bishop as such; and in the following centuries the use of this model will be assumed to recount the life of other Bishop-saints, of whom Ambrose ends up being the emblematic model. Furthermore, Paulinus gives credit to Augustine, who had urged him to compose the text. And we know that the Bishop of Hippo not only nurtured a profound gratitude toward the one who had conferred baptism on him, but was, moreover, indebted to Ambrose for many theological points which he had further elaborated and presented in ordered synthesis. Thus through Augustine the reflection of the Bishop of Milan entered into the theological tradition of the West.[23] In the following centuries we find Ambrose still present in the revival of his teaching on virginity, which the Medieval and modern periods have constantly validated. And even the Protestant Reformation, in seeking masters who would guarantee it a genuine return to the origins, willingly drew on Ambrose.[24] If we take for example the *Lectures on the Letter to the Romans* by Luther, so important in the evolution of the author's thought, we discover, alongside citations or allusions to the writings of the Bishop, one of his noble definitions as well: in fact, commenting on the verse "Since we have gifts that differ according to the grace given to us, let us exercise them:... if one is a teacher, in teaching" (Rm 12:7), Luther explains: "Many have the grace of teaching, even if they are deprived of great culture; others have both:

these are the better," and this is exemplified with the names of Augustine, Ambrose, and Jerome.[25] Already the faithful who listened to the preaching of Ambrose had manifested their appreciation in actions, which Augustine had expressed in his writings, and which the centuries have not rendered less true.

Now it is time to turn one last time to Ambrose: to this man who appears fully realized in a life's pursuit that he had not personally chosen and which he accepted only after obstinate opposition and serious reflection. He had come from the security of a noble senatorial inheritance, in the course of which he acquired the best of ancient Roman tradition along with the Catholic faith of his ancestors and family, which had nurtured in him the strong convictions ever since childhood and adolescence. Milan would have recognized in him a faithful protector, a patron who remained present in his community in a thousand ways which historically or ideally connected him to themselves. Along with the Milanese Church the whole of Christianity venerated him for his sanctity, seeing in him the figure of a believer worthy of esteem and imitation, a disciple who had made the word and the grace of the Gospel shine forth in his life.

But one does not truly grasp Ambrose or his message, if one does not perceive in him that unifying core which was precisely his episcopal ministry. Gérard Nauroy, in a suggestive text, has emphasized the richness of his character and his qualities: Ambrose, he asserts, "knew how to reconcile rare qualities united in the one saint: authority, perspicacity, and the spirit of decision on the part of a high official in the service of the Roman state; an ability then offered to the service of the Church with humility, a spirit of renunciation of the world, the interiority of a mystic and master of asceticism, of the monastic life and the most rigorous spirituality; the inflexible determination to confront Emperors; and the untiring activity, notwithstanding a body quite weak and sickly (represented in the mosaic image of S. Vittore in Ciel d'oro), but at the same time the compassion and availability of a man the door of whose work room always remained open."[26] When taken together, the various qualities here recalled describe the figure and the ministry of the Bishop: in relationship to this figure and this ministry each characteristic is motivated, structured, specified, and realized. In this sense Ambrose does not conform to the mold of a Bishop; it is more that on his genial personality and his availability to believers that the ideal Bishop was molded. That is why his frankness and originality have been harmed, in subsequent tradition, by certain interpretations unconsciously driven by the intent to revise and compare Ambrose to this or that image of a Bishop: unfortunately resulting in a caricature of the real figure.

Rather, Ambrose is the harmonious amalgam of all of these characteristics, even of those which, in an ideal construction, may seem to be contradictory and incompatible. He is at once the strong and gentle Bishop; the respecter of the state while being imperious in confronting sovereigns; patient in converting the Arians that he had found in the city and combative against every one of their demands; near to his people and in a customary relationship with Emperors; a man of pardon and of chastisement; studiously capable of profound concentration and a most active laborer who makes decisions and accepts the consequences.

At the beginning of his life the symbol of honey appears; alongside this we have seen developed the symbol of the whip. The Middle Ages were happy to present Ambrose with both of these contrasting images. Perhaps they weren't wrong... because, returning to use the expressions of the Bishop, we are able to attribute to him the figure of that perfect man who is described in the treatise *On Jacob and the Good Life*: a self-made man, he affirms, ought "to resist, like a strong soldier, the assaults of the gravest disasters and confront the battles; to direct the ship like a prudent helmsman during a storm," he is one who "has no fear during persecution, is not too soft when it comes to pain... but is like a strong athlete full of vigor, who renders blow for blow of his persecutor, not with the whip that kills, but with that of the word."[27] And, vice versa, the honey deposited on his lips should be ideally likened to his very charming word, because it was filled with the Lord of mercy who, with immense pleasure and condescending generosity, saves man, introducing him into his secrets. In his *Commentary on Psalm 118*, as if speaking of himself, Ambrose described "the mouth of the just" as "dripping with wisdom," from whom "outpours the *honey* of sweetness and of mercy." "The Church," he adds, "listens to the words of the just." And he already gave the reason: sweet are the words with which "are proclaimed the remission of sins, eternal life, even the resurrection from the dead" and so is indicated that "spiritual grace which permeates our most secret recesses."[28]

Perhaps the *whip* and the *honey*, the power and the mercy of Ambrose are still precious to us and so necessary. I propose them again in a poetic composition which evokes them and makes them current, the creation and gift of my friend Marco Ballarini, *Dottore* of the Biblioteca Ambrosiana.

> For whom is
> Your whip
> If not for us:
> New Arians
> Who of Christ
> Have made
> The least
> Of our gods?
> Yet
> What do we seek,
> At the root of all our
>   Interminable
> Wandering
> We orphans
>   And scattered
>   In the labyrinth
> Of an uninhabitable world,
> If not a father
> Who calls us back
> To the path of life
> And the law of the home?
>   Guide, then,
> Intercede,

Chapter XIX: Saint Ambrose

And do not tire in
    Your
        Impassioned
Mercy
Because of apparent indifference,
Fragile — useless —
Veil
Of our solitudes.

Endnotes

Chapter I: Episcopal Election of Governor Ambrose

[1] Ambrose, *On Penance*, II, 8, 67 & 73 (SAEMO 17, pp. 264-267).
[2] Ambrose, *Letter Outside the Collection*, 14 (Maur. 63) *to the Church of Vercelli*, 65 (SAEMO 21, pp. 296-297).
[3] The reader will be able to find a more thorough presentation on these events and on the doctrine here briefly outlined in the subsequent Chapter IV.
[4] Sozomen, *History of the Church*, VI, 24, 2-3 (SAEMO 24/I, p. 165).
[5] Cf. Elena Zocca, *La Vita Ambrosii alla luce dei rapport fra Paulino, Agostino e Ambrogio*, in *Nec timeo mori. Atti del Congresso internazionale di studi ambrosiani nel XVI centenario della morte di sant'Ambrogio. Milano, 4-11 aprile 1997*. Ed. L.F. Pizzolato and M. Rizzi, Milano, 1998, pp. 141-160 (esp. pp. 803-826).
[6] Cf. Paulinus, *Life of Ambrose*, I, 3 (SAEMO 24/II, pp. 28-31).
[7] Rufinus, *History of the Church*, XI, 11 (SAEMO 24/II, pp. 120-121).
[8] Cf. Paulinus, *Life of Ambrose* 6, 1-2 (SAEMO 24/II, pp. 34-35).
[9] Augustine, *Confessions*, VIII, 12, 29 (James J. O'Donnell, ed., Clarendon Press, Oxford, 1992), p. 101.
[10] Cf. Ambrose, *Letter 76* (Maur. 20) *to Marcellina*, 24 (SAEMO 21, pp. 150-151). For these observations and in general for the interpretation of the text of Paulinus on these proceedings I mostly follow Y.M. Duval, *Ambroise, de son élection à sa consécration* in *Ambrosius Episcopus. Atti del Congreso Internazionale di Studi Ambrosiani nel XVI centenario della elevazione di sant'Ambrogio alla cattedra episcopale, Milano 2-7 Dicembre 1974*, II, Milano, 1976 (Studia Patristica Mediolanensia, 7), pp. 243-283 to which I refer for the standing bibliography on the argument.
[11] Ambrose, *Commentary on the Gospel of Luke*, VIII, 73 (SAEMO 12, pp. 344-345).
[12] Cf. Paulinus, *Life of Ambrose*, 7, 1-9, 1 (SAEMO 24/II, pp. 34-39).
[13] Cf. L.F. Pizzolato, *Richerche su sant'Ambrogio. A Proposito di un Recente Libro di P. Courcelle*, "Aevum," 48 (1974), pp. 500-505.
[14] Paulinus, *Life of Ambrose*, 8, 2 (SAEMO 24/II, pp. 36-37).
[15] We have attestation of this in a law of which Ambrose himself, in 386, during the desperate contest with the court which I have already pointed out, supposedly reminds Valentinian II, the eponymous younger son of the Emperor: "In a case regarding the faith or any ecclesial order, the one who judges ought to be one who is neither unequal in rank nor dissimilar in legal status." Ambrose, *Letter 75* (Maur. 21) *to Valentinian II*, 2 (SAEMO 21, pp. 106-107).
[16] Rufinus, *History of the Church*, XI, 11 (SAEMO, 24/II, pp. 120-123). Ambrose too, in the letter to Valentinian II cited in the previous notation, supposedly reminded the young Emperor how the people had requested that his father appoint "the person that they now have as Bishop" and how he "guaranteed that there would be peace, if the one elected would accept the episcopacy." Ambrose, *Letter 75* (Maur. 21) *to Valentinian II*, 7 (SAEMO 21, pp. 108-109).
[17] Paulinus, *Life of Ambrose*, 9, 1 (SAEMO 24/II, pp. 38-39).
[18] Paulinus, *Life of Ambrose*, 9, 2 (SAEMO 24/II, pp. 38-39).
[19] Ambrose, *Letter Outside the Collection*, 14 (Maur. 63) *to the Church of Vercelli*, 65 (SAEMO 21, pp. 296-297).

[20] Paulinus, *Life of Ambrose*, 9, 3 (SAEMO 24/II, pp. 38-39).
[21] The date and the year of the episcopal ordination of Ambrose are definitively demonstrated in the study of O. Faller, *La data della consacrazione vescovile di sant'Ambrogio*, in *Ambrosiana, Scritti di Storia, Archeologia ed Arte Pubblicatin nel XVI Centenario della Nascita di Sant'Ambrogio. CCCXL-MCMXL*, Milan, 1942, pp. 97-112.
[22] Cf. B. Fisher, *Hat Ambrosius von Mailand in der Voche zwischen seiner Taufe und seiner Bishofskonsekration andere Weihe empfangen?* in *Kyriakon. Festschrift Johannes Quasten*, II, Münster i. W., 1970, pp. 527-531; É. Lamirande, *Paulin de Milan et la "Vita Ambrosii."* Aspects de la religion sous le Bas-Empire, Paris-Tournai-Montréal, 1983, p. 79, or *Cronologia ambrosiana. Bibliografia ambrosiana (1900-2000).* Ed. G. Visonà, Milano-Roma, 2004 (SAEMO 25-26, pp. 23-25).
[23] Paulinus, *Life of Ambrose*, 9, 2 (SAEMO 24/II, pp. 38-39).
[24] Augustine, *Confessions*, VIII, 2, 3 (O'Donnell, p. 89).
[25] Cf. H. Savon, *Simplicien, père d'Ambroise* "in accipienda gratia," in *Studia ambrosiana*, 1 (2007), pp. 147-159; C. Pasini, *Simpliciano e il vescovo Ambrogio*, ibid., pp. 45-65 (esp. p. 53).
[26] Cf. R. Pastè, *Da chi fu battezzato e consacrato S. Ambrogio (tradizione vercelese)*, "Ambrosius," 14 (1938), pp. 289-295; ibid., *Ancora: chi battezzò S. Ambrogio?*, "Ambrosius," 16 (1940), pp. 53-56.

Chapter II: Family Roots and His Youth

[1] Two sources come into consideration: *Letter 49* (Maur. 59) from Ambrose to the Bishop of Naples, Severinus, where in paragraphs 3-4 (SAEMO 20, pp. 80-81), the Bishop claims to be 53 years old (but this causes difficulties in placing the letter chronologically); and a lean reference derived from the biographer Paulinus regarding an assignment of the father of Ambrose "to the prefecture of Gaul" (but also in this case, as noted later in the text, this assignment was not able to be located precisely in the chronology). A complete examination of the various hypotheses and of the relative justifications is found in the *Cronologia ambrosiana. Bibliografia ambrosiana (190-2000).* Ed. G. Visonà, Milano-Roma, 2004 (SAEMO 25-26, pp. 15-20).
[2] Cf. H. Savon, *Ambroise de Milan (340-397)*, Paris, 1997, p. 31.
[3] Palladius, *Apology*, 115-116 (SC 267, pp. 300-301).
[4] "*Posito in administratione praefecturae Galliarum patre eius Ambrosio.*"
[5] Paulinus, *Life of Ambrose*, 4, 1 (SAEMO 24/II, pp. 32-33).
[6] Cf. M. de Dreuille, *S. Ambrogio della Massima. XII secoli di storia. La più antica casa religiosa di Roma*, Parma, 1996; P. Siniscalco, *Sant'Ambrogio e la Chiesa di Roma* in *Nec temo mori. Atti del Congresso internazionale di studi ambrosiani nel XVI centenario della morte di sant'Ambrogio. Milano, 4-11 aprile, 1997.* Ed. L.F. Pizzolato and M. Rizzi, Milan, 1998, pp. 141-160 (esp. pp. 142-144).
[7] Cf. H. Delehaye, *Trois dates du calendrier romain*, "Analecta sollandiana," 46 (1928), pp. 50-67 (esp. pp. 59-67).
[8] Ambrose, *On Virgins* III, 7, 38, & 37 (SAEMO 14/I, pp. 240-241).
[9] Ambrose, *Commendation to Virginity*, 12, 82 (SAEMO 14/II, pp. 262-263).
[10] Cf. F. Gori, in SAEMO 14/I, p. 205, n. 1, and *Cronologia ambrosiana*, op. cit., pp. 20-21.
[11] The two cited texts are: Ambrose, *On Virgins*, III, 1, 1-3, 14 (SAEMO 14/I, pp.

Endnotes

204-221) and Athanasius, *Letter to the Virgins* (CSCO 150, pp. 91-94; CSCO 151, pp. 72-76), while L. Dossi, *S. Ambrogio e S. Atanasio nel De virginibus,* "Acme," 4 (1951), pp. 241-262, has asserted on the track of L.-Th. Lefort, the strict dependence on Athanasius by the Ambrosian text, G. Rosso, *La "Lettera alle Virgini" Atanasio e Ambrogio,* "Augustinianum," 23 (1983), pp. 421-452, has somewhat revised the connection between the two texts: in any case the originality of the Ambrosian treatise *de Virginibus* had already been illustrated by Y.M. Duval, *L'originalité du de Virginibus dans le movement ascétique occidentale: Ambroise, Cyprien, Athanase,* in *Ambroise de Milan, XVI Centenaire de son élection épiscopale,* Paris, 1974, pp. 9-66.

[12] Paulinus, *Life of Ambrose* 4, 1-2 (SAEMO 24/II, pp. 32-33). This episode, datable no earlier than 353, affirms the date of birth at 340: it is, indeed, acceptable behavior for a boy of 13, but wouldn't be in a youth of 19 (which he would be if born in 334)!

[13] Ibid., 9, 4 (SAEMO 24/II, pp. 38-39).

[14] In ch. 8 of book II of *On Penance* (SAEMO 17, pp. 265-271), already cited in part, Ambrose accuses himself, affirming that he "was more remiss" because "called to the episcopacy from the clattering quarrels of the courts and from the dread of public administration" (68), going further imagining also that one might say of him: "Look at that one who has not been raised in the bosom of the Church, he has not been trained since childhood, but he has been torn from the tribunal, bound by the vanity of this age... he remains in the episcopacy not by his own worth" (72). These expressions, beyond the evident exaggerations, seem to me to be alluding to the growth of Ambrose from outside ecclesial life (because of the delay of his baptism) rather than from a wild youth.

[15] Cf. M. Forlin Patrucco-S. Roda, *Le lettere di Simmaco ad Ambrogio. Vent'anni di rapport amichevoli,* in *Ambrosius episcopus. Atti del Congresso internazionale di studi ambrosiani nel XVI centenario della elevazione di sant'Ambrogio alla cattedra episcopale, Milano 2-7 dicembre 1974,* II, Milan, 1976 (Studia Patristica Mediolanensia, 7), pp. 284-297 and my own *Chiesa di Milano e Sicilia. Punti di contratto dal IV all' VIII secolo,* in *Sicilia e Italia suburbicaria tra IV e VIII secolo. Atti del Convegno di Studi (Catania, 24-27 ottobre 1989),* Soveria Mannelli 1991, pp. 367-398 (esp. pp. 379-380).

[16] Cf. again my *Chiesa di Milano e Sicilia,* op. cit., pp. 368-380.

[17] Paulinus, *Life of Ambrose,* 5, 1-2 (SAEMO 24/II, pp. 32-35).

[18] Ibid., 8, 3 (SAEMO 24/II, pp. 36-37).

[19] Ibid., 3, 2-5 (SAEMO 24/II, pp. 30-33).

[20] Cf. I. Opelt, *Das Bienenwunder in der Ambrosiusbiographie des Paulinus von Mailand,* "Vigiliae Christianae," 22 (1968), pp. 38-44.

[21] Ambrose, *Commentary on the Gospel of Luke,* VIII, 74-75 (SAEMO 12, pp. 344-347).

[22] Ambrose, *On Penance,* II, 8, 73 (SAEMO 17, pp. 266-269).

[23] Cf. A. Ratti, *Il più antico ritratto di S. Ambrogio,* in *Ambrosiana. Scritti varii pubblicati nel XV centenario della morte di S. Ambrogio,* Milan, 1897; P. Courcelle, *Recherches sur saint Ambroise, "Vies" anciennes, culture, iconographie,* Paris, 1973, pp. 155-156. Alternately, quite critical, but perhaps with a preconceived attitude, N.B. McLynn, *Ambrose of Milan. Church and Court in a Christian Capital,* Berkeley, 1994, p. XVIII n. 16.

[24] A. Paredi, *Sant'Ambrogio,* op. cit., table I, comment and p. 159.

Chapter III: His Early Formation and "Father Simplician"

1. Ambrose, *On the Duties of the Clergy*, I, 1, 4 (SAEMO 13, pp. 24-25).
2. Ambrose, *On Virgins*, I, 1, 1-3 (SAEMO 14/I, pp. 100-103).
3. Paulinus, *Life of Ambrose*, 5, 1 (SAEMO 24/II, pp. 32-33). Cf. G. Maschio, *Ambrogio di Milano: note sulla formazione e sul metodo di lavoro*, Augustinianum, 49 (2009), pp. 145-175 (esp. pp. 145-151).
4. Cf. C. Somenzi, *Egesippo-Ambrogio. Formazione scholastica e Cristiana a Roma alla metà del IV secolo*, Milan, 2009 (Studia Patristica Mediolanensia, 27).
5. Cf. A. Paredi, *S. Gerolamo e S. Ambrogio*, in *Mélanges Eugène Tisserant*, V, Città del Vaticano, 1964 (Studi e Testi, 235), pp. 183-198; and my *Girolamo, santo*, in *Dizionario della Chiesa ambrosiana*, III, Milan, 1989, pp. 1471-1473.
6. Jerome, *Preface to the Books of Didymus on the Holy Spirit* (SAEMO 24/II, pp. 104-107).
7. Rufinus, *Apology Against Jerome*, II, 28 (SAEMO, 24/II, pp. 120-121).
8. Ambrose, *Commentary on Psalm 118*, IX, 20 (SAEMO 9, pp. 396-397).
9. Ambrose, for example, seeks to excuse the apostle Peter for having denied Jesus on the evening of Good Friday. The forced *apologia* of the Bishop tried to interpret the declaration of Peter "I do not know the man" in the sense in which the apostle was meant to deny that "he was a man whom he knew to be God"! (*Commentary on the Gospel of Luke*, X, 82, SAEMO 12, pp. 454-455). In this case we cannot contest Jerome when he says: "I know that certain ones, through devotion affected for the apostle Peter, interpret this passage saying that Peter did not deny God, but the man.... How futile this interpretation is; the reader should well understand: defending the apostle so to render God culpable of a lie. If in fact he had not denied him, then God lied when he had said: 'In truth, I tell you that this night, before the rooster crows, you will deny me three times.'" (*Commentary on Matthew*, IV, 27, SAEMO 24/II, pp. 112-113).
10. R. Cantalamessa, *Sant'Ambrogio di fronte ai grandi dibattiti teologici del suo secolo* in *Ambrosius episcopus. Atti del Congresso internazionale di studi ambrosiani nel XVI centenario della elevazione di sant'Ambrogio alla cattedra episcopale, Milano 2-7 dicembre, 1974*, I, Milan, 1976 (Studia Patristica Mediolanensia, 6), pp. 483-539 (esp. p. 539).
11. Augustine, *Confessions*, VIII, 2, 3 (O'Donnell, p. 89).
12. Cf. C. Pasini, *Simpliciano e il vescovo Ambrogio*, Studia Ambrosiana, 1 (2007), pp. 45-65. See also A. Solignac, *Il circolo neoplatonico Milanese al tempo della conversion di Agostino*, in *Agostino a Milano. Il battesimo. Agostino nelle terre di Ambrogio (22-24 aprile 1987)*, Palermo, 1988 (Augustiniana. Testi e Studi, 3), pp. 43-56 (esp. pp. 45-48).
13. Specifically, numbers 2, 3, 7, and 10 (respectively Maur. 65, 67, 37, and 38).
14. Gennadius, *Illustrious Men: Simplician*, 36 (CCEL/schaff/npnf203.txt. Cf. PL 58, coll. 1078-1079).
15. Solignac, *Il circolo neoplatonico*, op. cit., p. 47.
16. Specifically I, 2, 5-7, 24.
17. Augustine, *Confessions*, VI, 3, 3 (O'Donnell, p. 59).
18. Ambrose, *Commentary on Psalm 118*, XI, 9 (SAEMO 9, pp. 456-459).
19. Even if not everyone accepts the Ambrosian paternity of *On the Sacraments*. One synthesis of the positions is espoused in *Cronologia ambrosiana. Bibliografia ambrosiana (1900-2000)*. Ed. G. Visonà, Milano-Roma, 2004 (SAEMO 25-26, pp. 123-124, 132-133).

Endnotes

[20] Cf. G. Nauroy, *Le fouet et le miel. Le combat d'Ambroise en 386 contre l'arianisme milanais,* "Recherches Augustiniennes," 23 (1988), pp. 3-86 (esp. pp. 79-80).
[21] Ambrose, *Six Days of Creation,* V, 12, 36-37 (SAEMO 1, pp. 286-287).
[22] Ambrose, *Letter 32* (Maur. 48) *to Sabinus,* 1-3 (SAEMO 19, pp. 310-313). The letter is also important for the structure of the Ambrosian epistolary (cf. M. Zelzer in CSEL 82/II, pp. XVII-XVIII & XXVI).
[23] Ambrose, *Letter 7* (Maur. 37) *to Simplician,* 3 and 1-2 (SAEMO 19, pp. 72-73).

Chapter IV: "Take Heart, Heal the Ills of the People"

[1] Basil of Caesarea, *Letter 197 to Ambrose,* 1 (SAEMO, 24/I, p. 52). Concerning this letter, and especially paragraph 2, which most likely is not authentic (concerning the passage to Milan of the relics of Bishop Dionysius), permit me to refer back to that evidence in the introduction to SAEMO 24/I, pp. 35-49, and in the article *S. Dionigi, vescovo (+360c.),* in *Dizionario dei Santi della Chiesa di Milano,* Milan, 1995, pp. 58-63.
[2] Ibid., 1 (SAEMO, 24/I, p. 51).
[3] I reprise many dates from my *Le discussioni teologiche a Milano nei secoli dal IV al VIII,* in *Diocesi di Milano,* Brescia, 1990 (Storia religiosa della Lombardia, 9-10), pp. 43-82 (in particular pp. 46-55). See also C. Alzati, *Un cappadoce in Occidente durante le dispute trinitarie del IV secolo. Aussenzio di Milano,* idem, *Ambrosiana ecclesia. Studi su la Chiesa Milanese e l'Ecumene Cristiana fra tarda antichità e medioevo,* Milan, 1993 (Archivo Ambrosiano, 65), pp. 45-95. Concerning the arguments treated in this chapter, I take note of (and cite in detail, indicating in advance that in controversial cases I follow the interpretation that is deemed most plausible) D.H. Williams, *Ambrose of Milan and the End of the Nicene-Arian Conflicts,* Oxford, 1995; and C. Markschies, *Ambrosius von Mailand und die Trinitätstheologie. Kirchen-und theologiesgeschichtliche Studien zu Antiarianismus und Neunizänismus bei Ambrosius und im lateinischen Westen* (364-381 n. Chr.), Tübingen, 1995 (Beiträge zur historischen Theologie, 90).
[4] Resulting in the appellation of *homoean* attributed to the supporters of this doctrine (and, similarly, '*homoean*' used as an adjective).
[5] Gaudentius of Brescia, *Treatises, XXI,* 6-7 (DCO 02m/0370-0430, p. 999).
[6] Cf. M. Richard, *Saint Basile et la mission du diacre Sabinus,* "Analecta Bollandiana," 67 (1949), pp. 178-202.
[7] To whom Ambrose wrote letters numbered 27, 32, 33, 34, 37, 39, and 40 (respectively Maur. 58, 48, 49, 45, 47, 46, and 32).
[8] Jerome, *Letter 1 to Innocent,* 15 (NA/fathers/3001001.htm).
[9] Ambrose, *Letter Outside the Collection,* 14 (Maur. 63) *to the Curch of Vercelli,* 70 (SAEMO 21, pp. 298-299).
[10] Theophilus of Alexandria, *Letter to Flavian of Antioch,* fragment 1 (SAEMO 24/I, p. 213). Regarding this letter permit me to refer to my introduction in SAEMO 24/I, pp. 155-157.
[11] Ibid. (SAEMO 24/I, p. 213).
[12] Sometimes cited as an exception, there is the episode of the cleric who was not accepted by Ambrose, "because his comportment was somewhat improper," and who later "reneged on the faith at the time of the Arian persecution," that is during the events of 386 (*On the Duties of the Clergy* I, 18, 72; SAEMO 13, pp. 68-69): but one understands that this intervention of the Bishop does not have anything to do with our argument.

[13] For the specific connotation of the Trinitarian theology of Ambrose, see Markschies, *Ambrosius von Mailand*, op. cit. (Cf. in summary, p. 212, "The Trinitarian theology of Ambrose, on the surface not particularly original, in reality ought to be understood as a legitimate witness of a Latin neo-niceanism, crafted impromptu and totally personal; it is the testimony of a highly creative engagement with the theological tradition").

[14] Paulinus, *Life of Ambrose*, 11, 1-2 (SAEMO 24/II, pp. 38-41).

[15] Cf. R. Gryson in SC 267, pp. 107-121.

[16] Cf. Markschies, *Ambrosius von Mailand*, op. cit., p. 133.

[17] If it can be affirmed that the inspiration of Ambrose is possibly found in the *relatio* of the Council sent to the Emperors; and anyway this *relatio* was inserted in the publications of the epistolary of St. Ambrose, as *Letter Outside the Collection*, 7 *to the Emperors* (SAEMO 21, pp. 204-215); cf. M. Zelzer in CSEL 82/III, pp. XCI-XCV. For the opposing view, see again Markschies, *Ambrosius von Mailand*, op. cit., p. 165.

[18] Ambrose, *On the Holy Spirit* I, 1, 19-21 (SAEMO 16, pp. 70-71).

[19] Cf. Council of Aquileia, *Letter 2* = Ambrose, *Letter Outside the Collection*, 4 (Maur. 10) *to the Emperors*, 9-10 (SAEMO 21, pp. 346-347).

[20] Ambrose, *Letter Outside the Collection*, 5 (Maur. 11) *to the Emperors*, 3 (SAEMO 21, pp. 196-197).

[21] Ambrose, *On Faith*, I, Prologue, 1 (SAEMO 15, pp. 52-53).

[22] Ibid.

[23] For the dating of this work (and of those connected to it) I accept the reconstruction most commonly followed by scholars, even if these differ from the studies of Gunther Gottlieb (1973) which suggested a slightly later date (cf. Williams, *Ambrose of Milan*, op. cit., pp. 129-130, footnote 8).

[24] Ambrose, *On Faith*, I, 1, 8-10 (SAEMO 15, pp. 58-59).

[25] Ibid., III, 1, 1-2 (SAEMO 15, pp. 192-193).

[26] Gratian, *Letter of Emperor Gratian* (preface of the treatise *On the Holy Spirit*), 3 (SAEMO 16, pp. 48-49).

[27] Ambrose, *Letter Outside the Collection*, 12 (Maur. 1) *to Gratian*, 2 (SAEMO 21, pp. 242-243).

[28] R. Cantalamessa, *Sant'Ambrogio di fronte ai grandi dibattiti teologici del suo secolo*, in *Ambrosius episcopus. Atti del Congresso internazionale di studi ambrosiani nel XVI centenario della elevazione di Sant'Ambrogio alla cattedra episcopale, Milano 2-7 dicembre 1974*, I, Milan, 1976 (Studia Patristica Mediolanensia, 6), pp. 483-539 (in particular p. 539).

[29] Ambrose, *On Faith*, V, 3, 45-46 (SAEMO 15, pp. 356-357).

[30] Ibid., IV, 8, 91 (SAEMO 15, pp. 296-27).

[31] Ibid., II, 11, 89-90 (SAEMO 15, pp. 170-171).

[32] Ibid., II, 11, 90-95 (SAEMO 15, pp. 170-173).

Chapter V: Guide to Monks and Consecrated Virgins

[1] Francesco Petrarch, *On the Solitary Life*, II, 4 (F. Petrarch, *Opere latine*, ed. by A. Bufano, I, Torino, 1975, pp. 406-409).

[2] Andrea da Strumi, *Passione del santo martire milanese Arialdo*, 17, ed. by M. Navoni, Milan, 1994, "Di fronte e attraverso," 355, pp. 110-111.

Endnotes

3. It is located on the Via Peschiera, not far from the Arco di Pace.
4. Cf. F. Repetto-G. Rocca, *Sant'Ambrogio "ad Nemus,"* in *Dizionario degli Istituti di perfezione*, VIII, Rome, 1988, coll. 746-747.
5. Cf. Romite dell'Ordine di Sant'Ambrogio ad Nemis, *Il monastero di Santa Maria del Monte sopra Varese*, Gavirate-Varese, 2006 (La storia di Varese, IV, part 1).
6. Cf. G. Turazza, *Sant'Ambrogio ad Nemus in Milano. Notizie storiche dall'anno 357 al 1912*, Milan, 1914.
7. Sulpicius Severus, *Life of St. Martin*, 6, 4 (DCO 0360-0420).
8. Appearances notwithstanding, this is how one should understand the expression of Sulpicius Severus: "statuit sibi monasterium." (Translator's note: Pasini's source translates "monasterium" with "hermitage." Cf. *Vita di Martino. Vita di Ilarione. In memoria di Paola*, edited by A.A.R. Bastiaensen and J.W. Smit, Milan, 1975, Vite dei santi, 4, pp. 20-21 and 267.)
9. Augustine, *Confessions*, VIII, 6, 14-15 (O'Donnell, pp. 94-95).
10. Augustine, *Customs of the Catholic Church and Customs of the Manicheans*, I, 33, 70 (DCO 0354-0430. P. 1339-1340; cf. PL 32, coll. 1339-1340).
11. Ambrose, *Letter Outside the Collection*, 14 (Maur. 63) *to the Church of Vercelli*, 66 (SAEMO 21, pp. 296-297).
12. It might also be possible to recall the texts that Ambrose dedicated to the theme of solitude: cf. C. Somenzi, *Ambrogio e Scipione l'Africano: la fondazione Cristiana dell'otium negotiosum*, in *Nec timeo mori. Atti del Congresso internazionale di studi ambrosiani nel XVI centenario della morte di sant'Ambrogio. Milano, 4-11 aprile 1997*. Ed. L.F. Pizzolato and M. Rizzi, Milan, 1998, pp. 753-768.
13. Ambrose, *Letter 37* (Maur. 47) *to Sabinus*, 1 (SAEMO 20, pp. 40-41).
14. Paulinus, *Life of Ambrose*, 38, 1-5 (SAEMO 24/II, pp. 68-69).
15. Ibid., 47, 3 (SAEMO 24/II, pp. 78-79).
16. Cf. F. Gori, in SAEMO 14/I, pp. 44-46.
17. Cf. Jerome, *Letter 22 to Eustochium*, 22; *Letter 49 (48) to Pammachius*, 14 (SAEMO 24/II, pp. 104-105 and 108-111).
18. N.B. McLynn, *Ambrose of Milan. Church and Court in a Christian Capital*, Berkeley, 1994, pp. 60 and 62.
19. Ibid., p. 68.
20. G. Oggioni, *Matrimonio e verginità presso I Padri (fino a S. Agostino)*, in *Matrimonio e verginità. Saggi di teologia*, Venegono Inferiore, 1963, pp. 159-418 (esp. p. 286).
21. In wake of the Pauline affirmation: "It was not for Adam to be deceived, but the woman who, deceived, admits herself culpable of transgression" (1 Tm 2:14).
22. Ambrose, *On Instructions for Virgins*, 3, 16-5, 33 (SAEMO 14/II, pp. 122-135).
23. Cf. Y.M. Duval, *L'originalité du* De Virginibus *dans the movement ascétique occidentale: Ambroise, Cyprien, Athanase*, in *Ambroise de Milan. XVI Centenaire de son élection épiscopale*, Paris, 1974, pp. 9-66 (esp. p. 14).
24. Ambrose, *On Virgins*, I, 10, 57-58 (SAEMO 14/I, pp. 156-157).
25. Ambrose, *On Virginity*, 5, 25-26 (SAEMO 14/I, pp. 28-31).
26. Ambrose, *On Virgins*, I, 11, 65-66 (SAEMO 14/I, pp. 160-165).
27. For the citations on this last part and for their connection I have followed the *Costituzioni delle Romite dell'Ordine di S. Ambrogio ad Nemus*, S. Maria del Monte (Varese) 1988, n. 1-4.

[28] Ambrose, *On Virgins*, I, 5 (SAEMO 14/I, pp. 122-123).
[29] Ambrose, *Commendation to Virginity*, 9, 57 (SAEMO 14/II, pp. 244-245).
[30] Ibid., 9, 58 (SAEMO 14/II, pp. 244-245).
[31] Ambrose, *Commentary on Psalm 118*, VI, 8 (SAEMO 9, pp. 246-247).
[32] Ambrose, *On Virginity*, 16, 99 (SAEMO 14/I, pp. 78-81).

Chapter VI: Marcellina and Satyrus

[1] For the prefaces of the respective Masses for Saint Marcellina and for Saint Satyrus in the Ambrosian liturgy, cf. *Missale Ambrosianum iuxta ritum Sanctae Ecclesiae Mediolanensis, ex decreto Sacrosancti Oecumenici Concilii Vaticani II instauraturm*, Milan, 1981, n 347/6 and 393/6.

[2] Cf. M. Navoni, *Dai Longobardi ai Carolingi*, in *Diocesi di Milano*, Brescia-Gazzeda, 1990 (Storia religiosa della Lombardia, 9-10), pp. 83-121 (esp. pp. 97-98 and 109-113); E. Cattaneo, *La tradizione e il rito ambrosiani nell'ambiente Lombardomedioevale*, in *Ambrosius episcopus. Atti del Congresso internazionale di studi ambrosiani nel XVI centenario della elevazione di sant'Ambrogio alla cattedra episcopale, Milano 2-7 dicembre 1974*, II, Milan, 1976 (Studia Patristica Mediolanensia, 7, pp. 5-47, esp. 9-19).

[3] In this chapter I reaffirm many dates which I have already expressed in two articles: *S. Marcellina, vergine* (d. 400 c.e.) and *S. Satiro* (d. 378), in *Dizionario dei Santi della Chiesa di Milano*, Milan, 1995, pp. 84-91 and 124-128.

[4] I follow the position of Otto Faller (reaffirmed in CSEL 73, pp. 81*-89*), recorded (even if with doubts) in *Chronologia ambrosiana. Bibliografia ambrosiana (1900-2000)*. Ed. C. Visonà, Milan-Rome, 2004 (SAEMO 25-26, pp. 25-28); the dates of September 18, 377 or 378 are asserted respectively in J.-Ch. Picard, *Le souvenir des évêques. Sépultures, listes épiscopales et culte des évêques in Italie du Nord des origines au Xe siècle*, Rome, 1988 (Bibliothèque des Écoles françaises d'Athenes et de Rome, 268), p. 605; and in N.B. McLynn, *Ambrose of Milan. Church and Court in a Christian Capital*, Berkeley, 1994, p. 69. Other dates are collectively indicated ibid., n. 56. The interpretation of this author that has Ambrose exclusively a master of efficiency even in this context cannot be agreed with: "At one level, Satyrus' death was a godsend, giving Ambrose a privileged platform from which to address his people; he could thus assert a role for Satyrus — and for himself"! p. 76.

[5] Cf. O. Heiming, *Das Festdatum des hl. Satyrus von Mailand und die orientalische Quelle des Martyrologium Hieronymianum*, in *Orientalia Christiana Periodica*, 17 (1951), pp. 451-462.

[6] Perhaps even in this list the name Satyrus was not original. In fact, the *Martyrologium Hieronymianum* has derived this note with all probability from a Syriac source which it regularly used; in the Syriac text the name Castor may have been written twice because of an error and, since the terms Castor and Satyrus are written nearly identically, the second time it was interpreted as Satyrus.

[7] Ambrose, *On the Death of his Brother*, I, 20 (SAEMO 18, pp. 38-39).
[8] Ibid., I, 31 (SAEMO 18, pp. 46-47).
[9] Ibid., I, 58 (SAEMO 18, pp. 62-63).
[10] Ambrose, *On Virgins*, III, 7, 37 (SAEMO 14/I, pp. 240-241).
[11] Ambrose, *On the Death of his Brother* I, 76, 16, 41, and 54 respectively (SAEMO 18, pp. 72-73, 34-35, 52-53, and 60-61).
[12] Ibid., I, 8 and 20 (SAEMO 18, pp. 28-31 and 38-39).

Endnotes

[13] Ibid., I, 38 (SAEMO 18, pp. 50-51).
[14] Ibid., I, respectively 20, 24, 17, and 27 (SAEMO 18, pp. 38-39, 40-41, 36-37, and 42-43).
[15] Ibid., I, 43-44, and 48 (SAEMO 18, pp. 52-57).
[16] Ibid., I, 52 (SAEMO 18, pp. 58-59).
[17] Ambrose, *Epitaph for his brother Satyrus* (SAEMO 22, pp. 98-99).
[18] Cf. Dungalus, *Book against Claudius of Turin to the Emperors Ludovico and Lothario* (PL 105, col. 527).
[19] Ambrose, *Letter 76* (Maur. 20) *to Marcellina*, 1; *Letter 77* (Maur. 22), *to Marcellina*, intro. and 1; *Letter Outside the Collection*, 1 (Maur. 41) *to Marcellina*, 1 (SAEMO 21, pp. 136-137, 154-155 and 170-171).
[20] Cf. also for a certain assessment of what follows in the text, M. Zelzer, in CSEL 82/II, pp. XV-XXXIX and 82/III, pp. XIX-XXV and LXXXIV-LXXXVI.
[21] Cf. Ambrose, *Letter 56* (Maur. 5) *to Siagrius*, 21 (SAEMO 20, pp. 122-125).
[22] Cf. *Epitaph for Marcellina*, CIL 5, 623.
[23] Precisely in the marble Calendar of Naples and in the Greek Synaxaria: cf. H. Delehaye, *Quelques dates du Martyrologe hiéronymien*, "Analecta Bollandiana," 49 (1931), pp. 22-50 (esp. pp. 35-36).
[24] Cf. my *San Satiro e il suo culto a Milano*, in *Insula Ansperti. Il complesso monumentale di S. Satiro*, Milano, 1992, pp. 27-37; A. Ambrosioni, *Contributo alla storia della festa di san Satiro a Milano. A proposito di due documenti dell'Archivio di S. Ambrogio*, in *Richerche storiche sulla Chiesa ambrosiana*, III, Milan, 1972 (Archivo Ambrosiano, 23), pp. 71-96.
[25] It is situated at the top of Via Torino, set back a little way from the street.
[26] Cf. G. Figini, *Marcellina in Muggiano, chiesa di S.*, in *Dizionario della Chiesa ambrosiana*, III, Milan, 1989, p. 1875.
[27] Cf. G. Andreotti, *Marcelline*, in *Dizionario della Chiesa ambrosiana*, III, Milan, 1989, pp. 1882-1883.

Chapter VII: Aquileia: September 3, 381

[1] Council of Aquileia, *Acts* (SAEMO 21, pp. 350-351). Regarding the Council of Aquileia, cf. the *Introduction* in R. Gryson in SC 267; D.H. Williams, *Ambrose of Milan and the End of the Nicene-Arian Conflicts*, Oxford, 1995, pp. 154-184 (in reference to pages 169-172 numerous recent studies are recalled; see also pp. 185-190 for other aspects dealt with in this chapter).
*Translator's note: the Italian is *assise,* indicating that the 'Council' was effectively a court of law. Cf. the English *assize.*
[2] Council of Aquileia, *Acts*, respectively 6, 14 32, and 54 (SAEMO 21, pp. 354-345, 358-359, 370-371 and 384-385).
*Translator's note: Illiricum, including Serbia, Croatia, Bosnia/Herzegovina and Bulgaria, was part of the Western Empire. Raeteria is in Bulgaria, Singindunum is Belgrade.
[3] Ibid., 8-11 (SAEMO 21, pp. 354-357); the text has been simplified with the omission of the term "*saying*" that introduces the input of each speaker.
[4] Ibid., 18-21 (SAEMO 21, pp. 362-363): with the same simplification of the text.
[5] Ibid., 53 (SAEMO 21, pp. 382-283).
[6] Ibid., 42-43 (SAEMO 21, pp. 376-377).
[7] Palladius, *Apology,* 112 (SC 267, pp. 296-299).

[8] Ibid., 114 (SC 267, pp. 298-299).
*Translator's note: the word used here is "*Processo.*"
[9] Council of Aquileia, *Acts,* 51 (SAEMO 21, pp. 382-283).
[10] Palladius, *Apology,* 139 (SC 267, pp. 322-323).
[11] L. Cracco Ruggini, *Ambrogio e le opposizioni anticattoliche fra il 383 e il 390,* "Augustinianum," 14 (1974), pp. 409-449 (esp. p. 412).
[12] Cf. Council of Aquileia, *Letter 2* = Ambrose, *Letter Outside the Collection,* 4 (Maur. 13) *to the Emperors,* 8 (SAEMO 21, pp. 344-345).
[13] In the text the following three letters will be dealt with: Council of Aquileia, *Letter 1,* Ambrose, *Letter Outside the Collection,* 6 and *Letter Outside the Collection,* 9 (respectively Maur. 9, 12, and 13).
[14] Ambrose, *Letter Outside the Collection,* 9 (Maur. 13), *to Theodosius,* 6 (SAEMO 21, pp. 222-223).
[15] Cf. M. Simonetti, *La crisi ariana nel IV secolo,* Rome, 1975 (Studia ephemeridis "Augustinianum," 11), pp. 549-551.
[16] Ambrose himself never mentions Maximus again; as for Antioch, on the other hand, the Council of Capua of 392 wanted again to support Evagrius, successor of Paulinus, against Flavian.
[17] Ambrose, *Letter Outside the Collection,* 8 (Maur. 14) *to Theodosius,* 2 and 6 (SAEMO 21, pp. 214-217).
[18] Paulinus, *Life of Ambrose,* 18, 1-4 (SAEMO 24/II, pp. 44-47).
[19] It is not possible (or appropriate) to give a full explanation of these definitions here. I recall only that the term *hypostasis,* a simple transliteration of the Greek *hypostasis,* assumes the significance of "individual sustenance." On the themes which are taken up in the text, and again concerning the influence of Ambrose in the East (of which I will speak later), permit me to return to my introduction in SAEMO 24/I, pp. 55-88, and to my *Le discussion teologiche a Milano nei secoli dal IV al VII,* in *diocese di Milano,* Brescia, 1990 (Storia religiosa della Lombardia, 9-10), pp. 43-82 (esp. pp. 61-77) and *Ambrogio nella teologia posteriore greca. Un'indagine nei secoli Ve VI,* in *Nec temeo mori. Atti del Congresso internazionale di studi ambrosiani nel XVI centenario della morte di sant'Ambrogio. Milano, 4-11 aprile 1997.* Ed. L.F. Pizzolato e M. Rizzi, Milan, 1998, pp. 365-404.
[20] Ambrose, Hymn *On the Birth of the Lord,* strophe 5 (SAEMO 22, p. 48-49).
[21] Ambrose, *The Sacrament of the Incarnation of the Lord,* 5, 35-36 (SAEMO 16, pp. 396-399).
[22] Ambrose, *On Faith,* II, 9, 77 (SAEMO 15, pp. 164-165).
[23] The *canon* is a hymn of the Byzantine liturgy that may be sung in the *Divine Office* to the *Morning Lauds*: it was composed in 8 (or 9) *odes,* some designed in more strophes called *tropari.*
[24] Joseph the Hymnist, *Canon in Honor of St. Ambrose,* ode III, tropario 1 (SAEMO 24/I, pp. 356-357).

Chapter VIII: Roman Tradition and Christian Innovation

[1] Cf. F. Paschoud, *Cinq études sur Zosime,* Paris, 1975, pp. 88-93. (Cf. also Socrates Scholasticus, *History of the Church,* V, 11 and the relevant annotations in SAEMO 24/1, pp. 161-163.)
[2] Ambrose, *Commentary on Psalm 61,* 17 & 23-25 (SAEMO 8, pp. 296-7 & 304-309).

Endnotes

[3] Ambrose, *Letter 30* (Maur. 24) *to Valentinian* II, 7 (SAEMO 19, pp. 292-293).
[4] Rufinus, *History of the Church*, XI, 15 (SAEMO, 24/II, pp. 122-123).
[5] Paulinus, *Life of Ambrose*, 9, 2 (SAEMO 24/II, pp. 38-39).
[6] While amply studied, in the past and still today, I would prefer to locate this second mission two years later. The tone and the attitude that Ambrose uses in his encounter with the usurper is the same as found in a debate — the full detailing already referred to in the noted letter to Valentinian — leads me to prefer the later date. This isn't to clarify the uncertainty, nor to suggest one choice in preference to the other. The Priscillian affair, which we will discuss, is chronologically tied to this embassy. On the one hand, indeed, the phases of the process to which Priscillian was subjected cannot be dated with precision; on the other hand, Ambrose refers only to the presence of Bishops who wish to accuse and condemn Priscillian to death, without specifying any further details. For an examination of the different positions, cf. *Cronologia ambrosiana. Bibliografia ambrosiana (1900-2000)*. Ed. G. Visonà, Milan-Rome, 3004 (SAEMO 25-26), pp. 32-36.
[7] Ambrose, *Letter 30* (Maur. 24) *to Valentinian* II, 5-6 (SAEMO 19, pp. 290-293): for the sake of the dialogue the text was simplified with the omission of the *verba dicendi* which connect the contributions of each of the interlocutors.
[8] Ibid., 12 (SAEMO 19, pp. 296-297).
[9] Cf. Mazzarino, *Storia Sociale* cit., pp. 31-36.
[10] Ambrose, *Letter Outside the Collection*, 10 (Maur. 57) *to Eugenius*, 2 (SAEMO 21, pp. 224-225). In this interpretation I follow McLynn, *Ambrose of Milan*, cited, pp. 151-152.
[11] Ambrose, *Letter 72* (Maur. 17) *to Valentinian* II, 10 (SAEMO 21, pp. 44-45).
[12] Cf. L. Cracco Ruggini, *Ambrogio e le opposizioni anticattoliche fra il 383 e il 390*, "Augustinianum," 14 (1974), pp. 409-449 (in particular, pp. 434-436).
[13] Cf. again M. Forlin Patrucco-S. Roda, *Le lettere di Simmaco ad Ambrogio. Vent'anni di rapporti amichevoli*, in *Ambrosius episcopus. Atti del Congresso internazionale di studi ambrosiani nel XVI centenario della elevazione di sant'Ambrogio alla cattedra episcopale, Milano 2-7 dicembre, 1974*, II, Milano, 1976 (Studia Patristica Mediolanensia, 7) pp. 284-297; and my *Chiesa di Milano e Sicilia: punti di contatto dal IV all' VIII secolo*, in *Sicilia e Italia suburbicaria tra IV e VIII secolo. Atti del Convegno di Studi (Catania, 24-27 ottobre, 1989)*, Soveria Mannelli, 1991, pp. 367-398 (in particular, pp. 379-380).
[14] Symmachus, *Espistula – Letter* 72a in the epistolary of Ambrose (Maur. 17a), 20 (SAEMO 21, pp. 60-61).
[15] Ibid., 3 and 7 (SAEMO 21, pp. 50-53).
[16] Ibid., 5 and 10 (SAEMO 21, pp. 52-57).
   *Translator's note: that is, 382, when Gratian passed anti-pagan legislation without any influence from Ambrose.
[17] Ambrose, *Letter 72* (Maur. 17) *to Valentinian* II, 12-15 (SAEMO 21, pp. 44-47).
[18] Symmachus, *Relatio = Letter 72a* (Maur. 17a), 9 (SAEMO 21, pp. 54-55): Ambrose, *Letter 73* (Maur. 18) *to Valentinian* II, 4-5 (Ibid., pp. 62-65).
[19] Symmachus, *Relatio = Letter 72a* (Maur. 17a), 15-16 (SAEMO 21, pp. 59-60); Ambrose, *Letter 73* (Maur. 18) *to Valentinian* II, 19-21 (ibid., pp. 74-77).
[20] Ambrose, *Letter 73* (Maur. 18) *to Valentinian* II, 12 and 14 (SAEMO 21, pp. 68-73).
[21] Cf. M. Sordi, *L'atteggiamento di Ambrogio di fronte a Roma e al paganesimo*, in *Ambrosius episcopus. Atti del Congresso internazionale di studi ambrosiani nel XVI centenario della elevazione di sant'Ambrogio alla cattedra episcopale, Milano*

2-7 dicembre 1974, I, Milano, 1976 (Studia Patristica Mediolanensia, 6), pp. 203-229.
[22] Ambrose, Letter 73 (Maur. 18) to Valentinian II, 7 (SAEMO 21, pp. 61-67).
[23] Ibid., 23-29 (SAEMO 21, pp. 76-79).
[24] Cf. L. Cracco Ruggini, Ambrogio e le opposizioni, op. cit., pp. 438-439.
[25] Sozomen, History of the Church, VII, 25, 10-12 (SAEMO 24/I, pp. 174-175).
[26] Paulinus, Life of Ambrose, 48, 3 (SAEMO 24/II, pp. 78-79).

Chapter IX: A Contested Basilica and a People Bound by Their Bishop

[1] "In order that he might not be recognized, he changed his name; thus, since here (at Milan) there had been a Bishop Auxentius, to deceive the people that that one had also governed them, he changed himself to Auxentius." Ambrose, *Discourse Against Auxentius (Contra Auxentius) = Ep. 75a* (Maur. 21a), 22 (SAEMO 21, pp. 126-127). But Palladius of Ratiaria refers to him as "Auxentius of Durostorum" referring, it seems, to the period preceding his arrival at Milan: cf. Palladius, *Apology*, 140 (SC 267, pp. 322-325).
[2] Cf. D.H. Williams, *Ambrose of Milan and the End of the Nicene-Arian Conflicts*, Oxford, 1995, pp. 202-210.
[3] Ambrose, *Commentary on the Gospel of Luke*, VII, 52-53 (SAEMO 12, pp. 130-131).
[4] Ambrose, *On the Duties of the Clergy* I, 18, 72 (SAEMO, 13, pp. 68-69).
[5] Ambrose, *Discourse Against Auxentius = Letter 75a* (Maur. 21a), 37 (SAEMO 21, pp. 136-137).
[6] Ibid., 29 (SAEMO 21, pp. 130-133).
[7] Ibid., 16 (SAEMO 21, pp. 122-123).
[8] *Codex Theodosianus*, XVI, 1, 4 and in reduced form, XVI, 4, 1 (TLC/Theodosius/theo16.shtml; cf. L. De Giovanni, *Chiesa e Stato nel codice Teodosiano. Saggio sul libro XVI*, Naples, 1980, pp. 35-41).
[9] Rufinus, *History of the Church*, XI, 16 (SAEMO 24/II, pp. 122-125).
[10] Gaudentius of Brescia, *Treatises: Prefaces*, 1-6 (DCO 0370-0430, pp. 827-30).
[11] Cf. M. Magni, *Giovanni ale fonti, battistero di S.*, in *Dizionario della Chiesa ambrosiana*, III, Milan, 1989, p. 1444; M. David, *Maria Maggiore, basilica di S. (Prima del IX sec.)*, ibid., IV, Milan, 1990, pp. 2035-2037; idem, *Porziana, basilica*, ibid., V Milan, 1992, pp. 2931-2933; idem, *Stefano alle Fonti, battistero di S.*, ibid., VI, Milan, 1993, pp. 3556-3557; idem, *Tecla, basilica di S. (Sec. IV-VI)*, ibid., pp. 3640-3643.
[12] Scholars almost unanimously locate the events here described in 386, and as a consequence, fix the events retold in a letter from Ambrose to Marcellina (of whom he often speaks in the text) to the days immediately before Easter of that year. The dating of the *Discourse Against Auxentius* (and a letter from Valentinian to him, of which more will be said in the text), however, remains uncertain. Because I cannot believe that the deeds recounted in the letter to Marcellina correspond to those described in the *Discourse*, and therefore it (along with the letter by Valentinian) cannot be placed in the days immediately preceding Easter, I hold as valid the solution that the *Discourse* (and the events correlated to it) are earlier by several weeks, as has been re-proposed by G. Nauroy, *Le fouet et le miel. Le combat d' Ambroise en 386 contre l'arianisme milanais*, "Recherches Augustiniennes," 23 (1988), pp. 3-86. The hypothesis that transfers the *Discourse* to the period after Easter seems to me less acceptable, when by then there were no more motives

Endnotes

for requesting a church for baptismal celebrations; this interpretive line is nonetheless held by certain scholars, as, for example, G. Gottlieb, *Der Mailänder Kirchenstreit von 385-386. Datierung, Verlauf, Deutung,* "Museum Helveticum," 42 (1985), pp. 37-55; Williams, *Ambrose of Milan,* op. cit., pp. 210-215; McLynn, *Ambrose of Milan,* op. cit., pp. 196-208. A complete examination of the positions is referenced in *Cronologia ambrosiana. Bibliografia ambrosiana (1900-2000).* Ed. G. Visonà, Milan-Rome, 2004 (SAEMO 25-26), pp. 37-43.

[13] Ambrose, *Letter. 75* (Maur. 21) *to Valentinian II,* respectively 1-2, 4 and 12 (SAEMO 21, pp. 106-111).

[14] Ambrose, *Discourse Against Auxentius = Letter 75a* (Maur. 21a), 35-36 (SAEMO 21, pp. 134-137).

[15] Nauroy, *Le fouet et le miel,* op. cit., p. 44.

[16] Ambrose, *Discourse Against Auxentius = Letter 75a* (Maur. 21a), 4, 7, and 10 respectively (SAEMO 21, pp. 116-121).

[17] Ibid., respectively 2 8, and 16 (SAEMO 21, pp. 114-119 and 122-123); Paulinus, *Life of Ambrose* 12, 2-4 (SAEMO 24/II, pp. 40-41).

[18] Ambrose, *Letter 76* (Maur. 20) *to Marcellina,* 1 (SAEMO 21, pp. 136-137).

[19] In the brief homily on *Explanation of the Creed* (SAEMO 17, pp. 25-39) is found one of the catechesis that Ambrose used in a similar situation.

[20] Ambrose, *Letter 76* (Maur. 20) *to Marcellina,* 6 (SAEMO 21, pp. 138-141).

[21] Ibid., 8-10 (SAEMO 21, pp. 140-143).

[22] I accept the identifications proposed by Nauroy, *Le fouet et le miel,* op. cit., pp. 48-55.

[23] Ambrose, *Letter 76* (Maur. 20) *to Marcellina,* 11-13 (SAEMO 21, pp. 142-145).

[24] Ibid., 12 (SAEMO 21, pp. 142-143).

[25] Ibid., 22-24 (SAEMO 21, pp. 148-151).

[26] Maximus, *Letter to Valentinian II* (*Collectio Avellana,* 39), 3 and 7 (CSEL 35, 1, pp. 89-90).

[27] Ambrose, *Letter 76* (Maur. 20) *to Marcellina, 26* (SAEMO 21, pp. 152-153).

[28] Paulinus, *Life of Ambrose,* 13, 3 (SAEMO 24/II, pp. 42-43); Augustine, *The Confessions* IX, 7, 15 (NBA 1, pp. 270-271).

[29] Cf. *L'Introduction* of J. Fontaine and M.H. Jullien, in Ambroise de Milan, *Hymnes,* edited by J. Fontaine, Paris, 1992, pp. 11-123; I. Biffi, *La teologia degli inni di sant'Ambrogio,* "Ambrosius," 70 (1994), pp. 343-361.

[30] Ambrose, *Discourse Against Auxentius = Letter 75a* (Maur. 21a), 34 (SAEMO 21, pp. 134-135).

[31] They are all of 8 strophes, each of them composed of four verses; every verse is an iambic dimeter and therefore encompasses a total of 8 syllables, from the moment that each meter is made of two iambs (each of which comprises one brief and one long syllable).

[32] The phrase is explicitly copied on the similar phrase of Blaise Pascal: "*La vraie éloquence se moque de l'éloquence*" (true eloquence mocks eloquence). B. Pascal, *Pensees,* 4.

[33] J. Fontaine, *Prose et Poésie: l'interférence des genres et des styles dans la création littéraire d'Ambroise de Milan,* in *Ambrosius episcopus. Atti del Congresso internazionale di studi ambrosiani nel XVI centenario della elevazione di sant'Ambrogio alla cattedra episcopale, Milano 2-7 dicembre 1974,* I, Milan, 1976 (Studia Patristica Mediolanensia, 6), pp. 124-170 (esp. pp. 129 and 170).

³⁴ Ambrose, *On the Six Days of Creation,* V, 24, 89 (SAEMO 1, pp. 338-339). Here and in the preceding paragraph Ambrose takes up in poetic prose what the hymn expresses in verse.

³⁵ Ambrose, *Hymn ad gallicantum* (*the Chant of the Rooster*) (SAEMO 22, pp. 30-35).

*Lucifer is the name of the Morning Star

**Latin *petra* (rock) like the Greek πετρα, becomes "Peter."

³⁶ Ambrose, *On the Six Days of Creation,* III, 5, 23 (SAEMO 1, pp. 132-135).

Chapter X: "Because I Don't Deserve to be a Martyr, I Have Acquired These Martyrs for You"

¹ Cf. E. Dassmann, *Ambrosius und die Märtyrer,* "Jahrbuch für Antike und Christentum," 18 (1975), pp. 49-68 (the citations that follow are drawn from pp. 63, 66, and 68).

² Ambrose, *Commentary on Psalm 118,* XX, 46 (SAEMO 10, pp. 358-259).

³ Cf. Victricius of Rouen, *The Praise of the Saints,* 6 and 11 (CCL 64, pp 78 and 86).

⁴ Cf. Paulinus of Nola, *Songs, Carme XXVII,* vv. 436-437 (CSEL 30, p. 281). Cf. in general S. Constanza, *I rapporti tra Ambrogio e Paulino di Nola,* in *Ambrosius episcopus. Atti del Congresso internazionale di studi ambrosiani nel XVI centenario della elevazione di sant'Abrogio alla cattedra episcopale, Milano 2-7 dicembre 1974,* II, Milan, 1976 (Studia Patristica Mediolanesia, 7), pp. 220-232 (esp. p. 230).

⁵ Gaudentius of Brescia, *Treatises,* XVII, 12 (DCO, pp. 963-4).

⁶ In this chapter I claim many dates that I have already revealed in words regarding these three groups of martyrs: Ss. *Protaseo e Gervaso, martiri (III sec)* and *Nazaro e Celso, martiri (d. circa 303),* in *Dizionario dei Santi della Chiesa di Milano,* Milan, 1995, pp. 71-76 and 91-95; and *Vitale e Agricola, santi (III sec.),* in *Dizionario della Chiesa ambrosiana,* VI, Milan, 1993, pp. 3989-3994.

⁷ Ambrose, *Letter 77* (Maur. 22) *to Marcellina,* 1 (SAEMO 21, pp. 154-155).

⁸ Ibid., 13 (SAEMO 21, pp. 162-163).

⁹ Dassmann, *Ambrosius und die Märtyrer,* op. cit., p. 55.

¹⁰ Cf. E. Cattaneo-F. Reggiori, *La basilica di Sant'Ambrogio,* Milan, 1966; *La Basilica di S. Ambrogio: it tempio ininterrotto.* Ed. by M.L. Gatti Perer, Milan, 1995.

¹¹ Cf. M. Sannazaro, *Ad modum crucis: la basilica paleocristiana dei SS Apostoli e Nazaro,* Studia Ambrosiana, 2 (2008), pp. 131-153.

¹² Cf. ibid., p. 141.

¹³ Cf. Ambrose, *Commentary on the Gospel of Luke,* VII, 178 (SAEMO 12, pp. 228-231); Ambrose, *Hymn for Saints Victor, Nabor and Felix* (SAEMO 22, pp. 76-79) On these martyrs, cf. how I expressed this of *S. Vittore, martiri (d. 303 c.e.)* and *Ss. Nabore e Felice, martiri (d. 303 c.e.),* in *Dizionario dei Santi della Chiesa di Milano,* Milan, 1995, pp. 53-56 and 80-84.

¹⁴ Paulinus, *Life of Ambrose,* 14, 1 (SAEMO 24/II, pp. 42-43).

¹⁵ Ambrose, *Letter 77* (Maur. 22) *to Marcellina,* 1-2 and 12 (SAEMO 21, pp. 154-155 and 160-161).

¹⁶ Ibid., 13 (SAEMO 21, pp. 162-163).

¹⁷ Ibid., 7 and 12 (SAEMO 21, pp. 158-161).

¹⁸ Ibid., 10 and 12 (SAEMO 21, pp. 160-161).

¹⁹ Augustine, *Sermon 286 On the Birth of the Martyrs Protasius and Gervasius,* 5, 4

Endnotes

(DCO 0350-0430); cf. Augustine, *Confessions,* IX, 7, 16 (O'Donnell p. 109); Ambrose, *Letter 77* (Maur. 22) *to Marcellina,* 17 (SAEMO 21, pp. 164-165); Ambrose, *Hymn for the discovery of the saints Protasius and Gervasius* (SAEMO 22, pp. 80-85); Paulinus, *Life of Ambrose,* 14, 2 (SAEMO 24/II, pp. 42-43).

20 "They revealed themselves to the Bishop." Paulinus, *Life of Ambrose,* 14, 1 (SAEMO 24/II, pp. 42-43); "with a vision they were revealed to the Bishop." Augustine, *Confessions,* IX, 7, 16 (O'Donnell p. 109); "They were discovered because they were revealed to Bishop Ambrose in a dream." Augustine, *City of God,* XXII, 8, 2 (DCO 0350-0430).

21 Ambrose, *Letter 77* (Maur. 22) *to Marcellina,* 19-20 (SAEMO 21, pp. 164-167).

22 A. Paredi, *Politica di S. Ambrogio. Ne. XVI centenario della sua elevazione a vescovo di Milano.* 374ff. Milan, 1974, p. 89.

23 Cf. Paulinus, *Life of Ambrose* 29, 1-2 9 (SAEMO 24/II, pp. 58-61): even if the biographer erroneously speaks of a translation of both of these martyrs.

24 Cf. Ambrose, *Commendation to Virginity,* I, 1-3 and 5-8 (SAEMO 14/II, pp. 198-207).

25 Cf. Paulinus, *Life of Ambrose,* 32, 2-33, 2 (SAEMO 24/II, pp. 62-65).

26 Ambrose, *Inscription for the martyr Nazarius* (SAEMO 22, pp. 100-101).

27 Today the mortal remains of Saint Celsus are preserved in the adjoining Church of S. Maria dei Miracoli, under the altar of the third chapel in the right side of the building.

28 Ambrose, *Hymn for St. Agnes,* strophe 4 and 7-8 (SAEMO 22, pp. 72-75; the comment cited, ed. G. Biffi and of I. Biffi: ibid., p. 73).

29 On these legends, cf. U. Zanetti, *Les Passions des Ss. Nazaire, Gervais, Protais et Celse,* "Analecta Bollandiana," 97 (1979), pp. 69-88; ibid., *Les Passions grecques de S. Nazaire,* "Analecta Bollandiana," 105 (1987), pp. 303-384; and explained as such in the introduction in SAEMO 24/I, pp. 224-227. To this last one may be added C. Lanéry. *Le dossier des saints Nazaire, Celse, Gervais et Protais. Édition de la Passion* BHL 6043 (=3516), "Analecta Bollandiana," 128 (2010), pp. 241-280.

30 Cf. Pseudo Ambrose, *Letter 2 on the Rediscovery of Gervasius and Protasius* = BHL 3514 (PL 17, ed. 1879, coll. 821-825). The inversion of the names of the two martyrs is notable: it has been ascertained that the original (Milanese) order is "Protasius-Gervasius," while the inverse order "Gervasius-Protasius" denotes a use outside Milan.

31 Here I follow in particular the two principal Greek *Passions of the holy martyrs Nazarius, Protasius, Gervasius and Celsus* = BHG 1323 and 1323d (Zanetti, *Les Passions grecques de S. Nazaire,* op. cit., pp. 313-346 and 351-380). The conclusive citation: BHG 1323, 18 (ibid., pp. 345-346 and 379-380).

32 E. Dassmann, *Ambrosius und die Märtyrer,* op. cit., p. 63.

Chapter XI: Augustine, Son of the Church of Milan

1 Jacobus de Voragine, *Golden Legends, St. Augustine* (Jacobus de Voragine, *Leggenda aurea: Volgarizzamento toscano del Trecento,* ed. by A. Levasti, Florence, 1924-1926, pp. 1047-1048).
*Translator's note: The idiosyncratic spelling of Ambrose's name is retained to give the reader a little taste of the "vulgarized 13th c. Tuscan" copied by Pasini, but which cannot be reproduced in English. The Latin phrases are the first two lines of *Te Deum*: "We praise you, O God," "We proclaim you Lord."

[2] Cf. Hincmar of Reims, *Predestination of God and Free Will*, 29 (PL 125, col. 290); Landolfo Seniore, *History of Milan*, I, 9 (Cf. MGH, *Scriptores*, 8, pp. 41-42); Honorius of Autun, *Mirror of the Church* (PL 172, col. 995).

[3] Cf. M.L. Gatti Perer, *Iconografia agostiniana: il "Te Deum" e il battesimo di Agostino*, in *Agostino a Milano: il battesimo. Agostino nelle terre di Ambrogio (22-24 aprile 1987)*, Palermo 1988 (Augustiniana. Testi e Studi, 3), pp. 85-99; A. Cosma-V. Da Gai-G. Pittiglio, *Iconografia agostiniana. 1. Dalle origini al XIV secolo*, Rome, 2011 (NBA 46/1), pp. 86-88, 132-133, 137-138, 259-260.

[4] Cf. M.G. Mara, *Te Deum*, in *Nuovo Dizionario patristico e di antichità cristiane*, Genoa-Milan, 2006-2008, col. 5213.

[5] Augustine, *Confessions*, V, 13, 23 (O'Donnell, p. 56).

[6] Cf. G. Biffi, *Conversione di Agostino e vita di un Chiesa*, in *Agostino e la conversione Cristiana*, Palermo 1987 (Augustiniana. Testi e Studi, 1); pp. 23-34 (from which can be deduced many useful observations on the relations between Augustine and Ambrose).

[7] Augustine, *Confessions*, V, 13, 23 (O'Donnell, p. 56). Faustus was the Manichaean Bishop that Augustine had met at Carthage, still admired because of his eloquence and modesty but disappointing for the incapacity to respond to his questions.

[8] Cf. L.F. Pizzolato, *L'itinerario spirituale di Agostino a Milano*, in *Agostino a Milano*, op. cit., pp. 23-41.

[9] Augustine, *On Happiness*, 1, 4 (DCO 0354-0430).

[10] Augustine, *Letter 147, to Paulina*, 18-53 (esp. 23, 52); (FC Vol. 20). St. Augustine: *Letters*, Vol. 3 (131-164). Trans. W. Parsons, pp. 221-222; idem, *Against Julianus*, I, 3, 10 (DCO 0340-0430).

[11] Cf. Augustine, *Confessions*, VIII, 1, 1-5, 10 (O'Donnell, pp. 88-90, 92-23).

[12] Ibid., VI, 3, 3-4 (O'Donnell, pp. 59-60).

[13] Biffi, *Conversione di Agostino*, op. cit., pp. 26-27.

[14] Augustine, *Confessions*, VI, 1, 1-2 (O'Donnell, pp. 59-60).

[15] Ibid., IX, 5, 13 (O'Donnell, p. 108). It is also significant that in Augustine's own writings are preserved extracts from the lost *Commentary* by Ambrose *on the prophet Isaiah* (SAEMO 22, pp. 132-137).

[16] This theme is also developed in A. Caprioli, *La conversione. Un ritorno ad Agostino*, Milan, 1987, pp. 25-48.

[17] Augustine, *Confessions*, VIII, 1, 2 (O'Donnell, pp. 88-89); Biffi, *Conversion di Agostino*, op. cit., p. 29.

[18] Augustine, *Confessions*, V, 14, 24-25 (NBA 1, pp. 140-141).

[19] Cf. A. Solignac, *Il circolo neoplatonico Milanese al tempo della conversione di Agostino*, in *Agostino a Milano*, op. cit., pp. 43-56.

[20] Augustine, *Confessions*, IX, 7, 15 (O'Donnell, p. 109).
*The *Confessions* are addressed directly to God, hence the second person pronoun "Your" Spirit...

[21] Although the uncertainty regarding the identification of this location has not been fully resolved, it appears that the hypothesis that seems today to find the most credit locates Cassiciacum at Cassago, in Brianza, rather than at Casciago, in the vicinity of Varese (cf. L. Beretta, *Rus Cassiciacum: bilancio e aggiornamento della vexata quaestio*, in *Agostino e la conversione Cristiana*, op. cit., pp. 67-83; S. Colombo, *Ancora sul* Rus Cassiciacum *di Agostino*, ibid., pp. 85-92).

[22] Entitled: *La controversia academia, La felicità, L'ordine, I soliloqui, L'immortalità*

dell'anima; on these, and on certain letters of the same period from Augustine to Nebridius, see the work of G. Reale, L.F. Pizzolato, J. Doignon, J. Oroz Reta, G. Madec and G. Folliet in *L'opera letteraria di Agostino tra Cassiciacum e Milano. Agostino nelle terre di Ambrogio (1-4 ottobre 1986)*, Palermo, 1987 (Augustiniana. Testi e Studi, 2).

[23] Augustine, *Confessions,* IX, 6, 14 (O'Donnell, pp. 108-109).

[24] Cf. ibid., IX, 12, 32 (O'Donnell, p. 116); Augustine cited the first two strophes of the Hymn IV *"at the time of the Ascension"* (SAEMO 22, pp. 42-45).

[25] An example of a detailed indication in this sense, regarding the influence on his *Dialogues of Cassiciacum* on the part of the treatises of Ambrose, *On the Faith* and *On the Holy Spirit,* can be recalled in the recent study of N. Cipriani, *Le fonti cristiane della dottrina trinitaria nei primi Dialoghi di S.Agostino,* "Augustianianum," 34 (1994), pp. 253-312.

[26] Cf. V. Monachino, *S. Ambrogio e la cura pastorale a Milano nel IV secolo,* Milan, 1973, pp. 58-90.

[27] Ambrose, *On the Mysteries,* 1, 1 (SAEMO 17, pp. 136-137).

[28] Ambrose, *Explanation of the Creed,* 1 and 9 (SAEMO 17, pp. 26-27 and 38-39).

[29] Ambrose, *Inscription in the Baptistery* (SAEMO 22, pp. 96-99).

[30] Cf. M. Mirabella Roberti, *Milano romano,* Milan, 1984, pp. 96-102, and 115-119; idem, *I battisteri de sant'Ambrogio,* in *Agostino a Milano,* op. cit., pp. 77-83.

[31] Cf. J. Schmitz, *Die Taufe auf den Tod Jesu bei Ambrosius von Mailand. Ein Beispiel für den Einfluss der Theologie auf die Liturgie,* "Ecclesia Orans," 12 (1995), pp. 153-171.

[32] Ambrose, *On the Sacraments,* III, 1, 1; and II, 7, 20 and 23 (SAEMO 17, pp. 68-73).

[33] Ibid., IV, 4, 14-16 (SAEMO 17, pp. 92-95).

[34] Ibid., V, 4, 25 (SAEMO 17, pp. 114-115).

[35] From the *Orazione all' inizio dell'assemblea liturgica* of the Mass for Saint Augustine in the Ambrosian liturgy: cf. *Missale Ambrosianum iuxta ritum Sanctae Ecclesiae Mediolanensis, ex decreto Sacrosancti Oecumenici Concilii Vaticani II instauratum,* Milan, 1981, n. 383/2.

Chapter XII: Anti-Semitism?

[1] Cf. P. Courcelle, *Recherches sure saint Ambroise. "Vies" anciennes, culture, iconographie,* Paris, 1973, pp. 187-188 and table XXXVIII. (Cf. also pp. 102-103 and 139.)

[2] *Life and Deeds of Saint Ambrose,* 73-74 (SAEMO 24/II, pp. 208-211).

[3] Cf. Paulinus, *Life of Ambrose,* 48, 3 (SAEMO 24/II, pp. 78-79).

[4] Maximus of Turin, *Sermons,* 63, 3 (DCO 0370-0470).

[5] Ambrose, *Letter 74* (Maur. 40) *to Theodosius,* 25 (SAEMO 21, pp. 100-101).

[6] Cf. Sozomen, *History of the Church,* VII, 25, 9 (SAEMO 24/I, p. 174); Theodoret of Cyrus dramatizes the episode in *History of the Church,* V, 18, 20-25 (ibid., pp. 193-194).

[7] Cf. I. Ramelli, *Gnosi-Gnosticismo,* in *Nuovo dizionario patristico e di antichità cristiane,* Genoa-Milan, 2006-2008, coll. 2364-2380; C. Gianotto, *Valentino gnostico,* ibid., coll. 5530-5532.

[8] N.B. McLynn, *Ambrose of Milan. Church and Court in a Christian Capital,* Berkeley, 1994, pp. 301-302, proposes to locate this episode in the vicinity of Antioch, making play on the cult of the Maccabeans attested in that city. The hypothesis, how-

ever, does not seem to me to be sufficiently persuasive; in fact, even if Ambrose refers generically to a "temple in a country village" (Ambrose, *Letter 74* (Maur. 40) *to Theodosius*, 16 (SAEMO 21, pp. 96-97), the context (cf. Ambrose, *Letter Outside the Collection,* 1 (Maur. 41), *to Marcellina* 1 (SAEMO 21, pp. 170-171) seems to suggest a more precise geographical location with Callinicum. Also, the general interpretation of the precise dating by McLynn (pp. 298-309) is not acceptable to me, because of the habitual tone of suspicion that motivates him.

[9] Ambrose, *Letter 74* (Maur. 40) *to Theodosius,* 3 (SAEMO 21, pp 86-89). A double redaction of these letters exists; that already cited, which constitutes the form reviewed by the Bishop to be inserted in his epistolary, and the *Letter Outside the Collection,* 1a, that hands down the original form and which has been alluded to in the *Letter Outside the Collection,* 1 *to Marcellina* (of which I will speak later in this text). The variances between the two redactions are in any case relatively insignificant (they are indicated in SAEMO 21, p. 188).

[10] Ambrose, *Letter 74* (Maur. 40) *to Theodosius*, respectively 7, 10, and 20 (SAEMO 21, pp. 90-93 and 98-99).

[11] Ibid., 27 (SAEMO 21, pp. 102-103).

[12] Ambrose, *Letter Outside the Collection,* 1 (Maur. 41) *to Marcellina*, 3 and 12 (SAEMO 21, pp. 172-173 and 178-179).

[13] Ibid., respectively 9, 23, and 26 (SAEMO 21, pp. 176-177 and 185-186).

[14] Ibid., 27-28 (SAEMO 21, pp. 188-189).

[15] G. Nauroy, *Ambrogio di Milano,* in *Storia dei santi e della santità Cristiana,* III, Milan, 1991, pp. 70-81 (esp. p. 79).

[16] Cf. L. Cracco Ruggini, *Ambrogio e le opposizioni anticattoliche fra il 383 e il 390,* "Augustinianum," 14 (1974), pp. 409-449 (esp. p. 418).

[17] Cf. M. Simon, *Verus Israel. Étude sur les relations entre Chrétiens et Juifs dans l'Empire romain* (135-425), Paris, 1948, pp. 239-274; E. Cattaneo, *La religione a Milano nell'età di sant'Ambrogio,* Milano, 1974 (Archivio Ambrosiano, 25), pp. 41-45.

[18] Not forgetting that at Milan "the Jewish community was probably relatively notable." L. Cracco Ruggini, *Ebrei e Orientali nell'Italia Settentrionale fra il IV e il VI secolo d. Cr.,* "Studia et Documenta historiae et juris," 25 (1959), pp. 186-308 (esp. p. 217).

[19] Cf. L.F. Pizzolato, *La dottrina esegetica di sant'Ambrogio,* Milan, 1978 (Studia Patristica Mediolanensia, 9), pp. 43-87 (esp. 79-83).

[20] Ambrose, *On the Death of his Brother* II, 109 (SAEMO 18, pp. 144-145).

[21] Ambrose, *Explanation of 12 Psalms,* I, 41 (SAEMO 7, pp. 90-91).

[22] Ambrose, Letter 66 (Maur. 78) *to Horontianus,* I (SAEMO 20, pp. 184-185).

[23] Ambrose, *Commentary on the Gospel of Luke,* II, 49 and IV, 54 (SAEMO 11, pp. 190-191 and 342-343).

[24] Ambrose, *On the Six Days of Creation,* VI, 3, 15 (SAEMO 1, pp. 355-356).

[25] Cracco Ruggini, *Ambrogio e le opposizioni anticattoliche,* op. cit., p. 442.

[26] For these considerations certain intuitions are developed and laid out by V. Grossi, *Il Vangelo di Matteo nel rapport tra ebrei e cristiani (sec. II-V),* in R. Fabris, *Matteo,* Rome, 1982, pp. 577-587.

[27] Ambrose, *On Noah,* 19, 70 (SAEMO 2/1 pp. 452-455).

[28] Ambrose, *Commentary on the Gospel of Luke,* VI, 106 (SAEMO 12, pp. 90-91).

[29] Ibid., V, 79 (SAEMO 11, pp. 420-421).

Endnotes

Chapter XIII: An Effective Aid to Social Life

[1] For the theme taken up in this chapter cf. L. Cracco Ruggini, *Ambrogio di fronte alla compagine sociale del suo tempo*, in *Ambrosius episcopus. Atti del Congresso internazionale di studi ambrosiani nel XVI centenario della elevazione di sant'Ambrogio alla cattedra episcopale, Milano 2-7 dicembre 1974*, I, Milan, 1976 (Studia Patristica Mediolanensia, 6), pp. 230-265; V.R. Vasey, *The Social Ideas in the Works of St. Ambrose. A Study on De Nabuthe*, Rome, 1982 (Studia ephemeridis "Augustinianum," 17).

[2] Cf. *Cronologia ambrosiana. Bibliografia ambrosiana (1900-2000)*. Ed. G. Visona, Milan-Rome, 2004 (SAEMO 25-26), pp. 108-109.

[3] *Introduction* by F. Gori in SAEMO 6, p. 14.

[4] Ambrose alludes to the dish *matrice della scrofa*, used as an appetizer.

[5] Ambrose, *Elijah and the Fast*, 8, 24-25 (SAEMO 6, pp. 62-65).

[6] Cf. *Cronologia ambrosiana* op. cit., pp. 124-125 (*Naboth*), 135-136 (*Tobias*), 127-129 (*On the Duties of the Clergy*).

[7] Ambrose, *On Naboth*, 1, 2; and 12, 53 (SAEMO 6, pp. 130-133 and 172-173).

[8] Cf. the introduction of F. Gori in SAEMO 6, pp. 23-24; M.G. Mara, *Ricchi-ricchezza-beni*, in *Nuovo dizionario patristico e di antichita cristiane*, Genoa-Milan, 2006-2008, coll. 4506-4509.

[9] Ambrose, *On Naboth* 12, 50-52 (SAEMO 6, pp. 168-173).

[10] Ambrose, *On the Duties of the Clergy*, III, 6, 39, and 41 (SAEMO 13, pp. 296-301).

[11] Cf. M.G. Mara, *Usura*, in *Nuovo dizionario patristico e di antichità cristiane*, op. cit. coll. 5519-5520.

[12] Ambrose, *On Tobias*: 3, 9-10, 36 (SAEMO 6, pp. 204-207 and 230-233).

[13] Santo Mazzarino (cf. S. Mazzarino, *Storia sociale del vescovo Ambrogio*, Roma, 1989, p. 28) firmly insists that the wealth of Ambrose, from the very beginning, was used for the Church and for the poor. The legal transfer of the property would have happened only after 386, because in *Letter 76* (Maur. 20) *to Marcellina*, 8 (SAEMO 21, pp. 140-141) the full possession of those goods by the Bishop was still attested. In any case the substantial detachment of Ambrose from the property of the family, beginning with his ordination, is unchanging.

[14] Ambrose, *On the Duties of the Clergy*, II, 28, 136-139 and 142 (SAEMO 13, pp. 260-265).

[15] Augustine, *Confessions*, VI, 3, 3 (O'Donnell, pp. 59-60).

[16] Cf. Ambrose, *On the Duties of the Clergy*, II, 15: 69-72 and 16, 77 (SAEMO 13, pp. 222-227).

[17] Ambrose, *Commentary on Psalm 118*, VIII, 54 (SAEMO 9, pp. 368-369).

[18] Ambrose, *On the Duties of the Clergy*, II, 16, 76-78 (SAEMO 13, pp. 226-229).

[19] Cf. V. Monachino, *S. Ambrogio e la cura pastorale a Milano nel IV secolo*, Milan, 1973, pp. 279-301; G. Vismara, *Ancora sulla "episcopalism audientia" (Ambrogio arbitro o giudice?)*, "Studia et documenta historiae et iuris," 53 (1987), pp. 53-73.

[20] Ambrose, *Letter 24* (Maur. 82) *to Marcellus* (SAEMO 19, pp. 236-245). NB: the author cites no specific passages because he has selected elements from the entire letter.

[21] Ambrose, *On the Duties of the Clergy*, I, 1, 4 (SAEMO 13, 24-25).

Chapter XIV: "I Have Loved This Man"

[1] In Psalm 114 (116) the complete phrase is: "I have loved the Lord, because he has heard the voice of my prayer." Ambrose, after having commented on the psalm in its own appropriate meaning, in this part of his homily takes up the expression applying it to the Emperor.

[2] Ambrose, *On the Death of Theodosius*, 33-35 (SAEMO 18, pp. 234-235).

[3] Cf. P. Courcelle, *Recherches sur saint Ambroise, "Vies" anciennes, culture, iconographie,* Paris, 1973, pp. 193, 205, 212, 215, 216, 223-224, 229 and tables XLIV, LV, LXVII, LXXI, LXXII-LXXIII, LXXVIII, LXXXV-LXXXVI.

[4] Theodoret of Cyrus, *History of the Church,* V, 18, 2-22 (SAEMO 24/I, pp. 188-194; for a commentary on this passage cf. ibid., pp. 137-140).

[5] Paulinus, *Life of Ambrose,* 24, I (SAEMO 24/II, pp. 52-55); cf. Rufinus, *History of the Church,* XI, 18 (ibid., pp. 124-125).

[6] Here and in what follows of this reconstruction of the facts, I agree with one or another of the intuitions of N.B. McLynn, *Ambrose of Milan. Church and Court in a Christian Capital,* Berkeley, 1994, pp. 320-322 (but, as in other cases, I do not agree with his general reinterpretation of the event, which reduces the excessive punishment of Thessalonica to a cautious intervention that got out of hand in being carried out, and judges the public penance of the Emperor as the occasion offered to him by Ambrose to reclaim the favor of the crowd: cf. ibid., pp. 315-330).

[7] Concerning a "predetermined number" Sozomen speaks, *History of the Church,* VII, 25, 4 (SAEMO 24/I, p. 172).

[8] Paulinus, *Life of Ambrose,* 24, I (SAEMO 24/II, pp 52-55); cf. Ambrose *Letter Outside the Collection,* 11 (Maur. 51), *to Theodosius,* 16 (SAEMO 21, pp. 240-241).

[9] Ambrose, *Letter Outside the Collection,* 11 (Maur. 51) *to Theodosius,* 6 (SAEMO 21, pp. 234-235).

[10] Ibid., 6 (SAEMO 21, pp. 234-235).

[11] Ibid., 4-6 and 9 (SAEMO 21, pp. 234-237).

[12] Ibid., 11-13 and 17 (SAEMO 21, pp. 236-241).

[13] Cf. M. Zelzer, in CSEL 82/III, pp. LXXXIV-LXXXVI, CIX-CX, and CXXXI-CXXXII; for Hincmar of Reims, cf. his *Divorce of Lotharius and Teutberga, Quaestio* VII (PL 125, coll. 764-766).

[14] Cf. R. Gryson, *Le Prêtre selon saint Ambroise,* Louvain 1968 (Universitas Catholica Lovaniensis, Dissertationes, III, 2), pp. 275-290; V. Monachino, *S. Ambrogio e la cura pastorale a Milano nel IV secolo,* Milan, 1973, pp. 232-254.

[15] Ambrose, *On Penance,* I, 16, 90; and II, 10, 96 (SAEMO 17, pp. 224-225 and 276-277).

[16] Rufinus, *History of the Church,* XI, 18 (SAEMO 24/II, pp. 124-125); Ambrose, *On the Death of Theodosius,* 34 (SAEMO 18, pp. 234-235); Augustine, *City of God,* V, 26, 1 (NBA 5/I, pp. 396-399).

[17] Ambrose, *On Penance* II, 8, 73; and I, 6, 27-28 (SAEMO 17, pp. 266-269 and 188-191).

[18] Cf. ibid., II, 7, 54-57; and II, 3, 17-18 (SAEMO 17, pp. 256-259 and 238-241).

[19] Ambrose, *Commentary on Psalm 118,* XXII, 28-30 (SAEMO 10, pp. 416-417).

[20] *Codex Theodosianus,* IX, 40, 13 (http://ancientrome.ru/ius/library/codex/theod/liber09.htm#40 cf. Th. Mommsen-P.M. Meyer, *Theodosiani libri* XVI, Berlin 1905, I/2 p. 503); Rufinus, *History of the Church,* XI, 18 (SAEMO 24/II, pp. 124-125).

[21] Ambrose, *Letter 76* (Maur. 20) *to Marcellina,* 26 (SAEMO 21, pp. 152-153).

Endnotes

[22] G. Nauroy, *Ambrogio di Milano*, in *Storia dei santi e della santità Cristiana*, III, Milan, 1991, pp. 70-81 (esp. p. 80).

[23] A. Paredi, *S. Ambrogio e la sua età,* Milan, 1994, p. 431.

[24] M. Sordi, *La concezione politica di Ambrogio*, in *I Cristiani e l'Impero nel IV secolo. Colloquio sul Cristianesimo nel mondo antico*, Macerata, 1988 (Università degli Studi di Macerata, Pubblicazioni della Facoltà di Lettere e Filosofia, 47), pp. 143-154 (esp. p. 154); I have availed myself of this study also in the rest of this chapter.

[25] Ambrose, *On the Death of Theodosius*, 42, and 46 (SAEMO 18, pp. 240-245).

[26] Ibid., 47-48 and 50-51 (SAEMO 18, pp.244-249).

Chapter XV: In the Service of the Word

[1] Ambrose, *On the Six Days of Creation*, VI, 10, 75-76 (SAEMO 1, pp. 416-419).

[2] Biffi in SAEMO 1, pp. 419-421, n. 2.

[3] Cf. G. Nauroy, *Le fouet et le miel. Le combat d'Ambroise en 386 contre l'arianisme milanais,* "Recherches Augustiniennes," 23 (1988), pp. 3-86 (esp. 79-80).

[4] Cf. L.F. Pizzolato, *La dottrina esegetica di sant'Ambrogio,* Milan, 1978 (Studia Patristica Mediolanensia, 9); and above all G. Nauroy, *L'Écriture dans la Pastorale d'Ambroise de Milan*, in *Le monde latin antique et la Bible,* ed. J. Fontaine and Ch. Pietri, Paris, 1985 (Bible de tous les temps, 2) pp. 371-408 (from which I derive many dates in the course of this chapter).

[5] Ambrose, *On Cain and Abel*, II, 6, 22 (SAEMO 2/I, pp. 282-283).
*This phrase is not in the Latin.

[6] On the discovery of the Song of Songs in these years, thanks to the reading of the works of Origen, I will return in a later chapter.

[7] Because of this characteristic the *Commentary* of William of Saint-Thierry is added as an appendix to the *Opera Omnia* of St. Ambrose, in SAEMO 27.

[8] For this specific explanation I take up the interpretation formed by Nauroy, *L'Écriture dans la pastorale d'Ambroise,* op. cit., pp. 392-396.

[9] Ambrose, *Commentary on Psalm 118,* XVI, 20 and XIII, 23-24 (SAEMO 10, pp. 190-191 and 78-81).

[10] Ambrose, *On Joseph*, 4, 19 (SAEMO 3, pp. 360-363).

[11] Nauroy, *L'Écriture dans la pastorale d'Ambroise,* op. cit., p. 378.

[12] Ibid., p. 404.

[13] Ambrose, *On the Duties of the Clergy,* I, 22, 101 (SAEMO 13, pp. 84-85).

[14] Cf. Ambrose, *On the Six Days of Creation*, V, 24, 89 (SAEMO 1, pp. 338-339).

[15] Augustine, *Confessions,* VI, 3, 3 (O'Donnell, pp. 59-60).

[16] Ambrose, *Commentary on the Gospel of Luke,* VI, 78; and II, 33 (SAEMO 12, pp. 66-67 and 11, pp. 174-175).

[17] Ambrose, *On Isaac or the Soul,* 7, 57 (SAEMO 3, pp. 98-101).

[18] Ambrose, *On the Six Days of Creation*, III, 8, 36 (SAEMO I, pp. 146-149).

[19] Ibid., V, 11, 34 (SAEMO I, pp. 284-285).

[20] Ibid., V, 12, 37 (SAEMO I, pp. 288-289).

Chapter XVI: Concern for the Churches

[1] Paulinus, *Life of Ambrose* 38, 2 (SAEMO 24/II, pp. 68-69).

[2] Ambrose, *On the Death of Valentinian*, 25 and 27 (SAEMO 18, pp. 178-181).
*This phrase, in Latin, has a strong military ring: "service," as in "military service."
[3] Ambrose, *Letter 25* (Maur. 53) *to Theodosius*, 2 (SAEMO 19, pp. 246-247).
[4] Ambrose, *On the Death of Valentinian*, respectively: 46, 51, 53, and 75 (SAEMO 18, pp. 190-195 and 204-205).
[5] Ambrose, *Letter Outside the Collection*, 10 (Maur. 57) *to Eugenius*, 12 (SAEMO 21, pp. 230-231).
[6] Ibid., 1 and 12 (SAEMO 21, pp. 224-225 and 230-231).
[7] Leveraging the direct knowledge of Florence that Paulinus demonstrated in his *Life of Ambrose*, cf. É. Lamirande, *Paulin de Milan et la "Vita Ambrosii." Aspects de la religion sous le Bas-Empire*, Paris, 1983, p. 17.
[8] Ambrose, *Letter Outside the Collection*, 3 (Maur. 62) *to Theodosius*, 3 (SAEMO 21, pp. 194-195).
[9] Ambrose, *Letter Outside the Collection*, 2 (Maur. 61) *to Theodosius*, 4-5 and 7 (SAEMO 21, pp. 190-193).
[10] Paulinus records that, before his death, Theodosius had "confided to the Bishop" his children (Paulinus, *Life of Ambrose*, 32, I: SAEMO 24/II, pp. 62-63), that is, Honorarius and Galla Placidia, both present at Milan in that moment (also, if he intended to be inclusive, in a general consignment, also Arcadius).
[11] Ambrose, *On the Death of Theodosius*, 52-53 and 56 (SAEMO 18, pp. 248-251).
[12] For this part of the chapter I reclaim many dates from my *Le discussion teologiche a Milano nei secoli dal IV al VII*, in *Diocesi di Milano*, Brescia, 1990 (Storia religiosa della Lombardia, 9-10), pp. 43-82 (esp. 55-58).
[13] Ambrose, *Letter 70* (Maur. 56) *to Theophilus*, 7 (SAEMO 21, pp. 32-35).
[14] I follow the reconstruction suggested in the *Cronologia ambrosiana. Bibliografia ambrosiana (1900-2000)*. Ed. G. Visonà, Milan-Rome, 2004 (SAEMO 25-26), pp. 53-55, 77-78).
[15] Cf. Ambrose, *Letter 71* (Maur. 56a) *to Bishop Bonosus*, 4-5 (SAEMO 21, pp. 36-37).
[16] Ambrose, *The Education of a Virgin*, 7, 48-49 (SAEMO 14/II, pp. 148-149).
[17] Ambrose, *Letter Outside the Collection*, 15 (Maur. 42) *to Siricius*, 2-3 (SAEMO 21, pp. 326-329).
[18] L.F. Pizzolato, *Ambrogio a Firenze:* l'Exhortatio virginitatis, in *La presenza di sant'Ambrogio a Firenze. Convegno di studi abrosiani. Firenze 9 marzo 1994*, Firenze, 1994, pp. 7-21 (esp. p. 8).
[19] Ambrose, *Commendation to Virginity*, 14, 94 (SAEMO 14/II, pp. 270-271; cf. also ibid., n. 168); see also Pizzolato, *Ambrogio a Firenze*, op. cit., pp. 20-21.
[20] Cf. S. Costanza, *I rapporti tra Ambrogio e Paulino di Nola*, in *Ambrosius episcopus. Atti del Congresso internazionale di studi ambrosiani nel XVI centenario della elevazione di sant'Ambrogio alla cattedra episcopale, Milano 2-7 dicembre 1974*, II, Milan, 1976 (Studia Patristica Mediolanensia, 7), pp. 220-232.
[21] Cf. Paulinus of Nola, *Letter to Alipius* = *Ep. 24*, in the epistolary of Augustine, 4 (SAEMO 24/II, pp. 98-99).
[22] Ambrose *Letter 27* (Maur. 58) *to Sabinus*, 1 and 3 (SAEMO 19, pp. 252-255).
[23] Cf. M. Naldini, *Attività pastorale di s. Ambrogio. Firenze e i codici della Biblioteca Medicea Laurenziana*, in *La presenza di sant'Ambrogio*, op. cit. pp. 23-32 (esp. p. 24); and Pizzolato, *Ambrogio a Firenze*, op. cit. p. 8 n. 6.
[24] Cf. Paulinus, *Life of Ambrose*, 50, 1 (SAEMO 24/II, pp. 80-81).

Endnotes

[25] For much of what I present here, see the following: C. Alzati, *Metropoli e sedi episcopali fra tarda antichità e alto medioevo*, in *Chiesa e società. Apunti per una storia delle diocese lombarde*, Brescia, 1986 (Storia religiosa della Lombardia, 1), pp. 47-77 (esp. pp. 49-51).

[26] Cf. L. Chiodi, *Dall'introduzione del Cristianesimo al dominio franco*, in *Diocesi di Bergamo*, Brescia, 1988 (Storia religiosa della Lombardia, 2), pp. 13-37 (esp. p. 20).

[27] Gaudentius of Brescia, *Sermo* XVI, 2 and 9 (PLD 0956A-0958A). *The Latin term means "womb" or "belly."

[28] Cf. A. Zani, *"Ambrosius... tamquam Petri successor apostoli." Il riconoscimento di Gaudenzio di Brescia ad Ambrogio di Milano*, in *Pastor bonus in populo. Figura, ruolo e funzioni del vescovo nella Chiesa*, Rome, 1990, pp. 21-42.

[29] Cf. how I have already expressed this in *SS. Abbondio (V sec.) e Felice (IV sec.), vescovi*, in *Dizionario dei Santi della Chiesa di Milano*, Milan, 1995, pp. 117-121 (esp. 117-118).

[30] Ambrose, *Letter 5* (Maur. 4) *to Felix*, 1-2 (SAEMO 19, pp. 60-63).

[31] Ambrose, *Letter 43* (Maur. 3) *to Felix*, 2-3 (SAEMO 20, pp. 66-67).

[32] Ambrose, *Letter 5* (Maur. 5) *to Felix*, 6-7 (SAEMO 19, pp. 64-65).

[33] Ambrose, *On the Duties of the Clergy*, III, 22, 132-133 (SAEMO 13, pp. 354-355); cf. L.F. Pizzolato, *L'idea di amcizia nel mondo antico classico e cristiano*, Turin, 1993, pp. 269-276.

Chapter XVII: Effusive Fragrance and Sober Inebriation

[1] Jerome, *Prologue to Origen's Homilies on the Song of Songs* (SC 37 bis, p. 58).

[2] They see more than others the specific hints in this regard.

[3] Cf. P. Meloni, *Il profumo dell'immortalità. L'interpretazione patristica di Cantico 1,3*, Roma, 1975 (Verba Seniorum, n.s. 7) pp. 221-266.

*The Latin "odor" can be translated in various ways. As Pasini does in Italian, I translate it in the way that makes most sense in context, sic: odor = perfume, aroma, good odor, fragrance, even effulgence. We necessarily sacrifice the rhetorical repetitiveness of Ambrose's Latin.

[4] Ambrose, *Commentary on the Gospel of Luke*, VI, respectively 13-15, 20-21, and 25-27 (SAEMO 12, pp. 20-21 and 24-31).

[5] Ambrose, *On Virginity*, II, 61-62 and 65-66 (SAEMO 14/II, pp. 54-57.

[6] Ambrose, *Commentary on the Gospel of Luke*, VI, 28-29 and 33-34 (SAEMO 12 pp. 30-31 and 34-37).

[7] Ambrose, *On the Sacraments* IV, 1, 4 (SAEMO 17, pp. 88-89); *On the Mysteries*, 6: 29 (ibid., pp. 150-151).

[8] Ambrose, *Commentary on Psalm 118*, III, 8; and V, 9 (SAEMO 9, pp. 130-131 and 204-205).

[9] Cf. L.F. Pizzolato, *Ambrogio e Paulino di Nola: per una più precisa datazione dalla "Expositio psalmi CXVIII" di Ambrogio*, "Studi tardoantichi," 6 (1989 = *Polyanthema. Studi di litteratura Cristiana antica offerti a Salvatore Costanza*), pp. 333-345. For a more comprehensive examination, cf. *Cronologia ambrosiana. Bibliografia ambrosiana (1900-2000)*. Ed. G. Visonà, Milan-Rome, 2004 (SAEMO 25-26), pp. 99-101.

[10] *Introduzione*, L.F. Pizzolato in SAEMO 9, pp. 31 and 37.

[11] Ambrose, *On Isaac or the Soul*, 4, 17 (SAEMO 3, pp. 56-57).

[12] Cf. again Pizzolato, *Ambrogio e Paulino di Nola*, op. cit. For a more comprehensive examination, cf. *Cronologica ambrosiana*, op. cit., pp. 122-123.

[13] Cf. R. Iacoangeli, *Anima ed eternità nel "De Isaac" di Sant'Ambrogio*, in *Morte e immortalita nella catechesis dei Padri del III-IV secolo*, Rome, 1985 (Biblioteca di Scienze Religiose, 66), pp. 103-137.

[14] Ambrose, *On Isaac or the Soul* 8, 71-72 (SAEMO 3, pp. 114-115).

[15] Cf. E. Dassmann, *La Sobria ebbrezza dello Spirito. La Spiritualità di S. Ambrogio vescovo di Milano*, Varese, 1975 (subsequent citations are drawn from in pages 92 and 218).

[16] Ambrose, *Hymn II: in Aurora*, strophe 1-2 (SAEMO 22, pp. 34-37).

[17] Cf. G. Madec, *La centralité du Christ dans la spiritualité d'Ambroise*, in *Nec temeo mori. Atti del Congresso internazionale di studi ambrosiani nel XVI centenario della morte di sant'Ambrogio. Milano, 4-11 aprile 1997*. Ed. L.F. Pizzolato and M. Rizzi, Milan, 1998, pp. 207-220; K. Baus, *Das Gebet zu Christus bei hl. Ambrosius. Eine frömmigkeitsgeschichtliche Untersuchung*, Berlin-Vien 2000 (Theophaneia, 35). See as well G. Maschio, *La figura di Cristo nel "Commentary al salmo 118" di Ambrogio di Milano*, Rome, 2003 (Studia Ephermeridis Augustinianum, 88).

[18] Dassmann, *La Sobria Ebbrezza dello Spirito*, op. cit., pp. 232-233 and 224.

[19] Ambrose, *Hymn II: in Aurora*, strophe 6 (SAEMO 22, 36-39).

[20] Ambrose, *On the Sacraments*, V, 3, 15 and 17 (SAEMO 17, pp. 108-109).

[21] Ambrose, *Explanation of the 12 Psalms: Psalm I*, 33 (SAEMO 7, 78-81).

Chapter XVIII: The "Encounter"

[1] Paulinus, *Life of Ambrose*, 45, 1 (SAEMO 24/II, pp. 76-77).

[2] Ambrose, *Letter 5* (Maur. 4) *to Felix*, 1 (SAEMO 19 pp. 60-61); cf. Augustine, *Confessions*, VI, 3, 3 (NBAL 1, pp. 148-149).

[3] Ambrose, *On the Sacraments*, I, 6, 24 (SAEMO 17, pp. 54-57); *Second Apology for David*, 5, 28 (SAEMO 5, pp. 172-173).

[4] Ambrose, *On the Death of his Brother* I, 36 (SAEMO 18, pp. 48-49); *Letter 51* (Maur. 15) *To the Thessalonians*, 10 (SAEMO 20, pp. 90-91); *Letter Outside the Collection*, 11 (Maur. 51) *to Theodosius*, 5 (SAEMO 21, pp. 234-235).

[5] Cf. B. Ballabio, *La malatia di S. Ambrogio e in S. Ambrogio*, Milan, 1973, pp. 9-12.

[6] Paulinus, *Life of Ambrose*, 34, 3-4 (SAEMO 24/II, pp. 66-67).

[7] G. Nauroy, *Ambrogio di Milano*, in *Storia dei santi e della santità Cristiana*, III, Milan, 1991, pp. 70-81 (esp. p. 81).

[8] Paulinus, *Life of Ambrose*, 35, 1 (SAEMO 24/II, pp. 66-67).

[9] Ibid., 36, 1-2 (SAEMO 24/II, pp. 66-67).

[10] Ibid., 42, 1 (SAEMO 24/II, pp. 72-73).

[11] Ambrose, *Explanation of the 12 Psalms, Psalm 43, 96* (SAEMO 8, pp. 194-195).

[12] Cf. F. Braschi, *L'Explanatio psalmorum XII di Ambrogio: una proposta di lettura unitaria. Analisis tematica, contenuto teologico e contesto ecclesiale*, Rome, 2007 (Studia Ephemeridis Augustinianum, 105), p. 559. In this full treatment the author demonstrates how Ambrose himself had wanted to gather together a commentary on eleven psalms (save for the last one, Psalm 61), concluding, however, a revision of only seven, up to Psalm 43.

[13] Cf. where I have explained this in the article *S. Onorato di Vercelli, vescovo (IV cent.)*, in *Dizionario dei Santi della Chiesa di Milano*, Milan, 1995, pp. 160-163.

Endnotes

[14] Ambrose, *Letter Outside the Collection*, 14 (Maur. 63) *to the Church of Vercelli*, 7 (SAEMO 21, pp. 264-267).

[15] Going back to the first half of the 12th century is G. Colombo, *Per uno studio della Vita di S. Gaudenzio*, in *San Gaudenzio*, Novara, 1983, pp. 1-45 (esp. p. 27); suggesting instead the 9th century is J.Ch. Picard, *Le souvenir des évêques. Sépultures, listes épiscopales et culte des évêques en Italie du Nord des origins au Xe siècle*, Rome, 1988 (Bibliothèque des Ecoles francaises d'Athenes et de Rome, 268), pp. 636-637.

[16] G. Visonà, in *San Gaudenzio e le origini della Chiesa di Novara*, in *Il cristianesimo a Novara e sul territorio: le origini. Atti del Convegno, Novara 10 ottobre 1998, Novara 1999* (Studi storici, 14), pp. 137-159 (esp. p. 152). It can be asked whether this episode and the trip of Ambrose to Vercelli itself might not simply derive from the desire to attribute in some manner to Ambrose the origin of the diocese of Novara. As for the See of Vercelli, it could then be imagined that the letter written by Ambrose obtained its positive effect with the nomination of Honoratius, without the necessity of an intervention *in loco* on the part of the Bishop of Milan.

[17] *Life of Gaudentius* = BHL 3278, 11-12 (G. Colombo, *Edizione critica della "Vita Sancti Gaudentii,"* in *San Gadenzio*, op. cit., pp. 47-107, esp. pp. 80-83).

[18] Paulinus, *Life of Ambrose*, 45, 2 (SAEMO 24/II, pp. 76-77); Possidius, *Life of Augustine*, 27, 8 (ibid., pp. 102-103).

[19] Ambrose, *Explanation of the 12 Psalms, Psalm 43*, 12 & 14 (SAEMO 8, pp. 100-101 and 104-105).

[20] Paulinus, *Life of Ambrose*, 46, 1 (SAEMO 14/II, pp. 76-77).

[21] Ibid., 47, 1-3 (SAEMO 24/II, pp. 76-79).

[22] Ibid., 48, 1-3 (SAEMO 24/Ii, pp. 78-79).

[23] Ambrose, *On the Death of his Brother*, II, 132-134 (SAEMO 18, pp. 156-159).

[24] Ambrose, *On Virginity*, II, 2, 16-17 (SAEMO 14/I pp. 176-179).

[25] Being in strict connection with the treatise *On Isaac or the Soul*, probably dated to 396, this too on the *On the Good Death* may be referenced to the same period; earlier scholars had suggested dating the treatise to 386 (cf. R. Gryson, *Le Prêtre selon saint Ambroise*, Louvain 1968, Universitas Catolica Lovaniensis, Dissertationes, III, 2, p. 36) or later to 391 (A. Paredi, *S. Ambrogio e la sua età*, Milan, 1994, p. 530).

[26] Ambrose, *On the Good Death*, 2, 3 (SAEMO 3, pp. 130-131).

[27] Ibid., respectively, 11, 49; and 12, 52-55 and 57 (SAEMO 3, pp. 198-211).

Chapter XIX: Saint Ambrose

[1] Gregory of Tours, *The Miracles of St. Martin*, I, 5 (SAEMO 24/II, pp. 132-133).

[2] Florian, *Letter to Nicetius of Trier* (SAEMO 24/II, pp. 136-137); Gregory the Great, *Letter XI*, 6 *to the priests, deacons, and clerics of Milan* (MGH, *Epistulae*, 2, pp. 265-266).

[3] Cf. Ambrose, *Commentary on the Gospel of Luke*, VIII, 73 (SAEMO 12, pp. 344-345).

[4] Among the many exponents of this, cf. A. Paredi-M. Navoni, *S Ambrogio, vescovo e dottore della Chiesa*, in *Dizionario dei Santi della Chiesa di Milano*, Milan, 1995, pp. 186-195 (esp. the paragraphs *Culto liturgico* and *Leggende tradizioni* as cited in M. Navoni, pp. 193-198); E. Cattaneo, *La devozione a S. Ambrogio*, in *Ricerche storiche sulla Chiesa ambrosiana*, IV, Milan, 1974 (Archivio Ambrosiano, 27), pp. 85-110; idem, *La tradizione e il rito ambrosiani nell'ambiente Lombardo-medioeva-*

le, in *Ambrosius episcopus. Atti del Congresso internazionale di studi ambrosiani nel XVI centenario della elevazione di sant'Ambrogio alla cattedra episcopale, Milano 2-7, dicembre, 1974,* II, Milan, 1976 (Studia Patristica Mediolanensia, 7) pp. 5-47.

[5] Even today that market is perpetuated in the fair of the "oh bèj, oh bèj" which takes place in the days around December 7 in the streets adjacent to the Basilica of Saint Ambrose. [Translator's note: *oh bèj* means "how pretty!" and is the exclamation of children who are showered with little gifts, sweets, and chocolates.]

[6] Ambrose, *Letter 77* (Maur. 22) *to Marcellina,* 2 (SAEMO 21, pp. 153-156).

[7] Cf. A. Paredi, *S. Ambrogio e la sua età,* Milan, 1994, pp. 183 and 525; J.-Ch. Picard, *Le souvenir des évêques. Sépultures, listes épiscopales et culte des évêques en Italie du Nord des origins au Xe siècle,* Rome, 1988 (Bibliotèque des Écoles françaises d'Athènes et de Rome, 268), pp. 625-626.

[8] E. Apeciti, *Alcuni aspetti dell'episcopato di Luigi Nazari de Calabiana, arcivescovo di Milano (1867-1893). Vicende della Chiesa ambrosiana nella seconda metà del 1800,* Milan, 1992 (Archivio Ambrosiano, 66), p. 355 (cf. in general pp. 346-358).

[9] Alcuin, *On the Life of St. Willibrord/De Vita S. Willibrordi,* 32 (DCO 0735-0804).

[10] Landolfo Seniore, *History of Milan,* II, 2 (DCO 1050-1100); cf. also Cattaneo, *La tradizione e il rito ambrosiani,* op. cit., pp. 17-18, n. 37

[11] Galvano Fiamma, *Opuscolo sulle gesta di Azzone, Luchino e Giovanni Visconti,* XLIV, 168 (RIS, XII/4, p. 31).

[12] Cf. P. Courcelle, *Recherches sur saint Ambroise. "Vies" anciennes, culture, iconographie,* Paris, 1973, pp. 213-214 and tables LXVIII-LXIX.

[13] Cf. ibid., pp. 187-188 and table XXXVIII.

[14] Cf. ibid., pp. 158-159 and table IV for the identification of the whip, E. Bernasconi, *Il nostro somo padre (Nostrum parentem maximum). Vita di sant'Ambrogio illustrata coi cimeli della sua Basilica,* Milan, 1958, p. 219.

[15] Ambrose, *Against Auxentius = Letter 75a* (Maur. 21a), 23 (SAEMO 21, pp. 126-129). Other similar texts are recorded by L.F. Pizzolato, *Ricerce su s. Ambrogio. A proposito di un recente libro di P. Courcelle,* "Aevum," 48, pp. 500-505 (esp. pp. 504-505).

[16] Cattaneo, *La Devozione,* op. cit., p. 85.

[17] Cattaneo, *La Tradizione,* op. cit., p. 16.

[18] Giovanni di S. Martino, *Il convito o pasto dei monaci* (A. Bernareggi, *La più antica testimonianza dell'attribuzione a S. Ambrogio del rito Milanese,* "Ambrosius," 4, 1928, pp. 146-148).

[19] M. Navoni, *Ambrogio, santo (334c.-397),* in *Dizionario di Liturgia Ambrosiana,* Milan, 1996, pp. 7-26 (esp. p. 18).

[20] Cf. my *Le fonti greche su sant'Ambrogio,* Milan-Rome, 1990 (SAEMO 24/I) and *Ambrogio nella teologica posteriora greca. Un'indagine nei secoli Ve I,* in *Nec timeo mori. Atti del Congresso internazionale di studi ambrosiani nel XVI centenario della morte di sant'Ambrogio. Milano, 4-11 aprile 1997.* Ed. L.F. Pizzolato and M. Rizzi, Milan, 1998, pp. 365-404.

[21] Cf. Courcelle, *Recherches sur saint Ambroise,* op. cit., pp. 193, 205, 212, 215-216, 223-224, 227 and tables XLIV, LV, LXVII, LXXI-LXXIII, LXXVIII, LXXXV-LXXXVI, and (for that of Pierre Subleyras) p. 232 and table XCI.

[22] C. Mohrmann, *Introduzione,* in *Vita di Cipriano. Vita di Ambrogio. Vita di Agostino,* ed. A.A.R. Bastiaensen, Milano, 1975 (Vite dei santi, 3), pp. IX-LXIII (esp. p. XXXII).

Endnotes

[23] Cf. R. Crouse, *"Summae auctoritatis magister:"* the influence of St. Ambrose in medieval theology, in *Nec temeo mori,* op. cit., pp. 463-471.

[24] Cf. F. Buzzi, *La ricezione di Ambrogio a Wittenberg,* in *Nec temeo Mori,* op. cit., pp. 569-583.

[25] Luther, *Lectures on the Letter to the Romans,* 12, 7 (CCEL/l/luther/romans/pref_romans.html) trans. Bro. Andrew Thornton, OSB.

[26] G. Nauroy, *Ambrogio di Milano,* in *Storia dei santi e della santità Cristiana,* III, Milan, 1991, pp. 70-81 (esp. p. 70; from this page I have culled certain points for the conclusion of this chapter).

[27] Ambrose, *On Jacob and the Good Life,* I, 8, 36 (SAEMO 3, pp. 266-269).

[28] Ambrose, *Commentary on Psalm 118,* XIII, 22 and 25 (SAEMO 10, pp. 78-79 and 82-83).

Endnote Index of Works Cited

Here are all the works cited in this volume (or those to which I make allusion, indicated with "Cf."). The order is alphabetical by author and by work; at the end of the list are all the anonymous works. Page numbers do not specify the endnote number in which the citation is found.

The translator has included both an English version and, where otherwise the reference may be unclear, the Latin.

ALCUIN
On the Life of St. Willibrord/De
Vita S. Willibrordi, 32   310

AMBROSE
Commendation to Virginity
  I, 1-3 and 5-8   299
  9, 57   291
  9, 58   291
  12, 82   286
  14, 94   306
Commentary on Matthew
  IV, 27   288
Commentary on Psalm 61
  17 & 23-25   294
Commentary on Psalm 118
  III, 8; and V, 9   307
  VI, 8   291
  VIII, 54   303
  IX, 20   288
  XI, 9   288
  XIII, 22 and 25   311
  XVI, 20 and XIII, 23-24   305
  XX, 46   298
  XXII, 28-30   304
Commentary on the Gospel of Luke
  II, 49 and IV, 54   302
  V, 79   302
  VI, 13-15, 20-21, and 25-27   307
  VI, 28-29 and 33-34   307
  VI, 78; and II, 33   305
  VI, 106   302
  VII, 52-53   296
  VII, 178   298
  VIII, 73   309
  VIII, 74-75   287
  X, 82   288
Discourse Against Auxentius
  Letter 75a   296, 297, 310
Elijah and the Fast
  8, 24-25   303
Explanation of 12 Psalms
  I, 33   308
  I, 41   302
  43, 12 & 14   309
  43, 96   308
Explanation of the Creed
  1 and 9   301
Hymn for St. Agnes   299
Hymn for the discovery of the
  saints Protasius and Gervasius   298
Hymn of the Aurora
  strophe 1-2   308
  strophe 6   308
Hymn on the Birth of the Lord
  strophe 5   294
Inscription for the martyr Nazarius 299
Inscription in the Baptistery   301
Letters
  5 (Maur. 4)   307, 308
  5 (Maur. 5)   307
  7 (Maur. 37)   289
  24 (Maur. 82)   303
  25 (Maur. 53)   305
  30 (Maur. 24)   294, 295
  32 (Maur. 48)   289
  37 (Maur. 47)   291
  43 (Maur. 3)   307
  56 (Maur. 5)   293
  66 (Maur. 78)   302
  70 (Maur. 56)   306
  71 (Maur. 56a)   306
  72 (Maur. 17)   295
  73 (Maur. 18)   295
  74 (Maur. 40)   301, 302
  74 (Maur. 40)   301
  75a (Maur. 21a)   297
  75 (Maur. 21)   285, 296
  76 (Maur. 20)   285, 293, 297, 304
  77 (Maur. 22)   293, 298

Letter Outside the Collection
1 (Maur. 41)	293, 301, 302
2 (Maur. 61)	306
3 (Maur. 62)	306
4 (Maur. 10)	290
4 (Maur. 13)	294
5 (Maur. 11)	290
6	294
9 (Maur. 9, 12, and 13)	294
9 (Maur. 13)	294
10 (Maur. 57)	295
10 (Maur. 57)	305
11 (Maur. 51)	304
11 (Maur. 51)	308
12 (Maur. 1)	290
14 (Maur. 63)	285, 289, 291
14 (Maur. 63)	308
15 (Maur. 42)	306

On Cain and Abel
II, 6, 22	305

On Faith
I, Prologue, 1	290
I, 1, 8-10	290
II, 9, 77	294
II, 11, 89-90	290
II, 11, 90-95	290
V, 3, 45-46	290

On Instructions for Virgins
3, 16-5, 33	291

On Isaac or the Soul
4, 17	307
7, 57	305

On Jacob and the Good Life
I, 8, 36	311

On Joseph
4, 19	305

On Naboth
1, 2; and 12, 53	303
12, 50-52	303

On Noah
19, 70	302

On Penance
I, 6, 27-28	304
I, 16, 90	304
II, 3, 17-18	304
II, 7, 54-57	304
II, 8, 67 & 73	285
II, 8, 73	304
II, 8, 73	287
II, 10, 96	304

On the Death of his Brother
I, 58	292
I, 8 and 20	292
I, 20	292
31	292
I, 36	308
I, 38	292
I, 43-44, 48	292
I, 52	292
I, 76, 16, 41, 54	292
II, 109	302
II, 132-134	309
I, 20, 24, 17, and 27	292

On the Death of Theodosius
33-35	303
34	304
42, and 46	305
46, 51, 53, and 75	305
47-48 and 50-51	305
52-53 and 56	306

On the Death of Valentinian
25 and 27	305

On the Duties of the Clergy
I, 1, 4	288, 303
I, 18, 72	289, 296
I, 22, 101	305
II, 15, 69-72 and 16, 77	303
II, 16, 76-78	303
II, 28, 136-139 and 142	303
III, 6, 39, and 41	303
III, 22, 132-133	307

On the Good Death
2, 3	309
11, 49; and 12, 52-55 and 57	309

On the Holy Spirit
I, 1, 19-21	290

On the Mysteries
1, 1	301
6, 29	307

On the Sacraments
I, 6, 24	308
II, 7, 20 and 23	301
III, 1, 1	301
IV, 1, 4	307
IV, 4, 14-16	301
V, 3, 15 and 17	308
V, 4, 25	301

On Tobias
3, 9-10, 36	303

On Virginity
5, 25-26	291
16, 99	291
II, 2, 16-17	309
II, 61-62 and 65-66	307

On Virgins
I, 1, 1-3	288
I, 5	291
I, 10, 57-58	291
I, 11, 65-66	291
III, 1, 1-3, 14	286
III, 7, 37	292
III, 7, 38, & 37	286

Second Apology for David
5, 28	308

Endnote Index of Works Cited

Six Days of Creation
  III, 5, 23 — 297
  III, 8, 36 — 305
  V, 11, 34 — 305
  V, 12, 36-37 — 289
  V, 12, 37 — 305
  V, 24, 89 — 297, 305
  VI, 3, 15 — 302
  VI, 10, 75-76 — 305
The Education of a Virgin
  7, 48-49 — 306
The Sacrament of the Incarnation of the Lord
  5, 35-36 — 294
To the Thessalonians, 10 — 308

ANDREA DA STRUMI
Passion of the Holy Milanese Martyr Arialdo, 17 — 290

ATHANASIUS
Letter to the Virgins — 287

AUGUSTINE
City of God
  V, 26, 1 — 304
  XXII, 8, 2 — 298
Confessions
  V, 13, 23 — 300
  V, 14, 24-25 — 300
  VI, 1, 1-2 — 300
  VI, 3, 3 — 288, 303, 305, 308
  VI, 3, 3-4 — 300
  VIII, 1, 1-5, 10 — 300
  VIII, 1, 2 — 300
  VIII, 2, 3 — 286, 288
  VIII, 6, 14-15 — 291
  VIII, 12, 29 — 285
  IX, 5, 13 — 300
  IX, 6, 14 — 300
  IX, 7, 15 — 300
  IX, 7, 16 — 298
  IX, 12, 32 — 300
Customs of the Catholic Church and Customs of the Manicheans
  I, 33, 70 — 291
Letter 147, to Paulina, 18-53 — 300
On Happiness, 1, 4 — 300
Sermon 286 On the Birth of the Martyrs Protasius and Gervasius, 5, 4 — 298

BASIL OF CAESAREA
Letter 197, 1 — 289

COUNCIL OF AQUILEIA
Acts
  6, 14 32, 54 — 293
  8-11 — 293
  18-21 — 293
  42-43 — 293
  51 — 293
  53 — 293
Letter
  1 — 294

DUNGALUS
Book against Claudius of Turin to the Emperors Ludovico and Lothario — 293

FIAMMA, GALVANO
Opusculum on the Deeds of Azzone, Luchino and Giovanni Visconti, XLIV, 168 — 310

FLORIAN
Letter to Nicetius of Trier — 309

GAUDENTIUS OF BRESCIA
Sermo XVI, 2 and 9 — 307
Treatises
  Prefaces, 1-6 — 296
  XVII, 12 — 298
  XXI, 6-7 — 289

GENNADIUS
Illustrious Men: Simplician, 37 — 288

GIOVANNI DI S. MARTIONO
Il convito o pasto dei monaci — 310

GRATIAN
Letter of Emperor Gratian — 290

GREGORY OF TOURS
The Miracles of St. Martin, I, 5 — 309

GREGORY THE GREAT
Letter XI, 6 to the priests, deacons, and clerics of Milan — 309

HINCMAR OF REIMS
Divorce of Lotharius and Teutberga, Quaestio VII — 304
Predestination of God and Free Will, 29 — 299

HONORIUS OF AUTUN
Mirror of the Church — 299

JACOBUS DE VORAGINE
Golden Legends, St. Augustine — 299

JEROME OF STRIDON
Letter
  1, 15 — 289
  22, 22 — 291
  49 (48), 14 — 291
Preface to the Books of Didymus on the Holy Spirit — 288
Prologue to Origen's Homilies on the Song of Songs — 307

JOSEPH THE HYMNIST
Canon in Honor of St. Ambrose, ode III, tropario 1 — 294

LANDOLFO SENIORE
History of Milan, I, 9   299
LUTHER, MARTIN
Lectures on the Letter to the Romans, 12, 7   311
MAXIMUS
Letter to Valentinian II, 39, 3, 7   297
MAXIMUS OF TURIN
Sermons, 63, 3   301
PALLADIUS OF RATIARIA
Apology, 112   293
Apology, 115-116   286
Apology, 139   293
Apology, 140   296
PAULINUS OF MILAN
Life of Ambrose
1, 3   285
4, 1   286
4, 1-2   287
5, 1   288
5, 1-2   287
6, 1-2   285
7, 1-9, 1   285
8, 2   285
9, 1   285
9, 2   285, 286, 294
9, 3   286
11, 1-2   290
12, 2-4   297
13, 3   297
14, 1   298
14, 2   298
18, 1-4   294
24, I   304
29, 1-2, 9   299
32, 2-33, 2   299
32, I   306
34, 3-4   308
35, 1   308
36, 1-2   308
38, 1-5   291
38, 2   305
45, 1   308
45, 2   309
46, 1   309
47, 1-3   309
47, 3   291
48, 1-3   309
48, 3   301
50, 1   306
PAULINUS OF NOLA
Letter to Alipius - Ep. 24   306
Songs, Carme XXVII, vv. 436-437   298

PETRARCH, FRANCESCO
On the Solitary Life, II, 4   290
POSSIDIUS
Life of Augustine, 27, 8   309
RUFINUS OF AQUILEIA
Apology Against Jerome, II, 28   288
History of the Church
XI, 11   285
XI, 15   294
XI, 16   296
XI, 18   304
SOCRATES SCHOLASTICUS
History of the Church
V, 11   294
SOZOMEN
History of the Church
VI, 24, 2-3   285
VII, 25, 4   304
VII, 25, 9   301
SULPICIUS SEVERUS
Life of St. Martin
6, 4   291
SYMMACHUS
Epistula-Letter
3 and 7   295
5 and 10   295
72a   295
Relatio-Letter 72a   295
THEODORET OF CYRUS
History of the Church
V, 18, 2-22   304
V, 18, 20-25   301
THEOPHILUS OF ALEXANDRIA
Letter to Flavian of Antioch, 1   289
VICTRICIUS OF ROUEN
The Praise of the Saints
6 and 11   298
ANONYMOUS WORKS
Codex Theodosianus
IX, 40, 13   304
XVI, 1, 4   296
XVI, 4, 1   296
Epitaph for Marcellina   293
Life and Deeds of Saint Ambrose
73-74   301
Life of Gaudentius   309

Index of Names

The number indicates the page without specifying whether it is in reference to the text or a footnote; see also the preceding Index of Works Cited.
From antiquity to late Renaissance (and biblical personages)

A
Aaron 26
Abraham 265
Absalom 34
Acolius 256
Adam 64, 252, 265
Adeodatus 157, 166
Agnes 129, 133, 144, 145
Agricola 133, 134, 141, 142, 144, 231, 271
Ahab 183, 184
Alcuin 273
Alexander of Alexandria 84
Alipius 157, 166, 232
Ambrose (father of the saint) xv, 16-22
Ambrosia xvii, 62, 63, 229
Amos 39
Andragathus 99, 100
Andrea da Strumi 56
Andrew, Apostle 137, 271
Anemius xv, 46, 47
Angilberto II 271
Anisius of Thessalonica 229
Anna, mother of Tobias 34
Anolinus 146, 147
Ansperto 79
Anthony, hermit 4, 57
Apollinarius of Laodicea 94, 95
Arbogastes xvii, 223, 224, 225, 226
Arcadius, Emperor xvii, 167, 227
Arialdo 56
Arius of Alexandria 41, 84-86
Astasius 146
Athanasius of Alexandria 4, 18, 19, 31, 35, 41, 61, 94
Athanasius of Nisibus 45
Attilius Regulus 110, 112
Augustine xvi, 3, 5, 11, 19, 30-33, 57-59, 128, 140, 149, 150-159, 164, 166, 189, 202, 217, 232, 255, 261, 279, 280, 300
Auxentius (Mercurinus) of Durostorum xvi, 115-122, 275, 296
Auxentius of Milan xv, 1, 2, 3, 8, 10, 42-44, 57, 115, 228, 296

B
Balaam 25
Barbazianus 259
Basil of Caesarea 35, 39-41, 43, 54, 91
Bassianus of Lodi xvii, 236, 262
Bauto 107, 150
Benevolus 118
Bonhomini (Bonomi), Giovanni Francesco 12
Bonosius of Serdica (Niš) xvi, 228, 229, 230
Borromeo, Federico xi, 80
Butheric 197, 198

C
Caligula, Emperor 208
Camillus 110, 112
Cassiodorus 277
Castor, martyr 70, 292
Castulus 124
Castus 258
Catherine of Siena 80
Celsus, martyr 133, 135, 141-147, 257, 299
Cerealius 147
Charlemagne 273
Cicero 27, 183
Constans xv, 17, 108
Constantine, Emperor 16, 206, 207
Constantine II, Emperor xv, 16, 17
Constantius II, Emperor xv, 2, 8, 17, 41, 42, 105, 174
Cornelius, Pope 7
Cresconius 257
Cromatius 169
Cyprian of Carthage 7, 61

D
Dalmatius 119, 120, 121
Damasus, Pope xvi, 28, 48, 61, 92, 106, 223
David 34, 39, 96, 175, 200, 263
Decius, Emperor 139
Delfinus of Bordeaux 232
Deusdedit of Milan 270
Didymus the Blind 28, 29, 35, 51

317

Diocletian, Emperor xv, 17, 137, 139, 143
Dionysius of Milan xv, 2, 12, 41, 42, 44
Dominatorus of Bergamo 235
Dungalus 77, 293

E

Elijah 60, 125, 184
Epiphanius 277
Eucherius 81
Eugenius of Bologna 8
Eugenius, usurper xvii, 8, 15, 106, 113, 142, 223, 225, 226
Eusebius of Bologna 81, 85, 142
Eusebius of Caesarea 4, 28, 35, 277
Eusebius of Vercelli 12, 43, 58, 59, 259, 260
Eustacius 135, 142
Eustochium 61
Eustorgius of Milan 70, 71
Euthymius 122
Evagrius of Antioch 40, 43, 44, 228
Eve 64, 65

F

Faustus 152, 300
Felix, deacon 226
Felix, martyr 129, 133, 137, 138, 140, 141
Felix of Como 235-237, 255
Fiamma, Galvano 275
Flavian 113, 114
Flavian of Antioch 44, 45, 91, 92, 228
Florian 270
Fredrick Barbarossa 165
Fritigil 257, 258

G

Gabael 186
Galla 167
Galla Placidia 306
Gaudentius of Brescia 43, 118, 134, 135, 235
Gaudentius of Novara 259-261
Gennadius Massiliensis 32
Germinius of Sirmium 46
Gervasius, martyr xi, xvi, 24, 77, 127, 129, 133-146, 271, 272, 299
Goffredo da Bussero 80
Gratian, Emperor xv, xvi, 47-51, 62, 71, 81-83, 85, 88, 90, 93, 94, 99, 100, 102, 104, 106, 107, 109, 110, 113, 114, 117, 225-227, 295
Gratian, son of Theodosius 200

Gregory of Alexandria 42
Gregory of Nazianzus 35, 91
Gregory of Tours 269
Gregory the Great, Pope 270
Gregory VII, Pope 276

H

Hannibal 110
Helen 206, 207, 208
Herod 246
Herodias 125
Hilary of Poitiers 35, 43, 57, 129
Hincmar of Reims 149, 201
Homer 27
Honorarius, Bishop 274
Honorarius, Emperor xvii, 227
Honoratus of Milan 12
Honoratus of Vercelli xvii, 60, 235, 259, 260, 262
Honorius of Autun 149
Horontianus 176
Hyginus of Cordova 105

I

Indicia 78
Isaac 65, 265
Isaiah 155, 214
Isidore of Seville 22

J

Jacob 265
Jacobus de Voragine 149
Jerome of Stridon 28, 29, 35, 43, 51, 61, 230, 239, 280, 288
Jezebel 125, 183
John, Apostle 129, 137, 229, 249, 267
John Chrysostom 45
John Malalas 198
John the Baptist 125, 160, 218
Joseph, biblical patriarch 214
Joseph, husband of Mary 53, 229
Joseph the Hymnist 98
Josephus 27
Jovinian xvii, 61, 230, 231, 233, 259
Judas 100
Juliana xvii, 62, 142, 231, 232, 233
Julian the Apostate, Emperor 106
Julian Valens, Bishop of Pettau 48
Justina xv, 47, 48, 100, 115-117, 122, 125, 127, 167, 174, 277

L

Lamberto di Spoleto 274
Lampius of Barcelona 232
Landolfo Seniore 149, 274

Index of Names

Lawrence, martyr 129, 133, 231
Lawrence, son of Juliana 231, 232
Lazarus 203
Leonitus 7, 9
Liberius, Pope xv, 18, 19, 72
Lietus 192-194
Limenius of Vercelli 12, 259
Linus, Pope 146
Lucifer of Cagliari 76
Luther, Martin 279

M

Marcellina, sister of Ambrose xv, xvii, 4, 16-18, 22, 69, 70, 72-74, 77-80, 123, 135, 137, 171, 173, 188, 255, 271, 296
Marcellus, Bishop 192, 193, 194
Marcian 107
Marina Severus 47
Martinianus of Milan 97
Martin of Tours 7, 57, 269, 270
Mary, Virgin 65, 96, 207, 228-230, 243, 264
Maternus of Milan 137
Maximus, usurper xvi, 15, 99-105, 110, 113, 115, 126, 127, 166, 167, 174, 183, 223, 226
Maximus of Turin 166
Maximus the Cynic 91
Meletius of Antioch 40, 44, 91
Monica 154, 156, 158
Moses 26, 176, 252

N

Nabor, martyr 133, 137, 138, 140
Naboth 183
Nazarius, martyr xvii, 133, 141-147, 257
Nectarius of Constantinople 91, 92, 168
Nero, Emperor 146, 147, 208
Niceta of Remesiana 149
Nicetius of Trier 270
Novatian 201

O

Octavian Augustus, Emperor 105
Origen of Alexandria 4, 35, 61, 67, 212, 239

P

Palladius of Ratiaria xvi, 15, 49, 50, 52, 81-90, 115, 223
Pammachius 61
Paul, Apostle 10, 11, 38, 129, 176, 180, 194, 223, 240, 241, 252, 257, 261, 269

Paulinus of Antioch 40, 43, 44, 91, 228
Paulinus of Milan 3-9, 11, 13, 15, 16, 19-21, 26, 46, 47, 59, 60, 70, 73, 93, 94, 102, 114, 122, 128, 137, 140, 143, 158, 197, 198, 200, 201, 223, 226, 234, 255-258, 261-263, 278, 279, 286, 306
Paulinus of Nola 134, 232, 233
Pelagia of Antioch 133
Peter, Apostle 129, 131, 235, 288
Peter, Archbishop 79
Petrarch, Francesco 55, 56, 59
Philastrius of Brescia 10, 43, 235
Philo of Alexandria 35, 212
Pindar 22
Plato 22, 27
Plautus 181
Pliny the Younger 78
Pontician 57, 58
Possidius 261
Potiphar 214
Praetextatus, Vettius Agorius 107
Priscillian 104, 105, 295
Probus, Anicia Faltonia 21
Probus, Sextus Claudius Petronius 20, 21
Profuturus of Pavia 235, 259
Prosperus 75, 76
Protasius, martyr xi, xvi, 24, 77, 127, 129, 133-146, 271, 272, 299

R

Ramperto di Brescia 235
Rufinus, magister officiorum 196
Rufinus of Aquileia 3, 4, 8, 28, 29, 101, 118, 197, 201, 202, 204
Rumoridius 107

S

Sabinus of Milan 10, 40, 43, 59
Sabinus of Piacenza 37, 43, 85, 233
Sallust 27
Sarah 65
Sarmationes 259
Satyrus, brother of Ambrose xv, 16, 19-22, 69-80, 136, 255, 263, 271, 292
Scipio Africanus 110, 112
Sebastian, martyr 133
Secundus of Singidunum xvi, 52, 81, 84, 86, 87, 90, 223
Seneca 27
Severinus, Bishop of Naples 15, 286
Severus of Antioch 45, 97
Severus, the cured blind man 140

Siagrius, Consul 81
Siagrius of Verona 78
Simon the Pharisee 171, 172, 240
Simplician 11, 30-32, 37, 38, 78, 153, 156, 261, 262
Siricius, Pope 228, 230
Socrates Scholasticus 277
Solomon 220
Soteris, martyr xv, 17, 18, 19, 72, 133
Sozomen 2, 114, 167, 277
Stilicho xvii, 227, 257, 261
Sulpicius Severus 57
Symmachus, Quintus Aurelius xvi, 20, 99, 105-111, 113, 150, 151

T
Tatian 107
Tecla, martyr 133
Terasia 233
Terence 28
Tertullian 61
Theodobert I 274
Theodora of Alexandria 133
Theodoret of Cyrus 168, 196-198, 204, 205, 277, 278, 301
Theodoric 278
Theodorus, Flavius Manlius 31
Theodosius, Emperor xv, 4, 8, 48, 83, 84, 90-93, 102, 106, 113-115, 143, 166-174, 195-206, 210, 223-227, 239, 256, 257, 277, 278, 306
Theodosius II, Emperor 197
Theoduleus of Modena 257
Theophilus of Alexandria 44, 45, 228
Thomas, Apostle 137
Timasius 173
Tobias, son 34, 186

U
Ulfilas 115
Uranius 77
Ursicinus, martyr 145
Ursinus, antipope 48

V
Valens, Emperor xv, 47, 108
Valentinian I, Emperor xv, 8, 9, 43, 47, 48, 107, 108, 114, 120, 285
Valentinian II, Emperor xv, xvi, xvii, 47, 48, 90, 100-104, 107, 109, 113, 115, 118, 124-127, 150, 166, 167, 174, 223-227, 285, 295, 296
Valeria, martyr 145-147
Valerian, Emperor 139
Valerian of Aquileia 81, 169
Victor, Count 101
Victorinus, Marius 31
Victor, martyr 77, 129, 133, 137, 138
Victricius of Rouen 298
Virgil 27
Visconti, Lodrisio 274
Visconti, Luchino 274
Vitalis, martyr 77, 129, 133, 141, 142, 144, 145, 231, 271
Vittricius of Rouen 134
Volvinius 271

W
William of Saint-Thierry 212

X
Xenophon 27

Z
Zanobius of Florence 233, 234
Zechariah 218

Modern Era Bibliographical Index

A
Alzati, C. 289
Ambrosioni, A. 293
Andreotti, G. 293
Apeciti, E. 310

B
Ballabio, B. 308
Ballarini, M. 282
Bastiaensen, A.A.R. 291, 310
Beretta, L. 300
Bernareggi, A. 310
Biffi 305
Biffi, G. 154, 155, 299, 300
Biffi, I. 210, 297, 299
Biraghi, L. 80
Bufano, A. 290
Buzzi, F. 310

C
Cantalamessa, R. 30, 52, 288
Caprioli, A. 300
Cattaneo, E. 276, 292, 298, 302, 309, 310
Chiodi, L. 306
Cipriani, N. 301
Colombo, G. 308, 309
Colombo, S. 300
Costanza, S. 306, 307
Courcelle, P. 285, 287, 301, 303, 310
Cracco Ruggini, L. 89, 174, 177, 293, 295, 302

D
Dassmann, E. xiii, 134, 136, 249, 250, 251, 298, 299, 308
David, M. 296
De Giovanni, L. 296
Delehaye, H. 286, 293
Doignon, J. 300
Dossi, L. 287
Duval, Y.M. 285, 287, 291

F
Fabris, R. 302
Faller, O. 286, 292
Figini, G. 293
Fisher, B. 286
Folliet, G. 300
Fontaine, J. 129, 130, 297, 305
Forlin Patrucco, M. 287, 295
Fros, H. xxi

G
Gatti Perer, M.L. 298, 299
Gianotto, C. 301
Gori, F. 181, 286, 291, 303
Gottlieb, G. 290, 296
Grossi, V. 302
Gryson, R. 290, 293, 304, 309

H
Halkin, F. xxi
Heiming, O. 70, 292
Homes Dudden, F. xii, xiii

I
Iacoangeli, R. 307

J
Jullien, M.H. 297

K
Kirsch, J.P. 136

L
Lamirande, E. 286, 306
Lefort, L.-Th. 287
Levasti, A. 299

M
Madec, G. 300, 308
Magni, M. 296
Mara, M.G. 299, 303
Markschies, Chr. 289, 290
Mazzarino, S. 295, 303
McLynn, N.B. xiii, 287, 291, 292, 296, 301, 304
Meloni, P. 307
Meyer, P.M. 304
Migne, J.-P. xxi
Mirabella Roberti, M. 301
Mohrmann, C. 278, 310
Mommsen, Th. 304
Monachino, V. 301, 303, 304

N
Naldini, N. 306
Nauroy, G. 174, 205, 215, 216, 257, 280, 289, 296, 297, 302, 304, 305, 308, 311
Navoni, M. 277, 290, 292, 310
Nazari de Calabiana, L. 310

O
Odescalchi, B. 80
Oggioni, G. 62, 291

Opelt, I. 287
Oroz Reta, J. 300

P
Palanque, J.-R. xii, xiii
Paredi, A. xii, xiii, 24, 141, 206, 287, 288, 299, 304, 309, 310
Pascal, B. 297
Paschoud, F. 294
Pasini, C. 286, 288
Pastè, R. 286
Picard, J.-Ch. 292, 309, 310
Pietri, Ch. 305
Pizzolato, L.F. 231, 247, 285, 286, 291, 294, 300, 302, 305, 306, 307, 308, 310

R
Ramelli, I. 301
Ratti, A. 287
Reale, G. 300
Reggiori, F. 298
Repetto, F. 290
Richard, M. 289
Rizzi, M. 285, 286, 291, 294, 308, 310
Rocca, G. 290

Roda, S. 287, 295
Rosso, G. 287

S
Schmitz, J. 301
Simonetti, M. 294
Simon, M. 302
Smit, J.W. 291
Solignac, A. 32, 288, 300
Sordi, M. 206, 295, 304
Subleyras, P. 278, 310

T
Turazza, G. 291

V
Vasey, V.R. 302
Vismara, G. 303
Visonà, G. 286, 288, 292, 295, 296, 303, 306, 307, 309

W
Williams, D.H. 289, 290, 293, 296

Z
Zanetti, U. 299
Zani, A. 307
Zelzer, M. 289, 290, 293, 304

Index of Selected Topics

This index merely lists the pages where a topic is treated in some detail.

Altar of Victory Controversy 99, 105-113
Anti-Semitism 165-180
Apollinarianism 93-96
Appearance, Ambrose's 24
Arians/Arianism (this includes the various kinds of Arianism such as Homoeanism) 2, 41, 42, 45, 46, 49, 50, 81-90

Baptism, Ambrose's 9-12
Baptism/Sacrament of Initiation 159-162
Baptistery Inscription, Ambrose's 160, 161
Basilica Controversy 115-132
Bishop of Antioch Controversy 91-93, 228

Callinicum Controversy 165-180
Charity 188-194
Christology 41, 42, 49, 52-54, 85, 86, 95-97
Council of Aquilea 81-90

Death, Ambrose's 262
  meditation on 264-267
Doctrine 10, 42, 83, 87, 95, 136, 164, 229, 277

Embassy to Trier, Ambrose's 100-105
Emperor and Church 120, 121, 170-171, 205-208
Episcopal Election, Ambrose's 1-13
Eucharist 163-164, 251, 252, 269
Exegesis, Ambrose's 213-221

Holy Spirit 28, 29, 48-52, 90, 93, 128, 162, 203, 218, 235, 250-253

Homoeans/Homoeanism
  (see Arians/Arianism)
Hymns, Ambrose's 128-132, 149, 156, 157, 250, 251

Illness, Ambrose's 255-262

Jews/Judaism 165-180
Jovinian Condemnation 230, 231

Legends
  of the bees 21, 22, 281, 282
  of the whip 275, 276, 281, 282
  of the martyrs 145-147

Martyrs/Martyrdom 17, 18, 133-148
Monasticism/Hermits 57-60
Monophysitism 45, 95

Nature/Creation, Ambrose on 36, 37, 219-221

Ordination, Ambrose's 12-13

Paganism 105-114
Perfume, imagery of 68, 240-246
Priscillianism 104, 105

Social Injustice 180-188
Soul, journey of to God 248, 249

Thessalonica Massacre 195-208

Trinity 30, 49-52, 95, 116, 128

Virgins/Virginity 18, 60-68, 231, 232, 242, 243, 264

ST PAULS

This book was produced by ST PAULS/Alba House, the Society of St. Paul, an international religious congregation of priests and brothers dedicated to serving the Church through the communications media.

For information regarding this and associated ministries of the Pauline Family of Congregations, write to the Vocation Director, Society of St. Paul, 2187 Victory Blvd., Staten Island, New York 10314-6603. Phone (718) 982-5709; or E-mail: vocation@stpauls.us or check our internet site, www.vocationoffice.org